THE FOG OF PEACE AND WAR PLANNING

Military and Strategic Planning Under Uncertainty

Given both the importance and the difficulties involved in military planning, existing research has tended to focus almost exclusively on immediate pre-war and wartime periods surrounding the First and Second World Wars and has neglected peacetime periods and the specific challenges that planners must face. This volume sets out to examine and analyse how governments and military organizations planned for an uncertain and potentially threatening future during four different peacetime periods spanning from the beginning of the nineteenth century to the aftermath of the Second World War. For each period the authors have explored how the changing nature of military technology and hence of warfare affected military planning and provided a number of cases studies designed to illustrate the challenges and opportunities planners faced within their respective periods. Finally the book discusses what lessons can be drawn from past cases of military planning.

This book will be of foremost interest to students in military and strategic studies as well as military college staff, policymakers and think tank personnel.

Talbot C. Imlay is Associate Professor in the History Department at the Université Laval in Québec, Canada. He received his PhD in History from Yale University and is the author of *Facing the Second World War: Strategy, Politics, and Economics in Britain and France, 1938–1940* (2003).

Monica Duffy Toft is Associate Professor of Public Policy at the John F. Kennedy School of Government and the Assistant Director of the John M. Olin Institute for Strategic Studies, Harvard University. She is the author of *The Geography of Ethnic Violence: Identity, Interests, and the Indivisibility of Territory* (2003).

Cass Series: Strategy and History
Series Editors: Colin Gray and Williamson Murray

This new series will focus on the theory and practice of strategy. Following Clausewitz, strategy has been understood to mean the use made of force, and the threat of the use of force, for the ends of policy. This series is as interested in ideas as in historical cases of grand strategy and military strategy in action. All historical periods, near and past, and even future, are of interest. In addition to original monographs, the series will from time to time publish edited reprints of neglected classics as well as collections of essays.

THE FOG OF PEACE AND WAR PLANNING

Military and Strategic Planning under Uncertainty

Edited by

Talbot C. Imlay

and

Monica Duffy Toft

Routledge
Taylor & Francis Group

LONDON AND NEW YORK

First published 2006
by Routledge
2 Park Square, Milton Park, Abingdon, Oxon OX14 4RN

Simultaneously published in the USA and Canada
by Routledge
270 Madison Ave, New York, NY 10016

Routledge is an imprint of the Taylor & Francis Group, an informa business

© 2006 Talbot C. Imlay and Monica Duffy Toft

Typeset in Times New Roman by Taylor & Francis Books
Printed and bound in Great Britain by Antony Rowe Ltd, Chippenham, Wiltshire

British Library Cataloguing in Publication Data
A catalogue record for this book is available from the British Library
Library of Congress Cataloging in Publication Data
A catalog record of this book has been requested

ISBN 0–415–36697–6 ISBN 13 978–0–415–36697–7 (pbk)
ISBN 0–415–36696–8 ISBN 13 978–0–415–36696–0 (hbk)

TO OUR PARENTS,
JOAN AND WILLIAM DUFFY
AND
CAMILLE AND ROBERT IMLAY

CONTENTS

CONTENTS

TABLES

ILLUSTRATIONS

CONTRIBUTORS

Charles G. Cogan, PhD, is a senior research associate at the John F. Kennedy School of Government, Harvard University. A graduate of Harvard, then a journalist, and then a military officer, he spent thirty-seven years in the Central Intelligence Agency, twenty-three of them on assignments overseas. His latest book is *French Negotiating Behavior: Dealing with 'La Grande Nation'*.

John Ferris is a professor of history at the University of Calgary. He has written widely on military, strategic, diplomatic and intelligence history. Among his publications are *Men, Money and Diplomacy: The Evolution of British Strategic Policy, 1919–1926*, *The British Army and Signals Intelligence in the First World War*, and *A World History of Warfare* (co-edited with Christon Archer, Holger Herwig and Tim Travers).

Holger H. Herwig holds a dual position at the University of Calgary as professor of history and as Canada research chair in the Centre for Military and Strategic Studies. He has written the prize-winning *The First World War: Germany and Austria-Hungary 1914–1918*; his most recent work is *The Origins of World War I*, with Richard Hamilton.

Talbot C. Imlay is an associate professor of history at the University of Laval. He is the author of several articles and the monograph, *Facing the Second World War: Strategy, Politics and Economics in Britain and France, 1938–1940*.

Frederick W. Kagan is an associate professor of military history at the US Military Academy at West Point. He is the author of *The Military Reforms of Nicholas I: The Origins of the Modern Russian Army*, and co-editor of *The Military History of Tsarist Russia and The Military History of the Soviet Union*.

David Kaiser, a professor of strategy and policy at the Naval War College in Newport, Rhode Island, is the author of numerous articles and of five books, including *American Tragedy: Kennedy, Johnson and the Origins of the Vietnam War*.

Andrew F. Krepinevich, Jr., PhD, is an expert on defense and national security with extensive executive and strategic planning experience. He served in the US Army for twenty-one years, served on the personal staff of three secretaries of defense and was appointed to serve on the nine-member National Defense Panel. In addition to numerous monographs and opinion editorials, he is the author of *The Army and Vietnam* and *The Revolution in Military Affairs*.

Louise Richardson is executive dean at the Radcliffe Institute for Advanced Study, Harvard University, is an expert on international security, with an emphasis on terrorist movements. She is author of *When Allies Differ* and *What Terroists Want*, editor of *The Roots of Terrorism* and co-editor of *Democracy and Counter-terrorism: Lessons from the Past*. Richardson teaches at Harvard College, Graduate School, and Law School. She is co-editor of the SUNY Press terrorism series.

Lawrence Sondhaus is professor of history at the University of Indianapolis, where he directs the Institute for the Study of War and Diplomacy. He specializes in strategy and policy, with a focus on Germany and Austria in the years 1815–1918. His publications include *Navies in Modern World History* and seven other books on naval and military history.

David Stevenson professor of international history at the London School of Economics and Political Science, is the author of several books, including *Armaments and the Coming of War: Europe, 1904–1914* and *Cataclysm: the First World War as Political Tragedy* (UK edition is *1914–1918: the History of the First World War*).

John Tetsuro Sumida is the Major General Matthew C. Horner Chair of Military Theory at the US Marine Corps University and chair of the Department of the Army Historical Advisory Committee (2003–05). He is the author of numerous articles and the monographs *In Defence of Naval Supremacy: Finance, Technology, and British Naval Policy, 1889–1914* and *Inventing Grand Strategy and Teaching Command: The Classic Works of Alfred Thayer Mahan Reconsidered*.

Monica Duffy Toft is an associate professor of public policy at the Kennedy School of Government and the Assistant Director of the John M. Olin Institute for Strategic Studies, Harvard University. In addition to numerous articles and book chapters, Professor Toft is the author of *The Geography of Ethnic Violence: Identity, Interests, and the Indivisibility of Territory*.

ACKNOWLEDGMENTS

As with most major research projects, this book would not have been possible without the efforts of many people, but especially our contributors. When colleagues heard we were putting together an edited volume we received wishes of 'good luck.' With this group of scholars, however, good luck was not needed. Each provided drafts on time and submitted final versions of their essays in record time. No editor could have asked for a better team.

In lending moral and institutional support we would like to express our thanks to Samuel Huntington and Steve Rosen of the Olin Institute. As one of the last remaining arenas in academia that encourages political scientists and historians specializing in security issues to interact on a regular basis, the Olin Institute proved the ideal environment to produce this volume.

We would like to thank Jonathan Kirshner, Jack Levy, Paul Schroeder and Jack Snyder, who served as discussants at our second conference in which drafts were presented. Each provided helpful comments on several of the essays and provided invaluable guidance and wisdom on the broader topic.

For funding, we would like to thank Andrew Marshall at the Department of Defense, and Jorge Dominguez and James Cooney at the Weatherhead Center for International Affairs, Harvard University. Without their faith in the merits of this project, we could not have brought together such a fine team of scholars.

For help with editing and getting the manuscript out the door we are also grateful to Catherine Fratianni-Guevara, who remained enthusiastic from beginning to end.

Finally, we also thank our families and other colleagues (in some cases, one and the same) for their support and generosity in helping make this book a reality.

1

STRATEGIC AND MILITARY PLANNING UNDER THE FOG OF PEACE

Monica Duffy Toft and Talbot Imlay

Since the tragic events of 11 September 2001, the United States, with the support of various allies, has been at war against terrorism. Reflecting this situation, Congress has voted billions of dollars to fight the war. Reservists have been called up, armed forces deployed overseas, and a variety of measures have been taken, including military operations against the Taliban in Afghanistan and, more recently, a full-scale invasion of Iraq to overthrow Saddam Hussein's Baathist regime. Current debates focus on how to wage and win this war, not on where and when the next war will occur or on what shape it will take.

Despite this understandable preoccupation with the current war against terrorism, however, the United States and other countries cannot afford to ignore the possibility of major wars between sovereign states. Some scholars have argued that the staggering costs of interstate wars make them irrational and unthinkable – and therefore obsolete.[1] The events of 11 September might appear to confirm this view: the United States was attacked not by another country but by a non-state actor using highly unconventional weapons. Yet one should be careful before pronouncing the death of interstate war. It is hard to deny that the dynamics of an anarchic international system make such wars possible, even if they do not necessarily make them inevitable as pessimistic realists contend.[2] After all, the recent invasion of Iraq was a classic war between states, albeit states with very unequal military capabilities. Tensions with North Korea, moreover, could escalate to interstate war on the Korean Peninsula. If one accepts the continued possibility of interstate war, it follows that states have a responsibility to prepare and plan for them if only because the consequences of being caught ill-prepared are potentially disastrous.

Prudence alone then dictates that states and their militaries plan for the possibility of interstate war. But if the task of military planning is indispensable, it is also fraught with an uncertainty rooted in three basic problems: that of identifying friend and foe, that of understanding the nature of future war, and that of determining its timing.

Timing probably involves the greatest uncertainty. Aside from cases of deliberate aggression, planners cannot confidently know whether war will break out tomorrow, next week, next year, or in the next decade. Uncertainty about timing, in turn, exacerbates the uncertainty surrounding the nature of future war arising from the influence of such factors as technological developments. Given the pace of change, a war fought ten months from now promises to be radically different than one fought ten years from now. A key question for planners is determining what mix of old and new technologies and force structures will best counter future enemies on the battlefield.

Identifying likely enemies and allies is perhaps less uncertain than determining the timing and nature of war, since diplomacy, somewhat paradoxically, appears to be moving more slowly now than it did in the nineteenth century when alliances shifted with sometimes bewildering rapidity. Still, this type of uncertainty has in no way disappeared, as the current debate surrounding China's future intentions in Asia indicates. In short, uncertainty remains one of the few certainties for contemporary military planners.

For the United States, the inherent uncertainty of military planning is exacerbated by several additional factors. Since the end of the Cold War, the domestic perception of the level of *interstate* threat has been dropping, and with it the willingness to invest resources on military preparedness. Although 11 September and subsequent events have modified this situation, producing a sharp increase in US military budgets, in the long run it is unlikely that international terrorism will be seen to constitute a threat to the United States on the same scale as did the Soviet Union, justifying a proportional commitment of national resources. It is likely, in other words, that American armed forces will once again face constrained budgets. At the same time, the United States' position as the sole superpower means that its armed forces will be extremely busy in the near and longer-term future. In the absence of domestic consensus on what constitutes national security and the national interest beyond self-defense from attack by other states, US armed forces will have to be ready to respond to many different situations and not simply conventional combat. They will increasingly be called upon to assume a wide variety of tasks throughout the world that include active military operations, peace-keeping, and humanitarian aid. As recent events indicate, moreover, the United States must also be prepared to confront many different types of threats ranging from bio-terrorism to loose nuclear weapons and fissile material to information warfare. Such a diversity of threats and situations complicates immensely the task of military planning. Further complicating matters is the fact that US armed forces increasingly prepare to accomplish their various missions in cooperation with coalition partners who change from case to case. Each coalition partner presents different capabilities, which only adds to the difficulty of measuring the quantity and mix of forces needed for success. Taken together, these challenges make military planning for an uncertain future more difficult, perhaps more difficult than it has ever been in American history.

Given both the importance and the difficulties involved in military planning, surprisingly little research exists on the subject. By and large, scholarship on military planning focuses on immediate pre-war and wartime periods surrounding the First and Second World Wars.[3] The obvious example is the large body of work on the 1914 July Crisis that explores the extent to which precise military plans contributed directly to the outbreak of war by tying the hands of decision makers.[4] When not concerned with pre-war crises, work on military planning examines wartime periods, particularly the Second World War in which the emphasis is on how different strategies, doctrines, and operational practice contributed to achieving decisive success on the battlefield.[5] While both bodies of scholarship offer important insights into military planning, neither deals with peacetime periods when war is less immediate and palpable – and uncertainty therefore greater – than in immediate pre-war and wartime periods. Peacetime planners thus face different, though no less important, challenges than their pre-war and wartime counterparts. Put simply, military planning during peacetime, when there is no imminent threat of war, deserves to be examined on its own terms.

The Fog of Peace sets out to do precisely this. The origins of the volume lie in two conferences hosted by the John M. Olin Institute for Strategic Studies in order to examine how governments and military organizations in the past planned for an uncertain and potentially threatening future. The approach adopted was that of historical case studies. To be sure, other approaches might have been adopted, notably those that use quantitative and formal modeling tools. But we decided on historical case studies, not because we think this approach is inherently better than others but because we believe that detailed historical examination offers singular advantages in the study of peacetime military planning. In particular, case studies tell us about actual planners and planning – how planners went about their job. Accordingly, the participants, drawn from both history and political science, were invited to choose specific historical cases and to focus on individuals and military organizations responsible for military planning. Among the questions they were asked were: who were the military planners? Was planning *ad hoc* or more deliberate and organized? What kind of information did planners have available? What standards of assessment did they use? Were some planning efforts more successful than others in more accurately foreseeing the nature of future wars? And if so, why? Our aim in asking these questions of historical cases is to provide information that might be applied to current and future military efforts.

The bulk of the volume comprises of cases from four different peacetime periods – 1815–54, 1871–1914, 1919–39 and post-1945. Two considerations drove the selection of cases. One was diversity: eight cases spanning two centuries offer a rich empirical basis from which to draw upon. The second consideration concerned the evolution of warfare. The four time periods are each distinguished by the emergence of different types of military power. In the first set of cases from the 1815 to 1854 period, armies predominated; in the next two sets, covering the 1871 to 1914 and 1919 to 1939 periods, navies and then air forces figured prominently; and in the final set, beginning in 1945, nuclear weapons occupied the fore, ushering in the era of 'limited' warfare. Encompassing the four periods allows us to explore how the changing nature of military technology and hence of warfare affected military planning. All told, in their scope and diversity, the cases provide an excellent overview of the challenges confronting military planners over the last two hundred years.

The volume is organized chronologically, beginning with the first period, 1815–54, and ending with the last period covering the years after 1945. Each period consists of three chapters: the first chapter provides an overview of the period and circumstances under which military planning took place; the next two chapters are case studies designed to illustrate some of the challenges and opportunities planners faced within their respective periods. So, for example, the first section begins with Louise Richardson's overview chapter, followed by Frederick Kagan's case study of Russian military planning and Lawrence Sondhaus' case study of the German Confederation. The one exception to this organizing principle is the post-1945 period, which does not include an overview chapter because of the period's familiarity to likely readers of this volume.[6] The book ends with a discussion of possible lessons to be drawn from past cases of military planning.

I

Military planning will remain an uncertain enterprise. The future is too elusive to be imprisoned behind the bars of absolute predictability. But if uncertainty cannot be eliminated, it can be reduced. The 'fog of peace' can partially be lifted. Drawing on the various chapters in this volume, the remainder of the introduction discusses six factors that military planners must be aware of as they struggle to prepare for war under conditions of extreme uncertainty. The six factors are (1) historical shifts and changes; (2) the interstate system; (3) the nature of the political systems; (4) civil–military relations; (5) bureaucratic politics; and (6) individual planners.

At the most general level, military planners must consider broad forces or what French scholars of international relations term '*les forces profondes*.'[7] These large, impersonal forces work over a prolonged time period and range from climatic change on one end of the time-scale to industrialization, mass education, nationalism, and technological advances on the other end. The events of 11 September underscored the impact of another 'profound force' – religious extremism. These forces, however, pose not only threats but opportunities. As David Stevenson's chapter shows, changes in technology and transport compelled military planners to adapt their thinking. For example, advances in railroad transport sharply compressed the period from mobilization to battlefield, thus making conceivable such risky strategies as the Schlieffen plan. Post-1945 French planners, as Charles Cogan illustrates, labored to adapt the military to new domestic and international realities, among them the acceleration of de-colonization whose impact, given France's status as a leading colonial power, proved impossible to ignore. Similarly, Jon Sumida and John Ferris both discuss the challenges involved in planning for a possible war in the context of rapid technological advances in naval and air power. Ferris' equation of inter-war air power as a revolution in military affairs (RMA) is particularly intriguing given the current debate on whether such developments as network-centered warfare, which the US military is currently pursuing, constitute an RMA. While the inter-war Royal Air Force (RAF) embraced an RMA, most notably in its support of strategic bombing, it did not do so at the expense of all else. Then as now, in a rapidly changing world military planners must combine vision with flexibility.

A second set of broad factors involves the structure of the international system. Political scientists have long investigated the effect of different distributions of power on international politics. Which, they ask, is more stable or unstable: a uni-polar, bi-polar or multi-polar system? Do states balance, bandwagon or hide when confronted with powerful and threatening rivals?[8] Lawrence Sondhaus addresses these questions in his chapter on the German Confederation in the first half of the nineteenth century. The Confederation's eventual failure stemmed from its inability to control the rivalry between Austria and Prussia, two great powers whose ambitions in Central Europe precluded a stable German and European order. Bipolarity, in this case, proved unstable. Frederick Kagan and David Kaiser raise similar issues regarding Russia/Soviet Union, in Kagan's chapter as one great power among several and in Kaiser's chapter as one of two super powers. In both cases, Russia and the Soviet Union appeared to be expansionist powers and it is worth asking to what extent structure encouraged or inhibited Russian and Soviet leaders. In the present period, with the United States endowed with unrivalled military and economic power, not to mention considerable 'soft power' in such domains as culture and political ideology, it is worth considering the effects of such a structure not only for American military planners but also for their counterparts in other countries.[9]

Regime type emerges from the volume's chapters as a third factor. A growing political science literature is dedicated to the 'democratic peace' thesis that democracies do not fight each other and its corollary that a world comprised of democracies would be peaceful.[10] A variant of this thesis contends that democracies wage wars better and more successfully than non-democracies.[11] Recent work by historians on the First and Second World Wars, comparing such things as the organization of home fronts and levels of economic mobilization, support this claim, although many more comparative studies are needed before confident conclusions can be made.[12] But if the precise relationship between democracy and war remains debatable, it is clear that regime type influences military planning. As Holger Herwig shows, Imperial Germany's autocratic ruling structure magnified the impact of Kaiser Wilhelm's impulsive behavior and inhibited coordinated and responsible military planning. The result was disastrous for Germany and Europe. Discussing the inter-war period, Talbot Imlay draws attention to the unique nature of the Nazi regime whose expansionist and millenarian aims determined its attitude toward the possibility and nature of war. A great deal of the confusion and tragedy that characterized the diplomacy of the 1930s stemmed from the simple fact – clearer in retrospect than at the time – that Nazi Germany was not like other states. Although current military planners need to guard against false analogies that equate too easily Hitler and Nazism (or Stalin and Stalinist communism) with present-day leaders and regimes, the continued existence of non-democratic regimes – not to mention the uncertain consequences of democracy's spread – indicates that regime type is as relevant for military planners today as it was earlier.[13]

Civil–military relations is a fourth factor influencing military planning. Much of the literature on the subject contends that tensions between civilian and military leaders are unavoidable due to the different backgrounds, interests and outlooks of the two groups.[14] Military planning, in this view, is also a contested process in which civilians and military officers often work at cross-purposes. Studies of US defense policy after 1945, which underscore the struggles between military leaders who justified demands for greater spending by expanding their services' mission, and groups of civilian officials who sought to restrain military ambitions and ballooning budgets, support assumptions about the inescapable nature of civil–military tensions.[15] So too does Louise Richardson's chapter, which argues that in the first half of the nineteenth century diplomats (civilians) were more flexible and visionary in their planning efforts than their military counterparts. Interestingly, Kagan's chapter on Russian war planning suggests that tensions, while unavoidable, need not be debilitating. Military planning in Imperial Russia was based on a committee structure on which military officers *and* civilians served together, and that ensured the army's subordination to civil power, in this case the Tsar and his officials. In addition to sparing Russia the civil–military tensions that wracked Germany under Bismarck and his successors, as discussed in Herwig's chapter, this system fostered a more comprehensive planning effort than would have been possible from the military alone. Military planning, to paraphrase Georges Clemenceau, is too important a business to be left entirely to soldiers or civilians.

Military planning is affected not only by civil–military tensions but also by tensions among the military services, which leads us to our fifth factor, bureaucratic politics. Indeed, inter-service rivalries are so common as to be a fact of life in regimes of all types. During the Cold War, for example, competition between military services influenced the evolution of both US and Soviet defense policies.[16] Much of the scholarship on the subject focuses on budgetary and procurement issues, highlighting the battles fought between military services for larger budget shares. Military planning cannot help but be affected by these battles. Different services, possessing different capabilities and interests, are likely to conceive of future war in different, and even competing, ways. Thus Ferris demonstrates how the need to carve out an independent role influenced RAF planning during the inter-war period. Strategic bombing, by promising to bring enemies quickly to their knees, offered policy-makers not only a recipe for victory but one that undermined arguments for a large army and navy, thus in turn reinforcing the RAF's claim for increased resources. Similar claims by the US Air Force during the early Cold War, discussed in Kaiser's chapter, were partly rooted in turf warfare – hence the navy's violent opposition to a strategy that relied predominantly on atomic weapons before the introduction of the Trident submarine. Ferris and Kaiser's findings strengthen recent research on institutional culture suggesting that military services exert strong conformist pressures, shaping the way their members view the world.[17] Military planners, it appears, will conceive of future war in a way that highlights the role of their service at the expense of other services.

At the same time, the chapters also show that military services are not monoliths and that a good deal of disagreement often lurks behind the appearance of consensus. Krepinevich's chapter on the US Navy's development of aircraft carriers between the wars highlights intra-service divisions. Innovators found themselves opposed by proponents of a big-battleship navy who viewed carriers as at best a wasteful extravagance and at worst a threat to traditional missions and force structures. Intra-service divisions are also evident in Sumida's chapter, which discusses Admiral Sir John Fisher's efforts to impose a 'revolutionary conception of naval warfare' based not on the Dreadnought but on a combination of smaller battle cruisers and submarines. Fisher's grand conception, however, faced considerable opposition from outside *and* inside the navy. Interestingly, Ferris suggests that intra-service divisions benefited the inter-war British Royal Air Force (RAF) by preventing it from adopting one mission, strategic bombing, at the expense of all others. As a result, in 1939 the RAF possessed strategic air defense capabilities that proved vital to national survival during the Battle of Britain the following year. Given that modern military services are massive organizations combining numerous and often competing arms (e.g. infantry versus armor, bombers versus fighters, surface versus submarine warfare), military planning is an inherently political process in which competing viewpoints and interests confront one another. Whether this process can result either in paralysis or in a beneficial give-and-take dynamic – or in something in between – will depend on the extent to which there exists a culture of honesty and experimentation within a military service that encourages hard questions, the testing of assumptions, and the willingness to view mistakes as learning experiences and not as failures.

The individual is the final important factor that influences the dynamics of military planning. Hardcore structural theorists aside, most scholars would agree that individuals do affect international politics, sometimes decisively. One has only to think of Napoleon, Lincoln, or Hitler to make the point. Equally obvious, military planning is the work of people, although to be sure people in particular social, political and institutional contexts. As Sumida and Herwig show, it mattered that Admiral Fisher and Kaiser Wilhelm occupied the posts they did and not someone else. The question is, how can military organizations ensure that the best possible people occupy planning positions? Here, the scholarship on military innovation is helpful. Examining why particular military innovators are more successful than others, Barry Posen claims that civilian intervention is decisive, while Stephen Rosen argues that innovation is best carried out from within rather than against the system.[18] Both scholars, however, agree that it is possible to create conditions that make it more likely for innovators to succeed even if they disagree on what these conditions are. In terms of military planning, military organizations must learn how to strike a balance between encouraging visionary thought and avoiding recklessness.

Peacetime military planning is a large subject that could fill many volumes. Our task has been limited to the careful examination of a few crucial examples. For scholars, we hope to generate interest and debate in the subject of peacetime planning. For practitioners, we aim to provide guidelines – if not exactly spelling out what to do when planning under extreme uncertainty, this volume certainly holds important lessons on what *not* to do when attempting to pierce the fog of peace.

Notes

1 John Mueller, *Retreat from Doomsday: The Obsolescence of Major War* (New York: Basic Books, 1989); and Michael Mandelbaum, 'Is Major War Obsolete?' in *Survival*, vol. 40, no. 4, 1998–99, pp. 20–38.

2 For a recent pessimistic statement, see John Mearsheimer, *The Tragedy of Great Power Politics* (New York: W.W. Norton, 2001).

3 Cf. Williamson Murray and Allan R. Millett, eds, *Military Innovation in the Interwar Period* (Cambridge: Cambridge University Press, 1996).

4 Paul M. Kennedy, ed., *War Plans of the Great Powers, 1880–1914* (London: Allen & Unwin, 1979); Jack L. Snyder, *Ideology of the Offensive: Military Decision-Making and the Disasters of 1914* (Ithaca, NY: Cornell University Press, 1984); Steven E. Miller, ed., *Military Strategy and the Origins of the First World War* (Princeton, NJ: Princeton University Press, 1985); and Marc Trachtenberg, 'The Meaning of Mobilization in 1914' in *International Security*, vol. 15, no. 3, 1990, pp. 120–50.

5 John Mearsheimer, *Conventional Deterrence* (Ithaca, NY: Cornell University Press, 1983); Robert A. Doughty, *The Breaking Point: Sedan and the Fall of France 1940* (Hamden, CT: Archon Books, 1990); Robert A. Pape, *Bombing to Win: Air Power*

and Coercion in War (Ithaca, NY: Cornell University Press, 1996); and Karl-Heinz Frieser, *Blitzkrieg-Legende: der Westfeldzug 1940* (Munich: R. Oldenbourg, 1995). There is also a growing literature probing the extent to which Cold War military planners conceived of using nuclear weapons both on and off the battlefield. See David Alan Rosenberg, 'The Origins of Overkill: Nuclear Weapons and American Strategy, 1945–60' in *International Security*, vol. 7, no. 4, 1983, pp. 3–71; '"A Smoking Radiating Ruin at the End of Two Hours": Documents on American Plans for Nuclear War with the Soviet Union, 1954–55' in *International Security*, vol. 6, no. 3, 1981, pp. 3–38; Marc Trachtenberg, *History and Strategy* (Princeton, NJ: Princeton University Press, 1991); and John Lewis Gaddis *et al.*, eds, *Cold War Statesmen Confront the Bomb: Nuclear Diplomacy Since 1945* (Oxford: Oxford University Press, 1999).

6 Useful background material on the post-1945 period can be found in John Lewis Gaddis, *The Long Peace: Inquiries into the History of the Cold War* (Oxford: Oxford University Press, 1987); Maurice Vaïsse, *Les Relations internationales depuis 1945* (Paris: Colin, 1994); and Martin Walker, *The Cold War: A History* (New York: H. Holt, 1994).

7 Pierre Renouvin, *Histoire des relations internationales. Les crises du XXe siècle*, tomes 7–8 (Paris: Hachette, 1957–58); and Renouvin and Jean-Baptiste Duroselle, *Introduction to the History of International Relations* (New York: Praeger, 1967).

8 See Kenneth Waltz, *Theory of International Politics* (Reading, MA: Addison-Wesley, 1979); Robert O. Keohane, ed., *Neorealism and its Critics* (New York: Columbia University Press, 1986); Stephen Walt, *The Origins of Alliances* (Ithaca, NY: Cornell University Press, 1987); Joseph Grieco, 'Anarchy and the Limits of Cooperation' in *International Organization*, vol. 42, 1988, pp. 485–507; and Charles Glaser, 'Realists as Optimists: Cooperation as Self-Help' in *International Security*, no. 3, 1994, pp. 50–90.

9 For 'soft power,' see Joseph S. Nye, *Bound to Lead: The Changing Nature of American Power* (New York: Basic Books, 1990).

10 Michael Doyle, 'Kant, Liberal Legacies, and Foreign Affairs, Part I' in *Philosophy and Public Affairs*, vol. 12, no. 3, pp. 205–35; and Bruce M. Russett, *Grasping the Democratic Peace: Principles for a Post-Cold War World* (Princeton, NJ: Princeton University Press, 1993).

11 David Lake, 'Powerful Pacifists: Democratic states and war' in *American Political Science Review*, vol. 86, 1992, pp. 24–37; Allan C. Stam, *Win, Lose, or Draw: Domestic Politics and the Crucible of War* (Ann Arbor, MI: University of Michigan Press 1992), pp. 18, 65–8, 176–69; and Dan Reiter and Alan C. Stam III, 'Democracy, War Initiation, and Victory' in *American Political Science Review*, vol. 92, no. 2, 1998, pp. 377–89; 'Democracy and Battlefield Military Effectiveness' in *Journal of Conflict Resolution*, vol. 42, no. 3, 1998, pp. 259–77; *Democracies at War* (Princeton, NJ: Princeton University Press, 2002).

12 For comparative studies of the First World War, see Jay Winter and Lean-Louis Robert, *Capital Cities at War: Paris, London, Berlin, 1914–1919* (Cambridge: Cambridge University Press, 1997); and Jay Winter, 'Introduction' in Richard Wall and Jay Winter, eds, *The Upheaval of War: Family, Work and Welfare in Europe, 1914–1918* (Cambridge: Cambridge University Press, 1988). For the Second World War, see György Ránki, *The Economics of the Second World War* (Vienna: Bohlau Verlag, 1993); David Reynolds *et al.*, eds, *Allies at War: The Soviet, American, and British Experience, 1939–1945* (New York: St. Martin's Press, 1994); and Mark Harrison, ed., *The Economics of World War II: Six Great Powers in International Comparison* (Cambridge: Cambridge University Press, 1998).

13 For analogies, see Yuen Foong Khong, *Analogies at War: Korea, Munich, Dien Bien Phu, and the Vietnam Decisions of 1965* (Princeton, NJ: Princeton University Press, 1992). For the uncertain consequences of the spread of democracy, see Jack L. Snyder, *From Voting to Violence: Democratization and Nationalist Conflict* (New York: Norton, 2000).

14 Samuel P. Huntington, *The Soldier and the State: The Theory and Politics of Civil–Military Relations* (Cambridge, MA: Harvard University Press, 1957); Morris Janowitz, *The Professional Soldier: A Social and Political Portrait* (Glencoe, IL: Free Press, 1960); and Michael C. Desch, *Civilian Control of the Military: The Changing Security Environment* (Baltimore, MD: The Johns Hopkins University Press, 1999).

15 Melvyn P. Leffler, *A Preponderance of Power: National Security, the Truman Administration, and the Cold War* (Stanford, CA: Stanford University Press, 1992); and Michael J. Hogan, *A Cross of Iron: Harry S. Truman and the Origins of the National Security State* (Cambridge: Cambridge University Press, 1998).

16 Hogan, *A Cross of Iron*; and Kimberly M. Zisk, *Engaging the Enemy: Organization Theory and Soviet Military Innovation, 1955–1991* (Princeton, NJ: Princeton University Press, 1993).

17 Elizabeth Kier, *Imagining War: French and British Military Doctrine Between the Wars* (Princeton, NJ: Princeton University Press, 1997).

18 Barry Posen, *The Sources of Military Doctrine: France, Britain, and Germany Between the World Wars* (Ithaca, NY: Cornell University Press, 1984); and Stephen Peter Rosen, *Winning the Next War: Innovation and the Modern Military* (Ithaca, NY: Cornell University Press, 1991).

2

STRATEGIC AND MILITARY PLANNING, 1815–56

Louise Richardson

The Concert of Europe was brought into being by Article 6 of the Quadruple Alliance, which stated:

> To facilitate and to secure the execution of the present Treaty, and to consolidate the connections which at the present moment so closely unite the Four Sovereigns for the happiness of the world, the High Contracting Parties have agreed to renew their Meetings at fixed periods, either under the immediate auspices of the Sovereigns themselves, or by their respective Ministers, for the purposes of consulting upon their common interests, and for the considerations of the measures which at each of these periods shall be considered most salutary for the repose and prosperity of Nations, and for the maintenance of the Peace of Europe.[1]

With the signing of the treaty on 20 November 1815, the Concert of Europe was born. The idea of a concert or federation was not new, having been frequently mentioned by eighteenth-century publicists. The difference this time was the intervening experience of the war. The extraordinary destructiveness of the Napoleonic Wars and the inordinate difficulties experienced by the allies in forging an effective coalition against France demonstrated the need for more consistent collaboration among the great powers. The Concert of Europe was designed, therefore, to maintain stability after the Napoleonic Wars. The Peace of Paris and the Quadruple Alliance had stipulated the terms of the peace and the Concert was designed to maintain the order established by the peace.

The Concert was not simply a club of victors combining to protect their spoils, as evidenced by the generosity of the peace – even after the provocation of the 100 Days – and by the ease with which the defeated power, France, was integrated into the new system. Rather, the leaders of the great powers gathered at Vienna appear genuinely to have believed that along with their right to preside over Europe went the responsibility to maintain the European order. They believed that they had, in Castlereagh's words, 'not only a common interest but a common duty to attend to.'[2]

At Vienna, the great powers, Austria, Britain, Prussia, Russia and soon France, essentially established an oligarchy to manage their security relations. The members of this elite group, despite their considerable differences, had much in common. The revolution in France, and the use Napoleon had made of this revolution in waging a devastating war, had exposed the domestic vulnerabilities of all the great powers. There were differences on this point between the two western and more liberal powers and the three eastern and more conservative powers. Nevertheless, there was a powerful conservative consensus among the diplomats gathered at Vienna and a recognition of the acute need for their domestic legitimacy and their sovereignty to be recognized and reinforced. The revolution and the war that followed demonstrated that domestic and international politics could not entirely be divorced. At Vienna, however, the diplomats concentrated on regulating their international or rather their European affairs.

In performing this common duty the great powers developed a set of norms to serve as a code of conduct. They established rules of behavior to regulate the competition among themselves and followed a set of procedures designed to maintain order. These norms, rules and procedures were directed both internally and externally. The norms were addressed by these powers to one another, providing reassurance of their commitment to the common project and disavowing any intentions of defection. The rules were designed to ensure that the interests of each participant would be protected, again enhancing the benefits of cooperation and increasing the costs of defection. The procedures provided mechanisms for enhancing transparency, demonstrating continued commitment to cooperation, and reducing incentives for defection.

The norms were self-restraint, consultation, no unilateralism and constant assurances of commitment to the maintenance of stability. The rules of behavior included conference diplomacy, approval of territorial changes and respect for the status as well as the territorial interests of the others.[3] Finally, the members adopted a number of procedures designed to create an elaborate crisis-prevention system.[4] Perhaps the best example of the latter was the creation of the buffer states of the German Federation. This served not only the more traditional function of discouraging a French attack east, an Austrian attack north and a Prussian attack west, but also encouraged cooperative behavior by involving Austria and Prussia jointly in the management of this buffer zone.

Although the Concert had no resources to ensure compliance, states nevertheless repeatedly complied. Paul Schroeder has written on how this played out in practice. He described the forces at work as follows: 'Deterrence under the Vienna system took the form of moral and legal political pressure, the threat that reckless or unlawful behavior would cost the offending state status and voice within the system leading to isolation from it and the attendant loss of systemic awards and benefits.'[5] It was these forces which apparently deterred France from action in support of the Belgians and Egyptians and Russia from supporting the Greeks in three cases between the end of the Congress system and the outbreak of the revolutions of 1848. On several occasions in the same period the great powers chose to resist their own domestic opinion and act with their allies instead. Examples include Austria passing up potential gains in Italy, Britain and France resisting the temptation to support the rebels in Poland in 1830 and in Piedmont in 1848, and Tsar Nicholas deciding to make the Munchengratz agreement in 1833. The Concert could enjoy these successes, however, only because the major powers shared the fundamental belief in the legitimacy of the status quo.

The powerful consensus that united the three conservative eastern powers and the two liberal western powers was shattered by the revolutions of 1848 which paralyzed Austria and Prussia, transformed France into a radical republic, and deeply frightened, in the famous words of Palmerston, 'the only two Powers in Europe – that remain standing upright.'[6] Significantly, the revolutions were not accompanied by warfare. They did, however, undermine the Concert by bringing to power new governments and a new generation of leaders and revealing the folly of ignoring domestic opinion. The revolutions left a legacy of distrust among the great powers. Britain and Russia were wary of France, while Austria resented her dependence on Russia and Austro-Prussian relations deteriorated steadily. Ironically, when war did break out it was between the only two powers largely unaffected by the revolutions.

The Crimean War was, as has often been said, an unnecessary war. It was precisely the type of war that the Concert was designed to prevent and could have been prevented had the Concert's practices been followed. The war was essentially caused by misperception on the part of the Tsar and the combination of a divided government and an aroused public opinion in Britain. The war was made much worse by rampant incompetence on both sides. The Tsar believed, wrongly, that his limited and honorable motives would be clear to Aberdeen. Aberdeen was prepared to allow the Concert to impose a settlement, but Palmerston, with whom he shared power, was not, and so the two countries stumbled slowly into a very bloody war. The Crimean War marked a watershed in the nineteenth century. It was preceded by four decades of peace and succeeded by four wars in rapid succession.

Once the war was over, the necessary condition for the successful functioning of the Concert, acceptance of the underlying status quo, no longer existed. France, Russia and Prussia were now revisionist powers. Due to the internal upheavals they had experienced, they now preferred defection to cooperation. Louis Napoleon had hoped to overthrow the Vienna settlement even before the war, but his relative military success in the Crimean War emboldened his plans. Russia was deeply unhappy at the terms of the peace which, however moderate, spelled defeat. Prussia was shaken by the efforts of Austria to drag her into the war and worried that her great power status had been called into question. Austria and Britain remained the only two defenders of the Vienna settlement. But Austria, weakened by military expenditures and isolated by her role in the war, was unable, and Britain, reeling from her appalling performance in the war and with a public deeply opposed to continental commitments, was unwilling to defend the status quo.

The Concert as an Inter-war Period

The period 1815–56 is not generally considered to be an inter-war period. The term connotes a period beginning and ending with a major war between the main participants in the system under consideration. This particular international system, which was launched by the Napoleonic Wars and the resulting Vienna settlement, was not overturned by the war in the Crimea. Rather, the Crimean War was a testament to the erosion of the fundamental principles which had sustained the Concert. The war itself was a much less significant affair than either the Napoleonic War or the First World War, the two major clashes between the main players in the international system.

On this point it is fair to point out that there is very little agreement among historians as to when the Concert of Europe established in Vienna actually ended. My own view is that by the middle of the nineteenth century, the necessary conditions for the successful functioning of the Concert, which contemporary parlance would be called a security management institution, had evaporated. By definition, any period in history is an inter-war period as wars inevitably break out somewhere. But the period 1815 to 1856 is, I think, utterly different from the ideal-type inter-war period, as in the Europe of the 1920s and 1930s, which was so dominated by the recovery from war and the effort to resolve the issues left unfinished by the war. The Concert period has more in common with the prolonged period of uneasy peace that followed the Second World War, which also is hard to see as an inter-war period. The Concert also has much in common with the current international system and the efforts to integrate a defeated enemy into a new international order. The Concert of Europe, like the period after the Second World War and to a far lesser extent the present system, was marked by a self-conscious effort to construct a new world order.

In establishing an organizing principle for the Concert, the leading statesmen explicitly attempted to learn from the success of the final coalition in the war against Napoleon and from the failures of all the previous coalitions. The earlier coalitions had failed utterly in the attempt to forge a united and lasting front against Napoleon, partly because members of these coalitions were at least as suspicious of each other as they were of France. They regularly opted for opportunities to abandon the coalition in order to make a separate settlement with the enemy. In short, they behaved very much as states did, and were expected to do, in the eighteenth century.

The final coalition, however, was distinguishable from the others in the degree to which the statesmen were in constant personal communication. Castlereagh was not alone in believing that this fact was crucial to its success. In a letter to Liverpool he referred to 'the habits of confidential intercourse which a long residence with the principal actors has established.'[7] On another occasion Castlereagh made a similar point:

> It is impossible to have resided in allied headquarters even for the short period I have myself passed at them without perceiving how much the interests of the Confederacy are exposed to prejudice and disunion from the want of some central council of deliberation, where the authorized Ministers of the respective Powers may discuss face to face the measures in progress.[8]

In the words of his biographer, C.K. Webster, Castlereagh 'had learned the lesson of the closing years of the war as no other had done.'[9] There was, therefore, a very clear sense of learning from the experience of war and adapting the methods successful in wartime for the maintenance of peace. The existence of a shared common interest in stability was not in itself enough to prevent misunderstanding of the intentions of others, any more than the existence of a shared interest in victory against Napoleon had been. To reduce uncertainty and to help ascertain the real intentions of others it was thought necessary to meet and to do so at senior levels of government.

Impact of the Concert on Strategic and Military Planning

For the purposes of this project the key question is whether the reassurance provided by the functioning of the Concert was evident in the military and strategic planning of the participating powers. Were those developing military plans expecting another type of Napoleonic War with a real great power push for ascendancy in Europe? Or were they confident that the Concert would prevent, or at least provide adequate warning of such an attempt? Perhaps military plans were influenced by some altogether different considerations. There can be little doubt that in assessing the quality of diplomatic planning, the crafters of the Concert of Europe demonstrated a creativity, a willingness to learn and an ability to think in the long term that one would love to see present among contemporary political planners. Some displayed more skill than others and certainly Castlereagh, Metternich and Tallyrand, in their different ways, were extraordinarily skillful in playing their very different hands. Overall, however, the political leaders of Europe in 1815 displayed a remarkable willingness to contemplate new ways of conducting their affairs.

The type of foresight and creativity evident in the diplomatic sphere was, however, entirely absent from military and strategic planning in Europe in the period known as 'The Long Peace.' In the period after the Napoleonic Wars European armies largely reverted to the style of their eighteenth- century predecessors. An aristocratic officer corps whose only qualification was birth, led armies of long-serving and badly treated professional troops. This reversion to the ways of the *ancien régime* was easier for some than for others. In France, understandably enough, it was the most qualified. In practice if not in principle, even the French army abandoned the idea of a nation in arms and created a long-serving professional army. This army was not led by aristocrats but by professionals, but these too were quite separate from society at large and were quite happy to be employed in maintaining order at home rather than fighting abroad. The British, Russian and Austrian armies who had not had to transform their military structure to defeat Napoleon all experienced little difficulty in reverting to the ways of the eighteenth century. Only in Prussia were real reforms undertaken. These reforms had in fact been initiated before the defeat of Napoleon in the Army Law of 1814, which permitted conscription for three years and created a separate *landwehr* (reserve force) led by elected property owners. Devastating defeat in 1806 provided an impetus for significant reform of the Prussian army. The creation of a General Staff with responsibility for planning future campaigns in peacetime was considered a very radical step as was the idea that demonstrated competence must be a prerequisite for promotion. In time even these reforms were undermined, by the enforced retirement of the reformers, and the reestablishment of aristocratic control over the officer corps. Nevertheless the Prussian army in this period was unique in its commitment to training officers, evaluating its own performance and developing a rational method of self-administration.

With the sole exception of Prussia, therefore, military and strategic planning in Europe from 1815 to 1856 was no match for the new developments on the diplomatic front. The contrast between diplomatic innovation and military reaction was nowhere more in evidence than in Britain where the army remained impervious to change and isolated from society in the celebrated age of reform. Unlike Prussia, of course, Britain had been victorious against Napoleon and this fact seemed to legitimize the conservative impulses. Moreover the survival of the victor of Waterloo, Wellington, and the dominance he exercised over military matters ensured that all efforts at reform would be vigorously opposed.

There was no British equivalent of the Prussian General Staff in this period. The essence of strategic planning is the integration of political interests and military resources. But in Britain control over the army was itself a matter of dispute. Parliament retained control over the finances and the disciplinary code of the army but the Crown retained control, through the Horse Guards, of the command and organization of the army.

The army was administered by several different, and often competing, departments. The Secretary of State for War and the Colonies was responsible for the size of the army. The Secretary at War was responsible for army finances and for the annual Mutiny Act. The Treasury controlled army finances and the Commissariat department from which the army overseas received provisions. The Home Secretary was responsible for military questions in Great Britain. The Commander in Chief, based in the Horse Guards, was responsible for discipline and efficiency in the infantry and cavalry. The Commander in Chief was empowered to command the forces at home but had no control over the supply of arms, provisions and fortifications. These were controlled by the General of the Ordnance who was also responsible for the discipline and pay of the Royal Artillery and Royal Engineers. Nobody was responsible for coordinating the activities of these various entities.

The Duke of Wellington had created the office of Commander in Chief and until the outbreak of the Crimean War it was occupied either by himself or by a coterie of his aging henchmen, all veterans of the Peninsular War. They were staunchly loyal to the crown and bitterly resistant to all Parliamentary interference including calls for reform. The entrenched bureaucracy of the Horse Guards was protected throughout this period by the legitimacy they derived from the victory at Waterloo. In 1837 and again in 1849 the Duke of Wellington successfully resisted attempts to centralize military administration, fearing encroachments of the prerogatives and patronage of the Commander in Chief. He remained bound and determined to protect the army from Parliament.

There were a few issues during this period in which the duke was reluctantly forced to concede to Parliamentary and public pressure for reform. The barbarity of the military practice of flogging became a *cause célèbre* for reformers who eventually forced the duke, much against his will, first in 1829 to reduce the number permitted to be lashed to 300 and eventually after several interim steps to reduce the number to 50 in 1846. The practice was eventually abolished in 1881. Public revelations that the conditions in army barracks were worse than in Scottish poorhouses and English prisons aroused popular and Parliamentary outrage and induced some slow improvements in the living conditions in the army. The duke was also forced to concede in 1847 limits on the period of enlistment and in 1850 to require examinations before promotion for ensigns and lieutenants. Each of these reforms was bitterly contested and ultimately conceded in a strategic effort to preserve all the essential features of the army that had won in Waterloo. The age of reform in Britain did not extend to its army.

The absence of innovation in the army at this time was not only due to an entrenched and reactionary military establishment but also to a Parliamentary insistence on economy. The Napoleonic Wars had been exceedingly expensive and Parliament was committed in the aftermath to retrenchment. The army budget declined from £43 million in 1815, to £10.7 million in 1820, to under £8 million in 1836. In response to agitation by Chartists and invasion scares in the 1840s the budget rose to £9.5 million a year. These expenditures reflect declining numbers in the army which fell from 233,952 in 1815, to 102,539 in 1828, to 87,993 in 1838. The numbers rose in the 1840s to 116,434 in 1846 before declining again until the outbreak of the Crimean War.[10]

These figures amply demonstrate that successive British governments in this period did not contemplate and did not plan for deployment of a British army in Europe. Instead the army had three functions: first and foremost maintaining the Empire, second maintaining order at home, and third defending against a French invasion. The type of conflict that occurred in the Crimea, or any other major European commitment, was never anticipated. Small as the army was in this period at least two-thirds of it was committed overseas. In 1846, for example, with 103 infantry battalions and 100,600 men, the distribution of troops and regiments was: 23,000 (23) in India, 32,620 (54) elsewhere in the Empire, and 44,980 (35) in Britain.[11] The overseas deployment was significantly more expensive than that at home and in a review of military strategy that year Colonial Secretary Grey advocated a further shift away from imperial defense as a cost-saving measure.

With Wellington's death in 1852 the prospects for army reform were enhanced. The new Commander in Chief, Hardinge, under pressure from renewed fears of French invasion, proved open to change. He permitted the introduction of a more efficient rifle and established a musketry school to ensure its efficient use. He encouraged schemes for training junior officers and approved the purchase of land to establish a permanent army camp. Nevertheless, he never challenged the basic structure of the British army which was predicated on imperial and home defense and not on fighting a major European war. The army remained organized in small units around one battalion with no planning for large-scale action by brigades or divisions and no appreciation of the needs for the staff work or coordination essential in a major campaign.

The first line of British defense in this period was not the army but the navy. The British navy in this period enjoyed unrivaled supremacy in the seas. The navy too however had to adjust to the Parliamentary insistence on retrenchment in the period of the Concert of Europe. In 1815 the British navy had 214 ships of the line and 792 cruisers of all types. The admiralty proposed a peacetime goal of 100 ships of the line and 160 cruisers but even this proved optimistic. By 1835 the number of ships of the line fit for sail was fifty-eight.[12] Significant though this decline was, undoubtedly the British navy was unchallenged throughout this period even by its two closest rivals, the USA and France. It was through its navy not its army that Britain exercised ascendancy in this period. Others did not challenge her position in

18

part because the costs of doing so were so high and in part because the British navy did little to threaten the interests of others.

It is impossible to say with confidence that the existence of the Concert suffices to explain the absence of military planning for a new great power conflict in Europe. The occasional scares in Britain that France might be planning to invade suggest that the British were not completely confident of the good behavior of their European counterparts. Nevertheless the fact that there was no planning for a breakdown of relations suggests that there was a degree of confidence in the methods established to manage those relations.

Strategy of course is not simply about political planning and requires the integration of military and economic resources in furtherance of political objectives. The story of economic development is actually very different in each of the major powers in the nineteenth century, though the period of most dramatic change was actually the latter half of the century. As Paul Kennedy has pointed out, the combination of political stability, small-scale localized warfare, the growth of the international economy, the gradual impact of the Industrial Revolution and the slow modernization of military technology led to the ascendancy, even hegemony, of Britain by the middle of the century.[13]

The British economy was preeminent in the early and mid-nineteenth century. In the mid-nineteenth century Britain, with 2 per cent of the world's population and 10 per cent of Europe's, produced 53 per cent of the world's iron and 50 per cent of its coal and lignite. Britain was responsible for one-fifth of world commerce, two-fifths of the trade in manufactured goods and over one-third of the world's merchant navy.[14] The modernization that occurred in British industry and communications, however, was not replicated in the military. In the half century following the Vienna settlement, the armed services consumed only 2–3 per cent of GNP, significantly less than in both the eighteenth and twentieth centuries.[15] It is possible that both the faith in the Concert and the neglect of the military were products of something else, of the prevailing liberal philosophy of *laissez-faire* political economy associated with Adam Smith and Richard Cobden. This rationalist ideology greatly underestimated both the appeal and the likelihood of war. All these factors were mutually reinforcing as the Concert appeared to maintain the equilibrium, hence there was less need for military expenditures on forces that might not be needed, and the disinclination to intervene was strengthened. When Britain did choose to influence events abroad it did so through diplomacy and the application of the one aspect of the military in which it enjoyed a comparative advantage, the navy. While the actual strength of the navy declined steadily after 1815, its strength relative to its main competitors was overwhelming, equivalent, argues Kennedy, to the next three or four navies in fighting power. The disparity between Britain's military capacity and her extensive commitments and her global influence is striking.

The experience of the Crimean War revealed the weaknesses of the British self-confidence and the failure to make serious efforts at military reform. The army that faced Russia was very similar to the army that had faced Napoleon half a century earlier. Indeed the army commander, Raglan, had been Wellington's military secretary in the Peninsular War. The incompetence of the generals was compounded by the complete inability to provide logistical support in the form of medical supplies, shelter and transport for the troops. While the absence of reserve forces reduced the government to advertising for foreign mercenaries.[16] Soldiers starved to death a few miles from heavily provisioned ships due to lack of an efficient system of supply. In defense of the generals it should be said that most of them knew when they were dispatched to fight that they were utterly ill-equipped to do so. Most of the generals in fact opposed the operation but there was no mechanism in place through which they could voice their reservations.

The terrible suffering caused by the war and the public outcry to which it gave rise finally served as the catalyst for some serious rethinking of the nature of the military and some serious expenditures on its reform. British expenditures in the Crimea jumped from £9.1 million in 1853 to £76.3 million in 1854. Russia's jumped from £19.9 to £31.3 million in the same period.[17] Even with these expenditures, however, Britain was constrained by the behavior of its allies and, lacking the political or military will to fight to the finish, agreed to a compromise. This in turn served to reinforce the popular distrust of European entanglements at home and European distrust of British reliability abroad.

Russia

In the years between the Congress of Vienna and the Crimean War the steady ascent of Britain was matched by the steady decline of Russia, though the scale of the relative descent did not become apparent until the war. Just as Britain's growing wealth was not reflected in her small and relatively weak army so Russia's declining wealth was not initially reflected in her enormous and very powerful army. The Russian economy grew in the period between Vienna and the Crimea; on all the usual indicators there was a steady rate of growth. The problem for Russia was that the pace of growth among her rivals was considerably faster. While Russia's iron production, for example, doubled in the early nineteenth century, Britain's increased thirty-fold.[18] While Russia's total GNP increased, its per capita GNP dropped steadily behind.

The Russian army, in this period, however, appeared to be unrivaled in size and stature. It was engaged frequently and successfully in a number of small ventures in the Caucasus, in Turkestan, and in the suppression of the Hungarian rebellion in 1848. At the same time the Tsar declared himself willing and able to dispatch 400,000 troops to quell the revolt in Paris. The military elite were held in high regard by the Tsar and the mass conscripts were deemed reliable. Unlike the British army, the Russian army did not decrease in size during this period, a fact which could be attributed to lack of confidence in the Concert or to a return to the eighteenth-century ways of maintaining a vast peasant army.

While the war in the Crimea revealed the weaknesses of the British military the limitations that it revealed in the Russian military were even more glaring. Logistical problems were the biggest problem. Vast numbers of troops were pinned down, poorly trained, and badly armed. There were no railways south of Moscow which meant that it took often three months for troops from Moscow to reach the front – far longer than troops from Britain who arrived by sea. The Russian navy was seriously outclassed by the Anglo-French fleet. Medical and logistical support were even worse than the British. The army leadership appeared incapable of producing a coherent plan for the conduct of the war. The blockade, moreover, made it impossible for the government to finance the war. The longer the war dragged on the more apparent the inferiority of the Russian forces appeared. In the end Russia lost 480,000 men in this war. As in Britain, it was the shock of the revelations made by the war that proved the catalyst for reforms.

Prussia

Prussia was the least of the great powers in the period between the Vienna settlement and the Crimean War. It was surrounded by more powerful neighbors, with serious geographic disadvantages which were compounded by profound internal and inter-German problems. Prussia's unrivaled educational system, efficient administrative system and educated officer class could not compensate for these structural weaknesses. Indeed the Prussian military were at the forefront of considering military reforms in both tactics and strategy and in attempting to harness industrial developments to military technology. It was only after the structural problems were addressed in 1860, outside the inter-war period under consideration, that the Prussian potential in strategic planning could begin to be realized.

Austria

The Habsburg Empire was in an even more difficult position than Prussia. The leadership was in the unenviable and untenable position of defending the status quo in a changing world. The multiethnic and conservative society was bound to come under severe strain in an era of growing liberal nationalism. In the early part of the nineteenth century, however, these strains were not so obvious. What was obvious, however, was the acute financial hardships imposed by the protracted war against Napoleon. The paucity of the industrial and commercial base did little to alleviate the financial problems. Some regions did quite well but the empire as a whole fell behind Britain, France and Prussia in terms of per capita industrialization, production of iron and steel and other economic indicators.[19] The army, which was made up of as many nationalities as the Empire itself, suffered from this lack of resources. Whereas the army received 50 per cent of total revenues in 1817 this was reduced to 23 per cent in 1830 and 20 per cent by 1848, and even the funds which were allocated were inefficiently spent, due to the endemic corruption of the Austrian administration.[20] There was, in this period, no great military strategy evident in Austria – there was certainly no correlation between her military resources and the kind of wars in which she might be expected to engage. Reliance on the considerable diplomatic skill of Metternich could help for a while but only so long as the other great powers believed it to be in their interests for the Habsburg Empire to remain reasonably intact.

France

The Vienna settlement effectively kept French aspirations for European hegemony in check. France had lost about one and a half million men in the Napoleonic Wars and throughout the nineteenth century its population grew at a slower pace than that of its rivals. Economically too it was surpassed by Britain in all the economic indicators. In 1800 Britain's manufacturing output was level with France, by 1830 it was 182.5 per cent, by 1860 it was 251 per cent.[21] France remained more powerful than both Prussia and Austria but was far from being preeminent in Europe. France had both a large army, though smaller than Russia's, and a strong navy, though weaker than Britain's. The government could afford to invest in munitions and the armed forces generally and produced several military innovations in this period. Nevertheless, throughout the period under consideration here the French government had to content itself with being accepted as an equal power and was unable to elicit any support from the other powers for any revisions of the settlement of 1815.

Technological Developments

The striking domestic aspect of the period between the Vienna settlement and the Crimean War was that it witnessed technological developments that would in time transform the nature of warfare. The militaries were on the whole slow to seize upon these developments but by the end of the period they could no longer be avoided. Generally, only when civilian techniques had clearly surpassed those used by the military did the military change its ways. The development of the steam engine transformed transport both on land and on sea. Initially the military in both Britain and France were most interested in the resultant railway as a means of putting down disturbances in their big cities. Prussia benefited most from the railways which permitted the integration of its sprawling territories and permitted the rapid movement and supply of troops. Developments in communications, particularly the development of the telegraph, were to affect the conduct of warfare by permitting rapid communication between the field and the capital. This permitted both politicians and the public to have a greater say in the conduct of the war, as was amply demonstrated by the role of the British public in the Crimean War. The Prussians again made the most of these developments with Moltke's reorganization of the General Staff in 1857 and his establishment of strict bureaucratic efficiency. The Prussians too were the fastest in capitalizing on the French invention of the Minié bullet and rifle. Industrial techniques permitted them to re-bore their entire stock of muskets to turn them into rifles which could use Minié bullets in only two years.

Technological developments were most keenly felt in the maritime sphere. From the 1830s various private firms competed in building steam vessels that would quickly cross the Atlantic. In the 1840s propellers began to replace paddle wheels, iron hulls replaced wooden ones. Engines grew rapidly in size and power. The Royal Navy, with its supremacy assured since Trafalgar, and a fleet whose sail and design had served it well since the seventeenth century, was loath to change. This provided an opportunity for France to catch up with the British navy through superior technology. In 1837 France adopted shell guns. The following year Britain did the same. The French also initiated the use of steam engines in naval vessels, largely as a response to their humiliation at the hands of the Royal Navy during the Near Eastern Crisis. Technological developments thereafter were largely driven by the dynamic of the French trying to use technological advances to catch up with the British and the British adopting the French innovation.

Ultimately the Royal Navy prevailed, largely due to the willingness of the British public to make the necessary expenditures to preserve their naval superiority.

Conclusion

In looking back at the period 1815–56 it is clear that though there was a great deal of diplomatic skill in evidence in this period, there does not appear to have been as much skill in military and strategic planning. In each of the five great powers of the period there was a significant gap between the political aspirations of the governments and the military capacity to realize these ambitions. There was also in each country a considerable gap between the resources devoted to the military and the expectations to which the militaries were held. The experience of the Crimean War, for both the victors and the defeated, revealed at a terrible cost in human life and suffering the enormous shortfalls in military planning. Soldiers were poorly trained, badly led, and appallingly supported with logistics and medical facilities. Only the Prussian military was self-conscious about reform. The general conservatism of the other governments led, after the trauma of the Napoleonic Wars, not to a radical reevaluation of military principles but rather to a return to the military ways of the *ancien régime*. Statesmen appear to have concluded that the lessons to be learned from the war were primarily political rather than military. In learning from the wartime failure to forge effective coalitions the statesmen at Vienna showed considerable ingenuity and creativity but this was devoted to the creation of the new order. I can find little evidence to suggest that the same kind of innovative thinking and leadership was evident in military circles.

It was only in the latter half of the nineteenth century that the forces unleashed by industrialization and the new economy were harnessed for military developments. In defense of the military planners it should be pointed out that the pace of change in the period under review was altogether slower than in the second half of the nineteenth century. There can be no avoiding the conclusion however that the militaries were slower to change than they should have been.

In seeking to explain the failures of diplomatic and military planners in this period there appear to be a number of conclusions which hold true across the liberal and conservative regimes of Europe in the period. First, defeat appears to be a better teacher than victory. The one government to effect significant reforms was the Prussian government and they did so in the wake of a disastrous defeat at the hands of the French. In the British case, victory at Waterloo and the architects of that victory served as a bulwark against any change in the military establishment. Conversely poor performance by their armies in the Crimea served as an impetus to reform in Britain and Russia. Second, there is a natural inclination for inertia after an enormous expenditure of energy and resources. The resources of even the richest of the European governments were seriously depleted by the war and there was considerable pressure to reduce military expenditures once it was over. Third, domestic repercussions of external action require attention once the crisis has passed. The French Revolution had deeply shocked all the governments of Europe and all were preoccupied, after the defeat of Napoleon, with the need to ensure domestic stability. Fourth, in uncertainty there is a natural impulse to revert to the familiar. Far from learning from Napoleon's military stratagems in the wake of the shock he provided, European militaries retreated to the old familiar way of doing things. Finally, the relative security provided by the Concert of Europe reduced the incentive to plan for the type of eventuality the Concert was designed to prevent.

As to lessons for the planners of today, it is hard to say. There are some fairly obvious political lessons, like the importance of integrating a defeated power into the new order. The lesson for today would be to integrate Russia into NATO. The sensitivity of the early nineteenth-century statesmen to the status concerns and not just the territorial concerns of each other is another model worth emulating today. The lesson again would be to avoid unnecessary humiliation of Russia by, for example, engaging in military activities in an area formerly in her sphere of influence, or expanding our alliance to her doorstep. As to military planners the corollary to the Industrial Revolution is, of course, the revolution in information technology and the need for the military planners to seize the initiative in exploring the impact of this technological and information revolution on our military options and capacities. The final and again fairly obvious lesson is the importance of keeping a firm link between one's political aspirations and one's military capacities to achieve them.

Notes

1 Text of the treaty in Edward Hertslet, *The Map of Europe by Treaty* (London: Butterworths, 1875), p. 375.
2 Reference by Paul Gordon Lauren, 'Crisis Prevention in Nineteenth-Century Diplomacy,' in Alexander George, ed., *Managing U.S.–Soviet Rivalry: Problems of Crisis Prevention* (Boulder, CO: Westview Press, 1983), p. 56.
3 These rules are spelled out in Richard B. Elrod, 'The Concert of Europe: A Fresh Look at an International System,' *World Politics*, vol. 28, no. 2, 1976, pp. 163–7.
4 Paul Gordon Lauren has identified nine of these procedures ('Crisis Prevention in Nineteenth-Century Diplomacy,' pp. 31–64).
5 Paul Schroeder, 'Did the Vienna Settlement Rest on a Balance of Power?' *American Historical Review*, June 1992, pp. 699–700.
6 Referenced by Gordon A. Craig, 'The System of Alliances and the Balance of Power,' in J.P.T. Bury, ed., *The New Cambridge Modern History X* (Cambridge: Cambridge University Press, 1960), p. 260.
7 Castlereagh to Liverpool, 4 January 1815, as found in C.K.Webster, ed., *British Diplomacy 1813–1815: Select Documents Dealing with the Reconstruction of Europe* (London: Bell, 1921), p. 281.
8 Quoted in C.K.Webster, *Foreign Policy of Castlereagh 1812–1815* (London: Bell, 1931), p. 209.
9 Webster, *Foreign Policy of Castlereagh*, pp. 497–8.
10 Peter Burroughs, 'An Unreformed Army? 1815–68,' in David Chandler (eds), *The Oxford Illustrated History of the British Army* (Oxford: Oxford University Press, 1994), p. 164.
11 Burroughs, 'An Unreformed Army? 1815–68,' p. 164.
12 Paul M. Kennedy, *The Rise and Fall of British Naval Mastery* (London: Ashfield Press, 1994), p. 156.
13 Paul Kennedy, *The Rise and Fall of the Great Powers* (New York: Random House, 1987), pp. 143–5.
14 Kennedy, *The Rise and Fall of the Great Powers*, p. 151.
15 Kennedy, *The Rise and Fall of the Great Powers*, p. 153.
16 Kennedy, *The Rise and Fall of the Great Powers*, p. 176.
17 Kennedy, *The Rise and Fall of the Great Powers*, p. 176.
18 Kennedy, *The Rise and Fall of the Great Powers*, p. 171.
19 Kennedy, *The Rise and Fall of the Great Powers*, p. 165.
20 Kennedy, *The Rise and Fall of the Great Powers*, p. 165.
21 Kennedy, *The Rise and Fall of the Great Powers*, p. 168.

3

RUSSIAN WAR PLANNING, 1815–56

Frederick W. Kagan

War planning in the period 1815–56 was generally an informal and sporadic process. Although the Prussians had developed a sophisticated planning system run by professional military planners toward the end of this period, no other state in Europe did so. Russia certainly did not have a body of professional military planners, and Russian war planning normally focused on resolving imminent conflicts or crises. But though the system was informal and *ad hoc*, a careful study reveals that it functioned surprisingly well, at least for part of the period. In the first decade of the reign of Nicholas I (1825–55), Russia fought Persia and Turkey, suppressed a major Polish rebellion, and faced several major crises with other great powers. In each case, the tsar formed a committee to advise him consisting of very senior military officers and civilian statesmen. Each time the committee carefully considered the problem from the standpoints of military operations, grand strategy, economics, foreign policy, and domestic concerns. And each time the committee produced a carefully reasoned and well-supported proposal for a strategic course of action that Nicholas invariably adopted. The plans for military operations followed. Whatever flaws this system had, it was a complex and all-encompassing planning process that generally produced good results.

Russia's Changed Strategic Vision

The process of planning Russia's wars after 1815 was greatly complicated by the fact that the wars against Napoleon had shifted Russia's strategic vision in important ways. Throughout the seventeenth and eighteenth centuries, Russia's security concerns were aimed primarily to the north, northwest, and south. Sweden, Poland, and Turkey were the perennial threats, and a succession of Romanov tsars had conducted their military and foreign policies with those states in mind. Adventures further afield, such as Russia's participation in the Seven Years' War or the campaigns of 1798–1800 against revolutionary France, were aberrations. Many Russian leaders felt that such conflicts did not involve Russia's vital interests. Thus when Peter III took the

throne, he withdrew Russia from the Seven Years' War because he disapproved of Russia's involvement against Prussia. Similarly, when the war
against France took a bad turn in 1800, Russia simply withdrew. In the
words of one scholar,

> The fact that Russia had the now-decayed empires of Turkey and
> Persia as neighbours, and the smaller states and tribes of the
> Caucasus served as buffers against them, not only provided Russia
> with the kind of security, power, influence, and potential for gains
> in the Middle East comparable to Britain's overseas, but also,
> Russians believed, enhanced their choices in European politics. Like
> the British, they could either intervene or stay out and concentrate
> on areas where Russia had no competition.[1]

Such behavior stood in sharp contrast to the determination with which
Russia prosecuted her conflicts against Sweden, Poland, and Turkey, or with
which she involved herself in Western European problems after 1815. This
situation did not change rapidly even during Russia's first two campaigns
against Emperor Napoleon. Alexander I (1801–25), it is true, was more
deeply committed to maintaining the European order in general than his
predecessors had been, and he quickly recognized that Napoleonic France
posed a threat to that order, but he was slow to take action. A series of
Napoleonic provocations finally convinced him to involve Russia once again
directly in a war against France in 1805.[2] But Russia's commitment to that
war remained limited – only two contingents of troops constituting less than
25 per cent of the forces available to Alexander were sent to aid the
Austrians. When the war turned out badly, Alexander simply withdrew. The
same pattern was repeated almost exactly in the following year as Russian
contingents once again arrived too late to stave off the disaster that Prussia
had brought upon herself at the battles of Jena and Auerstädt. The end of
that campaign was marked by the signing of the Treaty of Tilsit, dramatically enough, on a raft on the river that formed the Russian border. The
symbolism was significant. For the first time, a Russian tsar was forced to
see that the Western European powers could pose real and meaningful
threats to the territorial integrity of the Russian state. The wars of Central
and Western Europe, in which Russia had lightheartedly involved herself or
from which she had withdrawn herself on a whim, were no longer whim-
sical. Sweden, finally defeated in 1809, had ceased to be a threat. Poland had
been abolished as a state by the Third Partition in 1795. Russian control of
the northern Black Sea littoral had been established at about the same time,
and the Ottoman Empire, therefore, had become a nuisance rather than a
threat. But in 1807 a large French army had driven into the Russian frontier
itself, and Alexander had felt obliged to call up a peasant militia of a type
not seen since the Polish invasions in the early seventeenth century. From

then on, Alexander regarded France as a major threat not only to the European order, but to Russia herself. The basis for Russian intervention in Europe's wars had shifted from one of opportunism to one of vital national interest.

The Treaty of Tilsit established less a peace than a truce. Alexander spent the half-decade it bought him attempting to put Russia's finances, armed forces, and state structure in order. By 1810 it had become clear to him that war with France was once again imminent, and he set out to prepare for it assiduously. A series of edicts swept away the old military structure and introduced a more modern, streamlined system based heavily on the French system that had brought Napoleon such success.[3] Teams of surveyors were sent to examine Russia's frontier in minutest detail, and fortresses and stockpiles were built all along the border.[4] A war with Turkey had begun in 1806, but was regarded as a distraction – so much so that Field Marshal M.I. Kutuzov, disgraced by the defeat at Austerlitz in 1805, was 'exiled' to the Turkish theater as punishment.

Napoleon's invasion of Russia in 1812 cemented Russia's turn to the west. For Alexander did not content himself with driving the invaders out, as many of his advisors recommended. Instead, he raised an enormous army, placed himself at the head of it, and led it in a triumphant march across all of Europe. In 1814 and 1815, for the first time in history, Russian armies stood in Paris.

After 1815, Alexander continued to regard the threat from the west as the primary danger to Russia. In 1816 one of Alexander's officers pointed out to him that there was considerable grumbling in the country about the failure to demobilize the army, which stood at more than 800,000 soldiers, easily three times as large as the standing force Russia had normally maintained before the wars against France. Alexander responded, 'Russia is in such a position that it must maintain an army the same size as the combined forces of Prussia and Austria; I do not take our other neighbors into account.'[5]

Nor was Alexander's concern confined to Central Europe. After 1815, he came to regard himself as the champion of the status quo and the enemy of revolution everywhere. When the Greeks rebelled against their Ottoman masters in 1821, Alexander absolutely refused to assist them despite the fact that they were his co-religionists fighting Russia's perennial arch-enemy. When the Piedmontese rebelled against their Austrian overlords that same year, however, Alexander proved quite willing to respond to Austrian requests for assistance in crushing the revolt.

Planning was done and orders sent out to create a Third Army (in addition to the First and Second Armies, which were the permanent standing forces) and to prepare it to march through Austria to aid in the suppression of the uprising. Not only was the composition of this army determined (it would consist of several infantry and cavalry corps drawn from the First Army, the Second Army, and the Army of Poland), but its units were set in motion toward the border. Other units were designated to 'backfill' the areas vacated by the elements of the new army. For a few weeks in the spring of 1821 it looked as though Russian armies would once again approach France. The crisis passed rapidly and the mobilization of the Third Army was cancelled, but Russia's deep involvement in the affairs of Western Europe was made very clear.[6]

This new focus on the west did not end with Alexander's death. When revolution broke out in Belgium in 1830 and the King of the Netherlands asked Nicholas for military assistance, he prepared his country to respond. Once again a Russian army, this time the Army of Poland under his elder brother, Grand Duke Constantine, would travel to the borders of France. In addition to that army, two infantry corps and two cavalry corps were also mobilized and sped toward the Russian frontier. Nicholas seemed to feel that a general revolutionary conflagration threatened Europe and that he would do best to stamp it out at the start. He was prepared to send 140,000 troops chasing across the continent to do it. Only the outbreak of revolution in Russian Poland itself caused the cancellation of this expedition, as Nicholas found more urgent tasks for the Army of Poland to attend to.[7]

The turn to the west was complicated and incomplete throughout this period, however. Between 1815 and 1856 Russia fought western states only once, during the Crimean War, and that conflict stemmed from a war that had been brewing between Russia and Turkey. The fact remains that throughout this period Russia's significant military operations were directed almost exclusively at traditional enemies: Persia, Turkey, and Poland. The Russo-Turkish and Russo-Polish Wars of this period do not seem in any obvious way different from Russia's wars in previous centuries.

Yet there was a change. Throughout the eighteenth century, conflict with Turkey involved Russia in negotiations with Austria; conflict with Poland in discussions with Prussia as well. The most significant European powers, France and England, played very minor roles in Russia's wars. After 1815 that changed. Although France and England actually sent forces against Russia only once in 1853, fear that one or the other or both states would intervene (whatever the unlikelihood of such intervention in reality) drove critical parts of Russian military planning in every war and crisis of this period. The initial threat from the west to which Alexander had responded, the danger of invasion by a European great land power, had evaporated in 1815. The threat had changed to the more nebulous danger that England or France or both might send expeditions against Russia while she fought one of her traditional foes. This period, therefore, was one of transition between the old threat calculus based on the northern and southern flanks, and the new threat calculus based on a land threat from the west, embodied by Germany at the end of the century. As in all periods of transition, the complexities were enormous and placed a great deal of strain on Russia's planning for war.

The Organizational Basis for War Planning

The period between the Napoleonic and the Crimean Wars was one of transition not only in international affairs, but in military organizational matters as well. Prussia's transformation of its military organization toward the end of this period would revolutionize the conduct of war. The effects of Russia's organizational reforms were less dramatic, but still significant.[8]

Alexander I had undertaken a series of reforms of the military administration before the climactic campaigns of 1812–14, but all of his efforts were incomplete, and many were mutually contradictory. In 1802 he established ministries in Russia for the first time, replacing the 'colleges' that Peter the Great had established almost a century before.[9] For a decade, however, the new war ministry had to co-exist with the bureaucratic organs of the old war college, resulting in confusion in the military administration and the diminution of the power of the war minister and his subordinates. Although the war college bureaucracy was finally abolished entirely in 1812, confusion remained. For the laws that abolished the war college also created a new position, Commander in Chief of a Large Active Army. The orders this commander issued were to be obeyed as though they originated with the tsar, and this commander had sweeping powers not only over the army he commanded, but over the civil government of the region within which that army happened to be operating. What is more, although Alexander ultimately appointed four commanders with these powers in 1812, no law or edict clarified their relationship to one another. Confusion within this organization was clearly reflected in the conduct of the campaign of 1812, as in the famous instance when P.I. Bagration refused to take orders from M.B. Barclay de Tolly on the grounds that they were equals in rank and commanding separate units. Moreover, the confusion between the commander's powers over the local logistics administrations and over those of the central military administration facilitated the inefficiency and corruption that flourished within the army and the war ministry throughout the rest of the wars against Napoleon.[10]

Throughout the reforms of 1812, war planning was not a major concern and no formal organs to conduct planning existed. Some important progress was, nevertheless, made in laying the groundwork for war planning in the future. The reforms of 1812 created a Military–Scientific Committee (*Voenno-uchenyi komitet* – VUA) that was tasked with gathering all available foreign works on military art and translating the best of them into Russian, with overseeing various experiments in military technology, and with a number of other functions. The archive of the VUA remains one of the best sources for Russian military history throughout the last century of the Imperial period. At the same time, the Military–Topographic Depot was charged with collecting and, when appropriate, commissioning maps of Russia and of the states on Russia's borders. The materials in both of these archives were clearly essential for the production of war plans, even if these agencies themselves were not charged with and did not undertake war planning.[11]

The reforms of 1812 were undone in the course of the final wars against France. In 1813 Alexander took the field with his armies, and, discovering that the structures he had created before the war were inadequate, he simply ignored them. He communicated his wishes concerning military operations through his chief of staff, P.M. Volkonskii, who effectively ran the Russian contingents in Western Europe in the tsar's name. When the wars were over, Alexander issued several decrees that simply made formal law from what had been informal practice. A new organ, the Main Staff of His Imperial Majesty, was formally created with Volkonskii at its head. It absorbed all of the operational elements of the war ministry which, henceforth, became merely an agency for overseeing the economic aspects of the army. Most importantly, the chiefs of staff of the armies, corps, and divisions received a dual subordination: they reported both to the commanders of their units and to the chiefs of staff of the units directly above them. The chiefs of staff of the First and Second Armies, thus, reported directly to Volkonskii. A staff system similar in structure to that of Prussia and, later, Germany came into being in Russia in 1816.[12]

There was still no agency responsible for war planning in the new structure, but the very prominence of the new senior staff officers encouraged a greater regard for this problem. For example, P.D. Kiselev, the chief of staff of the Second Army stationed along the borders of the Ottoman and Habsburg Empires, for the first time undertook a systematic study of previous campaigns against Turkey with an eye toward developing an appropriate plan for fighting against that state again.

The accession of Tsar Nicholas I in 1825 ushered in a period of great turbulence within Russia's military organization as well as her security situation. Persia, perceiving Russia's weakness in the wake of the abortive Decembrist Uprising of that year, attacked in 1826, hoping to seize back her former territories in the Caucasus. The Ottoman Empire, emboldened in part by Russia's weakness and in part by its own desperation, declared a *jihad* against Russia in 1827 and prepared for the war with Russia that followed in 1828. In 1830, the wave of liberal revolution finally reached Russia's Polish territories, and the Polish Rebellion lasted well into the following year.[13]

Although Russia was victorious in all of these conflicts, concerns about the complications emanating from Western Europe tarnished those victories. Nicholas was perennially terrified that delays in the advance of Russian troops would invite western intervention. He emerged from the Russo-Turkish War seriously shaken, from the Polish Rebellion convinced that Russia was in serious danger. The latter crisis in particular brought home to him most vividly the dangers Russia would face should England and France ever combine to fight Russia in defense of some border state. It was the clearest possible warning of the dangers of the Crimean War scenario, and it was examined at the time, as we shall see, though the most important lessons were not learned.

The war against Turkey also underlined the serious problems that had existed in the military organization established by Alexander. The dual-subordination of chief of staff of the Second Army, P.D. Kiselev, for example, as well as ambiguity about the role of Chief of the Main Staff of His Imperial Majesty I.I. Dibich, created a great deal of confusion. Kiselev, working directly with Dibich, circumvented Count P.Kh. Wittgenstein, the nominal commander of the army. Worse still, Dibich and Kiselev did not by any means always agree on the best way to conduct operations. Nicholas took the field with the army in 1828, further complicating matters, and a complex four-way correspondence sprang up among Kiselev, Dibich, Wittgenstein, and Nicholas that hindered both the planning and the conduct of ongoing operations. Nicholas solved the problem temporarily by sacking Wittgenstein, transferring Kiselev to a line command, leaving the theater of war, and placing Dibich in actual command of the armies in the theater. This change greatly aided the Russian campaign of 1829.

War Minister A.I. Chernyshev convinced Nicholas in the wake of that war, however, that a more permanent solution was necessary. Nicholas responded by once again reorganizing Russia's military administration. In a series of decrees issued between 1832 and 1836, Nicholas abolished the Main Staff of His Imperial Majesty (in peacetime – it would be reconstituted in wartime) and centralized the entire military administration under the control of the war minister. It was a sweeping and energetic reform that boded well for the long-term modernization of Russia's armies. By centralizing control of the entire military administration in the hands of the war minister, the reform permanently eliminated the problem of dual-subordination that plagues general staff-type organizations. The reform rationalized the military administration, made it more efficient and cost-effective, and placed it on a sound and coherent legal footing. The basic form of the new organization was so effective that it has remained the basis for the Russian and Soviet armies to this day.[14]

The more immediate consequences of the reform, however, were not entirely positive. The reforms' author, War Minister A.I. Chernyshev, lost interest in perfecting the administration once he had gained sole control of it. For the decade and a half following the end of the reforms in 1836, the war ministry and the army stagnated. Reforms of the combat units of the army itself, especially at the highest level, were conducted only half-heartedly and incompletely. By the end of Nicholas' reign, inefficiency and corruption were once again important factors degrading the effectiveness of Russia's military.

From the standpoint of war planning, the most serious problem with the reorganized military administration was the relative insignificance of the elements of a general staff, although a considerable amount of positive work essential for successful war planning was done. The newly reorganized war ministry contained a General Staff Department headed by the Quartermaster General. That department contained two sections, of which one was responsible for collecting and reviewing military historical, topographical, and statistical information about Russia and the other states of Europe, especially Russia's neighbors. The closest thing to a long-range planning cell, this section was charged with 'consideration of the defense and security of the borders of the Empire in general and in the higher relation.'[15] The General Staff Department also oversaw the activities of the Military–Topographical Depot. The work and effects of this department are hard to judge, but its existence does reflect a belief in the importance of long-range planning and of the collection and dissemination of information, both intelligence and academic, to the war planning process.

Other positive signs in this era were the founding of the General Staff Academy in 1832, clearly a critical step in the process of developing professional military planners and strategists, and the undertaking of an extremely impressive series of histories of the wars against Napoleon. The author of those histories, Lieutenant General A.I. Mikhailovskii-Danilevskii, was a member of the Military Council, the most senior formal collective body of military advisors in the state, and was asked to undertake the historical project by Nicholas himself. Mikhailovskii-Danilevskii used the enormous collection of documents available in the archives, and also sent questionnaires to surviving participants and interviewed others. Nicholas and War Minister Chernyshev read each draft of Mikhailovskii-Danilevskii's work, suggesting revisions and corrections. Their numerous comments on the drafts show how seriously they took the project.

War planning and the study of war in general, thus, was hardly neglected in the Russian war ministry in this period. But the professionalization of that study was only just beginning, and the results of these developments were not truly visible until the 1860s and the revolutionary reorganization of the army and the military administration that occurred under the leadership of War Minister D.A. Miliutin (who, incidentally, was asked to complete the last of Mikhailovskii-Danilevskii's histories upon the latter's death). Yet the General Staff Department held a relatively lowly position within the war ministry hierarchy, and it certainly could not compete in power and influence with the Prussian general staff that was also developing at this time. Chernyshev, moreover, who served as war minister from 1827 until 1852, was more concerned with administering the enormous establishment under his control than with planning.

Chernyshev also did not have operational control over the bulk of Russia's forces which belonged to the Commander in Chief of the Active Army, I.F. Paskevich, for most of this period. It was easy for him, therefore, to expect that Paskevich and his staff would do most of the planning.

Unfortunately, Paskevich had not really participated in the brief professionalization of the Russian staff system between 1816 and 1832 – he had simply held commands. What is more, he was possessed of an overbearing and overconfident personality, while his military skills and thinking were limited. He was an unfortunate choice for this important command, and his flaws helped stifle any prospect of serious war planning on the Active Army's own staff.

Overall, the reorganization of the military administration in Nicholas' reign laid important foundations for war planning within the war ministry bureaucracy, but did not make it a high priority. Planning throughout this period was conducted, therefore, either at the level of army staffs, or through the temporary creation of *ad hoc* committees to study possible courses of action during crises. Strange as it may seem, the latter method of planning was generally excellent and usually produced very good results.

Planning for War against Turkey, 1816–29

The Russo-Turkish War of 1806–12 ended with the Treaty of Bucharest – a peace designed to free Russia's forces to meet the impending war with Napoleon and to buy an exhausted Turkey time to recover. It was a peace unsatisfactory to both sides and difficult to enforce. With the conclusion of the wars against France, therefore, many leading officials in the Russian government turned their attention back to the unfinished business of Turkey, convinced that another war would follow relatively soon. A great number of war plans were developed by various individuals following the outbreak of the Greek Revolution against Turkey in 1821.

As a result, a number of experienced officers on their own initiative prepared a variety of concepts for a renewed campaign against Turkey. The authors of many of these plans would hold critical positions during the wars against Turkey in 1828–29. General I.I. Dibich would be the Chief of the Main Staff; General P.D. Kiselev would be chief of staff of the Second Army – the army that fought the war; and General E.F. Kankrin would be minister of finance.[16]

Of these, Kiselev was in the best position to write war plans, for he was chief of staff of the Second Army from 1819 until 1829. Throughout the 1820s he worked attentively on the problem, ultimately making use of the materials collected at the Military Topographic Depot and the Military–Scientific Committee and elsewhere, with the countenance of the Chief of the Main Staff of His Imperial Majesty. Using his own authority (he effectively ran the Second Army, since its nominal commander, General Wittgenstein, was a cipher with no influence at court), he sent spies to gather information about the Turkish fortresses, the road network in European Turkey, and the disposition and movement of Turkish forces. The fact that it was necessary to collect much of this information says a great deal about the informality of war planning before this period, for Russia had been fighting Turkey for decades, and the most recent campaign in European Turkey had ended only in 1812. The assiduousness with which Kiselev approached the task, however, revealed a streak of nascent professionalism which would serve both him and Russia well in the campaign that followed.

From the outset, Kiselev approached the problem from both an operational and a grand strategic perspective. In a memorandum of 1826, while the negotiations between Russia and Turkey that would lead to the Treaty of Akkerman of that year were underway, Kiselev pointed out the advantages that Russia would accrue by seizing the principalities of Moldavia and Wallachia. For both operational and grand strategic reasons, he advocated a preemptive strike in the event of the failure of negotiations. Operationally, the occupation of the principalities would allow for a much speedier beginning to any serious campaign against the Ottomans, would facilitate the rapid reduction of the feared Ottoman fortresses, and would provide a forward base from which to conduct serious reconnaissance of the foe. Grand strategically, Kiselev reasoned that such a bold move so early in Nicholas' reign could only have salutary effects on Russia's foreign policy in general.[17] The problem, as we shall see, is that Kiselev assumed that Russia would be pursuing specific military objectives, particularly the seizure of Constantinople, that Nicholas did not, in fact, desire to pursue. It is difficult for a theater staff officer to conduct a grand strategic appraisal of the problem facing him, and it is no surprise that Kiselev did not assess the situation quite correctly. His effort, however, was impressive.

As the war approached more clearly and imminently Kiselev turned his attention more carefully to the development of specific plans of operation and the preparation of the army for war. He worked out a detailed plan for mobilizing the Second Army. Measures of economy had stripped the force of most of its horses, which were as essential for armies in the nineteenth century as motor vehicles are for the armies of today. Without horses, cannon and equipment could not be moved and, above all, supplies could not be transported from collection points to the troops. Kiselev laid out in detail how many horses were needed, where they had to go, what they would cost, and how he intended to go about buying them. Similar attention was paid to other essential equipment of the army.[18]

Unfortunately, Nicholas' desire to save money overcame the advice of his officers. The Second Army was not authorized actually to begin buying horses until shortly before the campaign began. Similar delays bedeviled plans to purchase and move equipment and supplies. As a result, the frantic last-minute effort to buy thousands of horses drove the price of the animals up and created shortages. These shortages produced a ripple effect throughout the supply system. Kiselev had developed a clever plan to rely on the Black Sea Fleet to transport supplies from southern Ukraine to the ports along the Bulgarian coast. The boats brought the supplies to the ports, but there were no horses to transport them inland! Troops in and around the ports feasted while troops in the interior died of starvation.[19]

The situation was exacerbated by the confusion that resulted from the main staff system, discussed above. While Kiselev was working out the details in Tulchin, the Second Army headquarters, Chief of the Main Staff of His Imperial Majesty Dibich was developing his own plans in St. Petersburg – without bothering to consult Kiselev. Thus Kiselev developed a supply system intended to support the 100,000 soldiers he thought would be fighting – but Dibich actually sent 115,000. One historian has noted that the extremely high mortality rate among Russian soldiers from disease in 1828 was the only thing that saved the army from starvation.[20]

Thus confused, contradictory, and only partially implemented, it is no surprise that the war plans in 1828 did not create the preconditions for success in the campaign of that year. The Russian attack rapidly stalled as Turkish fortresses proved harder than expected to reduce, as the inadequacy of the force Nicholas had allocated to the campaign became apparent, and as administrative inefficiency and logistical disorganization began to take its toll. Nicholas had hoped and planned to end the campaign in 1828. Instead, the new year found his armies still working on reducing the Turkish fortresses guarding the crossings over the Danube. Worse still, rightly or wrongly Nicholas was becoming convinced that another poor campaign in 1829 would completely undermine Russia's international position and might even lead to English intervention in the war. He felt that he faced a real crisis, and he sought the advice of trusted subordinates to assist him in making a critical decision.

It is essential to keep in mind two things about Nicholas when studying his actions in this period. He was only 32 when the war broke out in 1828, three years after he had taken the throne, and he had not been raised to be tsar. That position by the law of succession in Russia had been supposed to go to his elder brother Constantine upon Alexander's death, but unbeknownst to Nicholas, Constantine had preemptively abdicated long before 1825.[21] The resulting confusion when Alexander died – Nicholas in St. Petersburg had the palace guard swear allegiance to Constantine, while the latter, living in Warsaw, had *his* guard swear allegiance to Nicholas – led to the Decembrist rebellion. The fact that Nicholas had not expected to be Russia's ruler, together with his comparative youth, made him relatively insecure and desirous of the advice of senior statesmen. He naturally welcomed a suggestion to convene a council of war, which he did in the form of the Committee of 19 November 1828.

Nicholas presided over this committee, which also included the superannuated General I.V. Vasil'chikov, who had suggested it, War Minister and Deputy Chief of the Main Staff of His Imperial Majesty, A.I. Chernyshev, Chairman of the State Council V.P. Kochubei, and Chief of the Main Staff of the First Army (which was not engaged in combat in the Balkans), Baron

K.F.Tol'. Nicholas was the youngest of those present by some ten years. He had been only 19 years old when the Napoleonic Wars had ended, and his elder brother had kept him entirely away from the fighting fronts. Even Chernyshev, the next youngest member of the group, had served as diplomat, spy, and combat commander in the wars against the French.[22]

The formation of the committee was, in part, a response to a series of stinging memoranda sent forward by Vasil'chikov, Chief of the Main Staff Dibich, the Commander of the Second Army P.Kh. Wittgenstein, and others. Their implied criticism seems to have stirred Nicholas to give some thought to exactly what he wanted to achieve in this war. He began the committee's first session, accordingly, with a clear statement of his aims:

> The goal of our current war with Turkey consists not in the conquest of Constantinople or in the overthrow of the sultan, but in the acquisition of as many guarantees as possible to drive the Ottoman Porte to the conclusion of a peace that will make possible henceforth the securing, in a firm and inflexible fashion, the precise execution of all privileges granted already by Turkey to Russia in preceding treaties.[23]

The absence of such a clear statement of goals during the planning phase was clearly one of the reasons for the confusion and inadequacy of the planning. This problem was remarked upon at the time: Kiselev, considering a war plan sent to him by Dibich, noted in 1827:

> The muster of troops into Corps or detachments, the preparation of supplies, of ammunition, and many other minor considerations depend *on the final goal of the war*, which cannot be determined without knowing the political relations of Russia to the other powers, and therefore the composition of *a plan of war*, without the necessary basis for this, would be a problematic proposition and completely useless.[24]

That Kiselev was correct was shown, in part, by the speedy success Russia's armies were able to achieve in 1829 when the goals of the war had been clearly spelled out, and the forces Nicholas was willing to use to achieve them determined precisely.

Nicholas, fearful of another failed campaign, imagined that he would conduct a war of delay and attrition in 1829. He would content himself with seizing the principalities of Moldavia and Wallachia and await the Turks' response. The committee, however, evaluated the foreign political situation in general, the nature of the theater of war, the problems of the internal organization and administration of the army, and the ultimate objectives of the campaign. It concluded that a war of attrition and delay was unwise and that only by striking aggressive blows could the campaign's objectives be attained without undue risk. Nicholas was convinced.

Several members of the committee called for an increase in the number of troops committed to the campaign, pointing out that the Russian forces had clearly not had the necessary strength to accomplish all the tasks necessary for success – which was a major cause of the failure of the campaign of 1828. Nicholas refused, citing the difficulties the Russians were having supplying the limited number of troops already in the theater. It appears that he was also afraid of concentrating too large a proportion of his army in the Balkans when he feared English and Austrian intervention on behalf of the Turks.[25] He set a ceiling on the troops he was willing to commit at 120,000, which the committee accepted perforce.

The committee then examined the state of play in the theater carefully, and developed a detailed plan. Russian forces would immediately attack two critical fortresses, Silistria and Shumla, and push along the Bulgarian coast toward Constantinople, hoping to force the sultan to terms before an attack on the Ottoman capital became necessary. Recognizing the difficulty they had had in taking Turkish fortresses rapidly in the previous year, the committee noted explicitly that Shumla had only to be masked, not necessarily taken.[26]

The campaign of 1828 had revealed a number of important problems in the organization of the highest level of leadership in the army, and Nicholas determined to resolve them. Nicholas placed Dibich himself, still Chief of the Main Staff of His Imperial Majesty, at the head of the armies in the theater, fired Wittgenstein, and transferred Kiselev to a line command. He also removed himself from the theater. The campaign of 1829 was brilliantly successful. Not only did the plan work well, but the enemy cooperated. For once forsaking their fortresses, the Turks amassed a large army in the field that Dibich was able to fall upon with a great deal of force. The result was the Battle of Kulevcha, which destroyed the Ottoman field army, allowed Dibich to take Adrianople, the capital of European Turkey, and, ultimately, forced the sultan to terms before any attack on Constantinople became necessary.

The planning process before the outbreak of the Russo-Turkish War had been problematic. Isolated individuals, some with access to the pertinent information, some without, had developed a series of mutually contradictory war plans without consulting one another. The chief of staff of the army that would fight the war had raised a variety of grand strategic issues that were not resolved before the war's beginning. He had developed a detailed war plan that was not in accord with the strategic vision of the war that would ultimately evolve. Even that plan, moreover, had been executed too late and partially. These planning problems resulted to a large extent from the confused organization of the army's command and staff structure. That confusion complicated not only the planning process, but also the execution of the plan. The result was a highly confused and unsuccessful campaign.

In the winter of 1828–29, however, Nicholas undertook a much more systematic and rational planning process for the following year's campaign. With a group of experienced advisors who could look at the war from a variety of perspectives, military and non-military, he had first enunciated a grand strategic vision. He had then worked with the group to produce a general plan for the prosecution of the campaign. That vision was communicated to the Chief of the Main Staff so that he could develop it into a detailed campaign plan that he was then put in charge of executing. Nicholas had created, for the moment, a highly effective system of war planning, and it produced immediately gratifying results.

This process of planning-by-committee became Nicholas' normal response to crisis. Russia's success in 1829 was so great that it appeared, for a time, to have undermined the sultan's ability to continue to rule his empire. Nicholas became concerned that the Ottoman Empire would collapse and he determined to fix upon Russia's best course of action in that eventuality. He convened, accordingly, another secret committee in September 1829 for the purpose of studying this question. This committee consisted of A.N. Golitsyn, a senior statesman with no military position, P.A. Tolstoi, one of the most senior of Nicholas' military advisors, Count Nessel'rode, Russia's foreign minister, D.V. Dashkov, a civilian advisor, and A.I. Chernyshev, Deputy Chief of the Main Staff and war minister. It was chaired not by Nicholas, but by V.P. Kochubei, one of the most senior civilian statesmen.[27]

This committee examined the various issues raised by Turkey's apparent weakness, and came to some interesting conclusions. Foreign Minister Nessel'rode argued that it was essential for Russia to preserve the Porte, for 'any other order of things that might be substituted there could not equal for us the advantage of having a weak state for a neighbor.' Dashkov agreed: 'A policy setting for itself the goal of the fall of the Turkish Empire does not correspond with the true interests of Russia.' The committee concluded, accordingly:

1   The advantages presented by the maintenance of the Ottoman Empire in Europe surpass the inconveniences accompanying its existence.
2   In consequence of this the fall of the Ottoman Empire does not correspond with the true interests of Russia.
3   Common sense demands that we prevent that fall, having sought out all possible means remaining to us for the conclusion of an honorable peace.[28]

Nicholas not only accepted these recommendations – he acted upon them. First, they were transmitted to Dibich who was negotiating the final peace treaty with Turkey. Second, Chernyshev sought to embody the resolution of the committee in military planning. In December he wrote to Nicholas, 'The actual situation of the Ottoman Empire presents an appearance so little reassuring that, in the most direct interests of Russia it imposes upon [us] the obligation to consider . . . the possibility that the Ottoman dynasty will succumb to one of the crises that are always reborn [and] that do not cease to menace it.' He asked Nicholas to establish a force of some 30,000 men, together with the necessary transports, ready to move to the Dardanelles on a moment's notice in the event of danger.[29] In 1833, Mohammed Ali, the ruler of Egypt, nominally under Turkish suzerainty, rebelled and marched on Constantinople with a large army. He found Russian troops before him in Anatolia opposite the Straits. He withdrew and the sultan continued to rule.

In this case, we see a committee formed to consider and rule upon a long-term grand strategic vision, which was accepted by the tsar, fleshed out by relevant military authorities, and acted upon when it came to the test. The lack of continuity between the two committees is interesting, considering that both were concerned with the same basic issues. But in 1828 Nicholas had faced a fundamentally military dilemma, and he had convened some of his most trusted and experienced military officers in a panel to advise him. The problem of 1829 was basically diplomatic and grand strategic, and the make-up of the committee reflected that emphasis. One of the advantages of this *ad hoc* system of planning, thus, is that composition of the planning agency can be tailored to the specific situation. It does not force individuals with certain areas of expertise and modes of thought to prepare plans and address issues for all areas of concern to the state.

The Revolutions of 1830 and the Preview of the Crimean War

The wave of liberalism that swept across Europe in the late 1820s and early 1830s had a number of important consequences for Russia, imposing new planning challenges and highlighting new dangers. Throughout the 1820s, England had been relatively friendly to Russia's desire to maintain the status quo in Europe. With the ascendancy of the Whigs in the 1830s, England became a deadly enemy, eager to support liberalism and seeing Russia as the primary foe. France's turn to liberalism at the same time revolutionized the political and military scene. For the first time England could threaten Russia not merely with the Royal Navy and nuisance raiding, but with serious invasion supported by English ships and executed by French soldiers. At the same time, European unrest during and after the revolutions generated a number of possible *casus belli*, and it was not long before Nicholas was forced to confront the possibility of war with France and England together.

It is not at all clear that England or France would have gone to war with Russia in any of the crises of the 1830s and 1840s. Domestic difficulties and restrictions in both states militated strongly against such actions. For the purposes of the present study, however, that issue is irrelevant. It mattered only that Russia's leaders and planners believed that war with France and England was possible, at times likely, and that they had to respond to that danger in their planning. The discussion that follows proceeds explicitly from the standpoint of the planners and from their assumption, right or wrong, that a war between Russia and France and England was a possibility seriously to be reckoned with throughout this period.

The first crisis came at the end of 1830, when Russia's Polish subjects rebelled, taking advantage of the fact that Alexander I had permitted Poland to retain a large Polish army under nominal Russian control, but commanded by Polish officers. This force, together with irregular and guerrilla forces, rapidly posed a serious threat to Russian control not only over Poland proper, but also over the border territories in Ukraine and Lithuania. Nicholas responded by sending Dibich at the head of a powerful army to meet the danger, but Dibich and his forces did not immediately attain success. The Poles' determination, the guerrilla nature of some of the combat, and the fact that the army's rear areas could never be properly secured, all combined to inflict severe losses on Dibich's forces. Because casualties taken during the Russo-Persian and Russo-Turkish Wars had yet to be fully replaced, those forces, furthermore, had entered conflict under strength.

The crisis generated by the possible intervention of France and England (to Russian minds), together with the difficulties Dibich was encountering in suppressing the rebellion, forced Nicholas to solve grand strategic problems that had important domestic political consequences. He had to find a way both to make good the deficiencies in manpower of the army operating against the rebels and to form yet another reserve army behind it. Moreover, he had to accomplish both tasks without generating rebellion within his own territories.

Fear of rebellion within the Russian lands themselves was not unfounded. Recruitment during the wars against Persia and Turkey did not maintain the army at anything like full strength, but it had been more than enough to cause grumbling and discontent in the provinces. In this relation it is important to keep in mind that prior to the emancipation of the serfs in 1861, Russia's army was not recruited from its enormous population as a whole, but only from the population of serfs – a population about as large as that of the Austrian Empire at that time. But whereas the Austrians maintained an army of only a few hundred thousand men and fought no major wars in this period, the Russians supported a force of over 800,000 active troops and were fighting constantly. The burden on the peasantry of such recruitment was not light.

Worse still, there was no rural police force in Russia. The tsars relied upon the army itself to maintain order in the countryside. The combination of recruitment, which might generate rebellion, with redeployment of the army from the interior to the borders and Poland, which would take away the only force capable of suppressing that rebellion, was more than Nicholas could risk. Once again he formed a secret committee to study the matter and make recommendations. Some of its members had served on the previous committee: Golitsyn, Vasil'chikov, Chernyshev, and Dashkov. Others were new, including Zakrevskii, now the minister of internal affairs, Kankrin, minister of finance, and a number of other senior military and civil advisors. This time Nicholas proffered a solution he had developed on his own, which would create a reserve army that might have been barely adequate to the task at hand. He admonished the committee, however, to consider his proposal objectively and make whatever recommendations it saw fit.[30]

The committee once again considered the matter from all angles. It recommended that he take no action at that time, but delay the formation of his new forces until the annual fall recruiting season, despite warnings from the war minister and others that a considerable time would elapse from that point before the new troops were fit for combat. The most powerful argument that the committee used to defend this view was that the new drafts would alienate the peasantry and generate rebellions that the army would not then be able to suppress. Grand strategic considerations also entered the picture, however: '[the committee] found that the consequences of a strong armament on our part without evident necessity could be very grave.' Provoked by an increase in Russia's military power the cause for which was unclear, Russia's enemies might decide to pre-empt a supposed Russian attack by striking at Russia's allies, particularly Prussia, which was then the weakest state in Europe. The committee warned that Russia would not be able to meet such a challenge: 'in this way a measure that is unusual and not necessitated by any clear disasters may place powers friendly to us in difficulties, and even in danger, the consequences of which would be harmful for us ourselves as well.'[31] Grand strategic and domestic political considerations overrode immediate operational difficulties. Nicholas accepted the committee's recommendations and delayed action. Happily for him, the Polish Rebellion collapsed before the new drafts were necessary.

In this case, we see an *ad hoc* committee once again make a careful survey of the entire foreign political and grand strategic horizon before ruling on a military issue – and Nicholas accepted the ruling despite the fact that it ran counter to his initial recommendations and desires. The members of this committee who had served on the previous committees provided an important element of continuity, but the flexibility of this *ad hoc* planning system was once again clear. Obviously the matter under discussion affected the minister of internal affairs and the finance minister much more directly than the foreign minister. It helped that both of those officials had held senior positions within the military administration earlier in their careers. That the committee could not find a solution at all adequate for the military problem at hand was more ominous. If the rebellion had gone on, or if one of the other powers had intervened, it is quite clear that the forces Russia had available could not have met the challenge. For the first time a relatively effective planning process could suggest little more than that the problem go away – larger constraints prevented the recommendation of a true solution.

Nicholas' relief when the Polish crisis blew over in 1831 was not long-lived. Liberalism had struck in Turkey as well, with the result that Mohammed Ali, the ruler of Egypt, as already mentioned, menaced the Ottoman Empire with a large and effective army. The dispatch of Russian forces to defend the sultan in 1833 was effective – but highly dangerous. Throughout the operation Nicholas feared that England and France would intervene against him to prevent him from gaining a permanent ascendancy at Constantinople that he did not intend to seek. He was forced, therefore, to consider the very real possibility of war against England and France in a theater of war defined by the possessions of the Ottoman Empire – a situation close enough to what would eventually emerge in 1853 to be worth careful historical examination.

Planning for this eventuality proceeded somewhat differently from the previous cases. The initiative seems to have come either from Nicholas himself or from War Minister Chernyshev, and the planning seems to have been confined primarily to the organs of the war ministry and the main staff.[32] To begin with, Chernyshev looked to fairly recent historical examples of periods of hostility or potential hostility between Russia and England. Thus Russian plans for war with England in 1800, 1807–08, and 1828 were retrieved and examined. It became almost immediately apparent that those crises had borne little or no similarity to the situation in which Russia found herself in 1833.

In 1800, 1807, and 1808, England had been virtually without European allies that would have contemplated war with Russia. In the latter two years, in fact, Russia was allied with Napoleonic France by the Treaty of Tilsit. On none of these occasions did the Russians have to be worried about the possibility of a French army transported by British ships attacking Russia. The plans for defense in those years, therefore, focused almost exclusively on the strengthening and garrisoning of critical coastal fortresses. Even those plans, moreover, were cursory and inadequate, for the crises inevitably blew over long before they could be completed or implemented in any meaningful way. The situation in 1828 was little different. Hostile though England might be, she still did not have a large army, and there was little likelihood that France would support an attack on Russia in defense of Turkey, in whose territorial integrity she had little interest.

By 1833, however, Nicholas felt that the situation had changed. The liberal regime in France, he believed, would eagerly join with England in opposing Russian involvement again in Turkey. By that point, England and France had developed an *entente cordiale* in defense of liberalism, while the Holy Alliance (Russia, Austria, and Prussia), which Russia clearly led, seemed to them determined to maintain the status quo and suppress revolution everywhere. As a result, unlike in the previous cases, Nicholas clearly felt that he had to worry about the landing of a French army on Russian soil.

Detailed studies of what needed to be done to bring the coastal fortresses to a state of adequate readiness were developed. What is more, a careful analysis of what ground forces would be necessary to defend against Franco-British attack was made and the particular units that would comprise that force were designated. All this work, it appears, was carried out by the war ministry itself, calling upon other government agencies, civil and military, for information and assistance as required.

The difference between the nature of the planning for this crisis and that of the previous crises probably simply reflects the fact that this crisis had not yet taken place. England and France had not declared war or even begun war preparations, and so these considerations were simply in the nature of prudent preparations. In 1828, 1829, and 1831, on the contrary, the crisis under consideration was hot and getting hotter when the committee planners met. By all the signs it seems likely that a similar pattern would have been repeated in 1833 had the crisis been more protracted and serious.

In many respects, it is probably unfortunate for Russia that this last crisis blew over so quickly, for this was the one that most merited careful study. The war plans drawn up called for committing four out of Russia's eight deployable infantry corps to the defense of the coastline, while two other corps would remain behind in Poland (both to garrison the recently re-subjugated Poles and to defend against possible Austrian attack or French attack through Prussia). One corps would hold the Turkish frontier, while the last corps would remain in Moscow as a nominal reserve (although several weeks' march away from any likely theater of war). It was not thought that more than 15,000 troops or so could be supported in the Crimea. Chernyshev would have liked to have assigned an additional infantry division 'in the nature of a reserve to cover Odessa or Sevastopol as necessary. This measure was recognized as essential in the considerations made in 1833 but was not finally resolved upon because of the extreme difficulties that would beset then the supply of forces in the Novorossiisk area.'[33]

The proposed deployment clearly demonstrates the Mahanian principle that a land power is at a severe disadvantage when attempting to defend its coastline against a sea power, since it must be strong everywhere, whereas the naval power can choose when and where to mass forces. In this case, it is quite clear that Russia would not have been able to defend the Crimea or southern Ukraine against an Anglo-French assault supplied from the sea. It is also clear that the massive forces deployed along the Baltic littoral would not have sufficed to keep that area free from invaders. A small raiding party would have been rounded up in short order. A corps-sized attack, however, including French soldiers, might have achieved local superiorities of two or three to one in that critical region. That Anglo-British force might have hoped to defeat successive Russian forces piecemeal as they raced to the site of the attack. Russia's defenses, expensive though they promised to be, were by no means sure actually to defend.

The Crimean War

During the Crimean War, Russia deployed over 2.5 million men, 1.7 million of them in regular units. In place of the 15,000 or so troops it had been thought the Russians could support in the Crimea in 1833, there were over 320,000 Russian soldiers there by 1856 – over 440,000 including those deployed around the Black Sea littoral.[34]

This deployment, probably the largest armed force fielded in European history at that time, was inadequate. It came too late to deter the war or prevent the situation in the Crimea from collapsing. What is more, no coherent plan existed that would have allowed Russia to strike at her enemies. In other words, Nicholas had no means to use this enormous force, many times the size of the Franco-British forces, to achieve his ends. Once again it appears likely that, as in 1828, he had entered this conflict without even knowing exactly what his objectives were. The result was a humiliating Russian defeat.

It is not clear that careful planning in the 1830s could have solved the problem. The fact remains that Russia's surrender in the Crimean War resulted primarily from her bankruptcy following an enormously expensive war – Franco-British forces victorious at Sevastopol could hardly have expected to march from there to Kiev, let alone St. Petersburg, in the face of Russia's unfought millions. Nicholas had worked assiduously throughout his reign to correct Russia's finances, but here her backwardness caught up with him. While the Industrial Revolution was creating wealth in the west, Russia had yet to experience it to any great degree. While England, France, and Prussia modernized their economies, used their new wealth to build railways, and re-equipped their small armies with rifles, Nicholas could afford to do none of those things. Worst of all, the persistence of serfdom in Russia both severely constrained the manpower available to the army and prevented Nicholas from adopting a cadre-and-reserve system of manning as the Prussians had done. And, of course, serfdom was one of the main reasons why the Industrial Revolution did not make it to Russia.

Nicholas seems to have been aware of the evils of serfdom. He was definitely made aware of how badly the serf system constrained recruiting for the army, and he seems genuinely to have disliked the very institution of serfdom. For a variety of systemic reasons, however, he did not feel that he could abolish it. What could adequate long-range planning have done in such a circumstance?

The example of Prussia provides an intriguing basis for reflection on that question. That state, threatened on all sides by more powerful neighbors, deliberately worked to offset that disadvantage by building a dense and efficient rail network, suitable for military use. The state and especially the military was deeply involved in the development of that network, and the importance of that involvement was demonstrated in 1866, when Prussian armies destroyed those of Austria in a matter of weeks – thanks largely to a superior concentration on the battlefield made possible by Prussia's railways.[35]

The close examination of the problems in 1833 makes clear that one powerful aid to the situation would have been the development of an adequate inter-theater rail network in Russia. A large part of Russia's strategic problem was that the major possible theaters of war, Poland, Turkey, the Baltic littoral, and the Crimea, are separated from one another by hundreds of kilometers. Even a reserve placed in the center remained weeks away by foot from any given theater. Double-tracked rail lines running from St. Petersburg, Riga, Warsaw, Kishenev, Odessa, and Sevastopol to Moscow would have made it possible to contemplate shifting forces from one theater to another with relative rapidity. What is more, it would have greatly alleviated the horrific logistics problems the Russians faced in trying to maintain a large force on their own territory – the Crimea.

The failure to build these rail lines was mainly due to parsimony. Determined to balance his budgets and restore Russia's finances, Nicholas was simply unwilling to undertake construction on such a large scale. To be sure, Russia was far from wealthy in the 1830s and 1840s. The development of an adequate railroad network, on the other hand, might well have allowed Nicholas to reduce the size of his army, which was one of the largest single drains on the exchequer. But was this failure not at least as much the result of a failure to recognize the danger? Above all, Russia, like Prussia, needed a way to economize forces by being able to move them from theater to theater. Railways made that possible. The existence of a flourishing general staff in Prussia that took its primary mission to be long-range planning as well as detailed war planning in peacetime focused the attention of the Prussian state on solving this problem. The absence of any equivalent body in Russia was surely a major contributing factor to Russia's failure to address the problem.

At the same time, the Prussian system and, especially, the German general staff system into which it developed and which has become the model of military excellence to many, was seriously flawed. Run as it was purely by professional military specialists with little regard and sometimes even contempt for political concerns, it led Germany to catastrophe in 1914. There is much to be said, on the contrary, for the more informal and *ad hoc* system used in Russia in this period. Whenever it was called into being, an emergency committee examined the situation with an open mind and a clear head, looked for historical precedents, took the international scene and the domestic situation into account, and developed reasonable plans and programs that were, on the whole, successful.

Above all, it never subordinated the political concerns and goals of the state to military ones – most of the committees recommended courses of action harmful to the conduct of ongoing operations in light of what they felt to be more pressing foreign or domestic political issues. This focus even within the war planning groups on the interests of the state as a whole above the interests of the armed forces in particular is surely one of the reasons why the armed forces have never themselves been a threat to the Russian or even the Soviet state. The same cannot be said of Germany.

To be sure, the German general staff system developed, in large part, from the need to develop the incredibly complex and minute plans necessary for a large-scale mobilization by rail. By the third quarter of the nineteenth century all the major powers (except England) had imitated this system to a greater or lesser degree not merely because of Germany's success, but because only with such a system could war in that period be prepared for and fought. Yet the dispute between Helmuth von Moltke the Elder and Otto von Bismarck over the role of politics in war does not have an analogue in Russia. The traditions of the earlier part of the nineteenth century carried over to the latter part in both countries. In Russia, therefore, the army's interests remained subordinated to the state's throughout, whereas in Germany they were not. The attitude of the planners and the nature of war planning played an important role in these developments in both states.

Notes

1 Paul W. Schroeder, *The Transformation of European Politics 1763–1848* (Oxford: Clarendon Press, 1994), p. 242.
2 The best account of the diplomacy of this period is Schroeder, *op. cit.*
3 For a more detailed discussion of this issue see Frederick W. Kagan, *The Military Reforms of Nicholas I: The Origins of the Modern Russian Army* (New York: St. Martin's Press, 1999), chapter I; see also D.A. Skalon, ed., *Stolietie voennago ministerstva 1802–1902* (hereafter *SVM*) (St. Petersburg, 1902), vol. IV, part 1, book 2, section 1, chapter III (IV:1:2:1:III).
4 The documents relating to this effort are in E. Cazalas, trans., *La Guerre Nationale de 1812: Publication du Comité scientifique du Grand Etat-Major russe* (Paris: Henri Charles-Lavauzelle, 1904).
5 A.P. Zablotskii-Desiatovskii, *Graf P. D. Kiselev i ego vremia* (St. Petersburg, 1882), p. 30.
6 Russia's response to this crisis was discussed by Generals P.M. Volkonskii, Chief of the Main Staff of His Imperial Highness, A.A. Zakrevskii, Duty General of the Main Staff of His Imperial Highness (similar to the G3 of an American army staff today), and P.D. Kiselev, Chief of Staff of the Second Army. Their exchanges can be found in *Sbornik imperatorskago russkago istoricheskago obshchestva* (hereafter *SIRIO*), vols. 73 and 78, entries for 3 March–15 April.
7 N.K. Shil'der, *Imperator Nikolai Pervyi, ego zhizn' i tsarstvovanie* (St. Petersburg, 1902), vol. II, Appendix XXI, pp. 574–76. See also *SIRIO*, vol. 132 (1911), for

Nicholas' correspondence with Constantine, especially Nicholas to Constantine, 6/18 October 1830, p. 56.

 8 The military reforms conducted by Nicholas I from 1832 to 1836 and, to a lesser extent, those conducted earlier by Alexander I, are the subject of Kagan, *The Military Reforms of Nicholas I.*

 9 A Petrine College was theoretically run by a small group of directors in a literally collegial fashion. By the end of the eighteenth century, however, the war college was normally dominated by a single individual. The 'ministerial' system introduced by Alexander placed control over Russia's bureaucracies into the hands of individuals. These individuals were not 'ministers' in the western sense, however; they were responsible only to the tsar and not in any way to any representative or legislative body.

10 The fundamental laws that defined these reforms were *Polnoe Sobranie Zakonov Rossiiskoi Imperii, Series I* (hereafter *PSZ I*), no. 20,406, *On the Establishment of Ministries*, 8 September 1802; *PSZ I*, no. 24,686, *General Establishment of Ministries*, 25 June 1811; *PSZ I*, no. 24,971, *Supremely Confirmed Establishment of the War Ministry,* 27 January 1812; *PSZ I*, no. 24,975, *Establishment for the Administration of the Large Active Army*; and *PSZ I*, no. 25,012, *Decree Given to the War Minister about the Complement of the War Ministry,* 28 February 1812. For the problems of inefficiency and corruption in the military administration, see *SVM*, vol. III, part 6.

11 *PSZ I*, no. 24,971, *Supremely Confirmed Establishment of the War Ministry*, 'Polozhenie dlia Voennago Uchenago Komiteta' and 'Polozhenie dlia Voennago Topograficheskago Depo.'

12 The relevant legislation is *PSZ I*, no. 26,021, *On the Administration of the War Department*, 12 December 1815 and *PSZ I*, no. 26,022, *On the Rules According to Which the Commander in Chief Must Administer Armies in Peacetime*, 12 December 1815. The development of this system of command during the wars with Napoleon is described briefly in *SVM*:1:2:1 and in N.P. Glinoetskii, *Istoriia russkago general'nago shtaba*, vol. I (St. Petersburg, 1883).

13 There are no English language works on the Russo-Persian or Russo-Turkish Wars. Indeed there is no decent study of the former at all. The best work on the Russo-Turkish War is N.A. Epanchin, *Ocherk Pokhoda 1829 g. v Evropeiskoi Turtsii* (St. Petersburg, 1905). For the Polish Rebellion, see R.F. Leslie, *Polish Politics and the Revolution of November 1830* (London, 1956).

14 For a detailed discussion of these reforms, see Kagan, *The Military Reforms of Nicholas I.* The principal legislation is: *PSZ, Series II*, no. 5,318, *Supremely Confirmed Project of the Reorganization of the War Ministry*, 1 May 1832; *PSZ II*, no. 9,038, *Supremely Confirmed Establishment of the War Ministry*, 29 March 1836; and *PSZ II*, no. 9,039, *Supremely Confirmed Proposition about the Order of the Conduct of Affairs in the War Ministry*, 29 March , 1836.

15 *PSZ II*, no. 9,038, *Supremely Confirmed Establishment of the War Ministry*, 29 March 1836, Part I, §44.

16 These plans are discussed and some of them are reproduced in Epanchin, *op.cit.*, vol. I.

17 Epanchin, *op.cit.*, vol. I, p. 161. The memorandum is reproduced in the original French in appendix 13 of that volume.

18 Epanchin, *op.cit.*, vol. I, pp. 191ff.

19 Epanchin, *op.cit.*, vol. I, pp. 348ff.

20 Epanchin, *op.cit.*, vol. I, pp. 348ff.

21 The only English-language biography of Nicholas is W. Bruce Lincoln, *Nicholas I: Emperor and Autocrat of All the Russias* (DeKalb, IL: Northern Illinois University Press, 1989). Nicholas Riasanovsky, *Nicholas I and Official*

Nationality in Russia, 1825–1855 (Berkeley: University of California Press, 1967), has some important insights into Nicholas' personality, especially in chapter I. The massive biography written by N.K. Shil'der, *Imperator Nikolai Pervyi: Ego Zhizn' i Tsarstvovanie* (St. Petersburg, 1903), is not only insightful, but reproduces a great many primary sources for the period 1825–32 (it was not completed beyond that point).

22 There is no English-language biography of Chernyshev. The best sources are N.K. Shil'der, '"Svetleishii Kniaz" Aleksandr Ivanovich Chernyshev,' *Voenny sbornik*, no. 1 (1902); no. 2 (1902), pp. 30–46; no. 3 (1902), pp. 24–42; and no. 4 (1902), pp. 21–40, and A. I. Mikhailovskii-Danilevskii, 'Zhizneopisanie Kniazia Aleksandra Ivanovicha Chernysheva,' *Sbornik imperatorskago russkago istoricheskago obshchestva*, vol. 122, pp. 1–288. See also Bruce Menning, 'A.I. Chernyshev: A Russian Lycurgus,' *Canadian Slavonic Papers*, vol. XXX, no. 2, June 1988, pp. 192–219.

23 Epanchin, *op.cit.*, vol. II, pp. 23–30.

24 From 'The Report of G[eneral] A[djutant] Kiselev About Considerations Concerning the Composition of a Plan of War, Received from Count Dibich attached to Report No. 355,' read to and approved by Wittgenstein on 21 September 1827, reproduced in full as appendix 15 in Epanchin, *op.cit.*, vol. I.

25 See Kagan, *The Military Reforms of Nicholas I*, pp. 89ff.

26 From Chernyshev's *aide-mémoire* to the tsar of 26 November 1828 in Epanchin, *op.cit.*, vol. II, pp. 23–30.

27 The work of this committee is discussed in N.K. Shil'der, *Imperator Nikolai Pervyi*, pp. 250–51.

28 Shil'der, *Imperator Nikolai Pervyi*, pp. 250–51.

29 *SIRIO*, vol. 122, pp. 304–7.

30 The records of this committee are in the Russian State Military Historical Archive (RGVIA), *fond* VUA, *delo* 18,021, 'Matter with the Journals of the Secret Committee of 1831 for Finding Ways to Strengthen the Military Resources of Russia through a Recruit Draft and the Formation of New Forces'; *delo* 18,022, 'Matter Concerning Various Informations Presented to the Secret Committee Established in 1831 for Finding Means to Strengthen the Military Resources of Russia Through a Recruit Draft and the Formation of New Forces'; and *delo* 18,045, 'Affair Concerning Various Papers Remaining after the Death of A[ctual] P[rivy] C[ouncillor] Dashkov, Concerning the Affairs of the Secret Committee of 1831 for Finding Ways [. . .]'

31 RGVIA, *fond* VUA, *delo* 18,021, *listy* 149 (reverse)–150.

32 Records of Russia's planning for this crisis are in RGVIA, *fond* VUA, *delo* 1107, 'On the Composition of an Army Designated for War in the West and about Military Preparations in the Event of a Break with England and France.'

33 *Ibid., listy* 215–17.

34 M.I. Bogdanovich, *Istoricheskii ocherk deiatel'nosti voennago upravleniia v pervoe dvadtsati-piati-letie blagopoluchnago tsarstvovaniia Gosudaria Imperatora Aleksandra Nikolaevicha* (1855–80 gg.), vol. I, Appendix 4, and pp. 370–72.

35 For the best brief discussion of the development of railroads in Prussia see Dennis Showalter, *Railroads and Rifles: Soldiers, Technology, and the Unification of Germany* (Hamden, CT: Archon Books, 1976).

4

Austria, Prussia, and the German Confederation:

The Defense of Central Europe, 1815–54

Lawrence Sondhaus

For four decades after the defeat of Napoleon, the members of the victorious coalition of 1813–15 continued to view France as their most likely adversary in a future major war. In Austria and Prussia, royal absolutist regimes feared not just invasion by French armies but the ideological threats of liberalism and nationalism, born in the era of the French Revolution and Napoleon. To defend Central Europe against the French threat both militarily and politically, the Congress of Vienna (1814–15) agreed to create a confederation consisting of the two German great powers and the remaining German states.

On the map of Central Europe the German Confederation (*Deutscher Bund*) replaced the Holy Roman Empire, a loose collection of over 300 states of various sizes, which since its origins in the Middle Ages had failed to provide either the catalyst for a German nation-state or security for its members. After toppling the thousand-year *Reich* in 1806, Napoleon had simplified the geography of Germany to include Austria, Prussia, and less than forty smaller states, the latter brought under direct French domination in the short-lived Confederation of the Rhine (*Rheinbund*). At the Congress of Vienna, Austria's Prince Clemens von Metternich and other allied leaders chose not to resurrect the Holy Roman Empire, and thus avoided restoring most of the petty principalities eliminated by Napoleon. The founders of the German Confederation hoped the organization linking Austria, Prussia, and thirty-seven smaller states would succeed where the old *Reich* had failed, providing a credible defense for Central Europe.[1]

The Organization, Its Role and Its Powers

To run the Confederation, the German Federal Act (8 June 1815) created the federal diet (*Bundesrat*) at Frankfurt, a body consisting of ambassadors accredited to the organization by its members.[2] The boundaries of the Confederation, though not finalized until 1818, conformed generally to those of the defunct Holy Roman Empire. Just as Austria's Habsburg monarchs had served as emperors of the old *Reich*, Austria's representative in Frankfurt served as permanent president of the federal diet. The Federal Military Committee, established in April 1818 as a subcommittee of the federal diet, included the Austrian president of the diet along with diplomats representing Prussia, Bavaria, and four of the smaller states. The Federal Military Commission, established in March 1819, consisted of military men and was to serve as a source of technical expertise for the civilians on the committee. The commission included one Austrian, one Prussian, one Bavarian, and three representatives from the remaining smaller states. The Federal Military Committee was most relevant between 1818 and 1821, before the formulation of the Federal Military Constitution (9 April 1821). Thereafter, the committee served as the link between the federal diet and the Federal Military Commission, formally presenting the latter with requests for information or opinions, then conveying the results to the diet as a whole. In lieu of a permanent command structure or general staff, the commission held regular meetings – more so after 1830 than before – and served as a forum for the reevaluation of the Confederation's security situation. The federal diet almost always approved the commission's recommendations. Because the two German great powers ran their own military affairs and the smaller states usually balked at federal interference into theirs, the Federal Military Commission had relatively little influence over the standards by which the troops that would form the federal army upon mobilization were conscripted, trained, or equipped. The body had true authority only over the German federal fortresses.[3]

Created primarily as a defensive alliance, the German Confederation occupied a central place in the Congress of Vienna's scheme for containing future French aggression in Europe.[4] The federal states anchored the front line against France, flanked on the right wing by an enlarged kingdom of the Netherlands and on the left wing, south of neutral Switzerland, by an enlarged kingdom of Piedmont-Sardinia. An invasion of the Confederation itself would bring in the great-power armies of Austria and Prussia. In the event of a French invasion, Prussia – awarded the Rhineland and Westphalia in the settlement of 1814–15 – would bear the brunt of the fighting along the Rhine, while south of the Alps, behind Piedmont, Austria maintained its largest field army in its Italian possessions of Lombardy and Venetia, blocking an invasion route taken by French armies four times between 1796 and 1809. Russia, of course, stood behind both Austria and Prussia.

Such cooperation had little precedent during the wars of the French Revolution and Napoleon, when the Netherlands, northern Italy, and western Germany had been home to sister republics or satellite kingdoms collaborating with France. Among the great powers, Austria and Prussia had fought France as allies only from 1792 to 1795 and from 1813 to 1815. France had faced the combination of Austria, Prussia, and Russia only from 1813 to 1815. Indeed, the Central European rivalry between Austria and Prussia, which had made the Holy Roman Empire almost completely

51

irrelevant by the 1700s, reemerged after 1815 and finally destroyed the German Confederation in 1866. Yet in the establishment and consolidation of the Confederation, most Austrian and Prussian leaders recognized that, as policymakers of European great powers, they had much in common with each other. As absolute monarchies their countries formed a conservative bloc, with Russia, in the international arena; ideologically, they hoped to make the Confederation a bulwark of conservative order, using its institutions to suppress liberalism and nationalism especially at the leading German universities, many of which were located in the smaller states. They also shared a vision of the potential utility of the Confederation as a defensive alliance not only against a revival of the French threat in the west but, should relations with Russia deteriorate, against a future threat from the east. Thus, from 1815 through the outbreak of the Crimean War in 1854, Austria and Prussia usually cooperated, though often grudgingly, joining forces to overcome the particularism of the fiercely independent smaller German states. But the partnership had its limits, especially in military affairs, where Prussia's claims to a position of domination (owing to its geographic role as principal defender of western Germany against France) naturally were rejected by an Austria eager to preserve, and assert, its constitutional position as presiding power in the federal diet. Metternich recognized that the Confederation, if limited to a defensive alliance among sovereign states, would help preserve a loose Austrian hegemony over Central Europe; thus, he always objected to any Prussian military proposal aimed at creating a genuinely integrated federal army as a common German institution.[5]

Article 11 of the Federal Act of 1815 provided the constitutional foundation of the Confederation as a military alliance. Under its terms, an attack on any federal state was considered an attack on all, resulting in a federal war. During a federal war, individual states were barred from concluding separate treaties of peace or armistice with the enemy. Within the Confederation, members were bound not to go to war with one another and to submit all internal disputes to federal mediation. The federal guarantee of support did not apply to the non-German territories of Austria and Prussia. The obligations of the smaller states in the event of a war involving the northern Italian lands of Austria (most likely, against France) or the eastern lands of Austria or Prussia (against Russia) remained undefined.[6]

In any event, Article 11 was vague enough to warrant further clarification, and Metternich in particular was determined not to let military men work out the specifics. Because the Federal Act was also too vague to be workable in other areas, the Austrian chancellor sought to have the war and peace powers defined by a civilian commission tasked with elaborating upon the general powers of the Confederation.[7] Their efforts produced the Vienna Final Act (15 May 1820), which devoted seventeen of sixty-five articles to war and peace powers. The Confederation was given sweeping authority

to declare war, make peace, declare neutrality, enter into alliances, and negotiate treaties; individual members, again, were barred from concluding
separate peace treaties or armistices once a federal war had been declared.
Federal wars were limited to defensive conflicts to preserve the integrity of
member states. While an attack on one state was considered an attack on all,
to prevent the exploitation of this federal guarantee for offensive purposes,
members were prohibited from provoking foreign powers. The mediation
powers of the organization were expanded to cover all crises involving
member states; the federal diet was also empowered to investigate
complaints against individual states by foreign powers and to arrange resti-
tution when claims proved to be justified. The federal diet was empowered
to order a mobilization during a mediation attempt, before a state of war
ensued, and individual states were obligated to participate in military preparations whenever the danger of war existed. In cases where the majority
refused to approve federal military action, a minority of the Confederation's
members could cooperate in measures of common defense. To placate the
smaller states, which feared being drawn into the great-power conflicts of
Austria and Prussia, members who went to war as European powers were
not guaranteed federal support but could receive it by a majority vote of the
federal diet. Within the German federal army (*Bundesheer*), each state was
permitted to contribute more than its required number of troops.[8]

The latter clause was inserted in the treaty in order to enable Prussia, with
a federal population in 1815 of almost 8 million (of a total Prussian population of 10 million), to have a federal army contingent equal in size to that of
Austria, which had a federal population of over 9 million (of a total
Austrian population of 27 million). Earlier, Prussia's insistence upon military parity with Austria in any German military structure had complicated
the determination of which of their territories would be considered German.
The use of population figures to determine the size of the military contingents of the states contributed to three years of attempts to gerrymander the
eastern borders of the Confederation in order to equalize the federal populations of the two states, before the federal borders question was finally
resolved in 1818. The Federal Military Constitution of 9 April 1821 fixed
the minimum strength of the German federal army at 1 per cent of the
population of the Confederation based upon the federal census (*Matrikel*)
of 1819. The force of 301,637 men was to be subdivided into ten corps: three
Austrian (I, II, and III Corps, totaling 94,822 men), three Prussian (IV, V,
and VI Corps, 79,234 men), one Bavarian (VII Corps, 35,600 men), and
three consisting of troops from the remaining states (VIII, IX, and X Corps,
91,981 men). The law required Austria to make the largest contribution,
while Liechtenstein, contributing fifty-five men to VIII Corps, made the
smallest.[9] Although Article 3 of the Federal Military Constitution called for
a peacetime establishment for the *Bundesheer*, in fact it was not a standing
army, existing only on paper until the federal diet ordered it to mobilize. The

particularism of the small states would have hamstrung the army's operations if it had ever been called upon to fight. Article 5 stipulated that no state with a full corps could combine the troops of another state with its own, ensuring that the thirty-six smallest states would always pool their troops in three corps rather than be incorporated into an Austrian, Prussian, or Bavarian corps. Article 17 stipulated that the commanders of all troop contingents, no matter how small, would be appointed by the governments of the states providing them; thus, no troops from the smaller states would be under the direct command of generals and officers from Austria or Prussia. At the insistence of the smaller states, there was no permanent peacetime command structure; Article 13 empowered the federal diet to elect the supreme commander in case of war. Further provisions included the election of a second-in-command (federal lieutenant general) by the federal diet, a measure that, in effect, provided for a Prussian second-in-command in case an Austrian was supreme commander, and *vice versa*.[10]

The maintenance of the federal fortresses – initially at Luxembourg in the Grand Duchy of Luxembourg, Mainz in the Grand Duchy of Hesse (Hesse-Darmstadt), and Landau in the Bavarian Palatinate, with others constructed later at Rastatt in Baden and at Ulm in Württemberg – provided a tangible focus for federal military activity. The fortresses were the common property of the German Confederation,[11] maintained with the resources of a federal fortress fund and administered by the Federal Military Commission. Notwithstanding the level of general distrust toward the two great German powers by the smaller states, the latter were perfectly willing to have the former provide all or part of the manpower for the federal fortresses located on their soil. For example, Prussians garrisoned the fortress of Luxembourg, and both Austrians and Prussians served alongside local Hessian troops in the garrison at Mainz. The Bavarians provided their own garrison for Landau but were to be reinforced by troops from Baden in case of war.[12]

Planning for War During International Crises: 1830–32 and 1840–41

The German Confederation had no standing war plans after 1815. On two occasions – after the July Revolution of 1830 and during the Near Eastern Crisis of 1840 – revived fears of a French threat to Central Europe led to the drafting of an order of battle and mobilization plan, in each case valid only for the duration of the war scare. These plans were produced not under the auspices of federal authorities in Frankfurt but by *ad hoc* conferences in Berlin (in 1831–32) and Vienna (in 1840), led by high-ranking Austrian and Prussian generals. Political considerations dominated both conferences, but at a time when the Prussian army was leading Europe in the development of a general staff, military mapping, and war gaming,[13] Prussian military leaders felt a sense of urgency concerning military preparations which their Austrian counterparts, and in particular the Austrian chancellor, Metternich, seemed not to understand. Prussian proposals to strengthen the federal military organization, put forth during each of the two crises, were dismissed by the Austrians as political power plays for more Prussian influence within the Confederation – which they were. Unfortunately for the cause of defending Central Europe, the Prussian military planners of 1830–32 and 1840–41 either were allied with, or were themselves, ambitious political figures determined to make Prussia the catalyst for a German unification, excluding Austria, of the sort eventually achieved by Otto von Bismarck in the years 1866–71. During each crisis the clear political overtones of their initiatives for a more formidable Prussian-dominated German federal army doomed them to fail. They also suffered from the fact that their ambitions did not necessarily reflect those of their monarchs or a majority view among Prussia's civilian government ministers. Thus, in a number of respects the circumstances under which Prussia unified Germany in 1866–71 – with an Austria sufficiently weakened, a Prussia sufficiently strengthened, and a solidarity in Berlin among the monarchical, civilian, and military authorities (led by William I, Bismarck, and the elder Moltke, respectively) – did not exist in 1830–32 or 1840–41.

The July Revolution of 1830 in France sparked the first serious post-Napoleonic fears of a revived French threat to the German states. In August 1830, the Federal Military Commission proposed improvements to the federal fortress at Mainz and an increase in its garrison. This relatively mild precaution brought a protest from Württemberg, which feared that any federal military measures, no matter how defensive in nature, might provoke a French invasion of Germany. Both Bavaria and Württemberg rejected the notion that their troops should reinforce those of Prussia or Austria at Luxembourg and Mainz, and if the federal army were called upon to mobilize, they wanted the south Germans of VII and VIII Corps to be free to support a course favorable to their own governments. Along with most of the smaller German states, they feared that Austria and Prussia, acting as European powers, would draw them into a war against France; Bavaria and Württemberg even joined other states in discussions for a south German neutrality pact. Of course they knew that Prussian and especially Austrian aid would be indispensable as soon as the French crossed the Rhine, and thus wanted the best of both worlds: to be free from being drawn into an Austro-Prussian war against France but still able to claim protection if needed.[14]

The war scare heightened after Belgium rebelled against the Netherlands in late August 1830 and the new French government of King Louis Philippe formally warned foreign powers not to intervene against revolutionary movements in countries bordering France. A majority of senior German military leaders, all veterans of the Napoleonic Wars, at this stage favored war with France to uphold the overall Vienna settlement of 1815, but on both sides of the question the military leaders did not always agree with the civilian leaders of their own countries. For example, in Austria, Metternich obviously favored upholding the settlement of 1815, while Field Marshal Archduke Charles opposed any course risking war; in Bavaria, King Ludwig I and the civilian leadership adamantly opposed war, while Field Marshal Prince Karl Wrede favored it.[15] Complicating matters, during the late summer of 1830 the wave of revolution swept through the German states, forcing changes of government in Saxony, Hanover, Brunswick, and Hesse-Cassel. There was some brief discussion of a German federal military intervention in the latter, but only when armed mobs originating there threatened the neighboring state of Hesse-Darmstadt. Among the members of the Confederation, Luxembourg faced the most serious revolutionary threat, as its grand duke was King William I of the Netherlands, and it bordered rebel Belgium, whose new leaders claimed it as part of their new independent state (proclaimed in November 1830). The Confederation rejected William's appeal (in his capacity as a German grand duke) for help against the Belgian revolution, and also did nothing when Belgian troops occupied the entire grand duchy except the city of Luxembourg with its Prussian-garrisoned fortress. Nevertheless, any French military effort in support of Belgian ambitions to annex the grand duchy would have drawn the Confederation into a war against France. A conference of the five great powers, meeting in London from November 1830 to January 1831, agreed that Belgium would be independent of the Netherlands and perpetually neutral, but the unresolved issue of Luxembourg, and the fact that the Netherlands did not accept the London verdict (and, indeed, would not, until 1839), helped keep the war scare alive.[16]

Prussian foreign minister Count Christian von Bernstorff, supported by a faction of civilian and military leaders in Berlin, hoped to exploit the crisis to his country's advantage. In January 1831 he sent General Friedrich von Röder to Vienna to gain Austrian approval for a plan to have Prussia initiate military talks with the governments of the smaller German states to prepare for the possibility of war against France. Röder told the Austrians that Prussia would fight only a defensive war, but in such a war would contribute 200,000 troops rather than the roughly 80,000 required under the Federal Military Constitution. He also offered Prussian mediation in any military talks between Austria and the south German states, ostensibly to alleviate the austrophobia of the latter. He was instructed to offer Prussian troops to bolster both a right (northern) flank including the IX and X Corps, drawn from the smaller northern states, and a center including the VII (Bavarian) Corps and the VIII Corps, the latter drawn from Württemberg and smaller southern states. Austrian troops would form the left (southern) flank on their own. Under such a mobilization plan Prussians would dominate the federal army, and it would be difficult not to have a Prussian general as supreme commander. After dispatching Röder to Vienna, Bernstorff sent another of his military allies, General Baron

August Rühle von Lilienstern, to the south German capitals to promote the same plan.[17]

During Röder's mission to Vienna, word arrived of the Italian revolutions in Modena, Bologna, Ferrara, and Parma. Metternich resolved to intervene in the central Italian states, and in March 1831 General Count Johann Frimont led Austrian troops in a brief, successful campaign to crush the revolts.[18] Austria's intervention in central Italy only heightened tensions with France, which disapproved of the operation. With the army in Italy reinforced to a post-Napoleonic peak of 104,500 men,[19] military leaders in Vienna feared a general war would stretch the Austrian armed forces to the limit. Archduke Charles, whom Emperor Francis I wanted as German federal commander, was not optimistic about the loyalty of the south German states; *Feldmarschalleutnant* Baron Friedrich von Langenau, former Austrian representative on the Federal Military Commission, thought 130,000 to 150,000 Austrian troops would be needed in southern Germany alone, both to bolster the local military contingents and to ensure that the south German governments did not defect to the French camp, as they had during the Napoleonic Wars.[20] Yet such concerns did not drive the Austrians to agree to a greater Prussian role in the defense of the Confederation. Indeed, intelligence concerning Rühle's mission to the south German states made Metternich all the more determined to foil the Prussian power play. By the time Röder left Vienna in early April 1831, he had to concede to the Austrians an even north–south split of command of any forces in Germany. In return, Metternich agreed not to push for the immediate selection of Archduke Charles as federal field marshal; at the time, it was widely assumed that Charles had enough votes in the federal diet to be elected commander.[21]

In August 1831 the Dutch invasion of Belgium and French intervention to defend the Belgians sparked a renewal of talk of more specific military preparations in Germany. Bernstorff took advantage of south German (especially Bavarian) overtures for Prussian leadership on the matter, sending the state governments an encouraging circular note. Metternich reacted angrily, believing Austria and Prussia should reach an agreement first before conducting talks involving the smaller states. In September he sent General Count Karl von Clam-Martinitz to Berlin to negotiate with the Prussians. Upon his arrival Clam-Martinitz learned from Bernstorff's subordinate, Johann Ancillon, that not everyone in the Prussian cabinet supported the foreign minister's recent 'circular note' or the earlier missions of generals Röder to Vienna or Rühle to the south German capitals. King Frederick William III's influential adjutant General Job von Witzleben went out of his way to disavow any involvement in Bernstorff's courtship of the south German states, and reassured Clam-Martinitz that the king placed the highest priority on friendship with Austria.[22] Other opponents of Bernstorff included Field Marshal August Neidhardt von Gneisenau, likely Prussian field commander in case of war, and his protégé, General Karl von Clausewitz. In *On War* (1832), Clausewitz made a derogatory reference to Austria 'towing the German Confederation like a small vessel behind her,' confirming that, like Bernstorff, he viewed the organization as an ineffective one dominated by Vienna.[23] But, along with Gneisenau, he believed the overtures of cooperation to the south German states were too risky, in light of the fact that Prussia needed Austria as an ally in order to be secure against France. They considered Prussia too weak, in any event, to make a successful bid for some sort of closer union with the southern states at the expense of Austria and the Confederation. Like the majority of German military men who relished the thought of taking the field against France, Gneisenau and Clausewitz wanted war only in league with Austria and Russia, under conditions approximating those of the victorious campaigns of 1813–15. Both believed that any policy which fundamentally jeopardized Austro-Prussian relations was a bad one. As luck would have it, in 1831 they were posted not to the west but to the east, Gneisenau as commander of an army guarding Prussian Poland against a spillover of the revolution then raging in Russian Poland, Clausewitz as his chief of staff. Both men died of cholera later that year.[24]

Thus, during the winter of 1831–32, Austria's goal of maintaining a solidarity with Prussia to preserve the status quo in Germany continued to be jeopardized by Bernstorff's attempt to use the tense international atmosphere to Prussia's advantage, especially to build closer bonds with the south German states at Austria's expense. Austro-Prussian military talks were at a standstill, and Gneisenau and Clausewitz, Prussian opponents of Bernstorff's policy, were not around to lobby against it. Informed by Clam-Martinitz of the internal divisions in Berlin, Metternich finally went over Bernstorff's head directly to Frederick William III to break the impasse in Austria's favor. In March 1832 Bernstorff withdrew from the military discussions; in May, the pro-Austrian Ancillon replaced him as foreign minister. In disposing of Bernstorff, Metternich treated Prussia as he would have any small German state, appealing directly to a monarch to circumvent or remove a minister he found troublesome. Meanwhile, Clam-Martinitz remained in Berlin for negotiations with Prussia's General Karl von Knesebeck; in March, representatives of the smaller German states were invited to join them. As the talks proceeded, Austria in particular was determined to have the Confederation develop a strategy that would make it impossible for the south German states to defect to the French or declare their neutrality in case of a war.[25]

The so-called Berlin Conference of 1832 resulted in a military protocol signed on 3 December. It provided for the emergency mobilization of a provisional army including the VII, VIII, and IX Corps, backed by 30,000 Prussians and 70,000 Austrians, which would defend the Rhine frontier between Mainz and Basel. The final, fully mobilized army would look somewhat more like the Prussian proposal of 1831, with Austria and Prussia each contributing five corps instead of three. A northern force would consist of 60–70,000 Prussians plus the X Corps; a central army, of 90,000 Prussians, the 30,000 Bavarians of VII Corps, and the VIII and IX Corps; and a southern army, of 150,000 Austrians. In the order of battle, troops from Bavaria and Württemberg would be commanded by (and outnumbered by) Austrians in the provisional army, and by Prussians in the fully mobilized army.[26] Austria accepted the terms of 3 December 1832 because the south German states had persisted in their refusal to be subordinated directly to Austria in the ultimate order of battle. Yet, with Bernstorff out of the way and Ancillon directing Prussian foreign policy, Metternich no longer felt compelled to resist the Prussian military scheme as a political threat to Austria within the Confederation. Furthermore, during 1832 the representatives of Prussia and the south German states had joined the rest of the federal diet in approving Metternich's Six Articles, designed to strengthen the hand of the rulers of individual states *vis-à-vis* internal revolutionary threats, thereby reaffirming what the chancellor considered to be one of the primary purposes of the Confederation.[27]

The Berlin Conference took nine months to produce a German federal order of battle and mobilization plan, measures which then remained relevant for just five months, until the return of a general peace. As early as November 1831 Austria and Prussia had joined the other three great powers in resolving the Luxembourg question by agreeing to partition the grand duchy, giving the western portion to Belgium while retaining the rest (including the city of Luxembourg and its fortress) for William I of the Netherlands as a truncated state still within the German Confederation. A second French intervention in Belgium in November 1832, supported by a British naval blockade, finally led to a *de facto* Dutch acceptance of Belgian independence and the partition of Luxembourg in May 1833, when William I promised not to use force to resolve either question (although he withheld formal recognition of the changes until 1839).[28] In any event, the military planning reflected in the protocol of 3 December 1832 rested upon false political premises. The German Confederation had spent months in acrimonious planning for a French invasion of the German states, which the new regime of Louis Philippe had not threatened and had no intention of undertaking.[29]

The same would not be true during the war scare of 1840, which stemmed from a Near Eastern Crisis pitting the ambitious pasha of Egypt, Mehemet Ali, supported by France, against the Ottoman Empire, ultimately supported by the remaining four great powers. After the conflict gradually intensified throughout the 1830s, in March 1840 Louis Philippe increased tensions still more by appointing Adolphe Thiers as French premier. As was the case during the crisis of 1830–32, the war scare of 1840 brought to the surface a Prussian vision for Germany incompatible with the status quo of the German Confederation as established by Metternich after 1815. Prussia, once again, hoped to attract support from the smaller states with plans to strengthen the German federal military as a step toward greater Prussian-led integration, while Austria emphasized the advantages of maintaining the Confederation as a loose union of sovereign states in a defensive alliance.

The death of Frederick William III in May 1840, two months after Thiers came to power in France, left the Prussian throne and government in new hands as the European war scare intensified. The last surviving European ruler of the Napoleonic era, the old king had grown to value the Austro-Prussian partnership in German and European affairs. His willingness to sack Bernstorff in 1832 reflected the fact that, late in life, he had become a loyal supporter of Metternich's policies. His successor, Frederick William IV, admired Austria but harbored romantic German nationalist sentiments. The new king's most influential advisor, Colonel (later General) Joseph Maria von Radowitz, had served as Prussian military plenipotentiary to the German Confederation since 1836. More so than Bernstorff or his Prussian military allies, Röder and Rühle, in 1830–32, Radowitz was willing to risk war with France in order to arouse German nationalism to Prussia's benefit.[30]

The London agreement of 15 July 1840, in which Britain, Prussia, Austria, and Russia gave formal diplomatic support to the Ottoman Empire against Egypt, sparked a wave of nationalist fever in France. Thiers threatened to overturn the Vienna settlement of 1815, touching off a war scare on the Rhine. While Metternich's Austria sought to deal with the crisis as a European diplomatic problem, Prussia cast it as a German military problem. For the south German states, the crisis provoked a replay of the sentiments of 1830–32: after initial talk of regional neutrality, they looked to Prussia for military leadership, making it that much easier for ambitious Prussians to manipulate events to their country's advantage. After Metternich's diplomacy failed to defuse the crisis on a European level, Austria (as in 1831–32) opened bilateral military talks with Prussia, this time held in Vienna.[31]

The principal negotiators in Vienna in the autumn of 1840 were General Karl von Grolman of Prussia and *Feldmarschalleutnant* Karl von Ficquelmont of Austria. Colonel Radowitz was a member of the Prussian team and kept the south German governments informed of developments, continuing to advocate federal military preparations in a separate initiative. Acting on the precedent of the Berlin Conference of 1832, which had dealt with the same issues, the Vienna negotiations proceeded quickly and, to Metternich's surprise, also to Austria's advantage. In a draft treaty concluded on 28 November 1840, Prussia even pledged to declare war in case Austria's Italian territories were violated and to use Prussian influence to get the rest of the Confederation's members to do the same. The 1840 order of battle also favored Austria more than its precursor of 1832, as

Prussian negotiators conceded to the Austrians overall command of the Bavarian VII Corps and south German VIII Corps within a southern army on the upper Rhine. Austria's only concession was to agree to give the same two corps a measure of tactical autonomy.[32] The heightened level of popular German nationalism during the war scare of 1840 actually played into Austria's hands, as the public reaction against the French threat limited the freedom of action of the south German leaders. This time their neutrality talk evaporated very quickly, and no one seriously thought the south German states might defect to the French.[33]

But Radowitz remained a wild card in Austria's calculations. In December 1840, while ostensibly on a mission to the south German capitals to convey details of the Austro-Prussian agreement, he sent back to Berlin reports of pervasive anti-Austrian sentiment and, especially in the border state of Baden, a very strong desire to cooperate militarily with Prussia. The south German rulers grudgingly accepted a German federal guarantee of Lombardy-Venetia but rejected the idea of serving under or depending upon the Austrians. Reflecting his distrust in Radowitz, Metternich sent General Heinrich von Hess to follow the Prussian colonel through the south German capitals. Hess found that Radowitz had communicated his own version of the draft treaty of 28 November, emphasizing the role of Prussia in the German mobilization plans. Radowitz's version of the plan even increased the number of armies from three to four: a north German army and a middle Rhine army, each under Prussian leadership, a south German army (including VII and VIII Corps) bolstered by more Prussian troops, and a separate Austrian army, thus giving Prussia control over all German forces except the Austrians. According to the agreement of 28 November, the northern and middle Rhine armies, indeed, were to be led and dominated by Prussians, but the VII and VIII Corps were assigned to a single southern army under Austrian command and consisting primarily of Austrian troops. The Austrians considered the damage-control mission of Hess a success; afterward, their diplomats in the south German capitals reassured Metternich that Radowitz's mission had left the states more suspicious of Berlin than of Vienna.[34]

Returning to Berlin in January 1841, Radowitz persuaded Frederick William IV that the time was ripe to press for a strengthening of the German Confederation and Prussia's role within it, a goal to be achieved by exploiting the German nationalism unleashed by the war scare to reform the federal military establishment. The Prussians soon formally proposed that Austria and Prussia make a joint declaration to the federal diet, calling for federal military preparations and a federal diplomatic *démarche* to Paris demanding an explanation of recent mobilization measures by the French army. The Austrians were also sent Radowitz's proposals for a federal military budget, regular federal military inspections, and a reduction in the federal military mobilization period from four weeks to two, to which

Frederick William IV appended a personal appeal to Metternich for a peace-time military structure as the surest guarantee of the defense of Germany. Metternich recognized that the Prussian proposals would change the German Confederation to Austria's disadvantage and, more important at that moment, feared the adoption of such proposals in the midst of the ongoing international crisis would lead to war. He sent Hess to Berlin to attempt to restore the Austro-Prussian understanding of 28 November 1840 and rebut Radowitz's proposals. The Austrians considered the shortened mobilization proposal potentially ruinous for the finances of the individual states and a provocation to the French. The inspection proposal, if adopted, should apply only to the armies of the smaller German states, not to Prussia or Austria, and only for the duration of the present crisis. Perhaps overdramatizing the latter issue, Metternich expressed fears that any permanent federal inspection regimen binding on Austria would spell the end of the multinational Austrian army, requiring it formally to designate certain regiments as its German federal contingent, leading inevitably to Hungarian appeals for a national army under Hungarian officers, and perhaps even to Polish (Galician) and Italian (Lombardo-Venetian) ambitions along the same line.[35]

Before Hess arrived in Berlin, Frederick William IV sent another dispatch to Vienna at the end of January 1841, calling for a revision of the November draft treaty to separate the south German VII and VIII Corps from the Austrian army on the upper Rhine, ostensibly to assuage south German concerns about Austrian domination but, in effect, to make the actual agreement conform to the false version Radowitz had explicated in the south German capitals in December 1840. Reporting from Berlin in early February, Hess confirmed the king's attachment to the notions of federal military inspections and, especially, a shorter federal mobilization period. At the same time the Austrian ambassador in Berlin, Count Joseph von Trauttmansdorff, characterized the Prussian military demands of 1840–41 as only the latest in a series of power plays to unite the smaller German states under the leadership of Berlin and exclude Austria from German affairs, previous examples being the Prussian military position in 1830–32 and the establishment of the Zollverein (a Prussian-led German customs union including Bavaria, Württemberg, and Saxony) in 1834. Trauttmansdorff confirmed Radowitz's control over Frederick William IV and the relative impotence of the Prussian foreign minister, Heinrich von Werther. Indeed, the latter was reduced to parroting Radowitz's ideas, characterizing the military measures as a matter of German national honor. By February 1841, if not earlier, Metternich clearly considered the problem to be Radowitz, not the new Prussian king or his cabinet. He also expressed confidence that Radowitz's efforts would fail, but took no comfort in this conclusion owing to the damage the Prussian initiatives would cause to the common Austro-Prussian front in German as well as in European affairs.[36]

As a product of the war scare of 1840, the Prussian initiatives could be sustained only in an atmosphere of crisis. International developments did not work to Radowitz's favor, as the fall of Thiers at the end of October 1840 had brought to power a much less bellicose French ministry. The subsequent defeat of Egyptian forces led to a resolution of the Near Eastern Crisis, and the French army began to demobilize. Austria did its part by blocking Prussia's provocative proposals until the international situation changed for the better. Meanwhile, within the German Confederation, Metternich skillfully employed his own brand of nationalism, stressing a unity or unanimity of the states (*Einigkeit*) rather than the Prussian goal of national unification (*Einheit*). Because the former in no way threatened the sovereignty of the individual federal states, it was Austria's best weapon in its quest to drive a wedge between the Prussians and the south Germans, and to convince the latter of the wisdom of preserving the status quo. The Prussian proposals to have all states increase their military budgets and subject their troops to federal inspection also proved to be very unpopular with the smaller states. Of course, the reduction of international tensions made the draft treaty of 28 November 1840 a dead letter as well, eliminating the divisive issue of the disposition of the VII and VIII Corps in the federal order of battle.[37]

In Berlin, Hess refused to concede anything on the issues of the mobilization period or the inspections, even after Frederick William IV threatened a breach with Austria and an end to the German Confederation. As Hess prepared to leave for Vienna, Radowitz, recognizing that the course of events had weakened his hand, paid him a conciliatory call at the eleventh hour, offering to drop Prussia's other federal military initiatives if Austria agreed to a one-time military inspection during 1841. Metternich agreed. In March 1841, the two powers presented a common front to the federal diet, requesting that the Federal Military Commission discuss measures on how to bring federal forces to a wartime footing. In May the commission presented the federal diet with recommendations already agreed upon by Austria and Prussia, for a bill introducing guidelines not just for the federal inspection, but for the peacetime strength of individual contingents as well as their weaponry, uniforms, annual exercises, and leave policies. Furthermore, the three mixed corps (the VIII, IX, and X) were to be given one year to agree to a standardization of armament, common manuals of arms, and common military regulations. A month later, the federal diet approved the measures.[38]

German Federal Military Reforms: 1841–54

The federal military inspections of 1841 were the first of a series of modest efforts to reform or improve the defensive system of Germany, carried out sporadically over the next dozen years. The tours were conducted by thirty generals, ten from Austria and Prussia, twenty from the remaining states, operating in groups of three, with a general from one of the great powers accompanying two from the lesser states. The inspectors found only Austria and Prussia in compliance with federal standards, citing various deficiencies and proposing improvements for the contingents of the other states. For example, inspectors recommended that the Bavarians double the length of their basic training period and hold maneuvers annually rather than every other year, and that the Württembergers extend their term of active service and maintain more officers in commission. The inspection prompted some of the smaller states to improve their state of military readiness. A second federal inspection, held during 1846 at the insistence of Austria and Prussia, found better conditions than in 1841.[39] For the system of federal fortresses the war scare of 1840 had a more tangible result: in August 1842 the federal diet approved the construction of additional works at Rastatt in Baden and at Ulm in Württemberg, to supplement the existing fortresses at Luxembourg, Mainz, and Landau.[40]

After the revolutions of March 1848 the Federal Act of 1815 was suspended until May 1851. During this eventful interlude, the Frankfurt Parliament tried, and failed, to create a new federal German *Reich* under a constitutional monarchy. In Prussia, Radowitz, by then a general, again emerged as the leading proponent of a revitalization and unification of the German states under Prussian leadership, excluding Austria. His Prussian Union plan of 1849 nearly led to war between the two German powers in 1850, when a strong showing by the Austrian army, backed by the diplomatic support of Russia, compelled Prussia to back down. Discussions at Dresden between December 1850 and May 1851 found no better solution to the German question than to restore the Confederation under the terms of 1815. Even though Metternich had been forced into retirement in 1848, Radowitz's ultimate failure in 1849–50 ensured that the Austrian chancellor's original vision of the Confederation, as a loose union of sovereign states in a defensive alliance, would prevail, at least for another fifteen years.

Another inspection of the federal military contingents was conducted after the restoration of the Confederation, and by the end of 1851 discussions were underway for a revision of the Federal Military Constitution of 1821. Negotiations dragged on for more than three years, and the resulting revisions, approved by the federal diet on 4 January 1855, changed just five supplementary sections addressing the federal army's wartime strength, armament, peacetime standing, reserves, and mobilization of support personnel in the event of war. Left unchanged were the original twenty-four articles of the 1821 document as well as the corps and command structure, including the provision that there would be no supreme commander or federal military headquarters in peacetime. The need to increase the wartime strength of the federal army was the least controversial of the changes; rather than wait for the formulation of the reform package as a whole, in

March 1853 the federal diet resolved to raise the fixed minimum strength from 1 per cent to 1.166 per cent of the population of the Confederation, based upon the most recent federal census (*Matrikel*) of 1842. With the Crimean War escalating, in January 1854 new troop quotas were formalized which provided for a fully mobilized strength of 526,037 men, including 153,295 Austrians, 170,509 Prussians, 50,236 Bavarians, and 151,997 from the remaining states.[41] In addition to the slightly higher percentage formula, the new numbers reflected the growth of the federal population since 1821 (when the fully mobilized strength was projected at 301,637), the growth of Prussia's federal population (by 1842) to a level roughly equal to that of Austria, and Prussia exercising its right to contribute more than the required number of troops.

Upon agreeing to restore the German Confederation, Austria and Prussia on 16 May 1851 concluded a secret three-year defensive alliance, each guaranteeing the non-German lands of the other. The Austro-Prussian agreement of 1851 regarding the defense of their non-federal territories, like the abortive 1840 agreement by Prussia to guarantee Austria's Italian provinces, represented an effort to bring some clarity to the ambiguity in the military relationship between the German Confederation and the non-federal lands of Austria and Prussia, an ambiguity which had persisted even after the clarifications provided by the Vienna Final Act of 1820. The circumstances under which Austria and Prussia were obligated to support the other federal states were always clearer than those under which the other federal states were obligated to support Austria and Prussia. For example, if Austria or Prussia were involved in a war as a European power (not on behalf of the German Confederation), the federal states would not be required to lend support, but the issue of what would happen in such a war if a foreign army invading either country entered that country's federal territory remained unresolved. Would the war then automatically become a federal war, regardless of its non-federal or non-German origins? In their quest to interpret the federal constitution in a way that would obligate the smaller states to support them in the defense of their non-federal territories, Austria and Prussia did not help their case by refusing, until 1851, to guarantee each other's non-federal territories, and even then, doing so only in a short-term secret treaty.[42] As a consequence, throughout the period 1815–54 Lombardy and Venetia were considered to be Austria's most vulnerable territories and thus had the heaviest peacetime garrison of any provinces in Austria or Prussia.

Postscript: The Crimean War

The men planning for the security of Central Europe between 1815 and 1854 did not foresee that the next major European war would include Russia as the potential primary enemy. The precedent of the Napoleonic Wars, in which many of them had fought at least as junior officers, caused the military leaders involved in federal war planning in 1830–32 and 1840–41 to take for granted that any threat would come from France. Shadows of the Napoleonic past appeared in Austrian and Prussian fears that the smaller states, especially in southern Germany, might once again attempt to remain neutral or join the French, and in Austrian and Prussian suspicions of one another, reflecting the marked lack of Austro-Prussian cooperation against France during most of the period 1792–1815. Most Austrian and Prussian military men were politically conservative and few considered Russia, the bulwark of European conservatism, to be an enemy (and the few who did, did not want to fight Russia). Such sentiments ran even higher among the smaller German states, in particular Hesse-Darmstadt, Württemberg, Baden, and Brunswick, all of which had dynastic ties with the Romanovs.

The potential threat to Austria and Prussia posed by Russia, and its implications for the German Confederation as a military alliance, received significant attention only between 1815 and 1820, reflecting the fact that during those years Metternich feared Russia more than France.[43] Concerned that the smaller states might seek to keep the Confederation neutral in a war pitting Austria (with or without Prussia) against Russia, Metternich conspired to have the duchies of Auschwitz and Zator included in Austria's federal territory even though they had never been part of the defunct Holy Roman Empire (indeed, Austria had acquired them only recently, in the First Partition of Poland, 1772). By lying outright about the square mileage, population, and past history of the duchies, the Austrians succeeded in having them included in the German Confederation when the federal boundaries were defined in 1818. Strategically located at the western extreme of Austrian Galicia, near the headwaters of the Vistula and Oder rivers, Auschwitz and Zator guarded the approaches to the 'Moravian Gateway,' a break in the Carpathian Mountains that provided the most obvious invasion route for any army bearing down on Vienna from the direction of Russian Poland. As federal territory the duchies became a tripwire, and their violation by Russian troops would have enabled Austria to claim federal support in the earliest days of any war against Russia.[44]

As it became clear, by 1820, that Russia would stand with Austria and Prussia in a conservative eastern bloc of great powers, the issue of the Confederation's involvement in a war against Russia faded. Before 1854 the only mobilizations of Austrian or Prussian troops on the Russian border came in 1830–31, when both German powers feared the revolution in Russian Poland would spill over into their own Polish territories, and in 1846, when a rebellion originating in the Free City of Cracow spread to Austrian Galicia, prompting the Austrian occupation and annexation of Cracow, with Prussian and Russian approval. The possibility of a federal war against Russia reemerged only after the outbreak of the Crimean War in 1853, and the subsequent intervention of Britain and France on the side of the Ottoman Empire. Throughout the war Austrian foreign minister Count Karl von Buol-Schauenstein pursued an anti-Russian policy. Austria mobilized for war, then occupied the Danubian Principalities (Romania) after Russia evacuated the territory in June 1854, then concluded an alliance with Britain and France in December 1854, and, a year later, delivered an ultimatum to St. Petersburg which helped drive Russia to the peace table early in 1856. Buol's policy had the support of most Austrian civilian leaders but not Hess, by then chief of the general staff, or Count Karl Grunne, influential general-adjutant of the young Emperor Francis Joseph. The military leaders were not exactly pro-Russian, recognizing that Austria could not countenance the sweeping Russian gains in the Balkans which would follow a Turkish collapse, but they had little confidence in a positive outcome should Austria actually go to war. In Prussia both the civilian and military leaders were divided into pro- and anti-Russian camps, but virtually everyone agreed that neutrality would best serve Prussian interests.[45]

Throughout the conflict Prussia and the smaller German states feared Austria's actions would draw them into a war with Russia, but their response was to accede to Austrian demands for support against Russia in the hope that, as allies of Vienna, they could restrain Austria from actually going to war. The Austro-Prussian alliance of 1851 was renewed on 20 April 1854, for the duration of the Crimean War. In the federal diet three months later, Austria and Prussia pressured the rest of the Confederation to accede to the pact, rendering irrelevant the question of whether the rest of the federal states would be obligated to declare war on Russia if the non-federal lands of Austria or Prussia were violated.[46] After Austria took the Danubian Principalities, Prussia agreed to extend its guarantee of Austrian territory to cover the occupied provinces and joined with Austria to prod the Confederation into doing likewise.[47] Austro-Prussian negotiations were acrimonious throughout, and neither Buol nor Prussian minister–president Baron Otto von Manteuffel bargained in good faith or kept the other fully informed of negotiations with other countries.[48] Taking his cue from the Prussian initiatives of 1830–32 and 1840–41, in January 1855 Buol made overtures to the smaller German states for the Confederation to join Austria's mobilization against Russia, over Prussia's opposition. Buol also invited them to join Austria in bilateral treaties of alliance in the event that an Austro-Prussian breach made a formal federal mobilization impossible, promising to defend the states against Russia and give them a share of the spoils in the event of a victory. While these proposals were more of a ploy to force Prussia to join Austria in mobilizing (a step which Buol was certain would drive Russia to the peace table), they were greeted with indignation in the smaller German capitals as well as Berlin.[49] By the spring of 1855 the possibility existed that Prussia's representative in Frankfurt, Otto von Bismarck, might succeed in getting the federal diet to declare neutrality.[50] The fall of Sevastopol in September 1855 shifted momentum back in

Austria's favor, and the Austrian ultimatum to Russia, delivered in December 1855, gained the grudging support of Prussia and the smaller states.[51]

For the task of negotiating an Austro-Prussian military convention in conjunction with the April 1854 renewal of the alliance, the Austrians left nothing to chance, sending to Berlin their chief of the general staff, Hess, the leading Austrian military figure in the 1840–41 negotiations with Prussia. The convention obligated Austria to send 250,000 men and Prussia 200,000 to the eastern front in case of war with Russia, and provided for further consultation between the allies regarding operational planning. The language of the document made clear the primacy of political over military considerations. In the April documents the *casus foederis* for the alliance was defined as a Russian annexation of the Danubian Principalities (then still occcupied by Russia) or a move by Russian troops southward across the Balkan Mountains (i.e., through Turkish Bulgaria toward Constantinople). Before agreeing to these terms, Prussia received secret assurances from Russia that neither would happen.[52] In the prevailing atmosphere of mistrust, such cynical behavior was the rule rather than the exception. Berlin's strategy of using the alliance to restrain Austria from going to war against Russia was matched by a willingness on the part of Vienna (as seen in the Austrian alliance of December 1854 with Britain and France) to pursue a policy independent of Prussia and, should the Prussians side with Russia, against Prussia.[53]

After December 1854, with the Confederation having extended its guarantee to the Austrian-occupied Danubian Principalities and Buol pushing for a mobilization of the federal army, the issue arose of the appointment of a federal supreme commander. Frederick William IV's brother, Prince William (the future Prussian king and German emperor, William I) and Francis Joseph's cousin, Archduke Albrecht, were the two leading candidates, but on Manteuffel's instruction, Bismarck kept the federal diet from voting on the matter. In February 1855 the Austrian chairman of the Federal Military Commission, Major General Joseph von Schmerling, attempted to force the issue by having the commission recommend to the federal diet that a commander be elected; the Prussian representative, Major General Baron Heinrich von Reitzenstein, joined three other commission members in beating back the motion by a vote of 4 to 2. The commission did recommend, and the diet mandated, that the contingents of the individual German states be in such a condition of readiness as to be placed on a war footing within fourteen days. Expensive measures such as the purchase and maintenance of the full complement of horses needed for a mobilization remained in effect until after the fall of Sevastopol in September 1855.[54] Thus, the German federal army actually came closer to going to war in 1855 than it ever had in the years 1815–54, and for reasons unrelated to the defense of the Confederation. But far from providing a precedent for future cooperation, the Crimean War did irreparable harm to the Confederation as an alliance. Afterward Prussia did not renew its bilateral pact with Austria, and Prussia and the Confederation remained neutral in 1859 while Austria was defeated by France in northern Italy.[55] In 1866 the Confederation collapsed when Austria and Prussia finally went to war to determine the political future of Germany.

Implications

As an organization for the defense of Central Europe, the German Confederation had several advantages: its members included two of the five great powers of Europe, which, when acting together, could compel the thirty-seven smaller states to follow their lead; its German character offered the possibility of greater cohesion (at least greater than the more artificial European or North Atlantic ideals of present-day organizations); and all of its members shared a fear of a revival of French military power after the defeat of Napoleon. The Confederation also suffered serious disadvantages: the two great powers among its members tended to use the organization to advance or defend their own interests; Prussia ultimately wanted the Confederation to evolve in the direction of a federal state (*Bundesstaat*) rather than the federation of states (*Staatenbund*) favored by Austria; and the smaller states took full advantage of the Austro-Prussian rivalry to preserve their own independence and strengthen their own voices within the organization. From a purely military point of view, long before its ultimate collapse on the eve of the Austro-Prussian War of 1866, the Confederation as an alliance was hardly a model of success. Indeed, it provides a better example of how a peacetime alliance can be used to restrain, as well as to support, military action. For example, in the crisis of 1840, Austria managed to postpone federal action on bellicose Prussian proposals until a change of ministries in France and the defeat of Egypt in the Near East ended the war scare; later, during the Crimean War, Prussia sought to use its bilateral alliance with Austria, and the rest of the Confederation's accession to it, to prevent Austria from going to war with Russia.

As early as 1950 one historian compared the newly established United Nations, with its Security Council already paralyzed by the Cold War between the United States and Soviet Union, to the German Confederation, an organization similarly affected by a cold war between Austria and Prussia.[56] In the post-Cold War world, the history of the German Confederation as a peacetime military alliance serves as a cautionary tale for western military planners, especially against advocates of a dramatic eastward expansion of the North Atlantic Treaty Organization (NATO), to include not only the former Soviet satellites and non-Russian republics but Russia itself, or the subsuming of NATO within a Eurasian security partnership encompassing an expanded NATO and Russia. At ceremonies marking the creation of the NATO–Russia Council (28 May 2002), culminating a process begun in 1991, President George W. Bush observed that the council 'offers Russia a path toward forming an alliance with the [NATO] alliance against common security threats including terrorism.'[57] Yet while it serves the interests of the general peace to integrate a former adversary into the broader system of international relations (as the Concert of Europe had included France after 1818), the same does not necessarily hold true for an alliance. Each of the longest-lasting multilateral peacetime alliance systems of modern history – the Triple Alliance of 1882–1915, NATO since 1949, and the Warsaw Pact of 1955–91 – has had a clearly dominant member, strong enough to compel all other members to conform to the paradigm of behavior which it has established. For example, under the leadership of Imperial Germany, traditional enemies Austria-Hungary and Italy became allies, the former because it needed German assistance in case of war with Russia, the latter because it needed German assistance in case of war with France. Similarly, within NATO, under the leadership of the United States and in the common cause of containing the Soviet Union, France agreed to West German rearmament, traditional enemies Greece and Turkey became allies, and the alliance survived the endemic recalcitrance of a member as important as France. When a single alliance system includes two great powers, neither of them strong enough to truly dominate the other, the smaller or weaker allies cannot be controlled so easily. As we have seen in the examples from the German Confederation in 1830–32 and 1840–41, to assert their independence from Austrian domination the south German states courted Prussia; at the same time, to assert their independence from Prussian domination, northern states such as Hanover and Saxony had closer ties to Austria (and indeed, went down to defeat fighting on Austria's side in 1866). In any future Eurasian security structure based upon a more formal partnership between NATO and Russia, smaller or weaker eastern European countries such as Ukraine or Poland could be expected to seek the closest ties with the United States, while France, for example, could be expected to assert its independence from American domination by forming closer bonds with Russia. As was the case with Austria and Prussia, the traditional great-power rivalry between the United States and Russia would make it impossible for the two to cooperate consistently within any common security structure. Even in situations where the United States and Russia might be in agreement – for example, against a threat from an Islamic funda-mentalist state or group, or from China – many of the smaller countries would likely consider it none of their business and, like the smaller states of the German Confederation, do whatever they could to prevent the organiza-tion from acting.

Some have argued that the Confederation, though relatively weak and disorganized as a military alliance, nevertheless served Germany, and Europe, far better than the militarily powerful German nation-state that succeeded it after the unification process of 1866–71: it was strong enough as a military alliance to defend the German states if they had been attacked, but too weak to pursue an aggressive policy. In particular, the ambiguity surrounding the obligations of Austria and Prussia to defend one another's non-federal lands (except for the years 1851–56) and of the rest of the Confederation to defend the non-federal lands of Austria and Prussia (except for the years 1854–56) made it exceedingly difficult for Austria, Prussia, or their potential enemies to formulate offensive war plans, and thus served the preservation of peace.[58] Just as many of the European members of NATO, during and after the Cold War, have feared that the United States, acting as a global superpower, would embroil them in a conflict originating beyond Europe, the smaller states of the Confederation feared being drawn into a war which Austria or Prussia might fight for the sake of great-power interests rather than to defend Germany. Their refusal to undertake out-of-area commitments to support Austrian or Prussian positions internationally, compromised only temporarily during the Crimean War, served as a further restraining factor for the alliance. Similarly, NATO supported US-led interventions in Bosnia (1995) and Kosovo (1999), owing to the clear implications for European stability, and in Afghanistan (from 2003), considered a legitimate cause in the wake of the terrorist attacks of 11 September 2001 against the United States, but the alliance did not associate itself formally with either of the US-led invasions of Iraq (1991 and 2003), leaving the United States to fight those wars with coalitions including NATO members (far fewer of them, in the second Iraq war) but without the stamp of approval of the alliance as a whole. The dual great-power dynamic of a common NATO–Russia security organization would make it even more difficult to secure the consent and participation of members for such military operations. But the case may be made that such restraints are not necessarily a bad thing, and that a flawed alliance with a structure not conducive to decisive action, such as the German Confederation, can still serve the goals of its members, provided that those goals are clearly defensive in nature.

Notes

1   On the founding of the German Confederation see Enno E. Kraehe, *Metternich's German Policy, volume 2: The Congress of Vienna, 1814–1815* (Princeton, NJ: Princeton University Press, 1983), pp. 366–99.

2   For a full text of the Federal Act see Edward Hertslet, ed., *The Map of Europe by Treaty, 1814–1875*, 3 vols (London: Butterworth's, 1875), vol. 1, pp. 200–07, and for articles describing the German Confederation in the Treaty of Vienna (9 June 1815), pp. 243–48. German text of Federal Act in Philipp Anton Guido Meyer, comp., *Corpus Iuris Confoederationis Germanicae*, 3 vols, 3rd edn (Frankfurt: H.L. Brönner, 1859; reprint edn Scientia Verlag Aalen, 1978), vol. 2, pp. 1–7.

3   'Geschäftsordnung der technischen Militär-Commission der deutschen Bundesversammlung', 15 March 1819, text in Meyer, *Corpus Iuris Confoederationis*

Germanicae, vol. 2, pp. 78–80; see also Jürgen Angelow, *Von Wien nach Königgrätz: Die Sicherheitspolitik des Deutschen Bundes im europäischen Gleichgewicht, 1815–1866* (Munich: R. Oldenbourg Verlag, 1996), pp. 51–2; Loyd Lee, '1840, The Confederation, and German Military Reform', *The Consortium on Revolutionary Europe, 1750–1850: Proceedings, 1987* (Athens, GA, 1987), p. 575.

4 Paul W. Schroeder, *Metternich's Diplomacy at its Zenith, 1820–1823* (Austin, TX: University of Texas Press, 1962), p. 4.

5 On Metternich's goals in Central Europe see *ibid.*, p. 255.

6 Hertslet, *Map of Europe*, pp. 247–48; for German text see Johann Ludwig Klüber, ed., *Acten des Wiener Congresses in den Jahren 1814 und 1815*, 2 vols (Erlangen: J.J. Palm und Ernst Enke, 1815), vol. 2, pp. 383–84.

7 Metternich to Johann von Buol-Schauenstein (Austrian president of federal diet), 16 May 1818, Haus-Hof-und Staatsarchiv (HHStA), Gesandtschaftsarchiv (GSA), Frankfurt, Weisungen, fasc. 2.

8 Hertslet, *Map of Europe*, pp. 649–53. For the entire Vienna Final Act, see *ibid.*, pp. 636–57. German text in Meyer, *Corpus Iuris Confoederationis Germanicae*, vol. 2, pp. 101–11.

9 Heinrich Lutz, *Zwischen Habsburg und Preußen: Deutschland 1815–1866* (Berlin: Siedler Verlag, 1994), p. 62.

10 Text of Federal Military Constitution, 9 April 1821, in Meyer, *Corpus Iuris Confoederationis Germanicae*, vol. 2, pp. 133–46.

11 See Lutz, *Zwischen Habsburg und Preußen*, p. 63.

12 For the texts of a series of treaties signed between 1815 and 1820 establishing the original three federal fortresses and their garrisons, see Meyer, *Corpus Iuris Confoederationis Germanicae*, vol. 2, pp. 116–25; see also Lee, '1840, The Confederation, and German Military Reform', p. 576.

13 See Arden Bucholz, *Moltke, Schlieffen, and Prussian War Planning* (Providence, RI: Berg, 1991), pp. 18–38, *passim*.

14 Robert D. Billinger, Jr., *Metternich and the German Question: States' Rights and Federal Duties, 1820–1834* (Newark, DE: University of Delaware Press, 1991), p. 55; Lawrence J. Baack, *Christian Bernstorff and Prussia: Diplomacy and Reform Conservatism, 1818–1832* (New Brunswick, NJ: Rutgers University Press, 1980), p. 266.

15 Billinger, *Metternich and the German Question*, p. 61; Angelow, *Von Wien nach Königgrätz*, pp. 87–88, 94–95.

16 Paul W. Schroeder, *The Transformation of European Politics* (Oxford: Clarendon Press, 1994), pp. 680–83, 700; Angelow, *Von Wien nach Königgrätz*, pp. 88–90.

17 Billinger, *Metternich and the German Question*, pp. 71–72, 74.

18 Lawrence Sondhaus, *In the Service of the Emperor: Italians in the Austrian Armed Forces, 1814–1918* (Boulder, CO: East European Monographs, 1990), p. 26; Billinger, *Metternich and the German Question*, p. 73.

19 Sondhaus, *In the Service of the Emperor*, p. 27.

20 Billinger, *Metternich and the German Question*, p. 74.

21 Baack, *Christian Bernstorff and Prussia*, p. 269; Billinger, *Metternich and the German Question*, p. 75.

22 Baack, *Christian Bernstorff and Prussia*, pp. 283–7. According to Angelow (*Von Wien nach Königgrätz*, p. 99), Frederick William III had no advance knowledge of Bernstorff's circular note.

23 Karl von Clausewitz, *On War*, trans. J.J. Graham, ed. Anatol Rapoport (New York: Penguin Books, 1968), p. 379.

24 Baack, *Christian Bernstorff and Prussia*, p. 276; Roger Parkinson, *Clausewitz: A Biography* (New York: Stein & Day, 1971), pp. 321–29.

25 Billinger, *Metternich and the German Question*, pp. 129–40, *passim*.

26 Baack, *Christian Bernstorff and Prussia*, p. 295; Billinger, *Metternich and the German Question*, pp. 138–9.

27 Baack, *Christian Bernstorff and Prussia*, p. 295.

28 Schroeder, *The Transformation of European Politics*, pp. 690, 716–17.

29 Angelow, *Von Wien nach Königgrätz*, pp. 104–5.

30 Robert D. Billinger, Jr., 'They Sing the Best Songs Badly: Metternich, Frederick William IV, and the German Confederation during the War Scare of 1840–41', in Helmut Rumpler (ed.), *Deutscher Bund und Deutsche Frage, 1815–1866* (Vienna: Verlag für Geschichte und Politik, 1990), pp. 94–95. See also Roy A. Austensen, '*Einheit oder Einigkeit*? Another Look at Metternich's View of the German Dilemma', *German Studies Review*, 6 (1983), pp. 41–57.

31 Billinger, 'They Sing the Best Songs Badly', pp. 96–97.

32 *Ibid.*, p. 98.

33 Wolf D. Gruner, 'The German Confederation and the Rhine Crisis of 1840', *The Consortium on Revolutionary Europe, 1750–1850: Proceedings, 1987* (Athens, GA, 1987), pp. 554–55.

34 Billinger, 'They Sing the Best Songs Badly', pp. 98–101.

35 *Ibid.*, pp. 101–02, 106–07.

36 *Ibid.*, pp. 103–08.

37 *Ibid.*, pp. 108, 110–11. According to Gary P. Cox, 'The Crisis of 1840 in the Continuum of French Military Planning', *The Consortium on Revolutionary Europe, 1750–1850: Proceedings, 1987* (Athens, GA, 1987), pp. 561, 563, throughout much of the crisis of 1840, the French army's role was more observer than participant. As Thiers and his nationalist supporters in the political arena and the press fanned the flames, the army grew increasingly skeptical until in October 1840 the war minister, General Amedée Louis Despans de Cubières, 'admitted that the army was unready for the kind of war French foreign policy might provoke. . . . When the prime minister showed no signs of striving to relax tensions, the king, backed by the army, balked,' leading to the dismissal of Thiers and the end of the crisis of 1840.

38 Billinger, 'They Sing the Best Songs Badly', pp. 109–10, 112.

39 Lee, '1840, The Confederation, and German Military Reform', pp. 579–80, 583.

40 Meyer, *Corpus Iuris Confoederationis Germanicae*, protocols of 11 August 1842, vol. 2, pp. 405–06.

41 Text of revisions of Federal Military Constitution, 4 January 1855, in Meyer, *Corpus Iuris Confoederationis Germanicae*, vol. 2, pp. 622–33. See also Carl von Kaltenborn, *Geschichte der Deutschen Bundesverhältnisse und Einheitsbestrebungen von 1806 bis 1856*, 2 vols (Berlin: Verlag von Carl Heymann, 1857), vol. 1, p. 316; Angelow, *Von Wien nach Königgrätz*, pp. 162–63. The latter (on p. 164) gives slightly different figures for the new troop quotas.

42 In January 1818, Austria rejected a Prussian proposal to have the eastern non-federal provinces of Prussia linked to Austria and the rest of the Confederation in some sort of defensive arrangement (Buol to Metternich, 14 January 1818, HHStA, GSA, Frankfurt, Berichte 1818, fasc. 39). Prussia rejected the idea of a bilateral Austro-Prussian understanding covering its eastern provinces. See Metternich's Vortrag to Francis I, 13 January 1818, reprinted in Alfred Stern, *Geschichte Europas 1815 bis 1871*, 4 vols (Berlin: Verlag Wilhelm Hertz (1894)), vol. 1, pp. 633–34; see also *ibid.*, p. 326, and Brigitte Winkler-Seraphim, 'Das Verhältnis der preussischen Ostprovinzen, insbesondere Ostpreussens zum Deutschen Bund im 19. Jahrhundert', *Zeitschrift für Ostforschung*, 4 (1955), p. 340. Prussia likewise refused to enter into a bilateral arrangement guaranteeing Austria's non-federal lands.

43 Schroeder, *Metternich's Diplomacy at its Zenith*, p. 242.

44 The quest to include Auschwitz and Zator in Austria's federal territory, initiated in a letter from Austria's war minister, Field Marshal Prince Karl zu Schwarzenberg, to Metternich, 2 February 1817, is chronicled in correspondence in HHStA, Staatsakten, Deutsche Akten, fasc. 101–02, and in HHStA, GSA, Frankfurt, Weisungen, fasc. 2. Acknowledgement of the false nature of Austria's historical argument for including the duchies (that they were a part of Austrian Silesia and, thus, a part of the Holy Roman Empire from 1333 to 1772, and transferred to Austrian Galicia for administrative purposes when Galicia was annexed from Poland in 1772) is in Schwarzenberg to Metternich, 16 September 1818, Kriegsarchiv, Hofkriegsrat Akten 1818, Präsidialreihe 2–21, pp. 98, 116–20.

45 Angelow, *Von Wien nach Königgrätz*, pp. 169–70.

46 For the terms of the 20 April 1854 alliance see Paul W. Schroeder, *Austria, Great Britain, and the Crimean War: The Destruction of the European Concert* (Ithaca, NY: Cornell University Press, 1972), pp. 166–67. In the vote in the federal diet, 24 July 1854, all but Mecklenburg-Strelitz and Mecklenburg-Schwerin voted for the resolution. See *ibid*, p. 190.

47 Schroeder, *Austria, Great Britain, and the Crimean War*, pp. 229, 239.

48 On Manteuffel's double-dealing see *ibid.*, pp. 83, 86, 230.

49 *Ibid.*, pp. 240–41.

50 *Ibid.*, p. 296.

51 *Ibid.*, pp. 311, 330–32.

52 Angelow, *Von Wien nach Königgrätz*, p. 175.

53 *Ibid.*, p. 184.

54 *Ibid.*, pp. 184–89.

55 While Prussia remained neutral in 1859, 80% of the Prussian army was mobilized to defend western Germany against French attack and to support an armed mediation effort by Berlin. The inefficiencies of the Prussian army during this mobilization provided the impetus for the recently appointed chief of the general staff, Count Helmuth von Moltke, to make improvements in the army's use of railroads for future mobilizations, and for the prince regent (soon to be King William I) to present the Prussian *Landtag* with proposals for the expansion and reform of the army. Thus, for Prussia, the impact of the war of 1859 helped lay the foundation for victory in 1866 against Austria. The issue of the army bill led to the constitutional crisis which resulted in the appointment of Bismarck as minister–president in 1862 and the subsequent extralegal buildup of the Prussian army, while Moltke's more effective use of railroads in the 1866 mobilization was crucial to the defeat of Austria at Königgrätz. See Bucholz, *Moltke, Schlieffen, and Prussian War Planning*, pp. 40–47, *passim*.

56 Enno E. Kraehe, 'The United Nations in Light of the Experiences of the German Confederation', *South Atlantic Quarterly*, 49 (1950), pp. 138–49.

57 George W. Bush, 28 May 2002, 'The NATO–Russia Council offers Russia a path toward forming an alliance with the alliance', www.whitehouse.gov/new/releases/2002/20020528.html

58 This case has been made by Billinger ('They Sing the Best Songs Badly', p. 113) and, especially pertaining to Russia, by Enno E. Kraehe, 'From Rheinbund to Deutscher Bund: The Road to European Equilibrium', *The Consortium on Revolutionary Europe, 1750–1850: Proceedings, 1974* (Tallahassee, FL, 1977), p. 172.

5

STRATEGIC AND MILITARY PLANNING, 1871–1914

David Stevenson

[W]hen we discuss the question of future war, we always deal with it as a war between Great Powers. That is to say, primarily, the long talked-of, constantly postponed war between France and Germany for the lost provinces; and, secondly, that other war, the thought of which has gradually replaced that of the single-handed duel between France and Germany, viz. a war between the Triplice and the Franco-Russian Alliance. It is that war which constantly pre-occupies the mind of statesmen and sovereigns of Europe, and it is that war which, I maintain, has become absolutely impossible.[1]

The International Environment

In considering planning between 1871 and 1914 for major operations between modern armed forces, we must concentrate on Europe. It has been estimated that in 1913 the European countries still accounted for some 43 per cent of world economic output, the great majority of foreign investment, 59 per cent of imports, and 65 per cent of exports.[2] Directly or indirectly they ruled nearly all of Africa and Australasia and much of Asia. They vied for influence in the Near East and they scrambled for concessions in China. By the eve of the First World War their rivalries extended to most corners of the globe. The only big exception was the western hemisphere. There the United States upheld its traditional opposition to European involvement, supported if need be by one of the world's strongest navies and a steel production almost equalling Britain, France, and Germany's put together. German planners toyed with schemes for invading America's east coast, and the US Navy's General Board, established after 1898, drew up War Plans Orange and Black for hostilities against Japan and Germany respectively.[3] Yet America's land forces remained small and ill equipped, and their participation in a European war was discounted both in the European capitals and in Washington. In contrast, the six Great Powers of Britain, France, Germany, Austria-Hungary, Italy, and Russia accounted for some three-quarters of global defence spending.[4] Armed

conflict between them would be more devastating and have greater repercussions than it would anywhere else.

Throughout the period under discussion many commentators agreed that
such a conflict was both possible and likely in the foreseeable future.[5] Others
dissented, contending that technological advance and economic globalization were making war an anachronism. According to the Russian–Polish
banker, Ivan Bloch, in his *Is War Now Impossible?*, the growth in the size of
armies and in the firepower of modern weaponry meant a major European
conflict would be a long and bloody stalemate that would terminate in
bankruptcy, famine, and chaos. The best seller by the British radical journalist Norman Angell, *The Great Illusion*, agreed that commercial and
financial interdependence meant war could no longer be profitable, and that
if not necessarily impossible it was certainly irrational.[6] In reality the situation was sufficiently ambiguous to sustain both such optimistic and more
sombre prognoses. Economically Europe was indeed becoming unprecedent-
edly integrated, but as yet this process had done little to consolidate peace.

Commercial expansion was one of the most arresting features of the
epoch. In his *The Economic Consequences of the Peace*, John Maynard
Keynes recalled in retrospect how produce from across the world could be
delivered to the Edwardian breakfast table.[7] Growth in world trade per
capita between 1800 and 1913 averaged 33 per cent per decade and by the
latter date may have reached one-third of the value of world production.[8]
The United States remained largely self-sufficient, but Europe did not. By
1914 even primarily agrarian states such as Italy and the Habsburg
Monarchy habitually bought in foodstuffs, while Britain imported about
two-thirds of its food by calorific value and Germany one-fifth. Italian
industry depended on seaborne British coal, as did the homes and factories
of St. Petersburg. Even more striking was the interdependence between
traditional enemies in Western Europe's heartland. France's Lorraine steel
industry drew up to 40 per cent of its coking coal from the Ruhr, while the
latter purchased iron ore from Normandy and Lorraine. The coal, steel, and
engineering industries of eastern France, the Rhineland, and the Low
Countries were being bound together by cross-border flows of raw materials
and labour and by interlocking ownership.[9] Moreover, the rise of economic
interdependence presupposed increased political collaboration. European
states placed little restriction on labour migration, and tariffs on goods –
despite increasing after the 1870s – remained very low by historical standards. Governments created new institutions such as the International
Telegraphic Union (1865) and the Universal Postal Union (1874), they
permitted railway companies to co-ordinate timetables across borders, and
from the 1890s they provided a framework of stable and convertible curren-
cies through the international gold standard.[10] Even so, official co-operation
remained minimal. The gold standard, in contrast to post-1945 international
monetary arrangements, had no founding charter or central institutions.

States adhered to it at a time and an exchange rate of their choosing, and such 'management' of the regime as occurred was through intermittent bilateral co-operation between central banks.[11] When European tension rose before 1914, the Continental countries hoarded gold reserves, undermining the whole system.[12] Furthermore, many governments tried to exploit financial dependence as a diplomatic weapon. Even the British authorities, which rarely applied political pressure to City of London transactions, opposed funding for the German 'Berlin to Baghdad' railway project, which they feared would endanger Indian security. The Germans intermittently embargoed Russian borrowing whereas the French encouraged Russian bond flotations on the Paris Bourse while debarring German Government issues.[13] In short, greater economic integration did little to attenuate political enmities.

Other economic trends may have exacerbated them. It was once conventional to divide the nineteenth century into so-called Kondratiev or 'long' economic cycles – the 'Great Victorian Boom' of 1850–73, the 'Great Depression' of 1873–96, and renewed expansion down to 1914. It is doubtful whether the periodization was really so clear-cut, though it is true that 1873–96, in contrast with the periods preceding and following it, was a time of falling prices, and it contained (in the mid-1870s, mid-1880s, and early 1890s) more than its share of deep and prolonged recessions. Greater protectionism and economic nationalism were the consequences. The buoyant years from the late 1890s to 1914, in contrast, were much more favourable for government revenues. Economic and financial recovery was the precondition for an upsurge in expenditure on armaments. Second, unequal economic growth rates altered the international distribution of resources and contributed to political uncertainty. Leaving aside the economic challenge from the United States, which was massive but distant, the centre of gravity of European military potential shifted eastwards and away from the Atlantic toward the interior of the Continent. In 1870 the German states and France fought as approximate equals in population and industrial production; by 1914 Germany's population was over 50 per cent more than France's and its steel production four times bigger. In 1890 the United Kingdom produced twice as much steel as did Germany but by 1913 the proportions were reversed.[14] Yet Germany's manufacturing and demographic expansion was offset by that of Russia, which in the 1890s and after 1908 achieved very fast industrial growth indeed, and by 1914 rivalled Germany in defence spending. These tendencies were sufficiently visible (despite the absence at the time of Gross National Product indicators) to influence political calculations, encouraging Britain and France to combine against Germany, and Germany to contemplate a preventive strike against Russia. In these circumstances economic interdependence, far from making military force obsolete, might even encourage resort to it. The pre-1914 planners in the Royal Navy believed Germany's dependence on maritime trade made it more vulnerable to blockade than was Britain.[15] The Chief of the German General Staff from 1890 to 1905, Alfred von Schlieffen, accepted that economic integration precluded a long war, but concluded that a conflict must be decided by overwhelming initial blows.[16]

In the security and political domains as well as the economic, international institutions were feeble and co-operation was *ad hoc*. The nearest equivalent to an international security organization was the so-called Concert of Europe, but it was extremely informal. Like the gold standard system, it lacked a founding document, a secretariat, or any permanent existence. Politicians of the day referred to 'Europe' as a political entity (in Gladstone's case deferentially, in Bismarck's dismissively), but in practice the Concert meant little more than an understanding that after wars or during international tension the member states' representatives would meet to seek a consensus. Its purview covered Europe, Africa, and the Near East, and its core constituents were the European Great Powers. They used it to scale down Russia's gains after its 1877–78 war with Turkey (Berlin Congress, 1878), to negotiate a settlement to the 1905–06 Moroccan Crisis (Algeciras Conference, 1906), and to co-ordinate their responses to the 1912–13 First Balkan War (London Conference, 1912–13). Under the 1871 London Protocol, powers were supposed not to modify internationally agreed treaties without mutual consent. In practice, however, in the Bosnian annexation crisis of 1908–09 Austria-Hungary (backed by Germany) pushed through a unilateral alteration and rejected a conference to discuss the issue, and the same two powers attempted to do likewise in 1914. The conference machinery could meet and operate successfully only when all the powers wished to use it, and conferences tended to be most successful when bilateral diplomacy had established prior agreement between the participants.[17] Nor was there much pressure to strengthen the system. Some commentators advocated transferring sovereignty to European institutions (and the German Emperor Wilhelm II mused in private on the need for a United States of Europe against America), but such agitation had been stronger in the 1850s than it was before 1914.[18] More modestly, Anglo-Saxon liberals and Continental socialists demanded arms limitation and greater recourse to arbitration to resolve international disputes. The Hague Peace Conferences of 1899 and 1907, however, achieved nothing except resolutions in principle in favour of arbitration and arms limitation, together with the creation of a court of international justice that states remained free to disregard. The conferences contributed to the *ius in bello* (the law of conducting war) by strengthening the humanitarian requirements for the treatment of casualties, prisoners, and civilians and by regulating the use of maritime blockades. The *ius ad bellum* (the legal right to resort to war) remained untrammelled.[19]

Superficially, none the less, 1870–1914 was a period of peace. It witnessed no general wars, involving all or most of the powers. More limited conflicts involving two or three of them, of which a cluster had occurred between 1854 and 1871, were few and isolated. The Russo-Japanese War of 1904–05 was the outstanding example; the Russo-Turkish War of 1877–78 and the Sino-Japanese War of 1894–95 might be added to the list, though all three ended quickly. The Italo-Turkish War of 1911–12 and the South African War of 1899–1902 were also fought between substantial forces with modern equipment, but only in their early stages. Plenty of lower-intensity conflicts took place outside Europe to offset against the tranquillity within it, but the period witnessed no prolonged upheavals on the scale of the mid-century Indian Mutiny, American Civil War, or Taiping Rebellion. The absence of fighting, however, did not mean the absence of tension, and the seeming precariousness of peace, in an era of crises, secret diplomacy, and arms races, impressed many contemporaries.[20] Events were to vindicate their foreboding, though for much of the period the danger of war was low. To understand this paradox more fully we must divide the international politics of the period into three sub-phases, separated in approximately 1890 and 1905.[21]

In the 1870s and 1880s the main lines of tension within Europe as revealed in diplomatic confrontations were between France and Germany (crises in 1875 and 1887) and Russia and Austria-Hungary (1878 and 1885–87). A land arms race setting Germany and Austria-Hungary against France and Russia was already beginning. But Germany was widely recognized as the strongest military power in Europe and under Otto von Bismarck, Chancellor until his dismissal in 1890, its government was broadly satisfied with the status quo. Moreover, extra-European disputes over Africa, Asia and the Near East divided France from Italy and Britain from France and Russia, thus helping him to divide his potential enemies. France lacked Great Power allies (although in 1875 Britain and Russia warned Bismarck against attacking her again), and Britain fought shy of Continental involvement. Given that Bismarck had accomplished a *rapprochement* with Vienna after the Austro-Prussian War of 1866, his main task was to prevent Austria-Hungary's and Russia's rivalry in the Balkans from forcing him to choose between them. He succeeded, if with increasing difficulty, until he fell from office. During this period, therefore, Europe was dominated by German-led alliances, notably the Dual Alliance with Austria-Hungary (1879) and the Triple Alliance with Austria-Hungary and Italy (1882), both of which survived until 1914.

In contrast, the Three Emperors' League (1873, revived in 1881) of Germany, Austria-Hungary, and Russia broke up at the end of the 1880s, opening the way in the second sub-phase for France and Russia to conclude a political alliance and military convention in 1891–94. Europe was now polarized between a Franco-Russian and an Austro-German bloc, each arming and drawing up war plans against the other. Yet paradoxically the pace of land armament slackened in these years and the most dynamic arms race was at sea, between Britain on the one hand and France and Russia on the other. Britain's 1889 Naval Defence Act set the principle of a 'two-power standard' of equivalence to the next two strongest navies put together.[22] The most acute diplomatic crises of this period (Fashoda, 1898; Dogger Bank, 1904) squared off London against Paris or St. Petersburg, and the Franco-Russian Alliance became an anti-British as well as an anti-German combination. In the meantime France seemed on the road to *rapprochement* with Germany and Austria-Hungary with Russia, and in many ways it was the British who had most reason to feel vulnerable. As they were highly unlikely to retaliate by launching a preventive war, however, this disposition was not particularly dangerous.

Yet in the third period (after 1905) conditions deteriorated drastically. Germany and Austria-Hungary believed themselves by 1914 to be 'encircled' and on the losing end of a reinvigorated arms race. To a large extent the Germans, who after Bismarck's departure were less acquiescent in the European status quo, had themselves to blame. With their 1898 and 1900 Navy Laws they began creating a major battleship fleet in the North Sea, a project that had little relevance to their security needs and was primarily intended for diplomatic leverage against Britain, as well as to consolidate domestic support for the Hohenzollern monarchy.[23] Further, they sought to profit from Tsar Nicholas II's defeat at the hands of Japan in order to try to realign Europe by pressing Russia and France into entering a Continental bloc. Between them these initiatives triggered the formation by 1907 of the British–French–Russian 'Triple Entente', while at the same time a developing confrontation between Austria-Hungary and Serbia threatened the Germans' most reliable Great-Power ally.[24] The military balance similarly moved against them. Britain outspent and outbuilt Germany in the Anglo-German naval race, especially after it developed into a competition to acquire the new breed of all-big gun or 'dreadnought' capital ships. After 1912 Germany reduced its pace of naval construction, but its comparative neglect of its army handicapped it in the new land arms race that now took off between the Franco-Russian and the Austro-German blocs. In some ways the conditions of the 1880s were recreated, but in a much more dangerous form. More frequent and serious diplomatic crises divided France from Germany over Morocco (1905–06 and 1911), Russia from Austria-Hungary in the Balkans (1908–09, 1912–13), and Russia from Germany over the Turkish Straits (1913–14). After approximately 1911, military planners in France and Russia believed for the first time that they could risk a general European war with a reasonable prospect of winning it. Conversely their German counterparts feared that unless they struck within the next few years their prospects of victory (and with them their country's power/political leverage) would be irretrievably lost.[25]

The Role of Strategic Planners

Strategic planners in this period operated in the shadow of the mid-nineteenth-century military revolution. In the first instance this revolution was technological.[26] For two centuries the design of ships of the line and of muskets and cannon had changed little. But after 1840 iron replaced wood and steam replaced sail in Europe's navies, while armies were now transported to the front by rail and fought with rifled and breech-loading artillery and handguns. These spectacular developments were merely the overture for further rounds of innovation.[27] The revolution was also institutional, the other Powers seeking to emulate the formula that brought Prussia its triumphs in Bismarck's wars. Two organizational changes stand out: the switch to relatively short-service conscript armies (typically two to four years with the colours, the standing army being reinforced on mobilization by a much larger trained reserve) and the creation of general staffs on the Prussian model. From the 1870s most Continental European armies trained up an intellectual elite from among their officer corps to serve in central bureaux dedicated to intelligence gathering and assessment, military history and tactical doctrine, and operational planning. By the turn of the century navies were copying armies and Britain and America were following the Continental lead. In many ways these years were the formative period for modern strategic planning, and it was in the Prusso-German Great General Staff and its counterparts elsewhere – the *Etat-major de l'armée* in Paris, the *Glavnyi Shtab* in St. Petersburg, the *Generalstab* in Vienna, the *Stato Maggiore* in Rome – that such planning was concentrated.

It is important to understand the institutional context. The relationship between general staffs and war ministries was a critical variable. Planning for the 'next' war (as it was frequently referred to) entailed not simply devising a concentration plan such as France's Plan XVII. It also meant answering basic questions about the size and equipment of the prospective army, its organization and recruitment, and its doctrine and training. Naval planners had to determine the numbers and specifications of warships in each category, their personnel and deployment, and their supporting infrastructure onshore. Some of these matters could stay secret, but others required money and legislation. After 1871 all the European Great Powers except Russia had elected legislatures, and after 1906 Russia did too. Army recruitment arrangements and unit organization, as well as warship construction schedules, were normally embodied in legislation, expenditure heads being itemized in the annual budget. In 1883 the German authorities therefore separated out the general staff from responsibility to the war minister and made its chief directly answerable to the Emperor.[28] Whereas the minister had to defend budgets and legislation in the *Reichstag*, intelligence and operational planning were shielded from parliamentary scrutiny. A similar distinction between the *Reichsmarineamt* (Imperial Navy Office) and the *Admiralstab* (Admiralty Staff) operated for the fleet. This system meant that operational planning proceeded largely independently of the head of the civilian government, the Chancellor, who was responsible for overseeing foreign policy. To work well, it placed a premium on the co-ordinating role of the sovereign, which Wilhelm II was ill-equipped to furnish.[29] In Austria-Hungary too the general staff enjoyed independence from the war ministry and, especially after Franz Conrad von Hötzendorff replaced Friedrich Beck as Chief of the General Staff (CGS) in 1906, there was often friction between the two bodies. Conrad also tried more persistently than his German counterparts to influence diplomacy, although the Emperor Franz Joseph generally held him in check.[30] In the Entente countries, in contrast, general staffs were less independent, and political supervision of the military establishment was stronger. Russia did not create a German-style general staff until 1906, and the war minister Vladimir Sukhomlinov almost immediately clipped its wings, removing CGSs who challenged him.[31] French politicians deliberately kept the high command weak because of their fear of military intervention against the Third Republic: a fear heightened by the civil–military conflict provoked at the turn of the century by the Dreyfus Affair. The CGS in Paris (unlike in Berlin and Vienna) would not command the army in war, and was appointed by the war minister, the latter usually being a junior non-serving general whose tenure in office typically lasted only a few months. Only after the Agadir Crisis of 1911 did Joseph Joffre's appointment as CGS with stronger powers restore greater stability.[32] Finally, the British created the post of Chief of the Imperial General Staff in 1906, but not until Sir William Robertson's tenure in 1915–18 did it take on much political weight.[33]

Chiefs of the general staff therefore functioned as only one element within a complex and divided hierarchy. Whether men and weapons would be available for the deployments that they planned depended on the lobbying talents of war and navy ministers, on the sympathies of legislators, on tight-fisted finance ministers, and on the priority monarchs, premiers, and foreign secretaries gave to strategic preparedness. For much of the period between 1871 and 1914 domestic political forces worked to limit armaments rather than expand them. Between the 1890s and 1912, for example, the Prussian war ministry deliberately limited the growth of the German army for fear that a greater intake of socialist urban workers and progressive middle-class officers might make it less reliable for domestic repression.[34] The reforms of Richard Haldane, Secretary of State for War in the British Liberal Cabinet after 1905, created a British Expeditionary Force that could be dispatched rapidly to the Continent, but were also intended to (and did) cap army expenditure.[35] In Germany, Russia, and Austria-Hungary too, for much of the period, finance ministries successfully limited military expansion in order to prevent additional taxation and borrowing. Nor was manpower unconditionally available, as despite the fact that in Continental countries from the 1870s most able-bodied young men were legally liable for military service, many were not called up. In France a Radical ministry in 1905 replaced a three-year with a two-year service liability, overriding protests from the military authorities that doing so would diminish the standing army. In Austria-Hungary, expansion in the annual recruitment quota was blocked for a decade from 1902 to 1912 because the Hungarian authorities insisted on greater use of Magyar in the army as their condition for consenting.[36] Even within the defence budget that was available, armies and navies jockeyed for funds. In Britain the Liberal government had a sound strategic case for its decision to concentrate resources on the navy, which followed extended consideration of the risk of invasion in the Cabinet's Committee of Imperial Defence. But Germany after 1898 and Russia after 1906 boosted their battleship construction budgets largely because of the political advantages hoped for by Wilhelm II, Nicholas II, and their civilian advisers, rather than for the warships' value in any likely combat scenarios. For much of this period, in short, army strategic planners in particular were starved of resources, and had to make bricks without straw. When in 1905 Schlieffen drew up his celebrated blueprint for overwhelming France with a northward sweep round Paris, he knew that the German army lacked the strength to implement it.[37]

If military planners faced domestic as well as international political uncertainty, they had also to contend with a fast-moving technological environment. The new dynamism of the mid-nineteenth century slackened little after 1870. A major new development was the decline in importance of state arsenals and shipyards relative to private arms firms such as Krupp, Schneider, Vickers, and Skoda, which ran their own research laboratories and often exported their output across the alliance lines to potential enemies. But several major innovations originated with the strategic planners themselves. Examples included HMS *Dreadnought*, constructed for the Royal Navy in 1905–06, the quick-firing 75 mm field gun, developed for the French army in its own arsenals in 1897, and the *M-Gerät*, the massive 42 cm mortar built secretly by the Krupp firm for the German general staff and directed against the Belgian fortresses in 1914. In such an environment, while any one country's planners might be able to influence the pace and diffusion of technological change, none could control it. On the contrary, a new cycle of innovation followed the introduction in the 1880s of a range of smokeless high explosives to replace the traditional brown powder. At sea they enabled gunnery combat at much longer ranges and rescued the fortunes of the battleship, which had seemed threatened with obsolescence. Side-mounted quick-firing guns provided extra protection against torpedo-boat attack; triple-expansion engines added to speed and range; and the invention of tougher and lighter nickel-steel armour plate made it possible to protect the decks and superstructure without rendering ships top-heavy, thus making combat possible away from the shoreline and out on the high seas.[38] On land the new explosives, linked to the introduction of the magazine rifle, completed the small arms revolution begun in earlier decades. Still more significant was the application of quick-firing (i.e. recoil-less) mechanisms to the field gun, beginning with the French 75 mm, which fired up to twenty rounds per minute compared with its predecessor's four to six. It obliged all armies to replace their light artillery *in toto*. In the first decade of the twentieth century the pace of change accelerated still further. At sea the outstanding innovations were first submarines, and second dread-nought battleships and battle cruisers fitted with turbine engines (eventually oil- rather than coal-fired), all big-gun armament, and new fire-control systems, even if, as far as the latter were concerned, the Royal Navy failed to adopt the best available product.[39] On land the artillery applied quick-firing technology to heavy guns, and the Maxim machine gun (which dated from the 1880s) now became integrated into standard infantry equipment. Nor should we consider weaponry in isolation. Wireless was becoming the normal medium of communication between large warships, and field tele-phones between units on land. After 1906 most armies and navies acquired first dirigibles and then aircraft for reconnaissance, and armies arranged to requisition hundreds of cars and lorries if war came. None the less, the railway remained central to mobilization and concentration and this tech-nology too was continuing to advance. Since 1871 total European railway mileage had nearly trebled, compounding and superheating had improved locomotives' efficiency, and longer steel rails, automatic braking, and block signalling had permitted greater axle lengths and higher speeds. The opening train-based deployments of 1914 would dwarf those of fifty years before.[40] One elementary fact distinguishing any future European war from those in the past would be that the opposing armies were far larger.

In principle, in responding to the political and technological uncertainties that surrounded them, strategic planners could draw on the best available information about their likely adversaries and on lessons from previous conflicts. General staffs included intelligence and military history branches alongside their operational planning divisions. Civilian intelligence agencies of the post-1945 variety were almost unknown before 1914, although in 1909 Britain created the forerunner of MI6 in order to monitor German battleship building.[41] Nor was communications intelligence of much signifi-cance, although French and Russian code breakers were able to decrypt diplomatic telegrams (including, in the French case, German ones).[42] Pivotal in intelligence gathering were therefore the military and naval attachés whom the Powers assigned to their embassies and legations from the 1850s onwards. Some (notably Russian ones) ran agents in the host country; most were surprisingly free to travel to strategic zones and to pick up gossip.[43] In addition to the attachés, the Germans had a network of 'tension travellers' behind the French and Russian borders, who could be activated at times of crisis and did in fact report quite accurately on French and Russian prepara-tions in July 1914.[44] But much was available from open sources. It was hard to disguise how many battleships, fortresses, and railway lines were under construction, and the military press was often revealing about other matters. Recruiting bills, shipbuilding programmes, and budgets had to be presented to parliaments, and placed additional material in the public domain. Further information came from friends. The French and Russian general staffs exchanged information about Germany, as did the French and British attachés in Berlin after 1911; the German and Austrian military shared intelligence about Russia. The upshot was that European staffs knew fairly clearly before 1914 the size and heavy armament of their opponents' armies and warships, and were speedily alerted if anyone undertook extraordinary military measures. The Russians had the further advantage of familiarity with the Austro-Hungarian and possibly even German concentration plans because of their use as a double agent until his exposure in 1913 of Colonel Alfred Redl, head of Austrian counter-intelligence and later a corps commander on the Polish border.[45] But this was exceptional. The German general staff seems to have known little about French and Russian war plans.[46] The French general staff before 1914, although correctly expecting the Germans to make their main attack westwards and come via Belgium, underestimated both the strength of the German right flank and the extent of its northward wheel.[47] All the same, compared to the uncertain guidance offered by military history, that from intelligence sources was good.

In examining the influence of military history, we should begin with the mid-nineteenth-century wars. They gave navies little to go on, and some of the information that they did provide was misleading. Until the 1890s most warships were fitted with rams because the Austrians used ramming successfully in 1866 at the battle of Lissa.[48] As for armies, most general staffs (possibly excepting Britain's) tended to discount the American Civil War as campaigning by amateurs in remote and unfamiliar terrain. The examples of 1866 and 1870–71, with their demonstrations of quick and decisive victory, were the ones that mattered.[49] The evidence seemed clear that a well-trained and rapidly deployed conscript army could overwhelm an experienced professional one, and the Austrians, French, Russians, and Italians reorganized their recruitment and force structures in consequence.[50] It is not true, however, that the 1870 war showed unambiguously that the advantage now lay with the strategic offensive. On the contrary, even Helmuth von Moltke the Elder, the Chief of the Prusso-German Great General Staff from 1857 to 1888, was more impressed by the 'People's War' waged by the French Republican Government of National Defence in the winter of 1870–71 than by the initial victories over Napoleon III. During the 1870s and 1880s he planned to attack Russia rather than France first in the event of a two-front war, but increasingly he doubted whether such a war could be won.[51] The French, despite their rapid recovery from defeat (by 1890 they matched Germany in the number of railways leading to the common border), planned for a defensive strategy in another war, or for a counterstroke after parrying the initial blow. Only after 1911 did they plan to take the offensive straight away. Russia too, disappointed by its military performance in 1877–78 and with its military organization thoroughly disrupted in 1904–05, remained cautious and defensive in its strategic planning until 1912.[52]

By the turn of the century, however, Bismarck's wars were of fading relevance in a Europe where future Great-Power conflicts were likely to be fought between coalitions rather than as bilateral duels, and with much more formidable weapons and bigger forces. The campaigns in South Africa and Manchuria in 1899–1902 and 1904–05 might have assisted in constructing more reliable scenarios, but largely failed to do so. Both sides in South Africa fought with small-bore magazine rifles, and the Boers had quick-firing artillery. They were able to repulse British frontal attacks, as Bloch had predicted. Observers from Continental armies doubted the relevance of the experience, but partly in the light of the South African example the French army remodelled its tactical doctrine in 1904 (prescribing advances by small groups covering each other with fire), only later to revert to a doctrine of massed bayonet charges. In Britain, where a Royal Commission investigated the country's unsatisfactory military performance, the view prevailed that the attack should be pressed home whatever the cost and the revised 1912 Field Service Regulations made little concession to the minority of officers who advocated 'defensive tactics'.[53]

But for most European observers Manchuria far outweighed South Africa in significance. Unlike Britain and the Boers, moreover, Russia and Japan also engaged in naval combat. In engagements fought at ranges of 8,000 yards or more, the Japanese benefited from their warships' greater speed and the accuracy of their long-range guns. Though neither side had submarines, mines were used effectively and sank two Japanese battleships.[54] All the same, the Royal Navy did little to improve its minesweeping capacity, and although the war confirmed the Admiralty in the wisdom of their decision to build HMS *Dreadnought*, that decision had been taken beforehand. On land, the war had a more discernible impact. Not only did the defeated Russians set up commissions of inquiry into many aspects of the fighting,[55] but also dozens of foreign military observers witnessed the operations from both sides, and the French, British, and German armies produced multi-volume official histories.[56] As in 1870, however, the 'lessons' could be read in more than one way. The Russians had defended Port Arthur with trenches and machine guns, against which the besiegers hurled their infantry in sacrificial attacks. Yet despite suffering twice the Russians' casualties, the Japanese eventually captured the high ground overlooking the harbour, from where their artillery destroyed the Russian Pacific Fleet. In the wake of the conflict, the European armies expanded their provision for machine guns and field telephones, and all except the French followed the Japanese in adopting inconspicuous uniforms.[57] But in general their observers were

DAVID STEVENSON

impressed by the eventual Japanese success in taking Port Arthur and forcing the Russians to negotiate. In the new fire-swept battlefield, the offensive might be more costly than ever, and high morale and discipline were at a premium, but the side that attacked could still impose its will. According to Joffre, the campaign was a 'shining confirmation' of the importance of aggressive willpower in war; according to the German official history, 'the will to conquer, conquered'. To an extent, the European military read into the Manchurian auguries what they wished to see.[58]

This last point has an obvious bearing on the issue of how such information and analysis were used. The stock answer to the question of how effectively pre-First World War planners anticipated the future would be that their record was lamentable. By December 1914 the Continental armies had thrown away thousands of their best young men in abortive offensives and had all but exhausted their munitions stocks, with the result that the Germans had to break off the First Battle of Ypres, the Russians had to suspend attacking operations, and the French had to dust off their pre-quick firing guns. The best estimates of shell consumption, derived with 1904–05 experiences in mind, had proved grossly inadequate,[59] and having conscripted many of their munitions workers in August the armies now belatedly returned them to their factories. No one, except arguably Bloch (and even he also got much wrong), predicted the continuous entrenchments that formed along the Western Front or the months-long attrition battles of Verdun, the Somme, and Flanders. Neither the British nor the German navy had foreseen the potential of the submarine as a commerce raider, and no diplomat had predicted a decisive American intervention in a European conflict. By borrowing and by printing money governments financed unimagined levels of spending. The examples could go on. Yet the very universality of these failures of foresight suggest it may be unreasonable to expect strategic planners to have anticipated the evolution of the conflict in the unprecedented circumstances of stalemated war between two industrialized coalitions that prevailed after 1915. If we reformulate the question more restrictively to consider the planning for the opening phase of mobile campaigning, recent research has to some extent rehabilitated pre-1914 strategic planners from the uniformly bad press awarded them in older accounts. Indeed, it now appears that many military leaders doubted if a European war was likely to be over by Christmas, although they may not have disclosed this pessimism to their political chiefs.[60] It is best to begin with the Entente powers, who adopted a reactive posture in the July 1914 crisis, before turning to the military appraisals that underlay the Central Powers' initiative.

The Russian armed forces, in contrast with most other European forces, had been involved in major hostilities only a decade before. They had learned from the experience. In particular, a major reason for their defeat in 1904–05 had been their slow mobilization and concentration. In 1914, in contrast, not only was Poland much less distant than Manchuria, and far better served with railways, but also a major reform in 1910 had adopted a territorial mobilization system that significantly accelerated Russia's speed of readiness, as the Austrians and Germans well knew.[61] After 1909 the tsarist army expanded its re-equipment budget, investing among other things in heavy artillery and machine guns, and on the eve of war it was about to embark on a major programme of strategic railway construction. It is true that the St. Petersburg general staff would have preferred not to fight in 1914, and the Central Powers deliberately challenged Russia before its rearmament effort could reach fruition. None the less, it can be argued that the concentration plan implemented in 1914 (the 'G' variant of Plan XIX revised, dating from 1912) was a rational response to Russia's politico-strategic circumstances.[62] Russia's army (which was not overwhelmingly larger than those of the Central Powers, despite the size of its population) was divided between separate operations against Austria-Hungary and Germany. Yet failing to attack Austria-Hungary (though strategically prob-ably the preferable course) would have meant leaving the Serbs to their fate, whereas in the event Russia's advance in southern Poland not only assisted Serbia but also, in that it defeated the Austrians and occupied most of Galicia, was the most successful of the 1914 offensives. Conversely, invading East Prussia was an obvious move when German forces there were denuded and some action was essential to help the French, who had demanded an early offensive operation against German territory and were very materially assisted by it when two German corps were moved from the west. Notwithstanding Russia's rout at Tannenberg, Plan XIX revised therefore achieved several of its objectives.

If we consider Russia's allies, the British Expeditionary Force, despite the offensive bias of the new Field Service Regulations, had learned from the South African campaign and was well drilled in defensive tactics. Intensive planning made possible its transport to the battle zone before the Germans realized it had been embarked. Furthermore, in 1911–12 the leaders of the Royal Navy had abandoned an inappropriate strategy of close blockade and raids and bombardments along the German coast in favour of a distant blockade. So far from being indifferent to the threats posed by mines and torpedoes its leaders were almost hyper-cautious.[63] In the case of France, however, there are more justified grounds for criticism. It is true that – compared with most European countries – the French had not stinted on their army expenditure. They called up and trained a higher proportion of their young men than did any other power, and in 1914 they deployed an army of comparable size to Germany's (despite their smaller population) at about the same speed, thus avoiding the botched mobilization that had made their defeat in 1870 likely from the beginning. But against this their Plan XVII, adopted in early 1914, assumed an immediate attack into German territory with all available forces. This contrasted with the more prudent defensive–offensive conception of Plan XVI, i.e. identifying and containing the main German axis of advance before launching a counter-stroke. Furthermore, the dispositions of Plan XVII were less favourable than those of Plan XVI to meeting a German offensive directed through the whole of Belgium instead of just the Ardennes – which the French had failed to anticipate in consequence of probably avoidable intelligence failures that Joffre himself retrospectively acknowledged.[64] Although in the event he did pause before committing his main forces in August 1914, he still engaged them prematurely. They attacked with a reckless tactical doctrine, conspicuous uniforms, and little support from heavy field artillery, which France had lagged behind Germany in developing for fear it would impede mobility. Taken together, these deficiencies suggested that the French had learned the lessons of 1870 better than those of 1904–05, and they came dangerously close to losing once again in the opening round. Even so, their army, its commanders, and the supporting railway system were resilient enough to be able to rally after the opening defeats and to halt the Germans at the battle of the Marne, thus winning time for the Allies to muster their strength and making an indispensable contribution to their eventual triumph.

None of the Entente planners, however, counselled opening hostilities in 1914. Those who did were in the opposite camp. To start with Austria-Hungary, Conrad as CGS faced potential enemies on five borders – Russia, Romania, Serbia, Montenegro, and Italy – whereas his army was more starved of resources than that of almost any other power. It was also multi-ethnic, although its leaders judged correctly that most of it was reliable for the time being. In circumstances of such vulnerability, Conrad and his experts drew up a complex set of contingency plans for concentrations against Italy, against Serbia and Montenegro, and against both the latter plus Russia. Admittedly, as until 1912 they had envisaged Italy as the most likely enemy, they had invested in mountain-warfare equipment such as pike-grey uniforms that on the Polish plains were inappropriate. But their intelligence about both Russian and Italian capabilities was quite good. Conrad was aware that the Russian army had recovered fast from its 1905 defeat, and in early 1914 he modified his concentration plans so as to hold his forces further behind the frontier. With regard to Serbia, however, although his attachés correctly reported on the Serbs' heavy losses in money, men, rifles, and munitions in the Balkan Wars of 1912–13, they greatly underestimated their prospective enemy's morale and fighting skill. Furthermore, Conrad was so determined to finish off the Serbs that he committed his reserve units to the Balkan front in July 1914 before changing his mind under German pressure and sending them northwards against the Russians, whom he attacked without receiving the expected German support. Like the French, moreover, he exacerbated the scale of his army's opening disasters by an excessive commitment to the tactical offensive. But

Conrad understood the basic problem only too well. His army was simply too weak for the multi-front campaign it was attempting. Going onto the offensive therefore made sense only on the assumptions that Germany would fight as well and that its army would win. Over-optimism about the German rather than the Austrian army caused his downfall.[65]

In contrast to its ally, the German army was probably the best prepared of all the European forces for the initial campaigns. It had invested more heavily than its counterparts in heavy field artillery (including the fortress-smashing *M-Gerät*), in field howitzers and machine guns, and in training its troops in entrenching techniques. Staff rides in East Prussia had already envisaged the manoeuvres that would enable an outnumbered force to repel the Russian invaders. The principal critiques of the German army's war preparations have therefore centred on strategy, though here too the most recent research, based on new material from the former East German archives, has forced some reconsideration. Terence Zuber has argued that Schlieffen and the younger Moltke, CGSs from 1890 to 1905 and 1906 to 1914, had a defensive–offensive conception. So, far from staking everything on a right-flank wheel through Belgium and west of Paris, they retained a strong left flank with the aim of defeating an expected opening French offensive near the frontier before driving into the enemy heartland. Zuber's argument demonstrates that Schlieffen's oft-cited memorandum of 1905 was a sketch for a possible ideal campaign if the German army was strong enough, rather than being the actual German war plan. Yet it leaves unclear when the Germans adopted the strategy actually pursued in 1914, which was indeed for a broad sweep though Belgium beginning at the outset of hostilities before the French offensive had been contained.[66] This strategy is the more puzzling because of additional new evidence that Moltke and his advisers were well aware of the high readiness and morale of the French army and knew it was a formidable antagonist that would be unlikely to collapse quickly.[67] In his dealings with the German political authorities Moltke certainly pressed for war in 1914, urging Germany's high readiness following its massive army law of 1913 and the desirability of acting before French and Russian rearmament efforts took effect.[68] His conduct is difficult to reconcile with his private doubts that victory was attainable: unless he was serious in his repeated assertions that a massive European war was inevitable, and this being the case Germany should at least start it at the most favourable moment.

The conclusion prompted by this analysis is that the Triple Entente armed forces were quite well prepared for war and would have been still more so had not their enemies deliberately forced the issue before Britain, France, and Russia were fully ready. On the other side both the Austrian and German military chiefs understood their armies' weaknesses and the difficulty of achieving decisive victory in the opening campaigns. Largely for political reasons, they pressed for war regardless. Perhaps the most consistent failure of anticipation on both sides was a tactical one: an under-estimation of the casualties and of the munitions consumption entailed in assaulting prepared positions. Yet even on this count, as has been seen, most general staffs did realize after the Russo-Japanese war that technolog-ical developments had made the tactical offensive more problematic, and that a major war would mean very heavy casualties indeed. Some of the soldiers marching off in August 1914 may have supposed that they were going to a picnic, but their commanders did not. Furthermore, pre-war appraisals of the military balance were accurate in that the French and Russian general staffs after 1911 viewed the balance of forces as moving in their favour (this was one of the justifications used for Plan XVII) and the Austrians and Germans saw that it was moving against them.[69] Yet the logical deduction from the evidence that the two coalitions were approaching equilibrium was that a war between them would be long and evenly matched, especially as two coalitions would find it harder to nego-tiate a compromise peace than would two single governments. Instead the military professionals in France and Russia inferred that it was now possible to risk a European war (as it had not been previously) and those in Austria-Hungary and Germany inferred that if war must come it was better faced now than in 1917. The pre-1914 period supports the contention of 'power transition' theorists that a greater equality of power may actually encourage conflict rather than deter it.[70]

Conclusion

In many ways the picture of the 1871–1914 period presented here has been conservative. First, although Europe's global economic and political prepon-derance was beginning to diminish, this development had surprisingly few implications for military planners. By the early twentieth century Japan was a potential enemy for Russia, and America and Germany were beginning to view each other as possible antagonists. On the other hand Tokyo and St. Petersburg buried the hatchet after 1905 and the likelihood of an Anglo-American war, still conceivable in 1871, dwindled almost to vanishing point. In general the main threats to the national security of the European powers continued to come from each other. Second, the rapid growth of global trading and financial interdependence also had fewer implications than might have been expected. Despite the rise of a supra-national heavy indus-trial complex in the Rhine Basin, few in France or Germany considered that war between them was thereby rendered impossible. Even Britain, the country that might seem most exposed in the event of an international economic breakdown, had less to fear from a war against Germany (whose overseas possessions were few and whose navy could be bottled up in the North Sea) than it did from one against France and Russia, which until approximately 1904 seemed more probable. Foreign Secretary Sir Edward

Grey had this in mind when he told the House of Commons on 3 August 1914 that Britain stood to suffer little more from participating in a European war than if it stood aside. Third, through all the intricate diplomacy of these years, there remained an underlying consistency to the pattern of European Continental alignments. Italy, it is true, despite remaining nominally a member of the Triple Alliance, shifted from a primary hostility towards France in the 1880s and 1890s to a primary hostility towards Austria-Hungary after the turn of the century. Britain regarded Russia and/or France as its most likely antagonists in a major war between c.1878 and 1904–05, but Germany after the latter date. Yet France and Germany remained potential enemies throughout the period, as did Russia and Germany and Russia and Austria-Hungary. Their army planners operated in an environment of continuity and stability not to be matched again until after 1945. In 1914 the French and Russian general staffs implemented respectively the seventeenth and the nineteenth war plans they had drawn up against Germany since the 1870s. On the other hand, at no time was any of the European powers deliberately arming with a view to opening hostilities at a predetermined date. Certainly there were moments when tension was high and a Continental war seemed closer, notably during the later 1880s and in 1911–14. In the 1960s Professor Fritz Fischer suggested that the Berlin leaders had resolved in December 1912 to start such a war in eighteen months' time. Before his death, however, he retreated from this contention, and it now seems established that Germany made no such decision before July 1914, even though from about 1911 its leaders increasingly envisaged war as an option.[71] War planning in 1871–1914 remained contingency preparation for a hypothetical eventuality that might never become real. So far from the Continent being an armed camp, most European countries did not conscript all of their available manpower, and defence spending averaged between 3 and 5 per cent of net national product, much less than either in the late 1930s or between the 1950s and the 1980s.[72]

If these factors made for predictability in planning assumptions, greater uncertainty arose from the shifts in relative wealth and power potential away from Britain and France and towards first Germany and then Russia. A further imponderable was the progressive technical refinement of both army and naval weaponry and equipment. It was relatively easy for intelligence services to monitor the quantitative evolution of the military balance, but much harder to predict how soldiers and commanders would perform in the new conditions of combat – and the very length of time since major operations had last occurred in Europe heightened the uncertainty. The pointers given by the campaigns in South Africa and Manchuria were suggestive but ambiguous. On the whole they indicated that victory would still go to the side that maintained the tactical and strategic offensive, even though the price might be very high indeed. With this in mind, and conscious that the military balance might be moving irreparably against them, the military planners of Germany and Austria-Hungary urged war in 1914, and their counterparts in the Entente countries (more confident than in previous years) advised their governments to pick up the gauntlet. Repeated diplomatic trials of strength, belligerent nationalism, and instability in the Balkans and elsewhere had created a political atmosphere in which statesmen were now inclined to listen.

These reflections underline how far we have moved in ninety years. It is devoutly to be hoped that no strategic planners today consider an all-out Great-Power conflict to be inevitable or that we live in an 'inter-war' period. In fact the international strategic environment before 1914 resembled less the post-Gorbachev and post-9/11 era than the inter-bloc military confrontation during the Cold War, despite the absence of weapons of mass destruction,[73] and even though airpower and submersibles remained in their infancy. Before 1914, as before 1989, two coalitions opposed each other in Central Europe at high military readiness, gathering intelligence, conducting manoeuvres, and drafting war plans on the assumption that high-intensity conflict with the other was a plausible contingency that must be prepared for. The likely enemy was not in doubt. And to judge from what has been revealed of Warsaw Pact planning, its offensive bias bore disturbing similarities to that of Wilhelmine Germany.[74] These analogies have not been lost on political scientists, who from the Cuban Missile Crisis to the 1980s searched for lessons from the First World War's outbreak.[75]

In contrast, conditions since 1991 have been much more fluid. Analysts continue to debate the defining characteristics of the post-Cold War era: perhaps a return to traditional geopolitical Great-Power balancing, perhaps a leap into something quite new, an end of history or a clash of civilizations.[76] In fact it exhibits both familiar and novel elements, which is one of the reasons why it is so difficult to characterize. However, it clarifies exposition to take September 2001 as a watershed. The nearest historical parallel to the decade 1991–2001 may be the 1920s, when the victorious western powers were divided amongst themselves but none the less enjoyed a transient hegemony before a revisionist coalition emerged. Between 1871 and 1914 the relevant exemplar is the 1870s, when a triumphant Germany confronted a defeated France but remained secure while it kept its potential enemies divided. While Bismarck remained Chancellor he managed to isolate Paris by co-opting Austria-Hungary and Russia in a conservative ideological alignment, but even he found the task daunting. His rasher successors hastened the Russo-French alliance, antagonized St. Petersburg, and then underestimated Russia's potential for speedy recovery from its defeat by Japan. The 1870s and 1920s precedents lend strength to predictions that America's post-Cold War predominance may be transitory, and that in the medium term a balance of power between status quo and challenging states will re-emerge. The inexorable advance since the 1970s in China's modernization supports such a view, as does the more recent recovery in Russia. At some point a new point of 'power transition' between America and its antagonists may therefore loom, and experience warns that such moments can be dangerous. Indeed, in its 2002 statement, *The National Security Strategy of the United States*, the current administration foresaw such an eventuality and announced it would try to prevent it, by dissuading 'potential adversaries from pursuing a military build-up in hopes of surpassing or equalling the United States'.[77]

None the less, the post-1991 period has so far been remarkable for the absence of a revisionist challenge, and arguably the upsurge of international terrorism since 9/11 has created a more urgent threat that may indefinitely delay the re-emergence of geo-political rivalries. It also makes pre-First World War Europe seem still more remote. Certainly there were numerous terrorist 'outrages' in that period, and the July 1914 crisis began with the Sarajevo assassinations and with an Austro-Hungarian punishment expedition against the Serbian state whose military intelligence officers had armed the killers and assisted them across the border. Yet Russia's intervention on Serbia's behalf showed that even the conservative powers refused to suspend their rivalries and close ranks against the perpetrators. Inter-state conflict remained the key security threat for strategic planners of the epoch.

Many considerations therefore underline the differences between the early twenty-first century and the early twentieth. This is not to say that nothing of contemporary applicability can be learned from studying the latter. Many fundamental principles of strategic planning date from 1871–1914, including keeping plans under regular review, supporting them by sophisticated intelligence gathering, preparing economic and financial as well as operational blueprints, and co-ordinating military and civilian authorities through bodies such as Britain's Committee of Imperial Defence. In addition, the period is rich in instructive case histories. Professor Sumida's contribution to this volume traces the origins of the Royal Navy's ill-fated commitment to the battlecruiser, a revolutionary technological solution to Britain's defence exigencies across the globe that was ill prepared for fleet actions in the North Sea. Professor Herwig's examines the incoherence of Wilhelmine Germany's strategic planning, which would lead to disaster on a grander scale. Wider comparisons between the powers of that time and today's United States, however, require more caution. Since the end of the Cold War in Europe, the contingencies facing American planners have grown more diverse. In addition to the potential threats from terrorism and from 'rogue' states acquiring weapons of mass destruction, the United States will presumably wish to be able to intervene as a 'peacekeeper', at least in the western hemisphere and possibly outside. Even so, in the medium term the risk of armed conflict with first-rank powers may yet return to the agenda, perhaps with Russia over Transcaucasia or with China over Taiwan. In such a scenario, historical analogies will become much more relevant, among the most pertinent being those with Kuwait in 1990, the Falkland

Islands in 1982, or perhaps Poland in 1939, when unconvincing deterrent postures were combined with ambiguous political commitments. Among the pre-1914 powers, however, only the British Empire faced equally global dangers to its interests, and the parallels between Victorian Britain and late twentieth-century America have fascinated commentators for some time. Even so, the terms of the analysis have altered greatly since the pioneering studies by Paul Kennedy, Aaron Friedberg, Joseph Nye, and others a decade and more ago.[78] For the moment, not only has Soviet military power collapsed and Japan's economic potential stagnated, but America has also reduced its military 'overstretch' and its economy once more appears the world's most successful, despite the alarming growth of internal and international indebtedness. Although assisted by its rivals' weaknesses, the United States has shown unexpected resilience. At any rate until the troubled aftermath of the 2003 Iraq invasion, it has seemed no longer a declining power but one at a peak of relative strength, and a historic menace to such powers has been hubris.

Notes

1 Preface to Bloch, I.S., *Is War now Impossible? Being an Abridgement of the War of the Future in its Technical, Economic and Political Relations* (Aldershot: Gregg Revivals, 1991 [first published 1899]).

2 Hardach, G., *Der Erste Weltkrieg* (Munich: DTV, 1973), p. 295 (citing League of Nations statistics); Kenwood, A.G. and Lougheed, A.L., *The Growth of the International Economy, 1820–1960* (London: Allen & Unwin, 1971), p. 92.

3 Kennedy, P.M. (ed.), *War Plans of the Great Powers, 1880–1914* (London: Allen & Unwin, 1979), chapters 1–2.

4 Hobson, J.M., 'The Military–Extraction Gap and the Wary Titan: the Fiscal Sociology of British Defence Policy 1870–1913', *The Journal of European Economic History*, 22, 3 (1993), p. 501, table 1.

5 Clarke, I.F., *Voices Prophesying War, 1763–1984* (London: Oxford University Press, 1966); Pick, D. *War Machine: the Rationalization of Slaughter in the Modern Age* (New Haven: Yale University Press, 1993).

6 Angell, N., *The Great Illusion: a Study of the Relation of Military Power to National Advantage* (London: Heinemann, 1933 [first published as *Europe's Optical Illusion*, 1909]); cf. Weinroth, H., 'Norman Angell and *The Great Illusion*: an Episode in Pre-1914 Pacifism', *Historical Journal*, 17, 3 (1974), pp. 551–74.

7 Keynes, J.M., *The Economic Consequences of the Peace* (London: Macmillan, 1920), pp. 9–10.

8 Kenwood and Lougheed, *International Economy*, p. 91.

9 Strikwerda, C., 'The Troubled Origins of European Economic Integration: International Iron and Steel and Labor Migration in the Era of World War I', *American Historical Review*, 98, 4 (1993), pp. 1106–41.

10 Lyons, F.S.L., *Internationalism in Europe, 1815–1914* (Leyden: A.W. Sythoff, 1963).

11 Bloomfield, A.I., *Monetary Policy under the International Gold Standard, 1880–1914* (New York: Federal Reserve Bank of New York, 1959).

12 De Cecco, M., *Money and Empire: the International Gold Standard, 1890–1914* (Oxford: Blackwell, 1974).

13 Feis, H., *Europe: the World's Banker, 1870–1914* (New York: Council on Foreign Relations, 1964 [reprinted edition]), is the classic account.
14 Kennedy, P.M., *The Rise and Fall of the Great Powers: Economic Change and Military Conflict from 1500 to 2000* (London: Fontana, 1989), p. 257.
15 Offer, A., *The First World War: an Agrarian Interpretation* (Oxford: Oxford University Press, 1989), part 3.
16 Ritter, G., *The Schlieffen Plan: Critique of a Myth* (London: Wolff, 1958), p. 47.
17 Langhorne, R.T.B., *The Collapse of the Concert of Europe: International Politics 1890–1914* (London: Macmillan, 1981); Crampton, R.J., 'The Decline of the Concert of Europe in the Balkans, 1913–14', *Slavonic and East European Review*, 52, 128 (1974), pp. 393–419.
18 Renouvin, P., 'Les idées et les projets d'union européenne au XIXe siécle', *Carnegie Endowment for International Peace Bulletin*, 6 (1931), pp. 463–83.
19 Dülffer, J., *Regeln gegen den Krieg? Die Haager Friedenskonferenzen von 1899 und 1907 in der internationalen Politik* (Berlin: Ullstein, 1981); Best, G., *Humanity in Warfare: the Modern History of the International Law of Armed Conflicts* (London: Weidenfeld & Nicolson, 1983).
20 On crises, Dülffer, J., Krüger, M., and Wippich, R.H. (eds), *Vermiedene Kriege: Deeskalation von Konflikten der Grossmächte zwischen Krimkrieg und Erstem Weltkrieg (1856–1914)* (Munich: Oldenbourg, 1997).
21 For standard English-language diplomatic histories, see Taylor, A.J.P., *The Struggle for Mastery in Europe, 1848–1918* (Oxford: Oxford University Press, 1971); Bridge, F.R. and Bullen, R., *The Great Powers and the European States System, 1815–1914* (London: Longman, 1980). On the Triple Alliance, see Afflerbach, H., *Der Dreibund: Europäische Grossmacht-und Allianzpolitik vor dem Ersten Weltkrieg* (Vienna, Cologne, and Weimar: Böhlau, 2002).
22 For a discussion of this race from the British perspective, see Marder, A.J., *The Anatomy of British Sea Power: a History of British Naval Policy in the Pre-Dreadnought Era, 1880–1905* (London: Cass, 1964 [reprinted edition]).
23 The literature is enormous. See Steinberg, J., *Yesterday's Deterrent: Tirpitz and the Birth of the German Battle Fleet* (London: MacDonald, 1965); Berghahn, V.R., *Der Tirpitz-Plan: Genesis und Verfall einer innenpolitischen Krisenstrategie unter Wilhelm II* (Düsseldorf: Droste, 1971); Epkenhans, M., *Die Wilhelminische Flottenrüstung, 1908–1914: Weltmachstreben, industrieller Fortschritt, soziale Integration* (Munich: Oldenbourg, 1991); Herwig, H.H., *'Luxury' Fleet: the Imperial German Navy 1888–1918* (London and Atlantic Highlands, NJ: Allen & Unwin, 1987); Hobson, R., *Imperialism at Sea: Naval Strategic Thought, the Ideology of Sea Power, and the Tirpitz Plan, 1875–1914* (Boston: Brill, 2002); Lambi, I.N., *The Navy and German Power Politics, 1862–1914* (Boston: Allen & Unwin, 1984).
24 It is important to appreciate this change in the international environment in order to understand the argument presented in Professor Sumida's chapter in this volume.
25 On the pre-war land arms race, see Stevenson, D., *Armaments and the Coming of War: Europe, 1904–1914* (Oxford: Oxford University Press, 1996); Herrmann, D.G., *The Arming of Europe and the Making of the First World War* (Princeton: Princeton University Press, 1996).
26 A good survey can be found in McNeill, W.H., *The Pursuit of Power: Technology, Armed Force, and Society since AD 1000* (Oxford: Blackwell, 1983).
27 *Ibid*, Chapter 7.
28 For more information, see Craig, G.A., *The Politics of the Prussian Army, 1640–1945* (London: Oxford University Press, 1964); Meier-Welcke, H. and von Groote, H. (eds), *Handbuch der deutschen Militargeschichte, 1648–1939*, vol. 5 (Frankfurt, 1968).

29 For a fuller analysis of the German system, see Professor Herwig's chapter in this volume.

30 Williamson, S.R., *Austria-Hungary and the Origins of the First World War* (Basingstoke: Macmillan, 1991), chapter 3.

31 Stevenson, *Armaments*, p. 156.

32 Ralston, D.B., *The Army of the Republic: the Place of the Military in the Political Evolution of France, 1871–1914* (Cambridge, MA and London: MIT Press, 1967); Porch, D., *The March to the Marne: the French Army 1871–1914* (Cambridge: Cambridge University Press, 1981).

33 Gooch, J., *The Plans of War: the General Staff and British Military Strategy, c. 1900–1916* (London: Routledge & Kegan Paul, 1974).

34 Förster, S., *Der doppelte Militarismus: die deutsche Heeresrüstung zwischen Status-Quo-Sicherung und Aggression, 1890–1913* (Stuttgart: Steiner, 1985).

35 Spiers, E.M., *Haldane: an Army Reformer* (Edinburgh: Edinburgh University Press, 1980).

36 Stone, N., 'Army and Society in the Habsburg Monarchy, 1900–914', *Past & Present*, 33 (1966), pp. 95–111.

37 Ritter, *The Schlieffen Plan*, p. 141.

38 Lautenschläger, K., 'Technology and the Evolution of Naval Warfare', *International Security*, 8 (1983), pp. 3–51.

39 Sumida, J.T., *In Defence of Naval Supremacy: Finance, Technology, and British Naval Policy, 1889–1914* (Boston: Allen & Unwin, 1989).

40 Stevenson, D., 'War by Timetable? The Railway Race before 1914', *Past & Present*, 162 (1999), pp. 163–94.

41 Andrew, C.M., *Secret Service: the Making of the British Intelligence Community* (London: Heinemann, 1985), chapter 2; Hiley, N.P., 'The Failure of British Espionage against Germany, 1907–14', *Historical Journal*, 26, 4 (1983), pp. 867–89.

42 Andrew, C.M., 'France and the German Menace', in E.R. May (ed.), *Knowing One's Enemies: Intelligence Assessment before the Two World Wars* (Princeton: Princeton University Press, 1986), pp. 127–49. The essays in the first part of this volume are fundamental on pre-1914 intelligence.

43 Vagts, A., *The Military Attaché* (Princeton: Princeton University Press, 1967).

44 Trumpener, U., 'War Premeditated? German Intelligence Operations in July 1914',*Central European History*, 9 (1976), pp. 58–85.

45 Sked, A., 'A Patriot for Whom? Colonel Redl and a Question of Identity', *History Today*, 36 (July 1986), pp. 9–14; Markus, G., *Der Fall Redl* (Vienna and Munich: Amalthea, 1984).

46 Memoir by General von Tappen, 'Meine Kriegserinnerungen', p. 8, Bundesarchiv-Militärarchiv, Freiburg im Breisgau, W-10 / 50779.

47 Tanenbaum, J.K., 'French Estimates of German Operational War Plans', in May (ed.), *Knowing One's Enemies*, pp. 150–71.

48 McElwee, W., *The Art of War: Waterloo to Mons* (London, 1974), p. 263.

49 Luvaas, J., *The Military Legacy of the Civil War: the European Inheritance* (Lawrence, Kansas: University of Kansas Press, 1988 [new edition]); Förster, S. and Nagler, J. (eds) *On the Road to Total War: the American Civil War and the German Wars of Unification, 1861–1871* (Cambridge: Cambridge University Press, 1997); Craig, G.A., *The Battle of Königgrätz* (London: Weidenfeld & Nicolson, 1964); Howard, M.E., *The Franco-Prussian War: the German Invasion of France, 1870–71* (London: Hart-Davis, 1961); Audouin-Rouzeau, S., *1870: la France dans la guerre* (Paris: Armand Colin, 1989).

50 Ralston, *The Army of the Republic*, chapter 2; Mitchell, A., '"A Situation of Inferiority": French Military Reorganization after the Defeat of 1870', *American*

Historical Review, 86 (1981), pp. 49–62; Keep, J.C.H., *Soldiers of the Tsar: Army and Society in Russia, 1462–1874* (Oxford: Oxford University Press, 1985), chapter 15.

51 Förster, S., 'Facing "People's War: Moltke the Elder and Germany's Military Options after 1871"', *Journal of Strategic Studies*, 10, 2 (1987), pp. 209–30.

52 Snyder, J., *The Ideology of the Offensive: Military Decision Making and the Disasters of 1914* (Ithaca, NY: Cornell University Press, 1984), chapters 3 and 7.

53 Travers, T.H.E., 'Technology, Tactics, and Morale: Jean de Bloch, the Boer War, and British Military Theory, 1900–1914', *Journal of Modern History*, 51, 2 (1979), pp. 264–86.

54 Mackenzie, S.P., 'Willpower or Firepower? The Unlearned Military Lessons of the Russo-Japanese War', in D. Wells and S. Wilson, *The Russo-Japanese War in Cultural Perspective, 1904–05* (Basingstoke: Macmillan, 1999), pp. 30–40.

55 Reported on by the French military attaché, General Moulin, in *Service historique de l'armée de terre*, Vincennes, carton 7.N.1477.

56 See Mackenzie, 'Willpower or Firepower?' and Howard, M.E., 'Men against Fire: Expectations of War in 1914', *International Security*, 9, 1 (1984), pp. 48–57. For a military history of the war, see Westwood, J.N., *Russia against Japan, 1904–05: a New Look at the Russo-Japanese War* (Basingstoke: Macmillan, 1986).

57 Herrmann, *The Arming of Europe*, chapter 3.

58 Mackenzie, 'Willpower or Firepower?', pp. 33–4.

59 On the 'shell shortage', see Strachan, H.F.A., *The First World War. Vol. I: To Arms* (Oxford: Oxford University Press, 2001), pp. 993–1005.

60 For a review of the evidence, see *ibid.*, pp. 1005–14.

61 On the military reform, Fuller, W.C. Jr., *Strategy and Power in Russia, 1600–1914* (New York: Free Press, 1992), pp. 423–33; Stevenson, *Armaments*, pp. 151–8.

62 For contrasting interpretations see the essays by J. Snyder and S.D. Sagan in Miller, S.E., Lynn-Jones, S.M., and Van Evera, S. (eds), *Military Strategy and the Origins of the First World War* (Princeton: Princeton University Press, 1991 [revised edition]), pp. 20–58, 109–33; Menning, B.W., 'Pieces of the Puzzle: the Role of Iu. N. Danilov and M. V. Alekseev in Russian War Planning before 1914', *International History Review*, 25, 4 (2003), pp. 775–98.

63 For a general view on British preparations, see Williamson, S.R., *The Politics of Grand Strategy: Britain and France Prepare for War, 1904–1914* (Cambridge, MA: Harvard University Press, 1969); Marder, A.J., *From the Dreadnought to Scapa Flow: the Royal Navy in the Fisher Era, 1904–1914* (London: Oxford University Press, 1961); see also Gooch, *The Plans of War*; Offer, *The First World War*; Sumida, *In Defence of Naval Supremacy*, among many others.

64 Joffre, J.J.-C., *Mémoires du Maréchal Joffre 1910–1917*, 2 vols (Paris: Plon, 1932), vol. I, p. 250.

65 Rothenberg, G.E., *The Army of Francis Joseph* (West Lafayette, IN: Purdue University Press, 1976); Käs, F., 'Versuch einer Zusammenfassten Darstellung der Tätigkeit der Österreich-Ungarischen Generalstabes in der Zeit von 1906 bis 1914: unter Besonderer Berücksichtigung der Aufmarschplänen und Mobilmachungen', PhD thesis (Vienna, 1962); Stone, N., 'Die Mobilmachung der Österreichisch-Ungarischen Armee 1914', *Militärgeschichtliche Mitteilungen*, 16 / 2 (1974), pp. 67–95.

66 Zuber, T., 'The Schlieffen Plan Reconsidered', *War in History*, 6, 3 (1999), pp. 262–305.

67 Förster, S., 'Der deutsche Generalstab und die Illusion des kurzen Krieges, 1871–1914: Metakritik eines Mythos', *Militärgeschichtliche Mitteilungen*, 54, 1 (1995), pp. 61–95.

68 Mombauer, A., 'A Reluctant Military Leader? Helmuth von Moltke and the July Crisis of 1914', *War in History*, 6, 4 (1999), pp. 417–46; and the same author's *Helmuth von Moltke and the Origins of the First World War* (Cambridge: Cambridge University Press, 2001).

69 Stevenson, *Armaments* and Herrmann, *The Arming of Europe* both document this point.

70 DiCicco, J.M. and Levy, J.S., 'Power Shifts and Problem Shifts: the Evolution of the Power Transition Research Program', *Journal of Conflict Resolution*, 43, 6 (1999), pp. 675–704. I am indebted to Professor Levy for this reference.

71 Fischer, F., *War of Illusions: German Policies from 1911 to 1914* (London: Chatto & Windus, 1975 [originally published in German, 1969]); Fischer, F. 'Twenty-Five Years Later: Looking back at the "Fischer Controversy" and its Consequences', *Central European History*, 21 (1988), pp. 207–23.

72 Stevenson, *Armaments*, p. 6.

73 Poison gas manufacture was improvised after the outbreak of the 1914 war.

74 Kramer, M., 'Warsaw Pact Military Planning in Central Europe: Revelations from the East German Archives', Cold War International History Project (http://wwucs.si.edu / index / cfm?fuseaction = library.doc); Mastny, V., 'Taking Lyon on the Ninth Day? The 1964 Warsaw Pact Plan for Europe and related Documents', Parallel History Project (http://www.isn.ethz.ch / php / collections / coll _ 1.htm).

75 See for example the essays in Miller *et al.* (eds), *Military Strategy.*

76 For the classic statements, see Mearsheimer, J., 'Back to the Future: Instability in Europe after the Cold War', *International Security*, 15 (1993), pp. 5–56; Fukuyama, F., 'The End of History', *The National Interest*, 16 (1989), pp. 3–16; Huntington, S.P., 'The Clash of Civilisations', *Foreign Affairs*, 72 (1993), pp. 22–49.

77 Kayser, C. *et al.*, *War with Iraq: Costs, Consequences, and Alternatives* (Cambridge, MA: American Academy of Arts and Sciences, 2002).

78 Kennedy, *The Rise and Fall of the Great Powers*, pp. 290–99; Friedberg, A.L., *The Weary Titan: Britain and the Experience of Relative Decline, 1895–1905* (Princeton: Princeton University Press, 1988); Nye, J.S., *Bound to Lead: the Changing Nature of American Power* (New York: Basic Books, 1990).

6

COMMAND DECISION MAKING
Imperial Germany, 1871–1914

Holger H. Herwig

> The common soldiers form the foundations; the colonels and
> other senior officers are the pillars of a perfect military
> rotunda; they support the massive cupola; they also carry – if
> need be – a hollow Hercules, perched on top of the cupola,
> into the rains and the thunderstorms.
>
> (Georg Heinrich von Berenhorst, 1805)

To the casual observer, by 1900 the military establishment of Imperial
Germany had become the new universal model. In three astonishingly rapid
campaigns, Prussia–Germany had defeated Denmark (1864), Austria (1866),
and France (1870–71), and in the process united the three dozen or so
German states. From Japan to Chile, Prussian army regulations, manuals,
uniforms, and weapons were adopted; Prussian–German military missions
were dispatched to Tokyo and to Santiago, to Constantinople and to
Nanking. Krupp as well as Mauser agents scoured the globe for potential
customers of the tools of war. From musical instruments and harnesses to
coastal batteries and mountain artillery, no German product was too expensive or too obscure to attract foreign buyers. Be it the Prussian General Staff
or Artillery School, the Hanoverian Riding Institute or Blacksmith School,
no German institution escaped emulation and requests for instructors. In
time, some of the states that most enthusiastically embraced military 'things
German,' such as Chile, in turn sent their own Prussianized military
missions as surrogates for the Germans to neighboring states.[1]

Not even the disastrous outcomes of the two German-inspired world
wars in the twentieth century altered this fascination with the German military. In fact, quite the reverse occurred: Ludendorff and Hindenburg,
Manstein and Guderian became household words, especially in Anglo-
Saxon military establishments. In the wake of the American fiasco in
Vietnam, Carl von Clausewitz became the sage of American military
academies and war colleges; his book *On War* the bible of instruction. Only
in recent years has there been a partial reversal of this idolization of the
German military as a new generation of scholars has researched the military

decision-making process in Imperial Germany.[2] Their findings show what I here call a process of 'command decision making,' insofar as this, like a command economy, was at least in theory rigidly structured, centrally directed, and administered in semi-authoritarian fashion by a ruler and his managerial bureaucracy. And it was this small coterie of perhaps ten to twelve men who after 1871 were entrusted with planning for an uncertain and potentially threatening future.

Parameters

In analyzing German decision making between the Franco-Prussian War and the First World War, it must be remembered that Imperial Germany was not a centralized, but rather a federal, state. Unlike Canada and the United States, Germany had not come about as a result of a constitutional convention, but rather by military conquest on the part of one of its members, Prussia. Chancellor Otto von Bismarck had recognized the need for federalism in order to bring especially the three southern German states of Baden, Bavaria, and Württemberg into the German Empire. Accordingly, Imperial Germany possessed no unified army; Prussia, Saxony, Bavaria, and Württemberg after 1871 maintained their individual royal armies, each with its distinct uniforms, flags, training, traditions, and institutions. The Prussian king – German emperor in time of peace – possessed only an ill-defined right of 'inspection' over the other royal armies. Needless to stress, the Bavarian, Saxon, and Württemberg armies jealously guarded their peacetime distinctiveness.

The Imperial Navy, on the other hand, was the one truly *German* military institution. The darling of the Liberals of 1848–49, the Kaiserliche Marine flew the imperial German colors of black, white and red; it recruited its officers and ratings from all German states; and it was represented by a state secretary of the Navy Office in the German Parliament (*Reichstag*) rather than in the Prussian Diet (*Landtag*). As such, it was seen (and it depicted itself) as the most visible unifying force in Imperial Germany.

At the top of the Prussian command structure stood the Hohenzollern king–emperor, who exercised almost limitless powers in the military realm. Bismarck had crafted the Prussian–German political system deliberately so as to negate as far as possible the powers of Parliament when it came to military matters. Thus, Wilhelm I (after 1871) and then Wilhelm II (1888–1918) were the *de facto* commanders-in-chief of all Prussian land forces (as well as of the Imperial German Navy). The extent to which the Prussian war minister or state secretary of the Navy Office could steer passage of monetary bills through the German Parliament alone limited their authority. The existing military agreements with Bavaria, Saxony, and Württemberg and the generosity of Parliament constituted the principal brakes on the monarch's military powers.

The peculiar Prussian–German command decision-making process was firmly embedded first in the Constitution of the North German Confederation (16 April 1867) and then in the Constitution of the German *Reich* (16 April 1871). Specifically, Article 63 of the Constitution of 1871 enshrined the Prussian king–emperor as '*Bundesfeldherr*,' that is, as commander-in-chief of all federal land forces. 'The entire armed land forces of the Reich will be composed of a unified army, which will be placed under the command of the kaiser in war and in peace.'[3] It further granted the king–emperor operational control of the non-Prussian armies through the august institution of the Prussian General Staff (which was not embedded in the Constitution). Article 64 required all field and fortress commanders to pledge unquestioning obedience to the *Bundesfeldherr* by way of a personal oath of loyalty; further, it accorded the king–emperor absolute power to make all officer appointments, from subaltern to chief of the General Staff. Third, Article 11 of the Constitution of 1871 granted the Hohenzollern ruler exclusive power to declare war, which he exercised only once, on 31 July 1914. Mobilization of the federal armies and a subsequent declaration of war – except in case of an attack on the territorial sovereignty of the *Reich* – required the approval of both the imperial chancellor[4] and of the German Federal Council (*Bundesrat*), which also occurred only once, on 1 August 1914. The *Bundesrat* was not an 'upper house' in the sense of the United States Senate, the Prussian Upper House (*Herrenhaus*), or the British House of Lords, but rather a permanent assembly of the diplomatic representatives of the federal German states, in which Prussia enjoyed veto powers.[5] Likewise, the conclusion of peace rested with neither the *Reichstag* nor the *Bundesrat*, but rather solely with the king–emperor, who exercised this right only once, on 10 May 1871 in the Frankfurt Peace that ended the Franco-Prussian War. Neither the *Bundesrat* nor the *Reichstag* had been asked to ratify that accord.[6]

Of all the major European powers, Germany alone possessed a unicameral parliamentary system. The *Reichstag*, elected by universal male suffrage, was the only truly parliamentary institution in Imperial Germany. But its powers were sharply curtailed by the Constitution of 1871.[7] Under Article 23, it could neither initiate legislation nor remove unpopular ministers. Its primary power was that of the purse – that is, the right to approve or to reject the army budget every five or seven years. It also was empowered by the Constitution of 1871 to grant or to deny war credits, a right which it exercised on 4 August 1914. It could at no time even question, much less instruct, the monarch (through the federal government) concerning military or security policies, or personnel appointments and decision making.

The Constitution of 1871 further enshrined into law the Prussian army's hallowed division between 'command' and 'administrative' domains. The former, which pertained to the organization, training, discipline, appointments, promotions, and disposition of forces, remained exclusively with the king–emperor. The latter, which revolved around budgetary items such as recruitment, size, and the equipping of forces, was delegated by the king–emperor to the chancellor (by way of the minister of war). This required the consent of the *Reichstag*. Obviously, the dividing line between 'command' and 'administrative' domains was often blurred and the subject of bitter acrimony between the executive and legislative branches of government.

The officially used title 'Supreme War Lord' (*Oberster Kriegsherr*) for the king–emperor was not contained in either of the two Constitutions of 1867 or 1871, nor in the various military conventions that Prussia negotiated with the south German states in 1867 and 1871. It existed only in the form of the personal oath of allegiance that German officers and soldiers pledged to their king–emperor, 'His Majesty the German Emperor Wilhelm I, my Supreme War Lord.'[8] In addition, Kaiser Wilhelm II jealously guarded his active command role, or '*Kommandogewalt*,' at least up to 1914. This *Kommandogewalt* consisted as no clearly mandated constitutional power, but mainly as a political guiding principle, employed by Prussia's kings since the reign of Friedrich Wilhelm IV in the 1840s and 1850s. Over time, Wilhelm II especially sought strenuously to broaden these nebulous powers to command. He largely succeeded, as his chambers remained the first and last place of appeal. Ministers and generals could advise; the king–emperor alone decided.

The king–emperor was assisted in his awesome, all-encompassing command and decision-making role by about forty generals and eight admirals. Each of these enjoyed direct access (*Immediatstellung*) to the monarch; each could bypass his immediate superior(s) and approach the ruler directly. In a typical week in 1889, for example, Wilhelm II granted one private audience to the chancellor, one to the head of the Civil Cabinet, and eight to military officers. Three Prussian royal institutions – the War Ministry (finances, equipment), the Military Cabinet (personnel), and the General Staff (operational planning) – stood at the king's side in running the army. The Navy Office (material), Navy Cabinet (personnel), and High Command/Admiralty Staff (operational planning) likewise assisted the emperor in running the Imperial Navy.

At the top of the Prussian command structure, and immediately below the monarch, stood the commanding generals of the *Reich*'s twenty-four military districts.[9] Each of these commanders was directly responsible to the Supreme War Lord for all matters pertaining to command, leadership, and training of the troops in their district; and to the Prussian war minister for those relating to supply and equipment. The corps commanders occupied the highest command posts in the realm. They acted sovereignly in all matters of command authority, discipline, combat training, and administration. They approved all fitness reports (for the Military Cabinet) and rendered judgment in matters concerning the officer corps' concept of military 'honor.' In time of war, Germany's army field commanders would be selected from their ranks. Their deputies, in such an exigency, would assume the power to suppress any civilian unrest, to censor all mail and newspapers, and to oversee transportation and communications as well as police and the courts, according to the Prussian State-of-Siege Law of 4 June 1851.[10]

The Prussian War Ministry, established by General Gerhard von Scharnhorst in 1809, was entrusted with matters ranging from finances to training, armaments to equipment, and organization to the health of the troops.[11] Numbering some 600 to 700 officers by 1900, the *Kriegsministerium* consisted of five major bureaus. Kaiser Wilhelm II selected all his war ministers from the ranks of division commanders, all of whom had studied at the prestigious War Academy (*Kriegsakademie*) and served with the General Staff. The minister's most important task was to prepare the army budget and to win parliamentary approval of the funds requested.

In fact, the Prussian war minister owed triple allegiance: to the nation for its security, to Parliament for the outlay of military expenditures, and to the king–emperor as an active military officer. Although the war minister was a Prussian, he had to cajole the *Reichstag*, which was German, to fund the largely Prussian-dominated army. And although the *Kriegsminister* was the only military officer in Prussia responsible to Parliament, as an active officer on duty in the Prussian army he owed unquestioned obedience to the King of Prussia – and by extension to the German emperor. While directly responsible to the Prussian king for the combat readiness of the Prussian army, the war minister was also a plenipotentiary to the *Bundesrat* and as such had to answer to the *Reichstag* on fiscal matters. This dual personal loyalty to king and Parliament constituted a natural conflict of interest. In case of conflict with his Supreme War Lord (Wilhelm II), the war minister possessed neither leverage nor freedom of action as his personal oath of loyalty to the king–emperor was inviolate. In case of conflict with the *Reichstag*, he could but resign his ministerial portfolio (provided that the king–emperor had acceded to this request). The war minister commanded not a single troop contingent or formation, and was not formally involved in the formulation of national security matters; his sole authority was in financial and administrative matters. Simply put, the war minister's position was precarious and unrewarding.

The Prussian Military Cabinet, created by Kaiser Wilhelm I in 1883, served as the monarch's personnel bureau.[12] As an exclusive agent of the Crown, it was regarded almost universally with suspicion and often accused of being 'unconstitutional.' Its chief, usually a lieutenant general, dealt with all matters pertaining to appointments and promotions, punishments and dismissals, decorations and awards, honor and appeals. His role was purely advisory. In addition, the chief of the *Militärkabinett*, assisted by no more than ten officers and an equal number of civil servants, was responsible for drafting the king–emperor's commands and decrees. Like the Prussian war minister, the chief of the Military Cabinet came to his post only after distinguished service with a division or army corps and the General Staff. As the Supreme War Lord's primary liaison with every other institution of the Prussian army, the chief of the Military Cabinet enjoyed a potentially influential position. Yet, like all other active officers, his sole allegiance was to the king–emperor. He could be challenged in personnel matters neither by Parliament nor by other department heads, but only by the monarch.

The Military Cabinet's greatest power lay in deciding promotions and appointments. Each year, every one of the Prussian army's 29,000 officers, from the lowest second lieutenant to the twenty-four army corps commanders, underwent formal evaluation by way of rigorous fitness reports (*Qualifikationsberichte*). Each report arrived at the Military Cabinet; each was given careful attention. With regard to senior postings such as corps commanders, fortress governors, and high-level staff appointments, the final decision in all cases rested with the king–emperor. The latter usually accepted the recommendations submitted by the chief of the Military Cabinet. But not always. The most celebrated rebuke occurred in 1906, when Wilhelm II insisted against the advice of the chief of the Military Cabinet (General Dietrich von Hülsen-Häseler) on appointing General Helmuth von Moltke (the Younger) as chief of the General Staff.

Undoubtedly, the Prussian General Staff was the army's premier (and most often emulated) institution.[13] The chief of the *Generalstab* enjoyed his seemingly august powers largely by tradition and example. He commanded not a single soldier, battalion, regiment, division, or corps. He could issue no formal orders, purchase no equipment, and authorize no war plan. His selection of personnel had to be cleared with the Military Cabinet; the War Ministry dictated his influence on the army's strength, organization, training, and equipment; his operational plans required the monarch's approval. His position was not embedded in the Constitution.

In essence, the chief of the General Staff was but 'the first advisor of the Imperial Supreme Commander.'[14] His primary function was to advise the king–emperor, at whose pleasure he served, on military planning and policy. No more; no less. That his influence far exceeded his modest formal role was due to the victorious campaigns of Helmuth von Moltke (the Elder); the General Staff's drive for intellectual and operational excellence; the chief's superior bearing and demeanor; and the fact that virtually every senior commander had come up through its ranks. In reality, the General Staff consisted of two entities: the Great General Staff in Berlin, which served its chief as a support cohort, and the Troop General Staff, which assisted divisional, corps, and fortress commanders in carrying out their command and training functions.

In time of peace, the chief of the General Staff formulated strategic and operational contingency war plans, devised and evaluated the annual maneuvers, gathered and evaluated military intelligence, maintained railroad schedules, worked out potential mobilization schemes, supervised the writing of military history, and oversaw the War Academy. His work was at all times subject to approval by the king–emperor. In time of war, the chief of the General Staff directed mobilization and then operational planning. The *Generalstab* grew from the small cadre of fifteen officers, which the Elder Moltke had taken into the field in 1870, into a bureaucratic labyrinth of about 650 officers by 1914. Noted by the distinct burgundy stripes on their uniform pants, the officers of the General Staff saw themselves, in Bismarck's words, as 'demi-gods.' They were all volunteers, were at times favored in advancement and promotion, and were routinely rotated between field and staff commands.

At the federal level, Article 53 of the Constitution of 1871 called for the creation of a unified, federal navy under the direct command of the German emperor. 'The Navy of the Empire is united under the supreme command of the Kaiser.'[15] Indeed, the *Kaiserliche Marine* was the only *German* branch of the armed forces. After the kaiser's reorganization of the navy in March 1889, its decentralized decision-making structure closely paralleled that of the Prussian army. Administrative matters as well as construction and maintenance of naval material were supervised by a state secretary of the Navy Office, who was responsible (by way of the imperial chancellor) to the *Reichstag*. Like the Prussian war minister, the state secretary of the Navy Office was both an active officer and a federal official who had to defend budgetary policy before the *Reichstag*. Strategy, operations, and tactics were relegated to a new chief of the High Command of the Navy – changed again in 1899 to an Admiralty Staff.[16] And as a parallel to the Prussian Military Cabinet, Wilhelm II in 1889 also created a Navy Cabinet to supervise personnel matters. As the junior service, the navy not surprisingly adopted many of the education, training, and ceremonial trappings of the Prussian army.

Process and Planners

Decision making in Imperial Germany, then, was both simple and complex. In 1898 Germany's leading constitutional authority, Paul Laband, at the request of Admiral Alfred von Tirpitz, state secretary of the Navy Office, attempted to summarize that process. While carefully avoiding defining the extra-constitutional term *Kommandogewalt*, Laband nevertheless firmly stated that 'the execution of Kommandogewalt is not governed by laws,' and that 'the Bundesrat and the Reichstag have no right of co-determination or control over it.' Nor, Laband went on, was Wilhelm II's power to command 'covered by the responsibility of the Reich Chancellor, or his authorised representative.' Military supreme command, both in peace and in war, was the 'absolutely personal prerogative' of the king–emperor, as was the 'direction of foreign policy.' The only control on the Supreme War Lord's powers were 'considerations imposed by the budgetary rights' of the *Reichstag*. In short, the king–emperor possessed sweeping, almost unlimited extra-constitutional powers in the areas of foreign and military powers. He alone decided the organization of the armed forces, their staffing, their war planning, and their deployment, in complete accordance with his own designs. 'There is but one man in charge of the Reich,' Wilhelm II declared at Düsseldorf in May 1891, 'and I will not tolerate any other.'[17]

Given the king–emperor's Olympian stature in the military realm, it is only fair to ask, (a) to what degree Wilhelm II lived up to his self-defined responsibilities, and (b) who guided him in reaching imperial decisions? There are two ways to run a 'command decision-making' process effectively. First, the monarch, to whom the system had been especially tailored, needs to be an enlightened despot, a man such as King Friedrich Wilhelm I (1713–40) or King Friedrich Wilhelm II (1740–86). Given that the king–emperor had sole decision-making rights in foreign and military policy, it would have required that Wilhelm II devote between ten and twelve hours a day to his duties. Second, the command process could have been run in the manner of Kaiser Wilhelm I, that is, for the ruler to surrender decision making to an enlightened chancellor, such as Bismarck, and his state secretaries. Thereby, the monarch could retain the right to make the final decision, without having to be involved in the entire deliberative process.

Wilhelm II did neither. As soon as he ascended to the throne in 1888, the kaiser made it known that he wished to be his own 'Officer of the Watch of the Ship of State,' his 'own Bismarck.' Apart from clinging to an ancient, mystical notion of the divine right of kings, Wilhelm II had his own notion concerning the distribution of power in the *Reich*. In September 1891 he committed that notion to paper in the Golden Book of the City of Munich: 'Suprema lex regis voluntas.'[18] That same year, Wilhelm II let it be known that he wished to be his own chief of the General Staff as well. Denouncing the Elder Moltke and Bismarck as 'pygmies' and 'lackeys' who had merely been his grandfather's 'tools' (*Handlanger*), Wilhelm II announced that Moltke's successor would be 'no more than a kind of amanuensis to me.' A horrified General Alfred Count von Waldersee, the Elder Moltke's successor as chief of the General Staff, noted: 'He wants to be his own General Staff chief. God preserve the fatherland.'[19] Each year, Wilhelm counted the number of signatures that he appended to state papers – including the promotion and appointment of each one of the Prussian army's 29,000 officers – and thus assured himself (and his retinue) of his centrality to the system.

As time went on, Wilhelm II tired of the work required of him and retreated more and more into a carnival-like world of ceaseless public spectacle. Diarist after diarist recalled that the kaiser reveled in multiple uniform changes each and every day, and that he flitted about his seventy-five official residences and castles endlessly. Wilhelm attended the opera *The Flying*

Dutchman in the uniform of an admiral and the ballet *Swan Lake* in that of a Cossack general; he received St. James's ambassador wearing the uniform of a British admiral of the fleet. Regattas at Cowes and Kiel, fox hunts at Donaueschingen and stag hunts at Rominten, passed for state work. As did the sometimes 200 days per year that Wilhelm II spent on the royal yacht *Hohenzollern.* 'He is not faithful to duty,' Admiral Georg Alexander von Müller, chief of the Navy Cabinet, quickly noticed, 'or else he would devote more of his time to the serious problems of his occupation.'[20]

As far as delegating power to responsible state servants went, Wilhelm II preferred to surround himself with the pliant scions of ancient Junker clans and to use them as a sounding board for his imperial aspirations. To be sure, he started well on 7 July 1888 when, just weeks after his accession to the throne, the new kaiser established a 'Headquarters of His Majesty the Kaiser and King' by All-Highest Cabinet Order.[21] This new headquarters, or *maison militaire*, consisted of high-ranking adjutants and generals *à la suite* and was designed to serve as a supreme advisory board to the monarch on military and security matters. Its creation underscored yet again the extra-constitutionality of the imperial command system. But the Cabinet Order establishing the *maison militaire* contained no mention of its functions, duties, or responsibilities. In time, it became a posh sinecure for officers from Wilhelm II's favorite Palace Guards and Life Guards; eventually, it simply withered and died. More ominously, in 1897 the kaiser dissolved the joint-services Home Defense Commission (*Landesverteidigungskommission*), composed of admirals and generals entrusted with the coordination of joint defense policies. It was never replaced with an analogous organization.[22] And only once, in 1904, did Wilhelm II conduct combined army–navy maneuvers (in the Baltic region).

The truth of the matter is that the kaiser would tolerate no advisory board as this might have curtailed his powers to command, the cherished extra-constitutional *Kommandogewalt*. From 1888 to 1918, there existed no single institution at which military and naval, diplomatic and financial policies could be coordinated, no equivalent to the British Committee on Imperial Defence, the French Conseil Supérieur de la Guerre, the American National Security Council, or even the Austro-Hungarian Common Council of Ministers. Ultimate authority in military and naval affairs rested exclusively with the king–emperor.

As to the men who were closest to the king–emperor in Imperial Germany's 'command decision making,' the ruling elite in terms of social origin came from an incredibly small, homogeneous aristocratic class. Of the 'men of 1914,' Chancellor Theobald von Bethmann Hollweg could trace his family back to the year 1416; War Minister Erich von Falkenhayn to 1504; and State Secretary of the Foreign Office Gottlieb von Jagow to 1268. The German branch of the Moltke clan was first mentioned in official documents in the year 1254. With regard to the generals, most had been born the sons of East Elbian landed squires and army officers. Almost all had attended cadet school at Lichterfelde, served in their father's regiment, and then had volunteered for study at the War Academy, before seeking duty with the General Staff. Very few, if any, had attended university or studied politics and economics. Of Prussia's highest-ranking officers in 1914 – field marshals, colonel generals, and corps commanders – 77 per cent belonged to the ancient nobility and 23 per cent to the newer titled nobility. Among active officers from ancient noble families on duty in 1914, there were forty-nine von Puttkamer, forty-four von Kleist, thirty-four von Zietewitz, thirty von Bonin, and twenty von Kemeke. These same families had lustily shed their blood on Frederick the Great's battlefields from 1740 to 1763.[23] The officer corps of the Imperial Navy, by contrast, was solidly middle class, men of education and modest means. Its most senior administrators and commanders (Capelle, Hipper, Hollmann, Ingenohl, Müller, Tirpitz) were burghers raised to the nobility of the robe (*Dienstadel*) so that their sons could enter the navy as nobles.[24] All swore a personal oath of allegiance to 'His Majesty the German Kaiser, Wilhelm II, my Supreme War Lord.'[25]

Wilhelm II's command role was most obvious at the annual army maneuvers, organized by the chief of the General Staff. There, the kaiser played to the hilt his stage role as Supreme War Lord.[26] Weeks of staff work were required just to transport the kaiser and his entourage to the maneuver area. Once there, Wilhelm II oversaw even the minutest of details in the war game. Each ended customarily with the kaiser leading a glorious cavalry charge for the winning side. And if that charge happened to run up against entrenched machine gunners, then they were simply ordered to change their colored arm bands and to join the celebrated cavalry charge! Given the long interwar peace between 1871 and 1914, such theatrics made a mockery of the army's premier opportunity to test its operational and tactical concepts.

Wilhelm II routinely evaluated the war game (a duty normally reserved for the chief of the General Staff) and to display his command role at times publicly criticized the *Generalstabschef*. In one celebrated case, Wilhelm openly criticized even the examination papers submitted by subalterns to the chief of the General Staff, which prompted General von Waldersee to submit his resignation. That the kaiser could lavish such time and detail on a relatively trivial matter at the height of the chancellor crisis of 1890, created by his decision to dismiss the *Reich*'s architect, Bismarck, reveals in spades Wilhelm's obsession with exercising his *Kommandogewalt*.[27]

In time, most senior planners realized that the only way to succeed was to play public lip service to the kaiser's command role – and then quietly and independently to conduct business as they saw it, knowing full well that Wilhelm II did not have the stamina for hard, sustained work. Alfred Count von Schlieffen was one of those who quickly learned how to side-step the kaiser's interference. In his first year as chief of the General Staff, Wilhelm II, who at the end of the annual maneuvers presented an evaluation that was diametrically opposed to that just rendered by Schlieffen, humiliated his *Generalstabschef* in front of his staff. Thereafter, Schlieffen learned to accept the kaiser and his bombast as a 'given,' as part of a God-willed reality.[28] In public, he acceded to the monarch's every wish; in private, he heaped ridicule and sarcasm on Wilhelm II. As for the navy, Alfred von Tirpitz developed a modern managerial style to circumvent the kaiser's obsession with ships and interference in operational matters. Each summer, Tirpitz took an intimate core of co-workers with him to his retreat at St. Blasien in the Black Forest, there to plan down to the most minute detail a new navy bill or supplement – and then in the fall to shower the new plans on the kaiser at his stag-slaying festival at Rominten in East Prussia.[29] The 'Schlieffen plan' and the 'Tirpitz plan' thus deserve closer examination in order to shed some light on how national defense policies evolved in Imperial Germany.

The Plans

German unification in 1871 represented, in the words of Britain's Conservative Opposition leader, Benjamin Disraeli, a veritable revolution, 'a greater political event than the French Revolution of last century.'[30] For the first time in modern history, Central Europe was united, under a Prussian Hohenzollern kaiser. No longer were the 360-odd states of the 'Germanies' to be the sporting field for France's armies. The Concert of Vienna system, fractured already during the Crimean War (1853–56), was now shattered. How would Europe reorder itself after 1871? Would France accept her defeat? Or would she seek revenge for the lost war? Put differently, would 1871 usher in a period of general European peace or just another inter-war period?

The Elder Moltke returned from France believing the latter to be the more likely scenario. While he left managing the 'fog of peace' to Bismarck, Moltke undertook two critical studies. First, he ordered the General Staff to investigate the campaigns of the Franco-Prussian War, and then to draw the 'lessons' from that conflict. Second, he immediately set about contingency planning for the future. The conflict with France had shown all of Carl von Clausewitz's intangibles (friction, interaction, escalation, the fog of war) to be at play. And there were two adversaries – one real, the other potential – to take into account. Put differently, Moltke's worst-case scenario was a possible Franco-Russian alliance that could involve the newly found *Reich* in a multi-front war. The French war had weakened radically his faith in future quick, decisive cabinet wars. 'Germany dare not hope to free itself in a short time from the one enemy by a quick and successful offensive in the west,' Moltke would conclude, 'in order thereafter to turn against another [enemy in the east].'[31] By the 1870s, the chief of the General Staff proposed to counter this potential two-front threat with a defensive–offensive strategy: Germany would mobilize 300,000 men against France and seek to defeat the

French in a series of pitched battles in Lorraine and the Saar; and it would put 360,000 soldiers in the field against Russia, seeking merely to disrupt Russian mobilization around Kovno and Warsaw. The *Reich* could hope for limited victories at best; 'it must be left to diplomacy to see if it can achieve a peace settlement.'[32]

Bismarck, for his part, as always sought a diplomatic solution to the *Reich*'s security concerns. After a brief period in which he trumpeted George Washington's warning against 'permanent alliances,' the iron chancellor in June 1877 convened a sort of 'retreat' at Bad Kissingen to plan the future. The 'retreat' amounted to Bismarck dictating to his son in brief, brilliant passages the *Reich*'s needs and concerns. France, Bismarck stated, taunted Germany with a 'nightmare of coalitions.' This could come about through a coalition of France, Britain, and (possibly) Austria-Hungary. Or, it could come about by an even 'greater danger,' a union of France, Russia, and Austria-Hungary. What to do? Bismarck ruled out further 'acquisition of territory,' being content with what the historian Ludwig Dehio called 'semi-hegemony' on the Continent. The *Reich* was 'satiated,' Bismarck decreed, it needed no more non-German ethnic subjects. Nor did he desire fleet and colonies. Germany, geographically wedged in between France and Russia, could not afford 'splendid isolation.' Bismarck's solution was simple: he desired 'a political landscape in which all the Powers, except France, need us and are prevented, by virtue of their relations towards each other, from the possibility of coalescing against us.'[33] Professional armed forces comprising 1 per cent of the population (of 45 million in 1880) would secure such an arrangement.

Bismarck next set out to augment this policy of alliance denial with one of alliance building: he wove a web of alliances with Austria-Hungary in 1879, Italy in 1882, Romania in 1883, and Russia in 1887. In the process, Bismarck, in the words of William L. Langer, made Berlin 'the focal point of international relations.'[34] For, whom could France turn to in case it sought *revanche* for 1871: Luxembourg, Liechtenstein, Monaco?

It is critical to appreciate that, regardless of past differences, Moltke and Bismarck worked hand-in-glove to secure the new *Reich*. Both understood that diplomacy alone could protect Germany's tenuous position of semi-hegemony in Central Europe, flanked by Russia in the east and France in the west. Both grasped the fact that no simple strategic-operational solution could resolve the dilemma of a two-front war. Both realized that war on the Continent would immediately involve Germany directly and detrimentally. This realization led to Moltke's prophetic warning in the *Reichstag* in 1890, that a future war could last seven or even thirty years. 'Woe to him that sets Europe on fire.'[35]

But the *Pax Germanica* of the 1880s was destroyed in short order in the following decade. In 1890 Moltke retired and Bismarck was fired. Kaiser Wilhelm II decided personally to lead Germans 'towards glorious times.' To that end, he demanded that Germany become a world power, with fleet and colonies; that the unpopular tie to Russia be dropped; and that he become the *arbiter mundi*. The new slogan of global politics (*Weltpolitik*) encapsulated this shift. Jettisoned in the process were caution and modesty and *Realpolitik*, the art of the possible. Germany was to be all things at once, and to be everywhere at once. France and Russia were to be challenged on the Continent, Britain and the United States at sea.

This radical shift toward the so-called 'New Course' came about because of the command decision-making role of one person: Wilhelm II. It was never debated at the highest councils – neither by the Home Defense Commission nor in the *maison militaire*, and certainly not by the Imperial Cabinet. Military and naval polices were never coordinated. No common budgetary strategies were ever hammered out. Diplomatic policy was never readjusted to reflect the radical shift in strategic policy. Financial policy at no time was fine-tuned to enable Germany to become the premier European power both on land and at sea. The end result was that Germany was bankrupt by about 1905, as three state secretaries of the Treasury resigned rather than bear responsibility for ever-greater mountains of debt. And that army and navy continued to pursue independent strategies, refusing to use even the chancellor's office as a clearing house for budgetary considerations. While coordinated planning may not have averted war in 1914, it certainly would have made plain to army and naval planners alike the limits of the *Reich*'s fiscal resources – and thus abilities to challenge the *Entente* both on land and on the high seas. In short, in what the historian Stig Förster has called the 'polychratic chaos' of Imperial Germany,[36] aims and means remained two disparate entities.

Given the kaiser's inability to undertake integrated war planning, the realization of his megalomaniac aspirations fell to a new cadre of professional generals and admirals, each of whom concentrated on his most immediate goal: operational planning. First among these was Alfred von Tirpitz, state secretary of the Navy Office, and the man entrusted with realizing the kaiser's dream of naval and world power. In Navy Laws of 1898 and 1900, augmented by Supplementary Laws of 1906, 1908, and 1912, Tirpitz strove to create a mammoth battle fleet of sixty capital ships, to be stationed in the North Sea.[37] In memoranda of 1888, 1891, and especially in Service Memorandum IX of 1894, Tirpitz defined his strategy in simple, yet powerful terms: to annihilate British sea power, if London proved unwilling to accord Germany its cherished 'place in the sun,' in a single Armageddon in the south central North Sea. 'In a war at sea, destruction of the enemy rather than territorial gain is the only goal.'[38] All of Tirpitz's smokescreen about building a 'risk fleet,' one that would simply deter British naval power, notwithstanding, such a powerful fleet stationed but a hundred miles off Britain's east coast could only be construed by London as a unilateral challenge to Britannia's sea control. The historian Paul M. Kennedy aptly likened the Tirpitz-fleet to a 'sharp knife, held gleaming and ready only a few inches away from the jugular vein of Germany's most likely enemy.'[39]

But how had this fleet come into being? How had it been financed? What operational goals had it been given, and by whom? In short, was the eventual High Sea Fleet in line with German material and financial capabilities? And what was to be its role in what by the 1890s was regarded in most civilian and military circles as an 'inter-war' period? Tirpitz's first task was to popularize the concept of a fleet. To this end, he had Alfred Thayer Mahan's *The Influence of Sea Power Upon History* translated, serialized in German journals, and 8,000 free copies distributed. The service journal *Marine-Rundschau* was turned into a popular magazine, and a naval annual, *Nauticus*, founded as well. Some 270 so-called 'fleet professors,' academics who lent their services to the Navy Office, roamed the land touting the virtues of sea power.[40] A Navy League was established with private funding and endowed with a journal, *Die Flotte*. Pastors and priests, federal princes and industrialists, were recruited to popularize the navy. *Reichstag* deputies were taken on cruises in the North and Baltic seas to witness first hand the glories of Neptune's kingdom. Massive public pressure was thus brought to bear on parliamentary deputies to pay for a navy and to support *Weltpolitik*. In a period of rapid social, economic, and bureaucratic change, deputies by and large struggled to stay abreast of popular demands and pressures.[41]

Second, Tirpitz formed a modern-day 'think tank' at his headquarters in Berlin. The navy's best and brightest gathered to plan down to the minutest detail what the navy needed – and what it could do for the country. During the summer, this coterie of aides (Capelle, Dähnhardt, Fischel, Heeringen, Hopman, Ingenohl, Scheer, and Trotha) joined Tirpitz at his residence at St. Blasien to finalize naval plans for the fall session of the *Reichstag*. On route from the Black Forest back to Berlin, they stopped off to see the kaiser at his fall stag hunt in East Prussia and overcame whatever technical critique Wilhelm II might have had with detailed briefs and plans. And in Berlin, they stood at Tirpitz's elbow, ready to supply any wavering *Reichstag* deputy with mountains of statistics and papers to shore up support for the fleet.

At heart, the Tirpitz plan came down to a *va banque* strategy, one that would take a generation to realize and one that would see Germany supplant Britain as the twentieth century's premier naval power. At a decisive audience with Wilhelm II at Rominten in September 1899, Tirpitz had described the future fleet as 'an absolute necessity for Germany, without which she will encounter ruin.' Tirpitz painted a clear picture of choices available in the new century: '4 world powers: Russia, England, America, and Germany.' Britain was the greatest threat, but one that could be overcome by superior German equipment, training, and organization – and by its 'unified leadership through the Monarch.'[42] In fact, Tirpitz offered the kaiser a dazzling vision: a Germany that in a single generation could make the leap from European land power to global maritime power. In the process, Tirpitz single-handedly added Britain to the ranks of Germany's likely adversaries. Bismarckian Germany had to fear no naval power. It had never had to plan for a major war at sea. Tirpitz changed that algebra.

But no true strategic concept lay behind the Tirpitz plan.[43] It speaks volumes for German decision making that the head of the Navy Office, a purely *administrative* bureaucrat, should envision and then realize a bold *strategic* national policy. There was never a 'grand council' of German naval leaders to hammer out Tirpitz's naval vision. Tirpitz, who feared that the Admiralty Staff, which was charged with developing naval strategy, might develop powers and independence akin to those of the General Staff, kept it powerless. For this reason, Tirpitz in 1903 vetoed an Admiralty Staff proposal to exchange officers with the General Staff. Four years later, Tirpitz persuaded Wilhelm II to reject an Admiralty Staff proposal that one-half of the Naval Academy graduates serve with the *Admiralstab*. And he again intervened with the kaiser to deny Admiralty Staff officers from wearing distinct pants stripes, like their General Staff brethren.[44] Indeed, it is indicative of the lack of coordinated naval planning that Tirpitz, a Berlin bureaucrat, in 1909 made the tactical decision to base the battle fleet on Helgoland – without bothering to consult either the Admiralty Staff, the Fleet Command, or the General Staff.

It is fair to say that Tirpitz never thought strategically. His was a grand political plan, not a strategic one. He simply expected the British, should they feel threatened by the German fleet, to descend into the Helgoland Bight and to offer battle. But Admiralty Staff chiefs knew better. As early as 1908, Vice Admiral Friedrich von Baudissin warned Tirpitz that the British might not simply steam into the Bight at the outbreak of a war. In 1909 Baudissin's successor, Admiral Max von Fischel, raised the key strategic issue: 'We are fighting for access to the ocean, whose entrances on that side of the North Sea are in England's hands. We are therefore basically the attacker, who is disputing the enemy's possessions.'[45] And in May 1914 Fleet Chief Admiral Friedrich von Ingenohl bluntly asked Tirpitz during the last peacetime naval maneuvers, 'What will you do if they do not come?'[46] It is indicative of Tirpitz's lack of strategic acumen that he could offer Ingenohl no reply. There was no flexibility in Tirpitz's planning, no fallback position in case the British refused to act according to his predictions.

At another level, the High Sea Fleet proved well beyond Germany's ability to pay (better, willingness to sacrifice) for it. Initially, Tirpitz indexed construction and maintenance costs for the fleet to the growth of the German economy.[47] And he opted to pay for it by way not of direct but rather indirect taxes – on consumer and luxury goods and services. But the never-ending upward spiral of construction costs – fueled especially by Britain's decision in 1905 to build super-battleships, beginning with HMS *Dreadnought* – forced Tirpitz up against the wall. German dreadnoughts increased in costs from 37 million Goldmark with the Nassau class of

1907–10, to 46 million with the Kaiser class of 1909–13, and finally to 50 million with the Bayern class of 1913–16. Overall, the navy's budget grew from 20 per cent of the army's outlays in 1898 to 53 per cent by 1911. And with no end in sight.

Obviously, army leaders were becoming alarmed at this escalating shift in scarce defense resources to the navy. What did Tirpitz hope to accomplish with his mighty fleet, in case of a general war on the Continent? The fleet, despite Tirpitz's promises, had attracted no new 'alliance partners.' Nor had it 'deterred' the British, who not only decided to maintain their numerical superiority in capital ships, but also to enhance their qualitative superiority with HMS *Dreadnought*.[48] Already in 1898, General von Waldersee, the Elder Moltke's successor as chief of the General Staff, had mused: 'What does the navy propose to do if the army is defeated, be it in the west or in the east?'[49] By 1905, that question had become not only fair, but also acute.

It fell to Alfred von Schlieffen to try to solve the *Reich*'s self-imposed isolation by military means. The basic contours of the Schlieffen plan are well enough known not to require detailed discussion here. Rather, of interest is the process by which the plan was devised. Who had input? Who did not? Was there even a formal operations plan? And if so, did it correspond to available force structure and financial resources? For, despite a bold claim by Terence Zuber that 'There never was a "Schlieffen plan",'[50] Germany's military leaders had no doubt as to its existence. In 1912 (as will be shown later) the kaiser formally asked his senior military planners whether they were prepared to execute the Schlieffen plan. In 1914 Helmuth von Moltke (the Younger), the Prussian chief of the General Staff, not only referred to Germany's 'one' operations plan, but attached Schlieffen's name firmly to it.[51] In August 1914 Moltke executed Schlieffen's grand design. General Wilhelm Groener, in charge of the Prussian army's critical railroad department, openly spoke of the 'great symphony' of the Schlieffen plan that same year.[52] By late fall 1914, General Erich von Falkenhayn, leaving his post of war minister for that of chief of the General Staff, sarcastically noted Moltke's intellectual bankruptcy. 'Schlieffen's notes are at an end and therewith also Moltke's wits.'[53] Subsequent military historians, such as the authors of the fourteen-volume official history *Der Weltkrieg 1914–1918*, have had no problems identifying that operations plan to have been Schlieffen's.

First off, Schlieffen developed his great memoranda concerning the conduct of a two-front war against France and Russia in relative isolation. In what obviously was going to be a war of coalitions, the Habsburg ally was almost absent in German thoughts. Schlieffen so distrusted the Austrian military that after 1896–97 he limited contact with their General Staff to annual New Year's greetings. Austria-Hungary's fate, he coldly asserted, would be decided not along the Bug but the Seine River.[54] At no time did Schlieffen (or his successor, the Younger Moltke) address the issue of a unified command in case of war. It speaks volumes for this utter lack of coordinated planning that Colonel Karl von Kageneck, the *Reich*'s military attaché at Vienna, on 1 August 1914 could cable the General Staff in Berlin: 'It is high time that the two general staffs consult now with absolute frankness with respect to mobilization, jump-off time, areas of assembly, and precise troop strength.'[55]

Second, Schlieffen paid little attention to available intelligence in formulating his rigid design. In an era in which civilian intelligence agencies were almost unknown, intelligence gathering fell to military and naval attachés as well as (in the German case) to a network of 'tension travelers' behind the French and Russian fronts.[56] Moreover, much of the required information could be gleaned from a variety of open sources, such as budgets, recruiting bills, shipbuilding programs, parliamentary debates, and the like. But Schlieffen chose to ignore this reality, and, according to Colonel Gerhard von Tappen, instead planned with almost no reference to what was known about either French or Russian war plans.[57]

Third, Schlieffen declined to bring other German planning agencies into his deliberations. As David Stevenson has pointed out in the preceding chapter, the relationship between General Staff and War Ministry was a critical variable; while the former devised the nation's war plans, the latter provided equipment and armaments. Planning for the 'next war' thus demanded close cooperation between these two agencies. But the Prussian War Ministry in Berlin apparently was kept ignorant of Schlieffen's plans until December 1912 – that is, until six years after the general's retirement.[58] Schlieffen never sought a face-to-face meeting with any of its chiefs to discuss force structure and size, preferring instead to exchange letters across town with the War Ministry.

Nor was the head of the civilian government, Chancellor von Bethmann Hollweg, officially informed of the great offensive 'wheel' in the west until December 1912.[59] For his part, the chancellor incredibly crowed even in his postwar memoirs that it was not his 'business' to have been involved in the formulation of the national strategy! 'The political leadership was not involved in the creation of the war plan.'[60] This situation is all the more incredible when one keeps in mind that the Schlieffen plan called for the war to begin with the violation of the neutrality of both Belgium and the Netherlands. At no time did kaiser, chancellor, and chief of the General Staff convene to debate national policy in case of war. 'Generally, there never took place during my entire period in office,' Bethmann Hollweg asserted, 'a sort of war council at which politics were brought into the military for and against.'[61] Given the kaiser's inability to act up to his responsibilities, it is little wonder that he never tackled the thorny issue of coordinating foreign and military policies.

Nor did coordinated planning improve under Schlieffen's successor. The Younger Moltke also preferred to keep national security planning within the confines of the 'red house on the Königsplatz,' as General Staff headquarters was popularly called, working primarily with his first quartermaster-general and leaving major department heads in the General Staff in the dark concerning his intentions and designs. Nor was Moltke eager to initiate frank exchanges of information and views with the general staffs of the various German royal armies outside Prussia. The Military Cabinet was a personnel bureau and the War Ministry an administrative bureau; the General Staff, in 'Julius' Moltke's view, alone was responsible with 'advising the Imperial Supreme Commander.'

The Imperial Navy also remained outside the planning loop. While the Admiralty Staff was probably aware of the planned violation of Belgian and Dutch neutrality by 1905, there was no direct planning between army and navy to coordinate their wartime strategies. Schlieffen did not even raise the possibility that the High Sea Fleet might interrupt British cross-Channel troop transports, either in his official contingency plans or even in his numerous writings in retirement.[62] British expeditionary forces – Schlieffen expected about 100,000 troops to cross the Channel – simply would be 'shut up' at Antwerp, 'together with the Belgians.' His successor, Moltke, also declined to address the possibility of naval action against British transports in the Channel. And while exchanges of officers between the Admiralty Staff and the General Staff had taken place sporadically, the junior service on occasion flatly refused the General Staff's requests to exchange intelligence data.[63]

Fourth, it is fair to state that the Schlieffen plan – like the Tirpitz plan before it – was never brought in line with Germany's capabilities. Schlieffen penned his great memoranda on the 'next' war without taking into account vital, non-operational factors. At no time did he seek to tailor his grand design to the *Reich*'s financial or industrial resources – to say nothing of coordinating it with the Imperial Navy. It would simply be a 'come-as-you-are war' in which the troops would live off the land and fend for themselves in Belgium and France as best they could. Schlieffen casually ignored force structure as well. When Colonel Erich Ludendorff, head of the Mobilization and Deployment Section of the General Staff, 'gamed' the Schlieffen plan in 1912, he discovered that the German armies lacked the strength to implement it. The fabled right wing of the 'wheel' through Belgium and along the English Channel was fully eight army corps (!) shy of strength requirement; and the seven to eight army corps that were to lay siege to Paris did not even exist on paper.[64] Part of the reason was that Germany was not willing to pay the price for universal male conscription: by 1914, about 5 million young men had escaped military training due to the *Reichstag*'s parsimony and the army's unwillingness to expand its officer corps beyond the traditional elites.

In fact, by 1911–13 there had emerged in Berlin two distinct visions of military policy. On the one hand, the General Staff, led by the energetic planning of Colonel Ludendorff, sought manpower enhancement in the form of an expansion of three corps, or about 300,000 men. The War Ministry, under General Josias von Heeringen, on the other hand, favored technological enhancement by way of additional firepower; it rejected manpower expansion on the ground that this would open up officer billets to 'undesirable circles.'[65] No compromise between the two visions was ever enacted. In 1914 the German armies were prepared for a traditional march on foot and horse (Field Regulations of 1906) for a war of maneuver and mobility. Even the Younger Moltke's 'small wheel' turn-in around Brussels required the troops to march 300 miles in 40 days – and to defeat the French, British, and Belgian armies in the process. Ammunition tables were forty years out of date, with the result that the German armies ran out of ammunition by October 1914. Trucks were woefully inadequate and rail capability too limited to handle the vast quantities of supplies required by a modern army corps – 130 tons of food and fodder per day, while standing still. In logistical terms, the Schlieffen plan, in the military historian Martin van Creveld's inimitable words, was 'the wheel that broke.'[66]

In the final analysis, neither admirals nor generals (nor civilian leaders) achieved their political–strategic objectives: annihilation of the British fleet in the south central North Sea; destruction of the French armies in the Seine basin; and the attainment of *Weltpolitik*. Neither army nor navy nor Chancery nor Foreign Office coordinated their various and diverse strategies. Neither Schlieffen nor Moltke involved other service agencies, both Prussian and non-Prussian, in their deliberations. Neither coordinated policy with their one loyal ally, Austria-Hungary. The civilians happily conceded that the formulation of national policy was not their 'business.' And at no time did kaiser, chancellor, war minister, chief of the General Staff, chief of the Admiralty Staff, and state secretary of the Navy Office meet to hammer out policy and strategy designs; instead, each jealously guarded his traditional military or civilian role, unwilling to surrender one iota of power or responsibility to a rival. Wilhelm II reveled in his cherished *Kommandogewalt*, blind to the reality that modern warfare required more than bluster and braggadocio. Force structures, finances, material resources, and industrial production were never coordinated for the 'next' war.

On the grand-strategic level, by way of both the Tirpitz plan and the Schlieffen plan, Germany attempted to become both a continental hegemon and a global sea power all in one generation. The *Reich* lacked both the resources and the solid leadership to attain either goal. Its security decisions concerning force structures, military doctrines, and international relations all too often were made through the prism of uncertainty. General Wilhelm Groener, Ludendorff's successor as first quartermaster-general, in May 1919 summarized the lost war for his General Staff officers:

> We struggled unconsciously for world dominion – naturally I can
> state this only in the most intimate of circles, but anyone who looks

at the situation relatively clearly and historically cannot be in doubt about this – *before* we had secured our continental position.[67]

Both army and navy had identified who the enemy was – France and Russia for the former, Britain for the latter. Both had undertaken independent contingency planning in case of war. Both had designed their force structures for such an eventuality. But in 1914, neither was prepared for the great hour of decision making.

Implications

Critics of this perhaps harsh portrayal of 'command decision making' under Kaiser Wilhelm II will undoubtedly point out that a 'war council' *did* take place on the eve of the Great War – on 8 December 1912, to be precise. Is this not evidence that the system worked? That Wilhelm II was able at the moment of crisis to pull all the strings of his decentralized command structure together? That civilian, military, and naval planners were able to coordinate their disparate and seemingly disintegrated strategies? The historian John C.G. Röhl has pointed out that in the wake of the 'war council,' *Reich* institutions inaugurated certain war-powers measures: to secure food and other stocks to feed both the civilian and the military sectors; to regulate the labor market; to set aside special funds to pay for the initial phases of mobilization; to increase the Reichsbank's gold reserves; and the like.[68]

The first observation that needs to be made is that this 'war council' stood out by its singularity. No system of 'war councils' was embedded in the Prussian–German constitutional system, and the so-called *Kriegsrat* on 8 December 1912 occurred simply because Wilhelm II called it into being. Second, it is instructive to note that neither the imperial chancellor nor the state secretary of the Foreign Office nor the Prussian war minister were invited to the meeting. This by itself negates the notion that a true 'war council' took place on 8 December 1912. And little came of the military discussions of that 8 December. After the kaiser allowed that in any future war, Britain would side with France and Russia – 'the Anglo-Saxons on the side of the Gauls and Slavs' – which could prompt Germany to conduct a Schlieffenesque offensive in the west, Wilhelm II demanded that the fleet prepare for the war with Britain; that the navy get ready to torpedo British troop convoys in the English Channel and to mine the Thames estuary; that Admiral von Tirpitz step up the production of U-boats; and that the Navy Office prepare the nation for war also with Russia.

Nothing of this sort happened. Tirpitz clung to his battleship grand design and simply demanded 'postponement of the great fight for one and a half years' in order to complete expansion of the Kaiser Wilhelm Canal and construction of the submarine pens on Helgoland Island. His propaganda apparatus undertook no major activity to popularize a war with Russia. The

Foreign Office launched no diplomatic offensive to shore up the kaiser's new vision of a war with Britain. And General von Moltke, who at the 'war council' had regarded a general European war 'to be inevitable, and the sooner the better,' instead became embroiled in a bitter (and losing) struggle with the Prussian War Ministry over an expansion of the army.[69] In short, the outcome of the putative 'war council' was, in the words of one of its participants, Admiral von Müller, 'apparently zero.'[70]

It is fair to state that the one 'war council' that ever took place under Kaiser Wilhelm II constituted mainly bluster.[71] Throughout his career, Wilhelm II was never able to live up to the primary responsibilities that the Constitution of 1871 bestowed upon him, or even to carry out effectively his role as commander-in-chief of Germany's armed forces. The strategic and operational plans of his army and navy were never coordinated; national finances were never rationally distributed to army and navy; and the *Reich*'s diplomatic position was never reassessed, and much less realigned, to buttress those military and naval strategies. Coordination of the Schlieffen plan and the Tirpitz plan was first and foremost the kaiser's duty; in this, he failed the nation utterly.

Yet, Germany went to war in August 1914. Why? And how? This 'leap into the dark,' as Chancellor von Bethmann Hollweg called it, was anything but a carefully orchestrated 'bid for world power' (Fritz Fischer), and more the result of a combination of fear and anxiety for the future on the part of a small coterie of senior officials who made the decision for war.[72] For years, they had seen Bismarck's *Pax Germanica* dissolve before their very eyes. Ever shriller nationalist appeals on the part of pressure groups had filled in the gap created by Wilhelm II's inability to rule. Foreign and military security policies had disintegrated, being replaced by individual service operations plans. The near total lack of civilian control had by default given greater weight to military considerations. The accompanying doctrines concerning a 'short war' and a 'cult of the offensive' had filled that void. Technical determinism had paralyzed what sober strategic planning still existed. It is little wonder that Count Leopold Berchtold, the Austro-Hungarian foreign minister, at the height of the July Crisis had cried out in despair: 'Who rules in Berlin? Moltke or Bethmann?'[73]

Perhaps most tragically, General von Moltke decided to jettison the 'inter-war' peace that had existed since 1871 out of despair about the present, fear about an uncertain future, and belief in the 'topos of inevitable war.'[74] While he feared what he called a 'horrible war,' one that could set European civilization back for decades, the chief of the General Staff nevertheless had pressed for war. A short, cleansing thunderstorm might lead not only to German territorial aggrandizement but perhaps even to national rejuvenation. As he put it to the German foreign secretary, Gottlieb von Jagow, in the spring of 1914, 'there was no alternative but to fight a preventive [*sic*] war so as to beat the enemy while we could still emerge fairly well from the struggle.'[75] Thus, while apprehensive about the course and nature of the coming war, Moltke nevertheless pushed to start it at what he considered to be the most propitious moment.[76] In 1914 a classic General Staff *tour de force*, one beset from the start with countless 'ifs' and based on enemy mistakes, tore apart the 'fog of peace.'

The political scientist Ned Lebow has suggested that the July Crisis of 1914 was a classic case of the causal relationship between cognitive impairment, miscalculation, and war.[77] In a well-researched chapter using the July Crisis as a case study, Lebow suggests that the 'cognitive distortions' of German political leaders, briefly discussed above, were the root cause of the great folly of war in 1914. They led, first and foremost, to the adoption of an unrealistic strategy (the so-called 'calculated risk') based on erroneous assumptions of how the other great powers would react to the Austro-Hungarian attempt to subjugate Serbia. As the crisis unfolded, these same 'cognitive distortions' prevented kaiser and chancellor, foreign secretary and chief of the General Staff, from realizing the grave extent of their miscalculations. And when all their rosy illusions were shattered at the end of July, the 'men of 1914' at Berlin suffered a 'dramatic loss of self-confidence,' which resulted in erratic and irresponsible behavior, and finally in war. If there is a lesson to be learned, surely it is that the outcome of such brinkmanship crises is the ability of governments to learn from the results of past behaviors and to modify subsequent behavior and policies. Crisis strategies, once discovered to be erroneous, demand constant and immediate reassessment. Severe time constraints leave no other choice. To maximize the probability of success, policy modifications must consist of a rapid and ongoing learning process. That, unfortunately, was not the case with Germany in July 1914.

In 1805 Georg Heinrich von Berenhorst, an insightful writer on the Prussian military system who had served with Frederick the Great, on the eve of the Prussian army's twin defeats at Jena and Auerstädt addressed the problem of leadership in the absence of an enlightened despot. In Berenhorst's formula, cited in the heading at the start of this chapter, the state could afford to carry 'a hollow Hercules,' if need be, because its 'perfect military rotunda' and 'massive cupola' were supported by a solid foundation of 'common soldiers' and by the sturdy pillars of 'colonels and other senior officers.'[78] For a quarter of a century, Wilhelm II had played at the role of Supreme Commander, aided and abetted by a coterie of sycophants and worshippers. When the Great Test came in 1914, the *Oberster Kriegsherr* revealed himself to be the quintessential 'hollow Hercules.' With the outbreak of war, Wilhelm moved off to the 'front' – in his case, Koblenz Castle on the Rhine River, where he dined on Frederick the Great's silver field service. On 20 August Wilhelm II ventured into the castle's gardens with the chief of the Military Cabinet, General Moriz von Lyncker, and the chief of the Navy Cabinet, Admiral Georg Alexander von Müller. The kaiser sat on one bench, the cabinet chiefs on another. Pathetically, Wilhelm II lamented: 'Am I already such a figure of contempt that no one wants to sit next to me any more?'[79]

Nor was this episode an isolated incident of senior military officers deprecating their Supreme War Lord's military command failure. In 1913 Colonel Ludendorff, operations and deployment chief in the General Staff, had commented on the Supreme War Lord's command authority: 'In case of war, the kaiser will not be asked.' Two years later, General Karl von Einem, a former war minister and then commander of the German Third Army, also reflected on the kaiser's *Kommandogewalt*: 'The truth is that we have not had a working head of state for the last century.'[80] Finally, it fell upon Imperial Germany's last chief of the General Staff, General Wilhelm Groener, on 9 November 1918 to inform the monarch that his army 'no longer stands behind Your Majesty.'[81] The 'perfect military rotunda,' to return to Berenhorst's analogy, was no longer willing to carry 'a hollow Hercules.'

Notes

1 See, for example, Holger H. Herwig, *Germany's Vision of Empire in Venezuela* (Princeton, 1986); and Wilhelm F. Sater and Holger H. Herwig, *The Grand Illusion: The Prussianization of the Chilean Army* (Lincoln and London, 1999).

2 See Holger H. Herwig, 'The Prussian Model and Military Planning Today,' *Joint Force Quarterly*, vol. 18, Spring 1998, pp. 67–75.

3 Ernst Rudolf Huber, *Deutsche Verfassungsgeschichte seit 1789*, volume 3, *Bismarck und das Reich* (Stuttgart, 1963), p. 989.

4 Huber, *Deutsche Verfassungsgeschichte*, vol. 3, pp. 821ff.

5 Huber, *Deutsche Verfassungsgeschichte*, vol. 3, pp. 849ff. Huber calls the Federal Council a 'princely aristocracy.'

6 Huber, *Deutsche Verfassungsgeschichte*, vol. 3, pp. 942–44.

7 Huber, *Deutsche Verfassungsgeschichte*, vol. 3, pp. 882ff.

8 See Wilhelm Deist, 'Kaiser Wilhelm II. als Oberster Kriegsherr,' in John C.G. Röhl, ed., *Der Ort Kaiser Wilhelms II. in der deutschen Geschichte* (Munich, 1991), p. 26.

9 See Wiegand Schmidt-Richberg, 'Die Regierungszeit Wilhelms II,' in *Handbuch zur deutschen Militärgeschichte 1648–1939*, Volume 3, Part 5, *Von der Entlassung Bismarcks bis zum Ende des Ersten Weltkrieges 1890–1918* (Munich, 1979), pp. 72–73.

10 Huber, *Deutsche Verfassungsgeschichte*, vol. 3, pp. 61–62.

11 Schmidt-Richberg, 'Die Regierunszeit Wilhelms II,' pp. 63–66.

12 Schmidt-Richberg, 'Die Regierunszeit Wilhelms II,' pp. 67–69; Huber, *Deutsche Verfassungsgeschichte*, vol. 3, pp. 818–19.

13 Schmidt-Richberg, 'Die Regierungszeit Wilhelms II,' pp. 69–72.

14 See Holger H. Herwig, 'The Dynamics of Necessity: German Military Policy during the First World War,' in Allan R. Millett and Williamson Murray, eds, *Military Effectiveness*, Volume 1, *The First World War* (Boston, 1988), pp. 81–82.

15 See Holger H. Herwig, *'Luxury' Fleet: The Imperial German Navy 1888–1918* (London, 1980), p. 21.

16 Huber, *Deutsche Verfassungsgeschichte*, vol. 3, pp. 838–39, 1004–06.

17 Cited in Wilhelm Deist, 'Kaiser Wilhelm II in the context of his military and naval entourage,' in John C.G. Röhl and Nicolaus Sombart, eds, *Kaiser Wilhelm II: New Interpretations. The Corfu Papers* (Cambridge, 1982), p. 171.

18 Cited in Michael Balfour, *Der Kaiser. Wilhelm II und seine Zeit* (Berlin, 1973), p. 164: 'The will of the king is supreme law.'
19 Cited in Arden Bucholz, *Moltke, Schlieffen, and Prussian War Planning* (New York and Oxford, 1991), p. 129.
20 Cited in Herwig, *'Luxury' Fleet*, p. 23.
21 Deist, 'Kaiser Wilhelm II,' p. 180.
22 Schmidt-Richberg, 'Die Regierungszeit Wilhelms II,' pp. 60–62.
23 See Walter Görlitz, *Die Junker. Adel und Bauer im deutschen Osten. Geschichtliche Bilanz von 7 Jahrhunderten* (Limburg, 1964), pp. 298–99, 319.
24 See Holger H. Herwig, *The German Naval Officer Corps: A Social and Political History 1890–1918* (Oxford, 1973), p. 76.
25 Herwig, *The German Naval Officer Corps*, p. 67.
26 See, for example, the 1903 recollections of Graf Robert Zedlitz-Trützschler, *Zwölf Jahe am deutschen Kaiserhof* (Berlin and Leipzig, 1925), pp. 42–43.
27 Deist, 'Kaiser Wilhelm II,' pp. 180–81.
28 Bucholz, *Moltke, Schlieffen*, pp. 128–9.
29 See Herwig, *'Luxury' Fleet*, chapters 2 and 3.
30 Speech of 9 February 1871, *Hansard: Parliamentary Debates*, 3rd Series, Volume 24, p. 81.
31 Cited in Gerhard Ritter, *Staatkunst und Kriegshandwerk. Das Problem des 'Militarismus' in Deutschland* (Munich, 1965), Volume 2, p. 244. See also Stig Förster, '"People's War": Moltke the Elder and Germany's Military Operations After 1871,' *Journal of Strategic Studies*, vol. 10, 1987, pp. 209–30.
32 See Graf Moltke, *Die deutschen Aufmarschpläne 1871–1890*, ed. Ferdinand von Schmerfeld (Berlin, 1928), pp. 64–66.
33 'Bad Kissingen Memorandum' of 15 June 1877, cited in Ralph R. Menning, *The Art of the Possible: Documents on Great Power Diplomacy, 1814–1914* (New York, 1996), pp. 185–86.
34 Cited in Menning, *The Art of the Possible*, p. 175.
35 Cited in Eberhard Kessel, *Moltke* (Stuttgart, 1957), pp. 747–48.
36 Stig Förster, 'Der deutsche Generalstab und die Illusion des kurzen Krieges, 1871–1914. Metakritik eines Mythos,' *Militärgeschichtliche Mitteilungen*, vol. 54, 1995, p. 92.
37 The best work on this remains Volker R. Berghahn, *Der Tirpitz-Plan. Genesis und Verfall einer innenpolitischen Krisenstrategie unter Wilhelm II* (Düsseldorf, 1971); see also Herwig, *'Luxury' Fleet*, chapter 3.
38 Alfred von Tirpitz, *Erinnerungen* (Leipzig, 1920), p. 112. Tirpitz's operational memoranda have been reproduced by Volker R. Berghahn and Wilhelm Deist, eds, *Rüstung im Zeichen der wilhelminischen Weltpolitik. Grundlegende Dokumente 1890–1914* (Düsseldorf, 1988), pp. 82ff.
39 Paul M. Kennedy, 'Tirpitz, England and the Second Navy Law of 1900: A Strategical Critique,' *Militärgeschichtliche Mitteilungen*, vol. 8, 1970, p. 38.
40 See J. Meyer, *Die Propaganda der deutschen Flottenbewegung 1897–1900* (Bern, 1967); and Wilhelm Deist, *Flottenpolitik und Flottenpropaganda. Das Nachrichtenbureau des Reichsmarineamtes 1897–1914* (Stuttgart, 1976).
41 For a general treatment of this phenomenon, see Samuel P. Huntington, *Political Order in Changing Societies* (New Haven and London, 1968), pp. 180–81; and in the German context, Stig Förster, *Der Doppelte Militarismus. Die Deutsche Heeresrüstungspolitik Zwischen Status-Quo-Sicherung und Aggression 1890–1913* (Stuttgart, 1985).
42 Kennedy, 'Tirpitz, England and the Second Navy Law,' pp. 34, 39, 40.
43 See Holger H. Herwig, 'From Tirpitz Plan to Schlieffen Plan: Some Observations on German Military Planning,' *Journal of Strategic Studies*, vol. 9, 1986, pp. 53–63.

44 See Herwig, 'The Dynamics of Necessity,' pp. 90–91.
45 Bundesarchiv-Militärarchiv, Admiralstab der Marine, PG 67304, A 1481 IV vom 18. 8. 1910. 'Ostsee oder Nordsee als Kriegsschauplatz.'
46 Cited in Albert Hopman, *Das Logbuch eines deutschen Seeoffiziers* (Berlin, 1924), p. 393.
47 See Peter-Christian Witt, *Die Finanzpolitik des Deutschen Reiches von 1903 bis 1913* (Lübeck and Hamburg, 1970); and Michael Epkenhans, *Die wilhelminische Flottenrüstung, 1908–1914. Weltmachtstreben, industrieller Fortschritt, soziale Integration* (Munich, 1991).
48 See Holger H. Herwig, 'Fisher, Tirpitz, and the Dreadnought,' *MHQ: The Quarterly Journal of Military History*, vol. 4, Autumn 1991, pp. 96–104.
49 Cited in Hans Mohs, ed., *General-Feldmarschall Alfred Graf von Waldersee in seinem militärischen Wirken* (Berlin, 1929), Volume 2, p. 388. Entry for 25 January 1898.
50 Terence Zuber, 'The Schlieffen Plan Reconsidered,' *War in History*, vol. 6 (July), 1999, pp. 262–305.
51 See Moltke's November 1914 memorandum in Eliza von Moltke, ed., *Generaloberst Helmuth von Moltke. Erinnerungen Briefe Dokumente 1877–1916. Ein Bild vom Kriegsausbruch, erster Kriegsführung und Persönlichkeit des ersten militärischen Führers des Krieges* (Stuttgart, 1922), pp. 16–17.
52 Cited in Holger H. Herwig, *The First World War: Germany and Austria-Hungary 1914–1918* (London, 1997), p. 44.
53 Cited in Hans von Zwehl, *Falkenhayn* (Berlin, 1926), p. 66.
54 See Herwig, 'From Tirpitz Plan to Schlieffen Plan,' p. 56.
55 Cited in Gordon A. Craig, 'The World War I Alliance of the Central Powers in Retrospect: The Military Cohesion of the Alliance,' *Journal of Modern History*, vol. 37, September 1965, pp. 337–38.
56 See Ulrich Trumpener, 'War Premeditated? German Intelligence Operations in July 1914,' *Central European History*, vol. 9, 1976, pp. 58–85.
57 See Bundesarchiv-Militrarchiv, Freiburg, W-10 / 50779, Kriegsgeschichtliche Forschungsanstalt des Heeres. Gerhard von Tappen, 'Meine Kriegserinnerungen,' p. 8.
58 Ritter, *Staatskunst und Kriegshandwerk*, vol. 2, p. 261.
59 Hermann von Kuhl, *Der deutsche Generalstab in Vorbereitung und Durchführung des Weltkrieges* (Berlin, 1920), Volume 1, p. 108.
60 Theobald von Bethmann Hollweg, *Betrachtungen zum Weltkriege* (Berlin, 1921), Volume 2, p. 7.
61 Hollweg, *Betrachtungen zum Weltkriege*, vol. 2, p. 7.
62 Gerhard Ritter, *Der Schlieffenplan. Kritik eines Mythos* (Munich, 1965), pp. 176, 182–92.
63 Ritter, *Der Schlieffenplan*, pp. 71–72 fn. 50, 198–99.
64 See Yehuda L. Wallach, *The Dogma of the Battle of Annihilation: The Theories of Clausewitz and Schlieffen and Their Impact on the German Conduct of Two World Wars* (Westport, CT and London, 1986), p. 58.
65 See Michael Geyer, *Deutsche Rüstungspolitik 1860–1980* (Frankfurt, 1984), pp. 90ff.
66 Martin van Creveld, *Supplying War: Logistics from Wallenstein to Patton* (Cambridge, 1977), p. 140.
67 Talk of 19 May 1919, cited in Fritz Fischer, *Krieg der Illusionen. Die deutsche Politik von 1911 bis 1914* (Düsseldorf, 1969), unnumbered frontispage.
68 John C.G. Röhl, *Kaiser, Hof und Staat. Wilhelm II. und die deutsche Politik* (Munich, 1987), pp. 198–202.

69 The war council has been reproduced and examined in excruciating detail by John C.G. Röhl, 'An der Schwelle zum Weltkrieg: Eine Dokumentation über den "Kriegsrat" vom 8. Dezember 1912,' *Militärgeschichtliche Mitteilungen*, vol. 21, 1977, pp. 77–134.

70 Cited in Görlitz, ed., *Der Kaiser . . . Aufzeichnungen des Chefs des Marinekabinetts Admiral Georg Alexander v. Müller über die Ära Wilhelms II.* (Göttingen, 1965), p. 125.

71 This should not, however, lead to the outrageous claim that the 'real' war council took place not at Potsdam on 8 December 1912, but rather at a meeting of the Committee of Imperial Defence at London on 23 August 1911, which 'set the course for a military confrontation between Britain and Germany.' Niall Ferguson, *The Pity of War* (New York, 1998), p. 65.

72 Bethmann's comment is in Kurt Riezler, *Tagebücher, Aufsätze, Dokumente*, ed. Karl-Dietrich Erdmann (Göttingen, 1972), p. 185. See also Fritz Fischer, *Griff nach der Weltmacht. Die Kriegszielpolitik des kaiserlichen Deutschland 1914 / 18* (Düsseldorf, 1961).

73 Cited in Franz Conrad von Hötzendorf, *Aus meiner Dienstzeit 1906–1918*, 5 vols (Vienna, Leizpig, and Munich, 1921–25), Volume 4, pp. 152ff.

74 See Wolfgang Mommsen, 'The Topos of Inevitable War in Germany in the Decade before 1914,' in Volker R. Berghahn and Martin Kitchen, eds, *Germany in the Age of Total War* (London, 1981), pp. 23–45.

75 Auswärtiges Amt-Politisches Archiv, Bonn, Nachlass Jagow, Volume 8, pp. 69ff.

76 See A. Mombauer, 'A Reluctant Military Leader? Helmuth von Moltke and the July Crisis of 1914,' *War in History*, vol. 6, 1999, pp. 417–46; and Mombauer, *Helmuth von Moltke and the Origins of the First World War* (Cambridge, 2001).

77 Richard Ned Lebow, *Between War and Peace: The Nature of International Crisis* (Baltimore, MD and London, 1981), pp. 119–47.

78 Georg Heinrich von Berenhorst, *Betrachtungen über die Kriegskunst* (Leipzig, 1827; Osnabrück, 1978), p. 511.

79 Cited in Walter Görlitz, ed., *Regierte der Kaiser? Kriegstagebücher, Aufzeichnungen und Briefe des Chefs des Marine-Kabinetts Admiral George Alexander v. Müller 1914–1918* (Göttingen, 1959), p. 50.

80 Einem to his wife, 23 March 1915, in Wilhelm Deist, ed., *Militär und Innenpolitik im Weltkrieg 1914–1918* (Düsseldorf, 1970), Volume 2, pp. 1135–36.

81 Cited in Kuno Graf von Westarp, *Das Ende der Monarchie am 9. November 1918* (Stollhamm, 1952), p. 46.

7

BRITISH PREPARATION FOR
GLOBAL NAVAL WAR, 1904–14

Directed Revolution or Critical Problem Solving?

John Tetsuro Sumida

Between 1904 and 1914, Britain's fleet was transformed by radical changes in warship design initiated by the Admiralty. The driving force behind the policy of technical innovation was Admiral Sir John Fisher, the navy's service chief (First Sea Lord). The apparent centerpiece of Fisher's scheme was the adoption of a novel kind of battleship that achieved substantial increases in speed and fire power at relatively low cost by exploiting the latest advances in steam and ordnance engineering. The first of the line was HMS *Dreadnought*, which was commissioned in 1906. The advent of the much-improved battleship upset the building program of Germany, Britain's single most dangerous naval rival. Fisher then responded to rapid German construction of similar units with even more heavily armed dreadnoughts in larger numbers. During the First World War, Royal Navy containment of the German battle fleet seemed to depend upon the quantitative and qualitative superiority of its capital ships. The so-called 'Dreadnought Revolution' has thus been viewed as a successful attempt to combine intelligent manipulation of technology with far-sighted strategic purpose.

Recent historical scholarship, however, has invalidated the basic premises upon which this proposition has rested. In the first place, Fisher was opposed to the further construction of any kind of battleship, including those of the dreadnought type, because he believed that defense against invasion could be entrusted to the submarine and fast surface torpedo craft, while trade and colonial territory was to be protected by a new type of super cruiser that was to become known as the battle cruiser. Fisher's actual force structure objective, in other words, was the replacement of the conventional battle fleet and cruiser squadrons with flotilla defense at home and battle cruiser control in distant seas. In the second place, Fisher wanted the Royal Navy to be able to defend British home waters, extended lines of maritime supply, and far-flung empire against even a hostile coalition of major naval powers, not just to contain the German threat in the North Sea. The German challenge, in short, was not the focal point of British naval policy, but one of several major concerns.[1]

The British fear of having to fight a global naval war against a superior combination of naval powers prior to 1914 was justifiable. That the First

World War was fought under much more favorable circumstances should not obscure the fact that the Admiralty needed to prepare for a range of possibilities, not a solitary certainty. Appreciation of the difficulty and complexity of Britain's strategic situation, moreover, casts a different light on the nature of the warship procurement aspect of Admiralty planning. The present chapter will thus assess British naval preparations during the early twentieth century in terms of the exigencies of the time, and not, as so often has been the case in the past, with respect to what happened afterwards. In place of the view that British policymakers chose the right technical solution to an obvious strategic problem, this study will argue that they were driven to radical technical expedients in order to address a worst-case strategic contingency that never came to pass, but nonetheless had to be taken into account.

Alfred Thayer Mahan's *The Influence of Sea Power upon History, 1660–1783* was the most widely read and influential study of naval strategy of the late nineteenth and early twentieth century. Nearly half the book was devoted to the American Revolution, a conflict in which Britain was opposed by a coalition of continental powers that possessed powerful navies. According to Mahan's account, it was Britain's need to maintain control of home waters and distant seas that prompted the division of her fleet, which exposed it to defeat in detail. In spite of the faulty deployments of her opponents, Britain thus lost the war and a considerable part of her empire. In this manner, Mahan delineated the fundamental problem of British naval strategy, namely the danger posed by a hostile alliance that could threaten British interests around the world.[2]

Geography and economics determined Britain's basic defense requirements. Britain was an island, which meant that invasion was impossible if its navy controlled the surrounding waters. But from the seventeenth century onwards, a large and increasing proportion of Britain's wealth was derived from far-reaching maritime trade and possession of territory scattered across the globe, the protection of which depended upon its ability to command distant seas as well as those at home. During the nineteenth century, military and economic changes magnified the dangers of invasion and interdiction of lines of maritime communication. Conscription inflated the size of the armies of potential European enemies, while Britain continued to rely on a much smaller professional land force. Population growth and industrialization made Britain dependent upon the ability to import food and raw materials, and export manufactures. By the early twentieth century, therefore, loss of naval supremacy would have exposed Britain to attack by armies that were much larger than its own on the one hand, and on the other starvation, economic collapse, and imperial dismemberment.

The costs of maintaining Britain's naval supremacy increased greatly during the late nineteenth century. Industrial and fiscal development enabled continental great powers to build up-to-date warships in significant numbers. Swift advances in armament, armor, and propulsion rendered mechanically sound warships obsolete after only a few years' service. Britain was thus compelled to build a larger fleet and to replace ships more frequently with upgraded units that were usually more expensive than their predecessors. The expansion of the fleet was accompanied by higher expenditure on manning, fuel, ammunition, and base facilities. In 1904, British naval spending each year was more than twice the amount it had been in 1889. Peacetime army expenditures during the same period had also nearly doubled, and the high costs of fighting a major colonial war in South Africa burdened the Treasury with large debts. These circumstances provoked serious political dissatisfaction, which clouded the prospects of future defense budgets. But even had the funds been forthcoming, there were other grounds for concern about the future of Britain's naval position.[3]

By the early twentieth century, the improvement of torpedoes threatened the tactical viability of the battleship. The introduction of gyroscopes and better methods of propulsion increased torpedo accuracy, speed, and range, which made them as likely to hit their targets as heavy caliber guns at existing battle ranges. The thick armor of battleships was situated to deflect projectiles fired at or above the waterline, and thus offered no protection against torpedoes, whose impact occurred against the lower hull. And unlike big guns, torpedo-launching gear could be mounted in small warships that were relatively cheap and simple to build. These factors had troubling implications. Britain had measured the state of its naval security largely in terms of battleships on the presumption that naval supremacy could only be maintained or contested by a fleet of such vessels. The characteristics of the latest torpedoes, however, meant that cruisers equipped with them might be no less potent than battleships in a sea fight, and that battleships could be sunk by flotilla. Uncertainty about the efficacy and vulnerability of the Royal Navy's primary weapons system raised doubt about its capacity to defend Britain's vital maritime interests.[4]

Manpower shortages posed no less critical worries. The Royal Navy was made up of volunteers and depended upon reenlistments to provide sufficient numbers of the skilled and experienced men essential to the efficient working of a modern warship. By the turn of the century, however, the rapid expansion of the fleet had created personnel requirements that exceeded supply at existing pay rates. The greater technical sophistication of new fighting vessels, moreover, increased demand for trained mechanics, a category of worker that was in especially short supply. Large 'across-the-board' increases in pay were out of the question given the greater spending in other areas. The danger of subverting discipline through pay anomalies limited resort to selective augmentation of salaries for technical specialists. The navy thus faced the prospect of not being able to recruit men in the numbers needed in the not too distant future if fleet expansion continued, and the inadequate retention of skilled labor meant that the existing fleet was manned by an increasingly less capable work force.[5]

The Anglo-Japanese alliance of 1902, which called for joint belligerency in the event that either party was attacked by two others, redressed British naval weaknesses in Asian waters *vis-à-vis* France and Russia, but was accompanied by the danger of involvement in a major war precipitated by Japanese action. This contingency did not come to pass in 1904 when Japan attacked Russia because France remained neutral. The British government, nonetheless, believed that hostilities with France and Russia, and perhaps even Germany as well, were possible and even likely. Moreover, Russian victory – which the British expected – would result in a less favorable naval situation in the Far East. While all these issues were in play, the cabinet informed the Admiralty that significant cuts in naval spending were imminent. The combination of international crisis and downturn in the navy's fiscal outlook prompted Lord Selborne, the civilian naval minister (First Lord), to seek a radical change in the direction of British naval policy.[6]

For several years prior to 1904, Selborne had tried to keep expenditure within bounds while building large numbers of up-to-date warships and making provision for the adequate manning of the fleet. But in spite of his pleas to his service colleagues on the board of Admiralty for administrative economies, spending had continued to increase and indeed had accelerated. During this time, Selborne was impressed by Admiral Sir John Fisher's forceful and imaginative approach to the solution of certain manning problems. Fisher, for his part, assured Selborne that if he was given the authority he could both increase the fighting efficiency of the fleet and reduce naval expenditure. In the spring of 1904, Selborne informed Fisher that he would succeed the current service chief of the navy. Just prior to Fisher's assumption of office in the fall, Selborne shifted responsibility for large issues of policy and the fighting power of the fleet from the board as a whole to the First Sea Lord in particular. The Admiralty, moreover, at this date had no formal naval staff, which might have restricted the new chief executive's freedom of action. Thus empowered and unencumbered, Fisher acted as he had promised.[7]

Fisher achieved large savings in the short run through administrative reforms, the sale of obsolete warships, and changes in manning. The unanticipated annihilation of the Russian battle fleet by the Japanese enabled Britain to reduce projected building programs, which resulted in further reductions in naval spending. Two years after Fisher became First Sea Lord, the naval world was stunned by the completion of *Dreadnought*, a battleship that was faster and more powerful than any other. The advent of *Dreadnought* disrupted foreign battleship programs by forcing cancellation of ongoing projects or completion of obsolescent units before work on new model vessels could begin, which extended Britain's period of relaxed new construction. But dreadnoughts were more expensive than their conventional predecessors, which meant that once Britain's naval rivals recovered their stride in capital ship design, the game of matching foreign building was bound to resume and require even greater outlays of cash than before. From the start, however, Fisher had a very different outcome in mind.[8]

Fisher came to the Admiralty with a revolutionary conception of naval warfare that he believed would solve Britain's manifold difficulties in one fell swoop. He was convinced that submarines were practically immune to attack from warships and could find and sink troop transports easily in the narrow seas around Britain. Fisher also believed that a monopoly of new methods of gunnery would enable British battle cruisers to fight at distances that were greater than the effective range of torpedoes and enemy big-guns, which would allow them to avoid torpedoes and engage battleships with impunity in spite of their relatively weak armor because they could supposedly hit before being hit. These same innovative gunnery techniques were also to enable battle cruisers to maneuver at high speed in small groups instead of moving in the large formations along steady courses characteristic of battleship tactics, and so their vulnerability to torpedo fire would be further decreased.[9]

Fisher's strategy was to defend the British Isles with flotilla only, which would free the surface fleet of battle cruisers to deploy abroad, concentrated in overwhelming force by the just-invented radio communications. A flotilla that was numerous enough to discourage invasion would be much less costly to build and maintain than a battle fleet large enough to do the same job. The battle cruiser's combination of superior speed and fire power would enable it to run down and destroy inferior cruisers and battleships as well, doing the work of larger numbers of conventional cruisers and battleships. In theory at least, flotilla defense at home and battle cruiser power projection abroad would use fewer men, ships, and maintenance facilities than the old system of home and foreign station battleship fleets, and large flocks of less-capable cruisers.[10]

Daring technological innovation was crucial to the viability of Fisher's vision. Submarines were still experimental. Turbine propulsion, which was required to provide battle cruisers with high speed, had never been mounted in a large warship. Replacement of mixed batteries of big guns and quick-firers by an all big-gun armament and the adoption of advanced gunnery instruments, both of which were needed to enable battle cruisers to hit their targets before they could be struck in return, were untried. Fisher authorized new submarines of larger size and better performance, and funded the secret development of observing and computing devices that aimed naval artillery accurately even when fighting ranges were much longer than had been standard in the past. Although he was opposed to the further construction of battleships, he probably viewed *Dreadnought* as a test bed for turbine engines and the all-big-gun armament. Three battle cruisers ordered in the same program year were scheduled for completion nearly two years after the new model battleship, which would allow ample time to modify the design of the former should trials of the latter reveal shortcomings that would make such a course desirable.[11]

Dreadnought's trials proved the technical practicability of turbines and the all-big-gun system. But in addition, the mere fact that it was much faster and more powerful than existing battleships delayed foreign new construction as described previously. This enabled the Admiralty to reduce large warship construction, which demonstrated that seizure of the technical initiative could work to Britain's financial advantage. Fisher thus concluded that the adoption of capital ships that were considerably faster and more powerful than *Dreadnought* would have a similar effect. Battle cruisers that were much swifter and more heavily gunned than those underway, Fisher hoped, would constitute a second naval technical leap forward that would compromise foreign capital ship programs and again enable Britain to build less and save money. The completion and successful trials in 1908 of the first generation of battle cruisers, the Invincible class, convinced the First Sea Lord that his vision was practicable.[12]

There were, however, setbacks in other areas. In 1902, the Admiralty had made an agreement with Vickers, the large armaments firm, to build submarines for the navy on a monopoly basis in return for assuming responsibility for all research and development costs for new designs. Government suspicion, however, that Vickers was charging excessively high prices – which were well founded – disrupted orders for the new model submarines required to implement Fisher's flotilla defense scheme, with the result that the first unit did not begin trials until late 1908. Moreover, development of the advanced gunnery instruments upon which the battle cruiser's ability to hit before it could be hit in return was delayed by a serious division of opinion within the Ordnance Department. The result was that Admiralty support for the project was suspended in the spring of 1908 in spite of the fact that preliminary trials were extremely promising.[13]

For Fisher, however, perhaps the most worrisome problem was not technical, but financial. In 1905, the Conservative government had resigned and from 1906 its Liberal successor, after a smashing victory at the polls, enjoyed an overwhelming majority in Parliament. In spite of the fact that naval spending had dropped by more than 10 per cent in 1905, the new cabinet insisted upon further sharp reductions in order to provide funds for an ambitious program of social reform. The international circumstances described above justified reduced naval construction in 1906, 1907, and 1908, which provided large savings. But the smaller big ship programs, which were from one-quarter to one-half the size of that of 1905 (the first to be made up of dreadnoughts), jeopardized the fiscal health of large naval shipbuilders and ordnance manufacturers. This was a serious problem because the Royal Navy depended upon these firms for research and development as well as the reserve building capacity that would be required should international conditions require a rapid increase in naval strength.[14]

Unlike many of his service colleagues on the Board of Admiralty, Fisher did not believe that the German navy on its own posed a critical threat to British naval security.[15] But he was willing to exploit rumors of accelerated German building to pressure the Liberal cabinet into substantial increases in the British capital ship program for 1909. For Fisher, there were two major issues at stake. In the first place, the proposed larger building schedule of six units – which was no less than three times the size of that of 1908 – would provide the orders needed to keep what he regarded as essential naval armaments companies in business. In the second place, Fisher intended that the entire program should consist of battle cruisers of unprecedented size, speed, and gun power. In the end, the cabinet agreed to measures that produced an eight-ship program, but Fisher was unable to carry his all battle cruiser initiative within the board, which resulted in orders for six battleships and only two battle cruisers. This outcome was somewhat mitigated by the addition of two battle cruisers ordered by Australia and New Zealand.[16]

Fisher's reforms and methods of running the navy created considerable opposition within and outside the service. His fight for more construction compromised his relations with the Liberal government, and this led him to resign in 1910. By then, however, the Royal Navy had over fifty submarines in commission, whose impressive performance in fleet maneuvers had convinced a majority of the Board of Admiralty that flotilla defense for short periods at least was viable. Moreover, the 1909 dreadnought crisis had not only resulted in large orders for British warship builders, but also precipitated a radical change in government tax policy that increased the income of the central government. This improvement in the financial situation was further magnified by recovery from economic recession, so that by 1913 the income of the British state was nearly a third greater than what it had been in 1908. As a consequence, the Royal Navy's big-ship programs, while smaller than that achieved in 1909, were never less than twice the size of 1908, which was enough to secure Fisher's industrial policy objectives.[17]

The translation of greater fiscal resources into large building programs enabled the Admiralty in the short run to maintain a force of major surface ships that was sufficient in number to defend home and foreign waters. The late start of Russia, France, Italy, and Austria-Hungary with respect to the construction of dreadnoughts meant that Britain could count on the effective deployment of older capital ships in the Mediterranean and Far East until 1913 or even later. Thus all the new model capital ships were available for use against the Germans. The strategic circumstances of the five years from 1909 to 1913 did not, therefore, require implementation of Fisher's battle cruiser scheme, and it was during this period that proponents of the traditional line of battle were able to restrict and then suspend the construction of battle cruisers, and put forward proposals for a new kind of battle fleet that provided a plausible if not wholly satisfactory antidote to the torpedo threat.

The concentration of all of the Royal Navy's dreadnoughts into a single battle fleet created a large and unwieldy formation that was highly vulnerable to torpedoes launched by enemy battleships, cruisers, and flotilla craft. Torpedo attacks from cruisers and destroyers could be prevented by screening the battle line with cruisers and destroyers, and torpedoes from enemy battleships might be avoided by a turn away. From 1910, the Admiralty thus began to consider seriously the development of what was called a 'Grand Fleet of Battle,' that is, a tactically integrated formation of capital ships (battleships and battle cruisers), cruisers, and flotilla. At the same time, the Royal Navy adopted methods of gunnery that supposedly would enable British battleships firing rapidly at medium ranges to score a large number of hits before torpedoes fired by enemy battleships could cross the distance between the opposed fleets. These expedients, however, depended upon the coordination of many units by slow and unreliable flag signaling, called for methods of aiming and firing that undermined efforts to shoot accurately when ranges were long, and risked disengagement before decisive harm could be inflicted on the enemy.[18]

By mid-1910, Reginald McKenna, the First Lord of the Admiralty, believed that Britain's heavy surface ships could be deployed away from home waters because immediate security against invasion would be guaranteed by flotilla defense, and radio communications would be capable of recalling the battle fleet quickly. McKenna had also reinstituted Admiralty support for the secret development of the advanced fire-control instruments that were required to give the Royal Navy a monopoly of long-range hitting. Trials of prototype equipment were mostly successful, but the change in emphasis from accuracy at long range to rapidity of fire at medium range called for by the Grand Fleet concept disrupted the adoption of gear that British battle cruisers needed in order to engage battleships or other battle cruisers without high risk of destruction because of their lack of heavy armor. Fisher, while not unaware of difficulties in gunnery, was confident that satisfactory solutions were within reach, and continued to press for the replacement of the battleship by battle cruisers that were even larger, faster, and more heavily armed than those ordered in 1909.[19]

In 1911, Winston Churchill became First Lord. He was enamored of Fisher's radical scheme, and thus called for the entire 1912 program to be devoted to improving battle cruisers. The opposition of senior officers who wanted to enhance the power of the conventional line of battle, however, resulted in the ordering of faster battleships and no battle cruisers. Fisher was outraged by this compromise, which produced capital ships that still were slower than battle cruisers and much more expensive. On the other hand, from 1913 onwards the coming into service of non-German dreadnoughts in quantity compelled Britain to continue building large surface ships in numbers adequate to provide security in distant seas as well as home waters.[20] This strained even the resources of a Treasury enriched by financial reform and economic prosperity. In 1914, the Admiralty thus in secret cancelled half the next year's battleship program and used the savings to increase submarine production, action that was intended to improve flotilla defense to the point that the surface fleet could if necessary be deployed in strength abroad without exposing Britain to invasion.[21]

But although the flotilla defense aspect of Fisher's radical concept of naval warfare was thus virtually accomplished, the development of a British monopoly of long-range hitting, upon which his vision of the battle cruiser depended, was finally wrecked in 1912 when the Admiralty refused to purchase certain perfected gunnery instruments. The high cost of this equipment was a major impediment to its adoption because by 1912, increases in spending on new warship construction had provoked calls from the Treasury for strict economies elsewhere in the naval budget. Moreover, Fisher's resignation two years before and the preoccupation with developing the Grand Fleet concept had greatly weakened support for the battle cruiser within the Admiralty; this meant less demand for a system of gunnery than had been intended in large part to compensate for the weak armor protection of the battle cruiser. Fisher, it needs to be said, was deceived about the actual state of gunnery affairs, and believed that the Royal Navy enjoyed a decisive gunnery advantage over foreign fleets when this was not the case.[22]

The outbreak of hostilities in August 1914 ended strategic uncertainty. Britain got something that was very close to a best strategic case, namely war against two naval powers with the assistance of three and later four naval powers. Deployment of the battle fleet abroad was unnecessary because allies were strong enough to maintain control of distant seas. Britain was thus doubly insured against invasion by flotilla defense and the presence of a battle fleet that was stronger than its German counterpart. Fisher, who was recalled to the First Sea Lordship by Churchill a few months after the outbreak of the conflict, promptly used the exigencies of war as a pretext to complete the implementation of his radical changes in British naval force structure. Within weeks of taking office, he placed large orders for submarines and five new battle cruisers that were faster and armed with larger guns than their predecessors. Fisher resigned over the Dardenelles operation in mid-1915, however, before he was able to implement an additional round of battle cruiser construction.[23]

In May 1916, a combination of an ill-advised German foray and British good fortune resulted in a collision between the two main battle fleets. In the ensuing battle of Jutland, unwieldy formation, risk-aversive tactics, and communications errors deprived the Royal Navy of a victory.[24] In addition, the failure to provide the battle cruisers with state-of-the art gunnery instruments as Fisher had planned, and ammunition-handling practices that allowed faster firing but also increased the likelihood of catastrophic explosion in the event of a hit, were major contributors to the loss of three British battle cruisers.[25] The commanders of the battle fleet diverted attention away from shortcomings in operational practice for which they were responsible by blaming these disasters on the supposed inadequacy of battle cruiser armor protection, which, when combined with their deployment at Jutland as an adjunct to the battle fleet, obscured their intended tactical mode of operation and strategic purpose.[26] In the following year, the near-decisive success of German unrestricted submarine attacks on British commerce overshadowed the pre-war development of the submarine as the primary instrument of flotilla defense.

Besides the reshaping of memory by *post facto* events, large naval interests were served during the war by telling the story of pre-war British naval policy in terms of dreadnought battleships and prescience about the Germans. In comparison with the army, which was engaged in heavy fighting, the battle fleet seemed idle, which raised questions about the value of a force that prior to hostilities had received the lion's share of defense spending, and that consumed armaments manufacturing output needed to fight the war on land. To meet such critical inquiries, the navy and its friends had to argue that the battle fleet was essential to prevent invasion and secure vital lines of maritime supply, which of course meant no mention of flotilla defense and battle cruiser power projection.[27] The Royal Navy's short-term embarrassment of riches, in other words, had to be disguised in order to preserve access to its sources of industrial supply and, with an eye to the post-war future, strengthen its title to a large share of the national purse. For Britain's naval strategic circumstances could alter, and the Royal Navy might once again be faced simultaneously with dire threats in both home waters and distant seas without certainty of assistance.

In 1807, British land and sea forces attacked Copenhagen in order to capture or destroy Danish warships that might soon be deployed against Britain in support of France and Russia. This preemptive strike on a neutral state in order to forestall the strengthening of a hostile Franco-Russian alliance inspired Fisher to suggest in late 1904 that the German battle fleet be 'Copenhagened.'[28] At this time, Britain was again faced with the possibility of having to fight the navies of France and Russia. The danger posed by Germany, therefore, was not that of a nascent dominant threat, but of an immediate menace that could tip the balance of naval power decisively against Britain if not eliminated. Fisher's proposal was not instigated by his fear of the German danger as it later developed, but prompted by its potential in the short-run to compromise Britain's naval command. In this case, as well as others, Fisher was reacting to the possibility that the Royal Navy would be faced by equal or superior numbers in geographically disparate seas.

Britain's need to protect valuable colonies and vital lines of maritime communications as well as home territory meant that her grand strategic perspective in the early twentieth century had to be global rather than regional. In 1904, the twin threats of war with a powerful naval coalition and of fiscal retrenchment, and certain advances in naval engineering, prompted Fisher to formulate a policy of fundamental technical and force structure change in order to provide adequate naval strength in both European and Asian waters at an affordable cost. Over the course of the next decade, technical setbacks delayed implementation, improvements in state finance allowed increased naval spending that was sufficient to maintain British naval supremacy with more or less conventional forces and deployments, and the prospect of support from strong naval allies in the event of war reduced the immediate need for a radical solution to the naval security problem. Nonetheless, the strategic, tactical, financial, and technical factors working in favor of Fisher's concept were strong, and his power and influence were such that it remained a significant factor at the Admiralty in spite of increased British attentiveness to the threat posed by the German navy in the North Sea.

Contingency in multiple forms made planning an extremely difficult problem for the Admiralty. At the level of foreign policy, Britain had to deal with the likelihood that yesterday's enemy might be tomorrow's ally, and *vice versa*, or that unanticipated military events might cause large if temporary shifts in the balance of power; the great danger was isolation and the formation of a hostile coalition of two or more powers that could pose serious threats in different parts of the world. The fiscal fortunes of the navy were also subject to wide swings. Within a decade, recession and recovery, changes in government, and major alterations in tax policy both forced radical reductions and allowed unprecedented increases in naval spending. And finally, technological innovation was a chronic source of uncertainty. The improvement of old weapons and the advent of new ones not only raised the question of whether or not warfare had been transformed to such a degree as to warrant fundamental changes in national defense policy, but could also create expectations that when unfulfilled invalidated basic assumptions about strategy and tactics.

Assessment of British planning for global naval war suggests three more general propositions. In the first place, worst case strategic contingencies must be engaged with solutions that are expensive or involve considerable risk. Policies of either sort thus generate considerable opposition, and in the absence of immediate and compelling circumstances justifying such action, are extremely difficult to implement. In the second place, financial limitation is a double-edged sword, both promoting and retarding radical change in military policy. Fiscal crisis can precipitate policy innovation, but can also simultaneously prevent spending on the development of technical advances that are crucial to its success. And in the third place, fundamental shifts in defense policy take years, during which time new weapons systems may be deployed in ways to maximize the value of old weapons systems. This creates transitional operational practices that may take on a life of their own, displacing the intended future.

The notion that Britain initiated a 'Dreadnought Revolution' in the early twentieth century was largely the result of drawing conclusions about Admiralty decision making without knowledge of the secret internal deliberations of the responsible leadership. Comprehensive, systematic, and rigorous study of once-classified official documents – which are the essential building blocks of any credible assessment of major policy – has provided a very different view of the matter.[29] The business of the Admiralty was not naval revolution – that is, coherent radical change to achieve a specific objective – but critical problem solving, which meant managing basic institutional function while dealing with continuously changing circumstances and preparing for a highly uncertain future. If there is a simple lesson to be learned from the story of British naval policy before the First World War, it is not that intelligent radical change in policy can be strategically beneficial, but that it is difficult, messy, unnecessary in the event, and can have large results that were not intended.

Notes

1 Jon Tetsuro Sumida, *In Defense of Naval Supremacy: Finance, Technology and British Naval Policy, 1889–1914* (Boston: Unwin Hyman, 1989; paperback edition, London: Routledge, 1993); and Nicholas A. Lambert, *Sir John Fisher's Naval Revolution* (Columbia: University of South Carolina Press, 1999).
2 Alfred Thayer Mahan, *The Influence of Sea Power upon History, 1660–1783* (Boston: Little, Brown, 1890), chapter 14.
3 Sumida, *In Defense of Naval Supremacy*, chapter 1.
4 Jon Tetsuro Sumida, 'The Quest for Reach: The Development of Long-Range Gunnery in the Royal Navy, 1901–12,' in Stephen D. Chiabotti, ed., *Military Transformation in the Industrial Age* (Chicago: Imprint Publications, 1996), pp. 49–96.
5 Jon Sumida, 'British Naval Administration and Policy in the Age of Fisher,' *Journal of Military History*, vol. 54, January 1990, pp. 8–11, and Lambert, *Fisher's Naval Revolution*, pp. 111–13.
6 George Monger, *The End of Isolation: British Foreign Policy 1900–1907* (London: Thomas Nelson, 1963), chapter 7; Jonathan Steinberg, 'The Copenhagen Complex,' *Journal of Contemporary History*, vol. 1, 1966, pp. 23–46; and Sumida, *In Defense of Naval Supremacy*, pp. 24–6.
7 Lambert, *Fisher's Naval Revolution*, pp. 90–94, and Sumida, *In Defense of Naval Supremacy*, pp. 26–27.
8 Lambert, *Fisher's Naval Revolution*, chapter 4, and Sumida, *In Defense of Naval Supremacy*, pp. 111–13.
9 Sumida, *In Defense of Naval Supremacy*, pp. 51–61, 158–62, 256–59; and Lambert, *Fisher's Naval Revolution*, pp. 116–17, 121–26.
10 Sumida, *In Defense of Naval Supremacy*, p. 330; and Lambert, *Fisher's Naval Revolution*, pp. 111–13.
11 Sumida, In *Defense of Naval Supremacy*, pp. 98–100, 111–15, 158–62; and Lambert, *Fisher's Naval Revolution*, pp. 154–57.
12 Sumida, *In Defense of Naval Supremacy*, pp. 158–62.

13 Sumida, *In Defense of Naval Supremacy*, pp. 126–38; and Lambert, *Fisher's Naval Revolution*, pp. 154–57, 182.

14 Sumida, *In Defense of Naval Supremacy*, pp. 111–15; Lambert, *Fisher's Naval Revolution*, pp. 129–54.

15 Ruddock F. Mackay, *Fisher of Kilverstone* (Oxford: Clarendon Press, 1973), pp. 370, 389–91. For the serious conflicts of interest that clouded Anglo-Russian relations, *detente* notwithstanding, see Keith Neilson, *Britain and the Last Tsar: British Policy and Russia, 1894–1917* (Oxford: Clarendon Press, 1995).

16 Sumida, *In Defense of Naval Supremacy*, pp. 162, 185–92; and Lambert, *Fisher's Naval Revolution*, p. 154.

17 Sumida, *In Defense of Naval Supremacy*, pp. 192–96; Lambert, *Fisher's Naval Revolution*, p. 195.

18 Sumida, 'The Quest for Reach' and Lambert, *Fisher's Naval Revolution*, pp. 211–21, 284–91.

19 Lambert, *Fisher's Naval Revolution*, p. 195, and Sumida, *In Defense of Naval Supremacy*, pp. 256–60.

20 Paul G. Halpern, *The Mediterranean Naval Situation, 1908–1914* (Cambridge, MA: Harvard University Press, 1971), chapters 1 and 2.

21 Lambert, *Fisher's Naval Revolution*, chapters 8 and 9.

22 Sumida, *In Defense of Naval Supremacy*, chapter 6.

23 Sumida, *In Defense of Naval Supremacy*, pp. 289–95; and Mackay, *Fisher of Kilverstone*, pp. 465–67.

24 Andrew Gordon, *The Rules of the Game: Jutland and British Naval Command* (Annapolis, MD: Naval Institute Press, 1996).

25 Nicholas A. Lambert, '"Our Bloody Ships" or "Our Bloody System"? Jutland and the Loss of the Battle Cruisers, 1916,' *Journal of Military History*, vol. 62, January 1998, pp. 29–55.

26 Arthur J. Marder, *From the Dreadnought to Scapa Flow*, 5 vols (London: Oxford University Press, 1961–78), vol. iii revised, pp. 208–9.

27 Marder, *Dreadnought to Scapa Flow*, vol. v, pp. 297–9; and Jon Tetsuro Sumida, 'Forging the Trident: British Naval Industrial Logistics, 1914–18,' in John A. Lynn, ed., *Feeding Mars: Logistics in Western Warfare from the Middle Ages to the Present* (Boulder, CO: Westview Press, 1993), pp. 217–49.

28 Steinberg, 'Copenhagan Complex,' and Mackay, *Fisher of Kilverstone*, pp. 19–20.

29 Jon Tetsuro Sumida, 'Sir John Fisher and the Dreadnought: The Sources of Naval Mythology,' *Journal of Military History*, vol. 59, October 1995, pp. 619–38; and Jon Tetsuro Sumida and David Alan Rosenberg, 'Machines, Men, Manufacturing, Management, and Money: The Study of Navies as Complex Organizations and the Transformation of Twentieth Century Naval History,' in John B. Hattendorf, ed., *Doing Naval History: Essays Toward Improvement* (Newport, RI: Naval War College Press, 1995), chapter 2.

8

STRATEGIC AND MILITARY PLANNING, 1919-39

Talbot Imlay

Military planners during the inter-war period laboured under the shadow of the Great War. In addition to untold human suffering, four long years of armed conflict wrought profound changes within and among states. What began in 1914 as a European war grew into a global conflict, involving belligerents from five continents, even if the bulk of the fighting occurred on European battlefields. The globalization of the war reflected Europe's loss of political and economic pre-eminence as hitherto rising countries, most notably the United States, emerged as undisputed great powers capable of decisively influencing world events. Within Europe and on its borderlands, the defeat of the central powers, together with the disintegration of four empires (the Russian, Austro-Hungarian, German, and Ottoman) and the creation of 'successor' states, remade geographical and political maps. The military landscape also changed with the growing use of weapons, such as the tank and the airplane, which promised to re-introduce mobility to the battlefield and to dissolve existing boundaries between civilians and combatants. Within belligerent countries, the Great War saw a remarkable increase in state power and capabilities as governments, compelled by the insatiable demands of modern industrial warfare, oversaw a massive mobilization of national resources. This unprecedented effort contributed to a reconfiguration of political, economic and social power within countries, with sometimes far-reaching consequences for international stability.

Interwar military planners had to take the Great War and its legacy into account when assessing the likelihood and nature of future war. The result was a great deal of uncertainty. Wartime and post-war geo-strategic, economic, political, and military developments meant that planners laboured in an environment of great flux characterized by rapid and sometimes revolutionary change. This chapter examines some of the developments that complicated the task of interwar military planners.

I

In geo-strategic terms, the Great War marked the end of Europe's pre-eminence in world politics as power and influence grew more diffused. The most obvious beneficiary of this process was the United States, which emerged as the leading great power. The transformation was most evident in the economic realm. In addition to the human loss and physical destruction, the Great War left Europe economically and financially exhausted: belligerents had pushed industrial production to the limit, liquidated significant portions of their foreign holdings, and gone into massive domestic and foreign debt. The United States, by contrast, was relatively and absolutely stronger at the war's end. Total manufacturing production for each of the European great powers dropped significantly between 1913 and 1920, while that of the United States rose by one-fifth. By the mid-1920s the United States alone accounted for almost 40 per cent of world manufacturing output. Less spectacular but still impressive was the growth of American commercial power after the war: in 1913 the total value of American exports was one-quarter the total for Europe (minus Russia); by 1925 the figure had climbed to 35 per cent. The United States' huge domestic market, moreover, ensured that American commercial policy, particularly tariffs, would have global ramifications. In the financial sphere, the United States went from being a debtor nation before 1914 to the world's leading creditor nation by 1919. That Britain and France had contracted much of this debt to finance their war efforts underscored the shift in power away from Europe to the United States.[1]

Some scholars contest the claim that the United States emerged as the leading great power after 1918. In particular, they maintain that Washington refrained from translating its economic strength into political and military power, in effect leaving Britain pre-eminent in the world throughout the interwar period.[2] While these scholars rightly warn against exaggerating the extent of US power after 1918, the Americans did wield unprecedented influence, especially in the economic and financial realms. Equally to the point, economics and politics during this period were increasingly interdependent, a factor that heightened the significance of the United States. The result is that other countries could not help but be affected by American decisions. Whether interventionist or isolationist or, more accurately, some combination of the two, the United States possessed an enormous capacity to shape events. Between the wars Washington might spurn responsibility, but it could not so easily abdicate power and influence.

The First World War, it has been argued, did not significantly alter the long-term evolution of the power balance among leading countries but at most accelerated by a few years pre-existing trends.[3] Yet if Europe's loss of pre-eminence appears inevitable in a longer perspective, the emergence of the United States onto the world scene after 1918 represented a strikingly new development at the time. Before the Great War the United States was a rising but still regional power. Afterwards it played a leading international role – as Woodrow Wilson's prominence during the Paris Peace Conference attests. Wilson's failure to convince Congress to accept the conference's handywork, moreover, did not produce an American withdrawal into isolation. Historians have effectively refuted the myth of interwar American isolationism, demonstrating that the United States remained deeply involved in European and world affairs during the 1920s, particularly through the exercise of financial power or 'dollar diplomacy'.[4] After 1918 American officials and bankers were at the centre of efforts to settle the thorny issues of war debts and reparations on which Europe's future economic and political stability rested. The success of the 1924 Dawes Plan on reparations, named after an American banker, owed a great deal to the influx of American investment capital into Europe and especially Germany. The result was a virtuous cycle financed by American dollars in which Germany paid reparations to Britain and France, thereby providing the two countries with the means to repay their war debts to the United States.[5]

Unfortunately, this virtuous cycle broke down at the end of the decade with the withdrawal of American investment capital from European to US domestic markets. This shift fuelled an over-heated Wall Street stock market that crashed in 1929, triggering an economic crisis within the United States marked by the rapid collapse of prices, production and demand, which in turn spurred a global crisis. No series of events underscored so clearly – or so disastrously – the prominent role of the United States between the wars. Ironically in this regard, economic depression strengthened isolationist forces within the United States that later in the decade would greatly constrain Roosevelt's more activist impulses.[6] But if the United States was undoubtedly more isolationist in the 1930s, it nevertheless continued to wield considerable influence, particularly in Europe. Significantly, the mounting possibility of war contributed greatly to this situation as Europeans sought to involve the United States more directly in the continent's affairs. In Britain and France, planners recognized that the outcome of another war would likely depend on the United States providing large-scale economic and other support, much as it had done during the Great War. Similarly, the United States increasingly factored into the calculations of Nazi Germany's leaders. Hitler, who viewed the world in terms of blocs, appears to have believed a war between a Eurasian bloc and the United States was inevitable at some time in the future, even if before 1941 he had no desire to precipitate events.[7]

The United States was not only a new and significant factor in international affairs after 1918 but also an uncertain one. Planners in other countries could never be sure of what role the Americans would play. During the 1920s American interventionism largely depended on private financial interests which themselves depended on the vagaries of domestic and international financial markets. The following decade, the recognition that the United States would critically influence the outcome of another war was counterbalanced by the uncertainty surrounding American policy. The combination of American domestic politics, in which isolationist and internationalist tendencies battled one another, and Roosevelt's elusive and cryptic nature left Europeans confused and frustrated.[8] In the end, it was Japan, with its surprise attack on Pearl Harbor, and Germany, with its unnecessary declaration of war, who forced the United States into World War II.

The United States was not the only country to benefit from the diffusion of power away from Europe after 1918. Japan also emerged from the Great War as a leading player, particularly in Asia. As with the United States, Japan's emergence onto the world stage did not occur overnight; but the Great War greatly accelerated the process. Japan's wartime economic boom, fuelled by Allied orders for Japanese goods, combined with the relative weakening of the Western colonial powers as a result of the war, left Japan as the dominant power in Asia. The 'Washington System', the name given to the regional order created by the series of multi-national agreements signed at the 1922 Washington Conference, confirmed this power shift. The treaties not only recognized Japan's leading role in the economic and political exploitation of Manchuria and northern China, but also effectively gave Japan naval supremacy in the Far East.[9] Unlike the United States, however, the Japanese grew discontented with the Washington System and its emphasis on 'cooperative diplomacy'. Beginning in 1931, the local Japanese army in Manchuria (the Kwantung Army) embarked on an expansionary course that produced an endless war of attrition against China. Significantly, Japan's 'Asian Quagmire' only inflated its ambitions as Japanese spokesmen began to speak in terms of a 'new order in East Asia' and, by 1940, of a 'Greater East Asia Co-Prosperity Sphere'.[10]

Expansionist aims brought Japan increasingly into conflict with the European colonial powers (Britain, France and Holland) and with the United States. Instrumental in establishing the Washington System, the Americans conceived of a regional order in the Far East based on peaceful economic cooperation and equal opportunity for all countries and for China in particular. No one country would be allowed to dominate. The problem was that the Japanese sought to construct, through intimidation and force, a closed and self-sufficient order in Southeast Asia that Japan could exploit to its benefit. Although war was not inevitable between the United States and Japan until well into 1941, their fundamental differences left little room for compromise. Tensions accordingly sharpened over the course of the 1930s. In the end, it was the inability of Washington and Tokyo to reconcile their opposing conceptions of regional order that prompted Japanese leaders to gamble on a high-risk solution – war with the United States.[11]

Overall, the emergence of Japan constituted an uncertain factor in international politics. Before Pearl Harbor, it was unclear which path Japan would take. Although Japanese domestic politics grew increasingly polarized during the 1930s, with militarists gaining the upper hand, it seemed possible that Japan might limit its ambitions, especially given the risk of war with the United States. Even if the Japanese chose to expand by force, it remained unclear whether they would direct their energies southwards, threatening American and European interests, or northwards against the Soviet Union. More generally, for European and American planners, Japan's strength and restlessness meant that planning was necessarily global in scope and that European events could not be considered in isolation. Both the British and the Americans in the 1930s found themselves confronted with simultaneous threats in Europe and the Far East. The result could sometimes be paralysis since decisions in one area inevitably impacted the situation in the other.[12] Meanwhile, the uncertainty of American policy exacerbated the situation facing European and especially British planners since the latter had to devise their own responses to various threats in ignorance of what the United States would do.

In addition to fostering a diffusion of power away from Europe, the Great War also produced important changes within Europe. If Europe – at least, Western Europe – initially appeared fairly stable, important sources of potential instability and thus of uncertainty could be detected. The most obvious was Germany's artificial weakness. Shrunken territorially, stripped of its colonies, militarily reduced to the status of a third-rate power, and burdened with heavy reparation obligations, Germany after Versailles was in no position to challenge anyone. Yet, as many contemporaries observed, Germany's economic and demographic resources alone made it a potential great and indeed dominant power in Europe. Indeed, the Nazis would use this potential as a springboard for their military conquests. Before then, if Germany appeared artificially weak during the 1920s, France, its primary rival, appeared deceptively strong. France's army might be the largest in Europe but the country was weaker demographically and economically than Germany. Indeed, for much of the interwar period France remained too powerful to acquiesce in major changes to the Versailles order, yet too weak to maintain this order without the help of others. The result was a good deal of hesitation, confusion, and uncertainty, not least in French policy.[13]

Britain's ambiguous position exacerbated the uncertainty caused by the artificial nature of the Franco-German balance of power. The British emerged from the Great War profoundly wary of continental entanglements that promised to drag them into another costly war. Reinforcing this perspective was the concern to safeguard the empire against internal and external threats, an empire, moreover, that grew markedly in size as a result of the Great War. Yet if the British sought to distance themselves from Europe, they could never detach themselves completely. Despite the recent claims of revisionist historians, British leaders before and after 1914 correctly recognized that Britain's physical security as well as the health of its liberal political and economic institutions depended on preventing

Imperial or Nazi Germany from completely dominating Europe.[14] As a result, the British were of two minds about the continent, which meant that British policy was profoundly ambivalent for most of the interwar period. Only at the last minute, in March 1939, did the British fully commit themselves to resisting Nazi Germany. Before then the possibility of an Anglo-German deal that would limit Germany's ambitions and allow Britain to retreat into isolation from continental affairs looked possible and, with Neville Chamberlain as Prime Minister from 1937, even likely.

Within Europe, two additional geo-strategic factors, both products of the Great War and its aftermath, contributed to uncertainty. One was the geographical re-ordering made necessary by the defeat and disintegration of the Austro-Hungarian, Russian, and German Empires. On the one hand, the emergence of new states such as Poland and Czechoslovakia and the enlargement of other states such as Romania and Yugoslavia (Serbia) promised to appease nationalist sentiments that had so destabilized Europe before 1914. On the other hand, the redrawing of maps often fostered nationalist tensions by creating new minorities who could look beyond their borders to a national home. Many of these states, moreover, were militarily weak and vulnerable, possessing multiple frontiers. The result was an unstable situation in eastern and central Europe, one that Germany and to a lesser extent Italy could exploit. Although the French sought to group these 'successor' states into a defensive alliance, they enjoyed little success, partly because of enduring differences among Poland, Czechoslovakia, and Romania, and partly because the French themselves could not decide whether these smaller states represented strategic assets or liabilities. The smaller states also embraced ambiguity, especially during the 1930s. Fearful of Germany's ambitions yet unable to rely on France (or Britain), eastern and central European leaders generally tried to steer a middle course. As a result, planners could not be sure of the role that these countries – and their valuable raw materials – would play in a future war.[15]

The Soviet Union constituted the other geo-strategic factor in Europe contributing to uncertainty. Wracked by revolution and civil war, Russia after 1917 effectively ceased to be a great power, a situation that created a great deal of confusion on its borders. This situation began to change with the consolidation of Bolshevik power in the early 1920s: the Soviet Union's size, demographic resources, and economic potential made it a latent if not actual great power. But if the Soviet Union could not be ignored, bolshevism greatly complicated matters. Following their defeat in the Soviet–Polish War of 1921–22, Soviet leaders temporarily abandoned the forceful spread of communist revolution and concentrated instead on strengthening the Soviet Union under the slogan of 'communism in one country'. Yet the ultimate aims of Soviet policy remained unclear. Were the Soviets sincere in their call for cooperation with non-communist countries? Or was Moscow's goal to embroil the capitalist world in war in order to reap the revolutionary benefits? Responses varied according to circumstances and one's political slant, but for planners the uncertainty surrounding Soviet policy and the Soviet Union's potential role in a European war remained constant.[16]

The Great War also had a tremendous economic impact at both the international and national levels. The end of the nineteenth century saw the beginning of a period of globalization marked by increasing outflows of capital, manufactured goods, technology, and people from developed countries (primarily western European) to the wider and less-developed world as well as increasing inflows of primary products from the latter to the former.[17] The Great War, however, disrupted this process of growing economic interdependence – a disruption that persisted well after 1945. While the 1920s saw attempts to restore the pre-war economic order symbolized by Britain's decision in 1925 to return to the gold standard, this restorative effort eventually failed. By the end of the decade economic nationalism was on the rise as states, conditioned partly by wartime experience, looked to solve economic problems themselves rather than through international cooperation. The result was the growth of tariff protection, trade restrictions, licences, and other controls aimed at regulating and limiting international exchanges. The Great Depression intensified the turn towards economic nationalism as countries reacted by creating exclusive trading blocs in which the expansion of intra-bloc trade failed to compensate for the general drop in global trade. A similar development occurred in the monetary realm as first Britain, then the United States, and finally France abandoned gold in favour of sterling, dollar, and franc zones or blocs.[18]

The rise of economic nationalism intensified competition between states and blocs. Economic gains increasingly were viewed in zero-sum terms, with a gain for one constituting a loss for the other. That this economic competition spilled over into the political realm is hardly surprising in a period of economic crisis. Mounting tensions during the 1930s, caused principally by the growing restlessness of Nazi Germany, Fascist Italy and Imperial Japan, powerfully reinforced the tendency towards zero-sum thinking. But competition not only heightened the risks of war; it also increased the uncertainty surrounding military planning. Economic nationalism was based on autarky, the principle that nations could become economically self-sufficient. In the context of modern war, however, the aim of self-sufficiency was chimerical since no state (or bloc) could meet the massive demands of war on its own. Waging war implied interdependence. If this represented a potential opportunity in wartime, for example by weakening an enemy through economic warfare, it also constituted a potential problem. For military planners, the tension between peacetime economic nationalism and wartime interdependence posed in acute form the question of access to foreign sources of raw materials (and other goods) needed for modern war. How reliable were existing sources? Did other potential sources exist? In a world divided into rival political and economic blocs, the uncertainty attached to this question complicated planning.

Economic developments at the national level, however, created the greatest uncertainty. The Great War's voracious demands for men, money and munitions compelled belligerent governments to intervene in the economy in unprecedented ways.[19] To varying extents, every belligerent experienced notable increases in state power and capacities as economic liberalism retreated before the new practice and conceptual apparatus of state-directed economic activity. Although the immediate post-war period saw efforts to roll back *étatiste* advances, success proved partial: having played a leading role in the wartime economy, governments afterwards found it tempting to play an activist economic role partly because democratic electorates now demanded as much from their political leaders. This new situation, moreover, undermined efforts to reorder the international economic system along pre-war lines. Before 1914 the self-regulating aspects of the system, notably the gold standard, rested on the independence of monetary policy from domestic political pressures. With this independence increasingly a relic of the past, financial disturbances, lacking a self-stabilizing mechanism, could easily transform themselves into crises. And crises, in turn, increased the pressure on national governments to intervene in economic matters.

Two factors during the 1930s further reinforced the interventionist tendencies of governments. One was the Great Depression. The deepening economic crisis prompted governments to experiment with various policies aimed at revitalizing the economy and alleviating hardship and suffering. After an initial period of deflationary policies, governments relaxed financial orthodoxy, increasing spending on public works and infrastructure projects in order to reflate the economy. More generally, during the 1930s proposals for rational economic planning came into vogue. Originally limited largely to socialists and trade unionists, support for planning grew to encompass much of the political centre and left.[20] By mid-decade another factor strengthened arguments for government intervention: the needs of rearmament. Bent on domination and conquest, the Nazi regime from its inception adopted an activist economic programme to boost arms production, which included controls on foreign exchange, wages and prices, investment, labour mobility, foreign commerce, and scarce raw materials.[21] Forced to respond, the French in 1936 nationalized their aircraft industry; two years later the British government abandoned 'business as usual' and the principle that rearmament should not interfere with the country's normal economic activity.[22] Overall, the urgent needs of rearmament prompted countries to embrace unorthodox economic practices whose features included a prominent part assigned to the state.

Resort to unorthodox economic practices greatly complicated the task of military planners by undermining the bases of economic analysis. Assessing a country's economic strength, a key component of its war-making ability, became increasingly difficult. Previously, an analyst could confidently have predicted that unorthodox methods – deficit financing, economic controls of various kinds, trade by barter, and other forms of state intervention – spelt economic ruin for those countries foolish enough to adopt them. At a time of increased state activity in the economy, however, the definition of sound economics grew far less certain as hitherto solid reference points crumbled. For several years after 1933, foreign observers had warned that Germany's flouting of orthodox economics would end in disaster. Yet by the end of the decade the same observers were less confident. Indeed, British and French assessments of the German economy in 1938–39 suggested that the regime's economic methods, combined with its 'authoritarian' political practices, strengthened rather than weakened Germany.[23] But even more important than shifting assessments is the underlying uncertainty that they reveal about Germany's economic strength. Paradoxically, the importance of economic strength in an age of total war stood in inverse relation to the ability of planners to assess this factor.

In addition to its geo-strategic and economic consequences, the Great War profoundly affected politics at both the international and national levels. Somewhat ironically, the need to reconstruct the international order after four years of death and destruction provided an opportunity to strengthen international solidarity. During the Paris Peace Conference, the leaders of the Big Four (the United States, France, Britain, and Italy) worked closely together. Although the defeated nations, principally Germany and revolutionary Russia, were excluded, Big Four cooperation represented a concert-type arrangement that might in time be expanded to include new members. The real innovation in international politics, however, was the creation of the League of Nations whose covenant was embedded in the different peace treaties themselves. Although owing much to the inspiration of Wilson, the League enjoyed important support among public and political opinion on both sides of the Atlantic.[24] To be sure, experienced statesmen and diplomats viewed sceptically the principle of 'collective security'; at the same time, the League's enforcement capabilities were only as strong as the will of its leading members, which excluded the United States – and initially the defeated states. Still, even the most hard-bitten *Realpolitiker* recognized that the League represented a new factor in international politics. Unlike before, there now existed a forum for the peaceful resolution of disputes as well as for the development of norms and procedures whose violation by nations entailed some political costs both at home and abroad.[25]

Hopes for international political cooperation, symbolized by the League, appeared well founded during the 1920s. The Dawes Plan on reparations and the Locarno accords paved the way for Germany's entry into the League in 1926, and for the remainder of the decade German, British and French leaders met regularly in Geneva, prompting journalists to speak favourably of a 'spirit of Locarno'. The League encouraged international cooperation in realms such as the international arms trade, finance, and trade; outside the League, leaders of the European steel industry, prodded by their national governments, formed the International Steel Entente in 1926 – a harbinger of the post-1945 European Coal and Steel Community, itself the precursor to a larger project of European economic and political integration.[26] Unfortunately, this growing cooperation did not survive the political and economic upheavals of the 1930s. The League's inability to respond effectively to Japanese, Italian, and German challenges fatally discredited the institution. Nothing better demonstrated the bankruptcy of collective security than the Munich Conference in September 1938, called to settle the escalating Czech crisis. Having excluded the Soviet Union from the deliberations, British and French leaders agreed to the transfer of the Sudetenland to Germany, blatantly ignoring Prague's protests. Afterwards, disunity between Paris, London and Moscow continued to undermine efforts to forge a combined response to the 'Fascist Challenge'.[27]

The changing nature of international politics during the interwar period provided yet another source of uncertainty for military planners. Before 1914, planners were confident that they understood the 'rules of the game'. Alliances and armaments, arms racing and balancing, crisis politics and, in the last resort, war were the accepted means by which states safeguarded and enhanced their security. After 1918 things were far less clear. New organizations, most notably the League, and developing norms of state behaviour, particularly those against aggressive war, had to be considered. Yet it was unclear how much faith should be placed in these fledgling institutions. Would collective security prove viable or would it handicap states in providing for their own security? Even during the 1930s, which represented something of a reversion to pre-1914 power politics, uncertainty remained a factor. Despite the League's increasing marginalization, norms of peaceful behaviour never completely vanished. Governments thus found it necessary to sell foreign policies, especially those that risked or involved war, to their domestic publics in terms of self-defence and justice – an imperative that even the Nazi regime respected. Uncertainty necessarily resulted since it was difficult to know in advance what influence fledgling norms against aggressive war would have on one's own government or on that of others.[28]

Domestic political developments also produced uncertainty. Convinced that democracies were inherently peaceful, Wilson viewed the spread of democratic regimes as a guarantee of the League's ultimate success in preventing wars. In this regard, the democratic wave following the Great War fostered optimism as newly created or independent states in Central and Eastern Europe adopted democratic constitutions. Especially promising was the advent of the Weimar Republic. With Germany a democracy, European politics would no longer be disrupted by the aggressive designs of an autocratic–militarist regime. But if democracy appeared ascendant in Europe during the 1920s, the situation changed radically during the 1930s. Economic depression exacerbated domestic divisions in many states, producing an unprecedented radicalization of politics often at the expense of democracy. One beneficiary was Soviet communism, which in the wake of capitalism's apparent failure appealed to large sections of the political centre and left who were often ignorant of actual conditions inside the Soviet Union.[29] Various forms of authoritarianism and fascism also attracted growing numbers. Across Europe, disgruntled politicians from the right and left formed new parties and movements that denounced democracy for its moderation, mediocrity, materialism and individualism. They preached instead the virtues of decisive action, even violence, group identity, and unity under an authoritarian and charismatic leader. During the interwar period, central and eastern European countries fell increasingly under the rule of authoritarian, although not necessarily fascist, rulers.[30]

The most portentous domestic political developments occurred within the future Axis powers. In Japan the military and its supporters, having gained the political upper hand, led the country into a series of wars on the Asian mainland. In Italy Mussolini's fascist regime shed its earlier prudence and in 1935 attacked Abyssinia, the first step in the creation of a Mediterranean empire. Even more disturbing was the Nazi seizure of power in Germany. Inspired by Hitler's racist, social Darwinist worldview, the Nazi regime set out by intimidation and conquest to remake Germany, Europe, and perhaps the world. The regime's determination to succeed, when harnessed to Germany's immense military and industrial potential, represented a revolutionary development that eliminated all hope for peaceful accommodation and cooperation with other countries. In Nazi Germany, and perhaps Fascist Italy, the domestic and foreign policy realms were mutually dependent: radical policies at home aimed at strengthening Germany for the upcoming European war that would not only revolutionize international politics, but also further radicalize domestic politics. The result would be a radicalizing dynamic of revolution and war.[31]

The radicalization of domestic politics heightened the uncertainty attached to military planning. Analysing the future policies of regimes based on new ideologies such as communism, fascism, and Nazism, posed unprecedented challenges. It was impossible to determine in advance the extent to which policies would be driven by ideological motives – whether world revolution or racial conquest. The vast extent and horrifying nature of Nazi Germany's ambitions might be clear after the fact, but this was not the case for most observers before 1939. Many intelligent people believed that Hitler's Germany, while certainly unpleasant and difficult, could be induced to cooperate peacefully with other countries. Only time proved them wrong. Similarly, the question of allying with the Soviet Union provoked intense debate in France and Britain as well as Germany because there was no obvious answer to the question of whether Moscow could be trusted. That these questions were themselves deeply politicized further hindered sober reflection. The overall result was a remarkable amount of uncertainty, which has to be kept in mind when examining the policy choices of different countries during the 1930s.

In addition to geo-strategic, economic and political factors, interwar planners also considered military factors. At the broadest level, the key question concerned the nature of future war. Not surprisingly, the Great War served as a model. Future wars would be total wars pitting nations and societies against one another; victory would go to the side that mobilized its resources in the fastest, most efficient, and comprehensive manner. Fielding massive armies was important but so too was equipping them with modern *matériel* and maintaining political support behind the war effort.[32] But if planners were confident about the broad contours of a future war, a great deal of uncertainty remained, especially when in the 1930s general staffs turned from broad conceptual planning to concrete preparations for a possible war. Translating the theory (or grand strategy) of total war into practice proved fraught with difficulties. For example, when the French began discussing the legal framework for total war, it soon became clear that the proposed legislation raised several contentious issues, including the role of women and the relationship of private industry to the state.[33] That the French Parliament ultimately contented itself with vague generalities highlights not only the weakness of the Third Republic's institutions but also the difficulties inherent in defining total war. The fact that so much of the effort and so many of the details lay beyond the immediate control of military planners only complicated their task.

Considerable uncertainty also surrounded the question of how a future war would be fought and, in particular, the role of the different services. With the exception of the British, interwar planners expected armies to be the dominant service, much as they had been in 1914–18. At the same time, however, army staffs during the 1920s faced a situation of declining resources stemming from overall budgetary cuts and from intense competition from other services, notably air forces. Planning was rendered still more difficult by the onus placed on waging a victorious war in such a way as to avoid human losses on the scale of 1914–18. How to reconcile these two imperatives was unclear. General staffs could place greater stress on the defensive, heeding the lesson that 'fire kills'; or they might emphasize the offensive, drawing attention to the successes of German and Allied offensives in 1918. Although army staffs debated these choices during the 1920s, the debate was somewhat artificial since the likelihood of great power war appeared distant.[34] While the growing possibility of war in the 1930s concentrated the minds of army staffs, it did not necessarily reduce uncertainty. Debates about the merits of defence over offence gave way to complex discussions about levels of implementation – tactical, operational, and strategic – as well as about the relationship between levels. The development of new weapons, such as the tank, and increased capabilities, notably motorization and communication, complicated matters still further. Integrating these developments into existing thinking and practice raised troublesome questions about the nature of the battlefield and about the relative advantages of defence and offence. At the same time, successive crises left army staffs in a quasi-permanent state of expectation, effectively limiting their ability to assess options. Subject to a bewildering array of events and developments, army staffs in the 1930s faced the prospect of war with the ground literally shifting beneath them.[35]

Uncertainty also weighed heavily on air forces, which emerged as independent services only in the interwar period. Fledgling air force staffs spent much of the 1920s fighting for survival and, not surprisingly, this situation coloured their outlook. Determined to resist the inglorious role of providing support for army (and naval) operations, air forces promoted strategic bombing – a proposal that offered them the starring role in a future war and promised to render their competitor services obsolete. If air bombardment could achieve victory by crippling a belligerent's home front, what need was there for armies and navies? That the vision far outran the means available did little to undermine the infatuation of air force staffs with strategic bombing in the 1920s. In the following decade, however, strategic bombing came increasingly into question. Their ambitions notwithstanding, air force staffs could not ignore completely the demands of other services, especially as the prospect of another war loomed ever larger. Pulled in different directions by the competing roles of battlefield support and strategic bombing (as well as strategic air defence), air force staffs committed themselves fully to neither with the result that both suffered.[36] Equally important, the approach of war made it increasingly difficult to ignore the gap between the theory of strategic bombing and existing capabilities. Recognizing realities, the German air force in 1937 effectively abandoned strategic bombing by cancelling the four-engine bomber. By then growing uncertainty had invaded thinking and practice in most air forces with the result that few planners could confidently predict the role that airpower would play in a future war.[37]

Uncertainty was also a factor for interwar navies. On the one hand, naval planners appeared relatively confident about the nature of future war. Ignoring the experience of the Great War, in which submarine warfare dominated, after 1918 naval staffs recommitted themselves to big-gun capital ships and decisive fleet battles. On the other hand, several factors undermined this apparent confidence. One factor was the effect of financial shortages and naval arms limitation agreements, most notably the 1922 Washington and 1930 London treaties. During the 1920s, naval staffs shelved expansion programmes, terminated on-going construction, and in some cases decommissioned warships, thereby creating a gulf between visions of naval warfare and available resources. While financial and political constraints weakened during the 1930s as navies embarked on impressive construction programmes, sparking naval arms races in the Mediterranean and the Pacific, navies faced mounting uncertainties regarding doctrine. Naval staffs remained focused on capital ships and fleet engagements, downplaying less glamorous tasks such as commerce raiding, blockade activities, and submarine warfare. Nevertheless, navies could not entirely ignore these facets of naval warfare, especially at a time when economic strength was viewed as vital to national power. As a result, naval staffs, like their air force counterparts, were increasingly uncertain about their future wartime roles and, in particular, about the balance to draw between traditional fleet encounters and more economically oriented tasks.[38] That naval war planners were often out of step with other services in the identification of threats further increased uncertainty. Thus, if the British navy looked to Japan as its principal enemy, the army focused on the empire and, to a lesser extent, Europe. Similarly, the Japanese navy concentrated on the United States and the Japanese army on Asian enemies, while the American navy focused on Japan far more than did the American army.[39]

Greater inter-service cooperation might have alleviated this problem. However, aside from Britain, where the Committee of Imperial Defence and its various sub-committees fostered a measure of cooperation, the military services in most countries worked in isolation from each other with predictably unfortunate results. Each service undertook strategic planning, operational and doctrinal development, and weapons acquisition largely in a vacuum. Given the nature of modern war, which demanded inter-service and inter-arms cooperation, this represented a serious weakness. Equally to the point of this chapter, service isolation exacerbated the uncertainty confronting planners as they sought to understand the nature of future war. The lack of institutionalized inter-service cooperation was nowhere more evident than in the realm of intelligence. The individual military services of each leading power possessed their own intelligence services but, aside from the creation by the British of a Joint Intelligence Committee on the eve of war, there existed no mechanism to coordinate the various intelligence activities within a nation. This dispersal of effort reinforced the pre-existing tendency of intelligence bureaus to focus on narrow military subjects, especially order-of-battle information.[40] The problem, of course, was that the all-encompassing nature of modern war demanded a more comprehensive understanding of national power than staff officers alone could provide.

Finally, the rapid pace of technological change in the military field constituted yet another factor contributing to the uncertainty of interwar military planners. The Great War saw the introduction of new or fledgling weapons such as the tank and the airplane. Although the wartime application of these weapons helped to overcome initial scepticism concerning their usefulness, they remained in the early stages of technological development well into the 1920s. However, as Richard Overy writes, the 'scientific threshold' accelerated during the 1930s as weapons systems made great technological strides. Airplanes, once flimsy wooden contraptions with limited range and carrying power, became modern single-wing, metallic machines with seemingly boundless capabilities. By the end of the decade, British and German scientists were working on jet engines. Tanks also became more powerful, faster, durable and lethal. Elsewhere, the British, the Americans, and the Germans all developed radar, whose potential for detection and target acquisition promised to alter profoundly the nature of warfare.[41] Military planners faced the formidable task of grasping technological change whose rapidity left little time for reflection. Integrating change also proved daunting. Frequent revisions to agreed-upon designs infuriated industrialists and hampered the onset of mass production. Equally worrisome, in a period of heightening international tensions, rapid technological change meant that countries might be saddled with obsolescent weapons if they misjudged the timing of war – as happened to the Soviet Union. Having begun large-scale production of weapons in the mid-1930s, the Soviets found themselves at a decided disadvantage in 1939.[42] Given the inherent vagaries of the international situation, however, correct choices depended on luck as much as on foresight.

II

This chapter has highlighted some of the national and international factors that complicated the task of interwar military planners. The overall effect of geo-strategic, economic, political, and military developments, many of them a legacy of the Great War, was to increase uncertainty, thereby undermining the ability of planners to pierce through the fog of peace. One might object that uncertainty always exists and that the inter-war years are no different from other peacetime periods. While there is some truth to this, uncertainty appears to have been especially prevalent between the two world wars due to the combined effects of developments in several realms. The Great War, a titanic four-year struggle pitting nations and societies against each other, profoundly upset reigning national and international orders. Change on such a scope necessarily bred uncertainty and confusion. In this regard, the inter-war period resembles the present day even if the threat of international terrorism was less evident then than now. The end of the Cold War, the collapse of the Soviet Union and its empire, the newly found independence of some states and the violent break-up of others, the hesitant forward march of the European Union, the emergence of the United States as the sole 'hyper-power', the advance of economic and financial globalization, the retreat of the state from national economies, the debate concerning the United Nations' proper role, the unsteady spread of democratic practices (not least in Russia), and the contested meanings of RMAs, together suggest that contemporary planners labour in a world fraught with uncertainty, much like their predecessors after 1919. Given the similarities between the two periods, it is worth examining more closely how earlier planners coped with relatively high degrees of uncertainty.

The following two chapters do just this by providing case studies of how particular groups of planners, those in the British air force and in the American navy, went about preparing their services for a possible, if not likely, war. While John Ferris probes the relationship between the evolution of theory, strategy, doctrine, and capabilities in the context of an RMA (the rapid development of air power), Andrew Krepinevich discusses the US navy's transformation from a battleship-dominated force to a carrier-based one. Both scholars, however, emphasize the complex and often contingent nature of developments that involved the inter-play of multiple factors, many of them beyond the control of individual services, and uncertain time horizons. Planners accordingly had to be flexible, imaginative and persistent in their efforts. These qualities are as indispensable now as they were then both to ensure that military services are not caught completely off-guard in a future war and to allow them to react quickly to unexpected situations given the inevitable gap between visions of the future and the future itself.

Notes

1 For economic figures, see Paul Kennedy, *The Rise and Fall of the Great Powers: Economic Change and Military Conflict from 1500 to 2000* (London: Unwin Hyman, 1988), pp. 280, 299; and Paul Bairoch, *Victoires et déboires*, vol. III, (Paris: Gallimard, 1997), pp. 21–24, 416–20.
2 See the special issue of the *International History Review*, vol. 13, no. 4, 1991 and especially B.J.C. McKercher, '"Our Most Dangerous Enemy": Great Britain Pre-Eminent in the 1930s', pp. 751–83; and *idem.*, *Transition of Power: Britain's Loss of Global Pre-Eminence to the United States, 1930–1945* (Cambridge: Cambridge University Press, 1999). Also see David Reynolds, *Britannia Overruled: British Policy and World Power in the Twentieth Century* (London: Longman, 2000), pp. 4–35.
3 Paul Kennedy, 'The First World War and the International Power System' in Steven E. Miller, ed., *Military Strategy and the Origins of the First World War* (Princeton, NJ: Princeton University Press, 1985), pp. 7–26.
4 Some of the earliest revisionist work challenging the notion of isolationism came from American scholars, and from New Left historians in particular, who sought to demonstrate the influence of economic factors on American foreign policy. The classic work is William Appleman Williams, *The Tragedy of American Diplomacy* (New York: Dell, 1962), pp. 118–61. Also see Melvyn Leffler, *The Elusive Quest: America's Pursuit of European Stability and French Security, 1919–1933* (Chapel Hill, NC: University of North Carolina Press, 1979).
5 For the financial diplomacy, see Stephen A. Schuker, *The End of French Predominance in Europe: The Financial Crisis of 1924 and the Adoption of the Dawes Plan* (Chapel Hill, NC: University of North Carolina Press, 1976); Denise Artaud, *La Question des dettes interalliées et la reconstruction de l'Europe (1917–1929)* (Lille: Université de Lille III, 1978); and Bruce Kent, *The Spoils of*

War: The Politics, Economics, and Diplomacy of Reparations, 1918–1932 (Oxford: Oxford University Press, 1989).

6 For good accounts of this period see David M. Kennedy, *Freedom from Fear: The American People in Depression and War, 1929–1945* (Oxford: Oxford University Press, 1999), pp. 387–422; and Robert Dallek, *Franklin D. Roosevelt and American Foreign Policy, 1932–1945* (Oxford: Oxford University Press, 1979).

7 Gerhard L. Weinberg, *World in the Balance: Behind the Scenes of World War II* (Hanover, NH: University Press of New England, 1981), pp. 53–95.

8 See the relevant chapters in Michael Hogan, ed., *Paths to Power: The Historiography of American Foreign Relations to 1941* (Cambridge: Cambridge University Press, 2000), pp. 176–295.

9 Akira Iriye, *After Imperialism: The Search for a New Order in the Far East, 1921–1931* (Cambridge, MA: Harvard University Press, 1965), *passim*.

10 Ikuhiko Hata, 'Continental Expansion' in Peter Duus, ed., *The Cambridge History of Japan, vol. 6, The Twentieth Century* (Cambridge: Cambridge University Press, 1988), pp. 280–85.

11 Akira Iriye, *The Origins of the Second World War in Asia and the Pacific* (London: Longman, 1987).

12 For the British policy, see Paul Haggie, *Britannia at Bay: The Defence of the British Empire Against Japan 1931–1941* (Oxford: Oxford University Press, 1981); and Anthony Best, *Britain, Japan and Pearl Harbor: Avoiding War in East Asia, 1936–41* (London: Routledge, 1995).

13 For comparative national resources, see Kennedy, *The Rise and Fall of the Great Powers*, pp. 291–320. For French policy, also see Anthony Adamthwaite, *Grandeur and Misery: France's Bid for Power in Europe, 1914–1940* (New York: Arnold, 1995).

14 For a revisionist argument concerning the First World War, see Niall Ferguson, *The Pity of War* (London: Penguin, 1998). For arguments concerning the Second World War, see John Charmley, *Churchill, The End of Glory: A Political Biography* (London: Hodder & Stoughton, 1993). An effective response to Charmley is in David Reynolds, 'Churchill the Appeaser? Between Hitler and Stalin in World War Two' in Michael Dockrill and B.J.C. McKercher, eds, *Diplomacy and World Power: Studies in British Foreign Policy, 1890–1950* (Cambridge: Cambridge University Press, 1996), pp. 197–220.

15 On this region, see Iván T. Berend, *The Crisis Zone of Europe: An Interpretation of East-Central European History in the First Half of the Twentieth Century* (Cambridge: Cambridge University Press, 1986); David E. Kaiser, *Economic Diplomacy and the Origins of the Second World War: Germany, Britain, France, and Eastern Europe* (Princeton, NJ: Princeton University Press, 1980); and Piotr S. Wandycz, *The Twilight of French Eastern Alliances, 1926–1936: French–Czechoslovak–Polish Relations from Locarno to the Remilitarization of the Rhineland* (Princeton, NJ: Princeton University Press, 1988).

16 On Soviet policy, see Jon Jacobson, *When the Soviet Union Entered World Politics* (Berkeley, CA: University of California Press, 1994); and Jonathan Haslam, *The Soviet Union and the Struggle for Collective Security in Europe, 1933–1939* (London: Macmillan, 1984).

17 For trade flows, see Angus Maddison, *L'économie mondiale 1820–1992: analyses et statistiques* (Paris: OCDE, 1995), pp. 252–53; for capital flows, see A.G. Kenwood and A.L Lougheed, *The Growth of the International Economy, 1820–1980* (London: Allen & Unwin, 1983), pp. 39–56.

18 John Gerard Ruggie, 'International Regimes, Transactions, and Change: Embedded Liberalism in the Postwar Economic Order' in *International Organization*, vol. 36, no. 2, 1982, pp. 379–415; and Barry Eichengreen, *Globalizing*

155

Capitalism: A History of the International Monetary System (Princeton, NJ: Princeton University Press, 1996), pp. 25–44.

19 The best study remains Gerald D. Feldman, *Army, Industry and Labor in Germany 1914–1918* (Princeton, NJ: Princeton University Press, 1966). Also see Hew Strachan, 'Economic Mobilization' in Strachan, *World War I: A History* (Oxford: Oxford University Press, 1998), pp. 135–48.

20 See Daniel Ritschel, *The Politics of Planning: The Debate on Economic Planning in Britain in the 1930s* (Oxford: Oxford University Press, 1997); Richard F. Kuisel, *Capitalism and the State in Modern France: Renovation and Economic Management in the Twentieth Century* (Cambridge: Cambridge University Press, 1981), pp. 93–127; and Alan Brinkley, *The End of Reform: New Deal Liberalism in Recession and War* (New York: Alfred A. Knopf, 1995).

21 Richard Overy, *War and Economy in the Third Reich* (Oxford: Oxford University Press, 1994); and Wilhelm Deist *et al.*, *Germany and the Second World War*, vol. 1 (Oxford: Oxford University Press, 1990), pp. 157–372.

22 For the French, see Herrick Chapman, *State Capitalism and Working-Class Radicalism in the French Aircraft Industry* (Berkeley, CA: University of California Press, 1991), pp. 101–47. For the British, see Robert Paul Shay, *British Rearmament in the Thirties: Politics and Profits* (Princeton, NJ: Princeton University Press, 1977).

23 To be sure, the actual state of Germany's war economy on the eve of war remains a subject of intense debate. For good starting points, see Overy, *War and Economy in the Third Reich*; and Timothy Mason, *Social Policy in the Third Reich: The Working Class and the 'National Community'* (Providence, RI: Berghahn, 1993). For French and British assessments, see Talbot Imlay, 'Allied Economic Intelligence and Strategy during the "Phony War"' in *Intelligence and National Security*, vol. 13, no. 4, 1998, pp. 107–32.

24 Donald S. Birn, *The League of Nations Union, 1918–1945* (Oxford: Oxford University Press, 1981); and Marvin Swartz, *The Union of Democratic Control in British Politics During the First World War* (Oxford: Oxford University Press, 1971).

25 Charles Maier, 'International Associationalism: The Social and Political Premises of Peacemaking after 1917 and 1945' in Paul Kennedy and William I Hitchcock, eds, *From War to Peace: Altered Strategic Landscapes in the Twentieth Century* (New Haven, CT: Yale University Press, 2000), pp. 36–52. Also see the special issue of *Relations Internationales*, no. 75, 1993, which is on the League.

26 For the arms trade, see David R. Stone, 'Imperialism and Sovereignty: The League of Nations' Drive to Control the Global Arms Trade' in *Journal of Contemporary History*, vol. 35, no. 2, 2000, pp. 213–20. For economic cooperation, see Éric Brussière, 'L'organisation économique de la SDN et la naissance du régionalisme économique' in *Relations Internationales*, no. 75, 1993, pp. 301–13. For the steel *entente*, see John Gillingham, *Coal, Steel, and the Rebirth of Europe, 1945–1955: The Germans and the French from Ruhr Conflict to Economic Community* (Cambridge: Cambridge University Press, 1991).

27 For an account of the run-up to war, see D.C. Watt, *How War Came:The Immediate Origins of the Second World War, 1938–1939* (London: Heinemann, 1989).

28 For a discussion of norms, see Martti Koskenniemi, *The Gentle Civilizer of Nations: The Rise and Fall of International Law, 1870–1960* (Cambridge: Cambridge University Press, 2002).

29 On the appeal of Soviet communism, see David Caute, *The Fellow Travelers: Intellectual Friends of Communism* (New Haven, CT: Yale University Press,

1988); and Sophie Cœuré, *La grande lueur à l'est: les Français et l'Union sovié-tique, 1917–1939* (Paris: Seuil, 1999).

30 On the inter-war 'crisis of democracy,' see Mark Mazower, *Dark Continent: Europe's Twentieth Century* (New York: Alfred A. Knopf, 1999), pp. 3–137; and T. Iván Berend, *Decades of Crisis: Central and Eastern Europe Before World War II* (Berkeley, CA: University of California Press, 1998).

31 For this dynamic, see MacGregor Knox, 'Conquest, Foreign and Domestic, in Fascist Italy and Nazi Germany' in *Journal of Modern History*, vol. 56, no. 1, 1986, pp. 1–57.

32 See Michael Howard, *War in European Society* (Oxford: Oxford University Press, 1976), pp. 112–15; and Alan Milward, *War, Economy and Society, 1939–1945* (Berkeley, CA: University of California Press, 1977), pp. 1–54.

33 On the gap between theory and practice, see Eugenia C. Kiesling, *Arming Against Hitler: France and the Limits of Military Planning* (Lawrence, KS: University Press of Kansas, 1996), pp. 1–40. Also see Roger Chickering, 'Total War: The Use and Abuse of a Concept' in Manfred F. Boemke, Roger Chickering and Stig Förster, eds, *Anticipating Total War: The German and American Experiences, 1871–1914* (Cambridge: Cambridge University Press, 1999), pp. 13–28.

34 On the French, see Judith M. Hughes, *To the Maginot Line: The Politics of French Military Preparation in the 1920s* (Cambridge, MA: Harvard University Press, 1971); and Elizabeth Kier, *Imagining War: French and British Military Doctrine between the Wars* (Princeton, NJ: Princeton University Press, 1997). For the Germans, see Gaines Post Jr., *The Civil–Military Fabric of Weimar Foreign Policy* (Princeton, NJ: Princeton University Press, 1973); and James S. Corum, *The Roots of Blitzkrieg: Hans von Seeckt and the German Military Reform* (Lawrence, KS: University Press of Kansas, 1992).

35 Valuable studies include J.P. Harris, *Men, Ideas and Tanks: British Military Thought and Armoured Forces, 1903–1939* (Manchester: Manchester University Press, 1995); Robert A. Doughty, *The Seeds of Disaster: The Development of French Army Doctrine, 1919–1939* (Hamden, CT: Archon Books, 1985); Deist, *Germany and the Second World War*, vol. 1; Karl-Heinz Frieser, *Blitzkrieg-Legende: der Westfeldzug 1940* (Munich: R. Oldenbourg, 1995); MacGregor Knox, *Hitler's Italian Allies: Royal Armed Forces, Fascist Regime, and the War of 1940–43* (Cambridge: Cambridge University Press, 2000); and Mary R. Habeck, *Storm of Steel: The Development of Armor Doctrine in Germany and the Soviet Union, 1919–1939* (Ithaca, NY: Cornell University Press, 2003).

36 See Richard Overy, *The Air War, 1939–1945* (London: Europa, 1980); Williamson Murray, *Strategy for Defeat: The Luftwaffe, 1933–1945* (Maxwell Air Force Base: Air University Press, 1983); Malcolm Smith, *British Air Strategy Between the Wars* (Oxford: Oxford University Press, 1984); Patrick Facon, *L'Armée de l'air dans la tourmente: la bataille de France, 1939–1940* (Paris: Economica, 1997); Michael S. Sherry, *The Rise of American Air Power: The Creation of Armageddon* (New Haven, CT: Yale University Press, 1987); and John Ferris' chapter in this volume.

37 See Tami Davis Biddle, *Rhetoric and Reality in Air Warfare: The Evolution of British and American Ideas about Strategic Bombing, 1914–1945* (Princeton, NJ: Princeton University Press, 2002).

38 Holger Herwig, 'Innovation Ignored: The Submarine Problem – Germany, Britain, and the United States, 1919–39' in W. Murray and A.R. Millett, eds, *Military Innovation in the Interwar Period* (Cambridge: Cambridge University Press, 1996), pp. 227–64.

39 See especially Reynolds M. Salerno, *March to the Oceans: The Mediterranean Origins of an Imperial War* (Ithaca, NY: Cornell University Press, 2002).

40 For intelligence, see Ernest May, ed., *Knowing One's Enemies: Intelligence Assessments Before World War II* (Princeton, NJ: Princeton University Press, 1984), pp. 503–42; and Williamson Murray and Allan R. Millett, eds, *Calculations: Net Assessment and the Coming of World War II* (New York: Free Press, 1992).

41 Richard Overy, 'Warfare in Europe Since 1918' in T.C.W. Blanning, ed., *The Oxford History of Modern Europe* (Oxford: Oxford University Press, 2000), p. 221. Also see the essays in Murray and Millett, eds, *Military Innovation in the Interwar Period*; and Stephen Peter Rosen, *Winning the Next War: Innovation and the Modern Military* (Ithaca, NY: Cornell University Press, 1991).

42 Earl F. Ziemke, 'The Soviet Armed Forces in the Interwar Period' in Allan R. Millett and Williamson Murray, eds, *Military Effectiveness*, Volume 1, *The First World War* (Boston: Allen & Unwin, 1988), p. 10; and David M. Glantz and Jonathan M. House, *When Titans Clashed: How the Red Army Stopped Hitler* (Lawrence, KS: University Press of Kansas, 1995).

9

CATCHING THE WAVE

The RAF Pursues a RMA, 1918–39

John Ferris

The policy of the Royal Air Force (RAF) between 1918–39 is usually read in a simplistic way. Assumptions about doctrine create presumptions about action – thus scholars argue that ideas on strategic bombing shaped all RAF policies and led straight toward specific forms of force structure and war planning. These views are false. RAF thinking about strategic bombing was not a 'doctrine,' with a close relationship between ideas, policies, strategies and forces – rather, it was a particular theory regarding how bombing would affect the will and economies of peoples, contained within a greater theory that airpower was producing a revolution in military affairs (RMA).[1] Granted, RAF ideas about bombing were flawed. Had they dictated its shape, the RAF would have been a bad service, but the relationship between ideas and force structures was not that simple. During the RAF's expansion programs of 1922–25 and 1936–39, an institution which wanted to establish a strategic bombing force instead created a fighter defense system, because this was faster and cheaper to build. The RAF combined a theory of strategic bombing with an air force centered on fighter defense, while an institution focused on strategic air warfare devoted as much of its attention toward replacing soldiers or warships in conventional roles. In theory, the RAF disparaged air interdiction or counter-force operations; in practice, major air exercises tested precisely these matters. Ideas shaped RAF policy, but more loosely than often is assumed. Two ideas were predominant: strategic bombing and a 'revolution in military affairs' (RMA). These ideas led in many, and often contradictory, directions.

The RAF of the inter-war years is often seen as impoverished and small compared to international rivals and its sister services, weaknesses explained by reference to Treasury control over military spending and the 'ten year rule' – the government's decision of August 1919 that Britain should not fund military programs which were needed simply to fight a major war which would occur before 1929. These alleged weaknesses and their causes have been much exaggerated.[2] The 'ten year rule,' for example, was an ambiguous and insignificant matter. It was one of a loose body of strategic principles accepted by the government, including an insistence that Britain concentrate its military resources on developing 'mechanical devices' to replace manpower in imperial defense ('substitution'), and on maintaining forces which could deter rivals in the short term or fight a major war in the middle term. These principles were a reasonable basis for strategic policy. None, including the 'ten year rule,' precluded effective planning or rearmament programs.[3] They were tailor made for the RAF; indeed, it was the first to formulate them. In late 1918 the Air Ministry wanted post-war Britain to maintain a large RAF as its first line of defense. It believed that during the foreseeable future, the world would be peaceful and Britain secure. Moreover, the RAF also believed it could get the funding needed to pursue its visions only if the Cabinet did not treat it in a 'parochial fashion,' but instead subsidized it at the expense of the Army and Royal Navy (RN). So to further this end, the Chief of the Air Staff (CAS), Frederick Sykes, urged the Cabinet to rest defense policy on an assumption like that of the 'ten year rule,' that 'it seems improbable that for some years there will be a great war between first-class powers.'[4] Though the RAF did not influence the government's strategic decisions of August 1919, it supported all the principles formulated at that time and already was on a 'ten year rule' imposed by the Air Minister, Winston Churchill.[5] These principles did much good to the RAF between 1919–34, helping it to develop an expensive rearmament program which treated other great powers as threats, and to seize roles from the older services which boosted RAF strength and finances.

Limitations of finance and decisions of grand strategy did affect British military policy, yet the RAF was in a fortunate situation. During the inter-war years, Britain invested a remarkable amount of its financial and economic strength, as well as its hopes, in the RAF, with the aim of being great in the air. It did so because politicians and the Treasury consistently regarded that aim as central to British strategy.[6] This was one of the few aims they did pursue consistently. The elaborate system which determined British decisions on strategic issues was weak in the center – the Cabinet and ministers did not normally control these issues, much less than their counterparts had done forty years before, and neither did mechanisms like the Committee for Imperial Defense or the Chiefs of Staff Committee. Individual politicians could dominate these issues and sometimes did so, but the key elements in strategic policy were the departments charged with handling specific tasks. Politics helped to determine strategy: ever fluctuating bureaucratic and political coalitions made a series of loosely connected decisions, which together added up to strategic policy, while departments determined their own aims and sought autonomy to pursue them. Here the RAF was the most successful of the fighting services. Ministers and the Treasury challenged its policy less than those of the Army and the RN, because they thought airpower posed a vital threat to Britain and also suited the principles they favored in defense policy. The RAF was less expensive than the Army and the RN, and its leaders ably exploited political opportunity. Their main aim, to develop air strength for the long term, coincided with the hopes of the Treasury and politicians to reduce defense spending in the short term. All three wished to limit the programs of the Army and the RN, and frequently combined against them. Ministers and officials did not necessarily share orthodox RAF views on strategic bombing, but they only began challenging them in 1937, when the RAF had been so successful that it was becoming the most costly of the fighting services.

The RAF was not always authorized to do everything it wished, but it had remarkable autonomy in formulating its policies and great resources with which to execute them. It had smaller budgets than it wanted, in some years perhaps less than it needed; but still it had much money to play with and usually more than most of its peers. RAF spending fell behind a serious rival only once, Germany between 1935–37. Otherwise, especially after considering arcane accounting procedures (between 1922–32, the Colonial Office, the government of India and the Admiralty provided a large hidden subsidy to the RAF by paying to maintain 25 per cent of its squadrons), Britain usually allocated as much money for airpower as any other state and more than most.[7] The RAF also did well compared to its fellow services. From 1922 to 1939, even during the lean years of 1929–34, the RAF grew steadily in estimates and strength, whereas the Army was hammered between 1922–39 and the RN between 1929–35. By 1926 the RAF had almost half of the Army's level of 'current effective' estimates, the true gauge of financial strength, and more by 1935. RAF strength was always great: it had 28 squadrons in 1922, 70 by 1929 and 135 by 1938. While never the largest air force on earth, quality multiplied its quantity to an unmatched degree, through unusual strength in organization, trained personnel, aircraft reserves, industrial capacity, links with science, and bases for expansion. Between 1918 and 1945, the RAF always ranked among the three most effective air forces on earth, usually second to none, often leader of the pack. None of this is to deny failures in the RAF. Rather the opposite: once it is understood that the service was well funded and controlled its own destinies, its failures must be judged more critically than when they can be excused away by the myth of the poor little RAF.

Compared to their counterparts in the Army and the RN, the RAF's leaders were unusually heterogeneous in origin and homogenous in experience. Their social status was less rarefied, with fewer grandees and more of the middling sort. They drew their sporting metaphors from football, not polo. These men came from many elements of the pre-war Army and colonial forces, and from young men of Britain and the Dominions who entered in 1914–15, all stamped by the Royal Flying Corps (RFC), the air service of the pre-war Army.[8] The older generation had become pilots before 1914, when that was deemed a risky profession, and the younger one in 1914–16, when it was even more so. They joined an exciting service with mixed status, unusual in its use of advanced technology and of officers as warriors – knights of the air who tinkered with engines. They had wide personal experience with the use and command of complex machinery at war, a murderous education on the western front and schooling in the only independent air force in the world. After the war, Army officers with the greatest expertise in technology, gunners and engineers, were off the high road to command – in the RAF, they were master. RAF leaders suffered from social and service insecurity, yet they thought they embodied every English virtue – character and brains: warriors, generals, managers, engineers, mechanics. During the inter-war years, no military service on earth had a higher quality of leadership. The older generation of these airmen, the CASs who carried the RAF from 1917 to 1937, were able by any standard. Frederick Sykes was a key figure in the development of airpower theory, Hugh Trenchard a brilliant politician and inspiring leader, John and Geoffrey Salmond and Charles Ellington all understood the possibilities of airpower well. The younger generation contained officers of outstanding ability like Charles Portal, Arthur Harris, and Hugh Dowding.[9]

During the inter-war years, RAF officers were few in number, shared remarkably similar professional backgrounds, and formulated policy in a consensual fashion, where junior officers had the opportunity to influence high policy – a pattern unlike those in the Army and the RN and in most contemporary military institutions. In 1923-24, for example, major conferences between all leading staff and operational commanders in Britain were called to formulate air doctrine and define the shape of the Home Defence Air Force (HDAF), the world's first strategic air force. Despite his reputation for intolerance, Trenchard abandoned his preferences on key issues, like the relative number of fighter versus bomber squadrons, when his subordinates rejected them.[10] In 1924, when the RAF considered major changes in the organization of carrier-borne aviation, it immediately solicited the views not just of all commanding officers but also of every naval aviation pilot![11] Again, RAF exercises were open-ended – the rules were not rigged, either side could lose, and usually air defense was judged to have done well against strategic bombers, contrary to the theory favored by the institution.[12]

RAF policy did not stem from analysis of foreign air activities or of the strength needed to fight specific wars – instead, a theory of air warfare preceded policy formation and threat assessment. This is not surprising. The RAF was created in 1917 precisely to pursue an RMA, though characteristically without being given the resources to do so. Officers, extrapolating from trends in technology and airpower, held *a priori* that an RMA was transforming power and war. As Sykes wrote in 1918,

> In future the existence of any nation will depend primarily upon its Air Power. . . . The Royal Air Force will in future be the first line of defense and offense of the British Empire. It is to her Air Fleet that

Britain must look to safeguard herself and her Dominions. Aviation enables us to think and act in the third dimension. In peace, the nation or nations which exploit this most fully will gain great advantages over those still thinking in two. In war the nation which is already in possession of this facility will obtain a transcendental if not decisive lead.

Air forces would strike 'the armies and navies of the opponent, his population as a whole, his national morale, and his industries, without which he cannot wage war,' and it would win independent of support from the other services.[13]

Such ideas echoed in RAF policy for thirty years. Before and during the Second World War, RAF officers viewed evidence on what airpower could do at present, through the prism of what their idea of the RMA predicted it would do in the future. In 1946, the head of Bomber Command, Arthur Harris, claimed that his forces alone had almost won that war and would have done so had other allied forces, like armies or navies, not been in the way.[14] Granted, the RAF did not speak with just one voice. In 1923 Ellington held that the RAF could not dominate British defense for decades: 'the main part of a national effort for defense should, for the present, be devoted to the Army and to aircraft capable of co-operating with it.'[15] Few RAF officers liked such conservative options, which would make airpower just another element of armies or navies, from preference and politics – after all, the Army and the RN did suggest such alternatives, along with dismemberment of the RAF. Still, many RAF officers were not revolutionaries but radicals, regarding airpower as a fundamental component of British power, equaling armies, navies and economic warfare in importance, altering their function but not displacing them. To confuse matters, when under pressure RAF revolutionaries were willing to make merely radical claims: even Trenchard could deny that he thought 'the Air was going to win a European war without the help of the Army and Navy and blockade etc.'[16] In 1937–38, when countering ministers' attacks on bombers and support for air defense, the Air Staff was able to reverse its real views, justifying strategic bombing forces on the grounds that they were 'an essential component in any sound system of air defense.'[17]

Nonetheless, faith in an RMA underlay all RAF policy. This faith had flaws. It was driven by technological determinism, it assumed that extrapolated trends would never end, and it exaggerated the speed and the result of this RMA. It led the RAF to pursue the technical and tactical possibilities likely to produce the most revolutionary results – but only if an uncertain number of uncertainties, 'known unknowns' and 'unknown unknowns' alike, could be overcome. The development of airpower was bound to be complicated. The RAF's experiments in strategic air warfare produced much fruit, both expected and unexpected, but, given the limits to its resources, only at the direct cost of possible developments in ground and maritime support.

This faith in an RMA also affected grand strategy. Because RAF thinkers referred to the role of airpower in the future conditional tense, their statements rested on the quicksand of speculation. They saw another great war as lying in the distant future, when technological changes would have affected the power of armies, navies and air forces in unforeseeable ways. Their assessments were based on arbitrary predictions about the effect of air power by unspecified dates, leading to vast, contradictory, unfalsifiable, even irresponsible, claims. In 1921 one Naval Staff officer complained bitterly that the RAF's case rested on claims of the '"if", "may" and "possibly" variety.'[18] Similarly, during 1940 the Army commander in Malaya reported that his RAF counterpart would not say 'anything definite as regards his plans or his capabilities: he claims to be able to do everything but will not, in the end, accept responsibility for or guarantee anything.'[19] Again, though no more than usual for military institutions, RAF officers assessed threats in a mechanistic and worst case fashion and often a cynical one, reaching its epitome during 1925–27 with the concept of an 'Afghan air menace,' exploited purely so as to increase the number of RAF squadrons maintained in India.[20] The fact that any air force was within reach of the British empire was taken to prove the intention and existence of an air threat; and no matter their doctrine, it was held that foreign airmen must either use their forces badly or like the British, who had discovered the natural way of airpower. In the 1920s the RAF interpreted France's development of a large air force for army support as proof that it posed a strategic bombing menace, and later did so again with the *Luftwaffe*.

The RAF's main objective was to survive as an independent service in control of all British airpower; to defend its autonomy and to strengthen its budgets. It was an institution with a vision looking for a role, one that the government would fund, so that it could repeat the process until it reached the millennium. The RAF always aimed to replace the Army and the RN in all their roles and become the dominant military institution on earth, but there was no direct route to this objective. So vast a theory and airy an aim could not guide immediate action: instead, opportunistic politics did so. At any point, the RAF emphasized one of its many aims over the rest, simply because that one seemed easier to sell, and its leaders contemplated many different futures. They aimed no more at strategic bombing than at entirely replacing the older services in their conventional roles. Precisely their failure to achieve the latter aim increased their focus on strategic bombing. Still, the RAF's claims that it could substitute for the Army in imperial defense gained squadrons and funding. It hoped to acquire much more by replacing the RN in the exercise of seapower, and thus realize its frequent claims that aircraft had superseded warships as the foundation of the British empire. In 1920–21 Trenchard argued that land-based bombers could replace fleets and the RAF pursued this aim through expensive policies – the development of bombs able to wreck battleships, and of airships and 'coastal reconnaissance' aircraft sufficient to replace cruisers in maritime reconnaissance, convoy escort and strike roles. It abandoned these aims only because airships and 'B-bombs' were technological failures, while the RN prevented the RAF from seizing its roles and funding.[21]

Despite these challenges, the RAF always assumed an RMA was occurring and that Britain must position itself to catch the wave. It prepared less for war against any power than for the greatest possible revolution in the forces useful against every power. It focused on air forces under its control which could dominate a strategic niche – most notably an HDAF, but also coastal reconnaissance and airships – rather than on those charged to support the Army and the RN and under their command. So too, major RAF expenditures on research and experiment centered on airships, 'B-bombs,' primitive guided missiles and radar. This approach was commendable but costly. Between 1924 and 1931, half the RAF's budget for research and development went just to two proposals which proved failures, airships and guided missiles, precisely when Britain fell behind in more elementary areas, like carrier–borne aircraft. Again, the RAF sustained a strong air–industrial complex for future eventualities, maintaining the largest number of firms it could feed without starvation, so to foster competitiveness, innovation and capacity. Only sixteen airframe and four engine manufacturers were allowed to tender designs or production contracts. The intention was to prevent one firm from dominating the market and to speed technical developments, because 'the number of aircraft manufacturing firms' was associated with 'progress in design.'[22] This approach was common among military services, but the RAF got the balance better than most; the RN tried to support more specialist firms than its orders could sustain, leading to their collapse between 1929 and 1931, while French air policy failed largely because it came to center on keeping many inefficient firms in intensive care, rather than profiting from the practice of triage. The triumph of the Spitfire occurred, conversely, because the Air Ministry knew how to marry the technical innovation of Supermarine to the wealth and expertise of Vickers.[23] By 1925 the Air Ministry had developed the basis for an industrial strategy which produced aircraft of remarkable quality and quantity during the Second World War, the 'shadow industry' scheme, whereby civilian engineering firms were joined as sub-contractors to established air concerns in the region, and retooled and reorganized in advance.[24] Still, the RAF's approach had problems. Once in the ring, firms could live comfortable lives, protected, as one air businessman said, from 'a basis of cut-throat competition.'[25] This contributed to their failures of the 1920s regarding the development of the monoplane.

Ultimately, the RAF prepared for its predictions; it shaped a force suited to the RMA which it anticipated. This caused its strengths and weaknesses during the Second World War. The RAF was good where it got the RMA right and bad where it did not, which meant that there was an opportunity cost. Since the RAF's idea of the RMA exceeded the reality of 1939, it delivered less than was possible in areas where airpower did not have a revolutionary effect.

Between 1918 and 1934, the RAF expected Britain to fight minor colonial campaigns during the foreseeable future, but no major wars. In 1919 Trenchard and in 1923 Ellington even doubted that any great war would occur within the next thirty years, or before 1950.[26] Admirals and generals perceived immediate threats against which Britain should prepare; airmen did not. They focused on the culmination of an RMA, rather than on wars that might occur during that process. These ideas were linked: in order to pursue their vision of an RMA, the RAF would need large funding, which could be endangered if the Army or the RN launched expensive programs against immediate threats. Granted, during 1921–33 the RAF used a 'French air menace' to justify the development of a strategic air force, but this was a political maneuver.[27] It held that all real threats were distant, and Britain could best defend its security by making medium–level investments in the RAF, to be financed by reducing large but by definition obsolescent armies and navies. It argued, for example, that battleships were 'an insurance for which we cannot afford to pay the premium' when trying to sink naval construction programs in 1920–21 and 1925.[28] Only around 1934, with the rise of Adolf Hitler, did the RAF believe serious threats might be imminent, and then it generally argued that Britain should respond by focusing its resources on the RAF, though Ellington prevented the worst possible consequences of this attitude by recognizing that the Army and the RN retained value and needed major funding.

Still, the RAF held that, in principle, any major airpower could threaten Britain and thought it knew how to fight a great war. It envisioned short wars with just one other power, whereas the RN thought of long conflicts against one enemy and the Army expected prolonged wars of attrition between coalitions. Though the RAF purported to be an imperial service, it was more Eurocentric than the Army or the RN in its definition of danger, being far less concerned with threats in Asia. Since contemporary aircraft had a small range, RAF assessments of threat focused on Europe, where most industrialized states were based, but it thought about great wars with powers elsewhere, and actively joined in when Whitehall authorized planning against Japan and the USSR. Here, RAF strategy was parasitical – it was less certain of who an enemy might be than how it would fight one – and politicized. As its contribution to the forces and planning for such wars, the RAF advocated the most independent possible air action, such as air strikes against Japanese battleships near Malaya or Soviet logistics in Afghanistan. The value of its contributions varied widely. RAF politics disrupted planning for the defense of Singapore, especially in 1940–41, when air authorities, thinking they had never had 'so good a wicket' to seize responsibility for the matter and the funds and prestige attached to it, grossly exaggerated their present ability to handle Japan.[29] In 1926–28, conversely, the RAF helped the Army to create a remarkable plan to use mechanized forces and air interdiction to stop a Russian invasion of Afghanistan.[30] Its contributions to strategic planning against Germany between 1934 and 1939 were intelligent, with other departments balancing its distortion of the significance of bombing. Ironically, until 1934, the RAF developed far more detailed plans for war against Turkey, because of the danger of hostilities in 1922–23 and 1925–26, than against the power it defined as an air menace.[31] War plans against France consisted essentially of an idea that every bomber the RAF could muster would attack Paris as often as possible. This reflected a general phenomenon; the RAF had a clear concept of how strategic bombing would work, which it did not apply in detail to any particular case.

The 'Trenchard doctrine,' emphasizing 'moral' factors and willpower as the true target of airpower, dominated RAF discussions about the mechanics and the aim of a bombing offensive.[32] As he put it,

> It is probable that any war on the European Continent in which we might be involved in the future would resolve itself virtually into a contest of morale between the respective civilian populations. By this is meant that there would be a tendency for the nationals of the power which suffered most from air attacks, or which lacked in moral tenacity, to bring such pressure to bear on their government as to result in military capitulation. Thus, the power that gains superiority in the air would have bombing superiority against ground objectives. It follows that if we could bomb the enemy more intensively and more continuously that [sic] he could bomb us the result might be an early offer of peace.[33]

According to this concept, when hostilities opened the belligerents would launch an all-out knockout blow by air.[34] This might break a people and their government, but air defense and accident would inflict heavy losses. If victory did not occur within a month, the weight of bombing would decline until new pilots and aircraft enabled a renewed effort. Air warfare could become spasmodic and last for a year or more but always, as one Air Minister, Lord Swinton, said in 1937, 'success will go to the nation which can most quickly overcome the will of his opponent to continue the fight.'[35]

RAF planning for strategic air warfare lacked just one thing: a strategy. It moved straight from theory to operations – what planners called strategy was merely the case of one operation following another. This attribute stemmed from the evidence and the ideas surrounding the theory. The RAF, as Ellington said in 1934, had to rely on 'pure guess-work' and 'arbitrary

assumptions' about every detail of strategic air warfare, 'as we have no practical experience of air warfare on a major scale under modern conditions to
provide us with definite conclusions capable of mathematical expression.'[36]
Detailed war planning must be speculative, thus pointless. Given the political–psychological considerations in British thinking about grand strategy
and airpower theory, discussions on how strategic bombers would fight a
war easily slipped into one about how they would deter war. Meanwhile, the
need for detailed planning was sapped by the concept that bombing would
win quickly and through metaphysical means, by wrecking the 'morale' of a
'nation.'

Notoriously, the 'Trenchard doctrine' defined enemy willpower as a better
target for air attack than its economy. Sometimes it is assumed that the RAF
simply ignored industrial targets, which distorted the shape of its forces. In
fact, RAF officers did not make a radical distinction in targeting between
morale and material. They always assumed that morale could not be struck
without hitting material, and *vice versa*. Even Trenchard held that only
attacks on material targets could damage morale.[37] In 1933, the commander
of RAF strategic bombers wished to attack Paris in case of war, because it
was the central node both of French will and aircraft production.[38] In
1936–39, when the Air Staff began detailed planning for strategic air war, it
wished to focus on precise and key economic targets, but soon found that
it lacked so much information on 'methods of bombing' that it could be sure
of few matters, while all of the targets it wished to hit were in major cities.[39]

RAF plans for strategic bombing were useless when war broke out, not
because of the choice between targets but due to the exaggeration of their
vulnerability. Though the RAF did distort the precision and effect of the
bombing of industrial targets, its argument was less that bombing was
strong than will was weak. Making crude assumptions about the collective
character of nations and crowds, especially of lower classes in urban
centers, RAF officers assumed that bombing would spark upheaval among
volatile peoples such as Jews in the East End or Frenchmen everywhere
(which helps to explain the pessimism regarding bombing of Germans,
whose morale was assumed to be rather British). Trenchard, like J.F.C.
Fuller and other military theorists who combined reactionary politics with
technological determinism and faith in dominant weapons, promoted not
total war but a mixture of medieval and futurist conflict – one of cham-
pions, fought between small elites of technologically trained members of
the upper classes, with the attacker throwing its will against the *hoi polloi*
below, winning by the demonstration of superiority rather than
destruction – an image reflected in the post–war image of the social origins
of fighter pilots during the Battle of Britain.[40] RAF thinking often drifted
toward the idea that merely to show the ability to bomb would be enough
to win, and perhaps deter war; since one could win by demonstration, why
think of damage, therefore, why plan for war? Ironically, the RAF never

formed a coherent case as to how bombing would affect morale, no doubt because it declined, for obvious political reasons, to espouse the most obvious means to do so, a naked policy of terror bombing against civilians. As one Air Staff officer noted, bombing could affect morale only through a policy of terror and noted, with a touch of prophecy, that 'no doubt with our usual skill at putting our enemies in the wrong in the eyes of the world, we shall see to it that the enemy is the first to transgress international laws.'[41] This need to avoid this political danger twisted the logic of strategy. Trenchard held that a bombing campaign against economic targets need not be 'indiscriminate' even if 98 per cent of bombs missed their targets and hit civilians! This was scarcely the means to foster serious debate.[42] Of course, in 1941 the RAF was happy when 2 per cent of its bombs landed within ten miles of their target.

Thus, strategy became sleight of hand. The RAF sold its vision of an RMA without developing a strong or falsifiable case for strategic bombing, which wrecked rational discussion of ends and means in air policy and grand strategy. The ideas that strategic bombing would deter war or determine its nature led Whitehall to fundamental miscalculations in diplomacy and in strategy and in the allocation of resources – to invest more money and hope than was wise in strategic bombing, at the expense of other arms. Thus, in the later 1930s, politicians preferred to produce hundreds of obsolete aircraft rather than help an Army suffocating from financial strangulation. Distorted faith in an airpower RMA shaped Britain's mistakes during the 'phoney war.' On 15 May 1940, politicians hoped to counter the looming debacle on the ground (stemming in part from the RAF's failures to prepare for air control over the battlefield), by throwing their bombers against German railways and oil refineries which, Prime Minister Churchill hoped, 'would cut Germany at its tap root.'[43] These attacks were futile. Identical errors haunted British strategic assessments in the Pacific during 1940–41.[44] More generally, between 1940 and 1945 the RAF was a strong service, in part because it received a disproportionately large share of national resources.

Yet bad process did not produce bad forces. The exaggerated fear of strategic bombing caused the unparalleled investments in air defense that made Fighter Command unbeatable in 1940 while in technical terms the RAF made good use of the resources it received for strategic bombing. Even had it abandoned the Trenchard doctrine and aimed to strike key nodes in enemy industry, by 1939 the shape of Bomber Command probably would not have been much different than it was – in fact, it was similar to that of the United States Army Air Force (USAAF), which did have a falsifiable doctrine emphasizing industrial targets. Given the technology of the day, a bombing force designed to attack material would be like one focused on civilians. The RAF's confusion over targets reflected their nature. In 1946, Harris also stated that he had aimed 'to weaken the enemy's will to resist and to deprive him of the weapons necessary to wage a successful war,' by inflicting 'the most severe material damage on German industrial cities.'[45] So to attack morale, he wrecked German material as much as the USAAF – which killed as many civilians as Bomber Command despite aiming at industry.

What is the overall verdict on the RAF during the inter-war years? Given the scale of the resources it received, the judgment must be critical, more so than regarding the RN and especially the Army, where government decisions crippled service policy. In meeting its primary objective, the development of air forces for strategic purposes, the RAF stood at the top of the class. Whatever its weaknesses, in 1939 Bomber Command stood alongside the USAAF in preparations for that difficult task and they raced neck and neck until 1945. Between 1943 and 1945, in technical terms, Britain led the world in strategic bombing – Bomber Command could place a more devastating conventional bomb-load more accurately than any other air force on earth; unlike the USAAF, it actually was capable of precision bombing. Yet that capacity also proved far less valuable than the RAF had hoped – perhaps a rational weapon for a stronger power in a war of attrition, but useful for Britain only as part of a great coalition and in conjunction with the USAAF (and *vice versa*) and unable to achieve quick, cheap, cost-effective and single-handed victory. For most of its duration, the Combined Bomber Offensive cost the attackers far more to mount than the defender to surmount, and Britain by itself could never have sustained that cost (neither could the United States).[46] Alone on earth, conversely, the RAF made strategic air defense effective. By 1917–18 Britain had established an advanced air defense system, which the RAF honed consistently over the next twenty years. It learned all the right lessons of the First World War and it was always able to handle any and every strategic bombing force which might have attacked Britain, whether in 1926, 1934 or 1938. Fighter Command in 1940 was not the product of the rebellion of one great captain, Air Vice Marshal Dowding, or of the Treasury and Thomas Inskip, against the system, but precisely of the system itself – of the institutional decision of the RAF over a fifteen-year period to develop air defense through regular and sizable investments.[47]

In every other area of air warfare, the record of 1939 is poor. By 1918, British aviation matched German in support for the Army and the RN and exceeded any other air force; in both it sank to third rate status by 1939, because the RAF chose to allow it. During the First World War, the essential function of airpower was the support of armies, especially of artillery, and inter-war armies had a real claim on such support. This was a great task and it absorbed the airforces of France, Italy, Germany and the USSR. Yet for the RAF to follow this path would be to abandon its vision and perhaps its existence. In 1919–21, it struggled over this issue with the Army, which struck to control all airpower outside naval aviation.[48] The RAF could not avoid this battle, which it won by 1922, and it proved pitiless in victory. Until

1939 it ignored the Army's demands for air support; it thought the idea absurd. Geoffrey Salmond argued, characteristically, 'if aerial forces are so powerful that by means of their offensive powers through explosions and gas, and other means of spreading destruction they so alter future warfare that the Army constitutes a "mopping up" party, it follows that the main part of a national effort for defense should be devoted to the air.'[49] In 1939 the RAF ranked perhaps fifth in the world as regards air support for armies, but its characteristic disjunction between theory and practice helped the RAF to salvage something from a bad situation. In theory, the RAF ignored army support, but in practice 'imperial policing' gave much of the RAF experience in ground support, which contributed to its remarkably rapid recovery from this failure during 1941.[50]

A greater tragedy for British airpower – the greatest of its history – lay in naval aviation. In 1917 the Royal Navy Air Service (RNAS) led the world in this practice, matching the Germans in the use of maritime strike aircraft from land bases, while also possessing a great lead in carrier aviation. Naval staff officers and commanders had an excellent and advanced idea of how to use such forces. However, this went to waste – the RNAS's amalgamation with the RFC deprived both the RN and the RAF of this expertise in maritime aviation. The only institution to profit was the Imperial Japanese Navy, because its air force was trained by British officers who used the RNAS as a model.[51] This failure occurred in an odd fashion.[52] Between 1919 and 1924 the RAF helped to develop naval aviation effectively, because anything less threatened disaster. Trenchard sought to appease the RN, fearing that if it attacked in conjunction with the Army, the RAF would be wrecked. From 1925, however, with the Army broken and the RN irreconcilable, the RAF increasingly ignored carrier aviation and thus damaged it. Meanwhile, when 'coastal reconnaissance' flights failed to seize funding from the RN, the RAF abandoned efforts to develop a maritime strike capacity based on land. Though it recouped the latter failure by 1942, the RAF was the primary culprit for the poor state of the Fleet Air Arm. Britain was weakest in naval aviation of the three great naval powers in 1939, for which it suffered and from which it did not recover during the Second World War.

During the inter-war years, the RAF expected Britain to fight just one major power at a time, with an RMA in airpower producing quick victory. Instead, a prolonged struggle of attrition between coalitions began in 1939, and airpower reshaped warfare without revolutionizing it. Whether the vision was worth the pursuit is open to question. Certainly Britain paid a heavy price for doing so. Conceivably, it would have gained as much through airpower had the RAF pursued a conservative approach between 1919 and 1939, simply honing the strong suits of British aviation in 1918 (naval strike, aircraft carriers, ground support and strategic air defense) and overcoming practical problems like those in aircrew training, focusing on optimal preparation for the middle term rather than on an RMA in the long run. Instead, the RAF lost British excellence in naval aviation and ground support, expanded existing strength in air defense, and created a good strategic bombing force that could not achieve the ends it predicted. The very existence of the RAF produced interservice battles that damaged the Army, the RN and Britain. The RAF triumphed in its single greatest task, air defense, but failed in the second, maritime air power; its excellence in strategic bombing was matched by poverty in ground support. Not that such a balance was unusual; in 1939 every air force was, at best, master of one domain. But British air enthusiasts had always promised so much more.

This record does not indicate that Britain received a sizable return on its large investment in airpower, until one accounts for one other aspect. When gauging the quality of military forces, writers focus too much on doctrine and not enough on institutions. Underneath the mediocre superstructure of doctrine and operational preparation lay the most professional air force on earth – a first-rate institution with an impressive ability to improve. By 1942, with painful effort, the RAF brought itself to strength in the areas where it was weak in 1939, while keeping its lead where it had led. In 1939, it stood at the rear of the pack in maritime strike forces and in the tactical or operational support of armies; by 1942, it had pulled to the front in army support and tied regarding maritime strike forces. The *Luftwaffe*, conversely, never equaled Britain in air defense, strategic bombing or maritime airpower. Only the United States matched this record, which is a remarkable feat, considering the disparity between British and American resources.

Judgment of the RAF is complicated because it was an air force like no other; never an average service, but one where triumph and tragedy marched hand in hand. By 1939 it was characterized by an extreme combination of failure, as in war planning, and success, as in the ability to learn. This rare situation emerged from the general attempt to force the pace of a revolution in the terms of power, combined with two developments that began simultaneously around 1934. Air Ministry technical staffs of the 1920s emphasized that the aircraft industry must match foreign developments, so RAF policy 'will not be deflected out of its way by some single advance,' while a regular program of orders ensured that at any time most British aircraft would be good, the remainder divided between obsolete and excellent.[53] Unfortunately, around 1934 Britain did lag in one advance, which rendered all its aircraft obsolescent all at once. Britain fell eighteen months behind Germany and the United States in the monoplane – key to the development of speed, range and firepower for aircraft – which caused a cascading series of problems. Without monoplanes, Britain possessed no modern aircraft between 1936 and 1938, fatal to a policy based on 'pure guess work' and little fact. In 1938–39, trials between Hurricanes, Spitfires and the best British bombers showed that every aspect of RAF planning must be recast, which was not completed until 1942. Arguably, between the wars the RAF had a good long-term policy which failed just once, in 1936–39 – that moment, unfortunately, when success was most essential. This produced an odd phenomenon in 1939–41: steadily rising superiority in airpower in those areas which the RAF defined as most significant, combined with disastrous weakness in all others. Had the RAF begun to receive high performance fighters and bombers eighteen months before it did, arguably it would have avoided most of its failures of 1940–41. Instead, the need to replace every RAF aircraft at once created problems for those fields or areas receiving the lowest priorities, producing misfortune for ground support and in the Middle East, and disaster at Singapore and for carrier-borne aviation. Against this, the RAF developed an unparalleled systematic ability to improve its performance, once it had hard facts. From 1934, through the Air Fighting Committee, the RAF was the first military service on earth to develop Operational Research, mathematically-based assessments of force structures and tactics, linked to practice with an Operational Development Unit, with the resulting praxis incorporated into all elements of planning. This was the root for the RAF's extraordinary learning curve during the Second World War.

So strong a performance proves the high quality of an organization. These successes occurred for precisely the same reasons as the failures – the RAF was an independent service charged to take an RMA as far as it could go. Measured by squadron slice, between the wars the RAF always was the world's most expensive air force, because its personnel were long-service volunteers backed by a full range of separate supporting services. Britain paid a premium for professionalism in the air and it received a return on its investment. In 1939 it possessed a force just past the threshold of excellence, with the world's largest cadre of good personnel ready to serve as a base for expansion, men able to learn fast and teach well; the quality of its units, establishments and officers was uniformly high, better than any other air force. Conversely, as the Air Minister, Kingsley Wood, said in 1939, massive and rapid expansion from a small base had made the *Luftwaffe* larger than the RAF but also 'likely to show the defects of its rapid growth when a heavy strain was put upon it.'[54] The RAF's base of power was multiplied by unmatched strength in three areas which together, if to a lesser degree, affected air warfare as the General Staff system had done land warfare between 1866 and 1871. The RAF had a close and fruitful link between scientists, engineers, firms and commanders, from which stemmed key successes like the development of radar and scientific air intelligence.[55] It pioneered a new form of learning, Operational Research, and new forms of command, control, communications and intelligence, which spread from air defense through every branch of the RAF between 1934 and 1941.[56] Not that mathematics was applied universally well: as one staff officer wrote in 1937, 'our present wastage rates are not, as I had thought, based on the experience of the last war.

They are really based on nothing at all.'[57] Between 1939 and 1945, the RAF made errors in important areas and sometimes disliked facing them. Still, it was unusually willing to scrutinize its operations and to learn from error. Institutionalized learning systems such as Operational Research sections at headquarters, combined with supple C3I systems, married knowledge to killing, helping Coastal Command, Bomber Command and the Desert Air Force move from impotence to proficiency toward victory.

Whether airpower produced an RMA before 1945, or RMAs ever happen, are open questions, but the RAF believed they would and did, and it confronted changes in war which can be termed revolutionary. Its experiences illustrate how an institution's attempts to pursue an RMA can affect its preparation for war. In such cases, it is easy to trip over one's feet, because these characteristics follow drummers with different beats – technology guiding an RMA, politics leading war. In following its drummer, the RAF jettisoned strengths which were sure to be useful, in order to concentrate on developments which it hoped would become more so. This approach stemmed from faith rather than fact, and its devotees ignored countervailing evidence, anticipated the apocalypse in every sign, and exaggerated the immediate value of this RMA. In the event, most of their predictions had not been realized by September 1939. One can justify in a simple way the RAF's pursuit of an RMA only if one concludes that a conservative approach would have produced a worse service in 1939–45, which is not necessarily so. Simplicity, however, is not a universal virtue. A complex form of judgment shows the significance of tiny changes in dates when assessing the efforts of any institution to pursue an RMA. In 1939, the RAF's position was poor – even air defense was just receiving first-rate fighters for the first time since 1934. Between 1942 and 1945, Britain led or was tied in every aspect of airpower except carrier-borne aviation. Again, Bomber Command was ordered to prepare for war in 1942. During 1939, it could not damage its enemy at all. By 1942 it was a million-man force with a thousand bombers and extraordinary technique, able to flatten small cities, to expand despite heavy casualties, with an impressive learning curve, murderously effective aircraft and ordnance entering production – but still unable to inflict significant damage on the enemy despite a heavy opportunity cost. Only by 1944 did this investment pay off at all, and even then not in a cost- effective fashion – Bomber Command was not an individual war winner, merely one of many forces delivering killing blows to the foe. By 1945, atomic weapons finally gave airpower the means to sustain an RMA; by 1961 land- and sea-based missiles usurped much of this power. Which of these dates is preeminent? Who could have predicted so radical a change in power over so short a period? Yet changes precisely of this scale and rapidity must characterize any successful RMA, which will hamper prediction of its practical value in the future.

Consideration of this case leads to broader questions about RMAs and the development of power. Contemporary students of military policy frequently emphasize the centrality of doctrine, asserting that innovation can occur only when an institution has falsifiable ideas that guide force structures, war planning and expenditures. Can institutions actually achieve this during the early stages of an RMA, or even just of a radical change in military affairs? In such cases, can they do more than formulate a vague unfalsifiable 'theory,' loosely linked to policies, one open to all the criticisms that may be offered about the RAF? Given the need to make so many guesses about so many independent but inter-related matters, can an institution in pursuit of an RMA even plan in a meaningful fashion? Will their gains really lie in the achievement of the aims they have in mind, or in unexpected spinoffs from the means they develop in order to achieve these ends? Can one pursue an RMA through a rational policy?

Notes

All material from files in the ADM, AIR, CAB and WO series are held at The National Archives United Kingdom, Kew Gardens, and are cited by permission of the Controller of Her Majesty's Stationery Office. Material from the Trenchard Papers is cited by permission of the copyright holders and by courtesy of the Royal Air Force Museum, Hendon.

1 For a discussion of these points, cf. John Ferris, '"The Air Force Brats" View of History: Recent Writings on the Royal Air Force, 1918–60,' *International History Review*, vol. 20, no. 1, January 1998.

2 Sir Charles Webster and Noble Frankland, *The Strategic Air Offensive Against Germany, 1939–1945, Vol. 1* (London, 1961), p. 21; H. Montgomery Hyde, *British Air Policy Between the Wars, 1919–1939* (London, 1976), pp. 58, 158; Tami Davis Biddle, 'British and American Approaches to Strategic Bombing: Their Origins and Implementation in the World War II Combined Bomber Offensive,' in John Gooch, ed., *Airpower, Theory and Practice* (London, 1995), p.101; Christina J.M. Goulter, *A Forgotten Offensive: Royal Air Force Coastal Command's Anti-Shipping Campaign, 1940–1945* (London, 1995), p. 39; Scot Robertson, *The Development of RAF Strategic Bombing Doctrine, 1919–1939* (Westport and London, 1995), pp. 25, 29–30, 37, 143.

3 John Robert Ferris, *Men, Money and Diplomac: The Evolution of British Strategic Policy, 1919–1926* (London and New York, 1989).

4 Memorandum by Sykes, 21.10.18, 'Considerations Affecting the Strength, Organization and Constitution of the Royal Air Force After the War,' *passim*, AIR 2 / 71; 60th Meeting of the Air Council, 13.11.18, AIR 6/13; GT 6477, 6478, CAB 24 / 71.

5 Minute by Churchill, 1.7.19, AIR 2 / 89.

6 David Edgerton, *England and the Aeroplane: An Essay on a Militant and Technological Nation* (London, 1991).

7 Ferris, *Men, Money, Diplomacy*, pp. 32–36, passim.

8 The best institutional study is Hugh Driver, *The Birth of Military Aviation: Britain, 1903–1914* (London, 1997).

9 Useful biographies of these officers include Andrew Boyle, *Trenchard, Man of Vision* (London, 1962), Eric Ash, *Sir Frederick Sykes and the Air Revolution* (London, 1998), Robert Wright, *Dowding and the Battle of Britain* (London, 1969) and Denis Richards, *Portal of Hungerford* (London, 1977).

10 John Ferris, 'Fighter Defence Before Fighter Command: The Rise of Strategic

Air Defence in Great Britain, 1917–34,' *Journal of Military History*, vol. 63, October 1999.

11 Minute by Trenchard, 6.11.24, *passim*, AIR 5 / 387.

12 Ferris, 'Fighter Defence Before Fighter Command'.

13 Memorandum by Sykes, 21.10.18, AIR 2 / 71 A. 6446.

14 Sir Arthur T. Harris (ed. Sebastian Cox), *Despatch on War Operations, 23rd February, 1942 to 8th May, 1945* (London: Frank Cass, 1995).

15 Memorandum by Ellington, 11.2.23, 'The Next War,' AIR 5 / 282.

16 Seventieth meeting of the COS, 30.5.28, CAB 53 / 2; Trenchard to Hankey, 2.5.28, CAB 21 / 314.

17 'Note on Secretary of State's Minute to C.A.S. of 26.9.1937,' AIR 9 / 50; 'The Strength of the Bomber Forces in Relation to the Principle of Parity,' Air Staff, 2.11.38, AIR 8 / 227.

18 Minute by Domville, 8.4.21, ADM 1 / 8605.

19 Dewing to Kennedy, 12.9.40, Bond to Dewing, 21.10.40, WO 106 / 2537; Bond to CIGS, tele, 15.7.40, No. 11216, *passim*, WO 106 / 2441.

20 'Air Staff Notes on Air Requirements to meet Afghan Air Menace,' 23.3.25, AIR 9 / 25; Trenchard to Chamier, 31.8.25, *passim*, AIR 5 / 608.

21 Memorandum by Trenchard, 'The Big Ship Controversy from the Air Point of View,' undated but circa December 1920–January 1921 by internal evidence, AIR 8 / 30; minute by Trenchard, 11.1.21, AIR 5 / 552; minute by DSR to AMSR, 7.10.26, *passim*, AIR 2 / 302; AIR 5 / 1341, AIR 2 / 310 and AIR 9 / 34, *passim*.

22 Minute by Bullock, 14.8.22, AIR 2 / 246 S.20211.

23 Sebastian Ritchie, *Industry and Air Power: The Expansion of British Military Aircraft Production, 1935–1941* (London, 1997).

24 'Report of the Committee on Mobilization Reserves,' 1925, AIR 5 / 406.

25 *Aviation*, XVI / 6, 11.2.24, 'Problems of Aircraft Production in Great Britain,' pp. 151–53.

26 Trenchard to Churchill, 30.7.19, Trenchard Papers, C / 11 / 1, Royal Air Force Museum, Hendon; memorandum by Ellington, 11.2.23, 'The Next War,' AIR 5 / 282.

27 John Ferris, 'The Theory of a "French Air Menace" and Anglo French Relations, 1919–25,' *Journal of Strategic Studies*, vol. 10 (1987).

28 Ninth meeting of the Bonar Law Committee, 26.1.21, CAB 16 / 37; 'Précis of lecture by C.A.S. on the Employment of Air Power in overseas defence,' January 1925, AIR 8 / 45.

29 Babington to Pierse, 13.4.40, AIR 2 / 7174; more broadly, cf. John Ferris, 'Student and Master: The United Kingdom, Japan, Airpower and the Fall of Singapore,' in Brian Farrell and Sandy Hunter, eds, *Singapore, Sixty Years On* (Singapore: Eastern Universities Press, 2002), and James Neidpath, *The Singapore Naval Base and the Defence of Britain's Eastern Empire, 1919–1941* (London, 1981).

30 'Minutes of Meeting Between C.A.S., D.C.A.S. and Colonel Muspratt,' 1.6.28, *passim*, AIR 5 / 608.

31 For RAF war plans against Turkey during the 'Chanak crisis,' cf. AIR 8 / 51, AIR 5 / 297, AIR 5 / 250 and AIR 5 / 266, and during the 'Mosul crisis,' cf. AIR 8 / 34 and AIR 9 / 42.

32 For important discussions of these issues cf. Michael Paris, *Winged Warfare, The Literature and Theory of Aerial Warfare in Britain, 1859–1917* (Manchester, 1992); Scot, Robertson, *The Development of RAF Strategic Bombing Doctrine, 1919–1939*; Barry Powers, *Strategy Without Slide Rule* (London, 1976); Malcolm Smith, *British Air Strategy Between the Wars* (Oxford, 1984); Allen D. English, 'The RAF Staff College and the Evolution of RAF Strategic Bombing Policy,

1922–9,' *Journal of Strategic Studies*, vol. 16, 1993. The outstanding account of strategic bombing theory and practice is Tami Davis Biddle, *Rhetoric and Reality in Air Warfare: The Evolution of British and American Ideas about Strategic Bombing, 1917–45* (Princeton, 2002).

33 Transcript of a speech by Trenchard to an Army Staff Exercise, April 1923, AIR 9 / 8.

34 Useful source references for the RAF's concept of strategic air warfare may be found in AIR 5 / 328, AIR 5 / 564, AIR 5 / 282, AIR 19 / 92, and COS 341, COS 344, CAB 53 / 24.

35 Swinton to Inskip, 4.11.37, AIR 2 / 226.

36 COS 553, CAB 53 / 30; 125th COS meeting, 4.5.34, CAB 53 / 4.

37 Briefing by Trenchard for lecture by Brook Popham, undated, circa December 1923 by internal evidence, AIR 5 / 328.

38 'Remarks by Air Vice Marshal Sir Tom Webb-Bowen ("A" Syndicate) at the Final Conference on 13.3.33,' memorandum by Brook Popham, undated, 'A.D.G.B. Staff Exercise, 13th / 15th March 1933,' AIR 2 / 675.

39 First meeting, Bombing Policy Sub-Committee, 22.3.38, First meeting, Transportation Targets Committee, 27.5.38, AIR 5 / 1143.

40 Edgerton, *England and the Aeroplane*.

41 Minutes by Higgins, July 1923, and Chamier, 10.1.24, AIR 5 / 328.

42 Seventieth COS meeting, 30.5.28, CAB 53 / 2.

43 WM (40), 123rd Conclusion, Minute 2, Confidential Annex 15.5.40, CAB 65 / 13.

44 Ferris, 'Student and Master'.

45 Harris, *Despatch on War Operations*, pp. 7, 22.

46 Williamson Murray, 'Reflections on the Combined Bomber Offensive,' *Militargeschichtliche Mitteilungen*, vol. 52, 1992; *idem*, 'Strategic Bombing: The British, American and German Experiences,' in Williamson Murray and Alan Millett, *Military Innovation in the Interwar Period* (Cambridge, 1996); Tami Davis Biddle, 'Sir Arthur Harris's Wars,' *International History Review*, 1999; W. Hays Park, '"Precision" and "Area" Bombing: Who Did Which, and When,' in John Gooch, ed., *Airpower, Theory and Practice* (London, 1995).

47 Ferris, 'Fighter Defence Before Fighter Command'.

48 Ferris, *Men, Money, Diplomacy*, pp. 63–74, 83–90.

49 Minute by Salmond, 13.4.23, AIR 5 / 382.

50 This is the topic of Bradley Gladman, PhD dissertation, University College, London.

51 John Ferris, 'A British "Unofficial" Aviation Mission and Japanese Naval Developments, 1919–29,' *Journal of Strategic Studies*, 5/3 (1982).

52 Geoffrey Till, *Air Power and the Royal Navy, 1914–1945. An Historical Survey* (London, 1979), is the best account for carrier aviation, and Goulter, *A Forgotten Offensive*, for land-based maritime strike forces.

53 Minute by Geoffrey Salmond, 18.4.25, AIR 5 / 406.

54 War Cabinet meeting, 30.9.39, WM (39), 32nd Conclusions, Minute 7, Confidential Annex, CAB 65 / 3.

55 Alan Beyerchen, 'From Radio to Radar: Interwar Military Adaptation to Technological Change in Germany, the United Kingdom, and the United States,' in Williamson Murray and Alan Millett, *Military Innovation in the Interwar Period* (Cambridge, 1996); David Zimmerman, *Britain's Shield: Radar and the Defeat of the Luftwaffe* (Stroud, 2001).

56 John Ferris, 'Airbandit! C3I and Strategic Air Defence During the First Battle of Britain,' in Michael Dockrill and David French, eds, *Strategy and Intelligence: British Policy During the First World War* (London, 1994); *idem*, 'Fighter Defence Before Fighter Command'; *idem*, 'Achieving Air Ascendancy: Challenge

and Response in British Air Defence, 1915–40,' in Sebastian Cox and Peter Grey, eds, *Air Power History: Turning Points from Kitty Hawk to Kosovo* (London, 2002).

57 Minute by F.O. 1, 22.6.37, AIR 5 / 1124.

10

TRANSFORMING TO VICTORY

The US Navy, Carrier Aviation, and Preparing for War in the Pacific

Andrew F. Krepinevich, Jr.

In the closing days of the First World War, navies measured strength by the striking power of their battleships. After the war, the United States planned to remain a great sea power by increasing the number of these powerful ships in its fleet. Nearly a quarter of a century later, the American Navy entered the Second World War as a 'battleship' force – albeit supplemented with eight aircraft carriers carrying a few hundred planes. During the course of the conflict, however, the United States relied almost exclusively on a new form of sea power – the carrier battle group, which combined the power of carriers, hundreds of ships, thousands of airplanes, and a revolutionary logistical system that spanned immense distances of ocean. The United States ended the war as the world's premier naval power with 41,000 planes, 28 large and 71 smaller carriers, but fewer than a dozen battleships. How did the US Navy master such a remarkable transformation?

Military Transformation

Understanding the Navy's evolution from a battleship fleet to a carrier force requires an appreciation for the difficult issues militaries face in preparing for the future, and the complex dynamics at work during periods of rapid change. This revolution at sea presents a classic case study in military transformation, exemplifying innovation on a scale sufficient to effect a military revolution.[1] Military revolutions witness the introduction of new capabilities that, when combined with innovative operational concepts and force structure, produce a discontinuous leap in effectiveness. During a military revolution, past performance is no assurance of continued success. Revolutions compel military organizations – even dominant ones – to restructure, often radically, or risk catastrophic failure. The measures of merit associated with military power also change in major, and perhaps even fundamental ways. To remain competitive, organizations must transform in order to adapt to different circumstances. Typically, this has meant exploiting rapidly emerging technologies to create new capabilities. Once acquired, new capabilities enable different kinds of operations that can yield remarkable increases in effectiveness within a relatively short period of time.

Recognizing the necessity of change is perhaps the first step in transformation. But acknowledging the need for transformation is one thing – successfully reconfiguring an armed force is quite another. Indeed, there are a number of issues that must be considered to account for an organization's success or failure. Historical analysis suggests the basic building blocks comprise the following:[2]

1 A vision that has the potential to inspire dramatic change.
2 The means to link the vision to a problem that must be solved or an opportunity that can be exploited at the operational or strategic level of war.
3 The ability of the organizational leadership to institutionalize the vision.
4 A transformation process which includes methods to validate the vision and reduce uncertainty, rethink attitudes toward new system procurement, and revise the measures of effectiveness used to determine optimum doctrine and force design.
5 The availability of sufficient human and material resources to support the transformation.

These five factors must be present to sustain the transformation.

Once this transformation begins, a military will reach a crossover – or break point – where investments in new capabilities begin to have a dominant influence on military affairs. At a minimum, for a break point to occur, the emerging capability must be executable at the operational level, affecting major forces during the conduct of a campaign.

The large body of scholarship concerning the evolution of the American carrier force offers a solid basis for illustrating the transformation profile of one of the truly significant military revolutions in modern times.

The Seeds of Transformation

Great Britain's Royal Navy, the preeminent naval power at the turn of the century and the United States' First World War ally, marked the way for the US Navy's transformation path. During the First World War, the Royal Navy aggressively explored the potential of aviation technology. Britain's admiralty deployed a number of sea-borne platforms for launching aircraft, culminating in 1918 with the deployment of *Argus*, a prototype for future carriers. The *Argus* demonstrated that the Royal Navy had largely solved two of the three basic challenges of carrier aviation – launching and recovering aircraft. The United States, inspired by the Royal Navy's wartime experience, directed its own transformation effort toward solving the third challenge – undertaking large-scale sustained air operations at sea.[3]

The scope of future naval air operations proved a subject of intense debate among American naval officers. A distinct minority envisioned a revolutionary new mission for aircraft – conducting powerful air strikes at extended ranges that could threaten the enemy fleet. Visionaries considered several transformation paths for the future of naval air power – zeppelins, seaplanes and long-range, land-based aircraft, planes carried on existing surface combatants, launched from submarines or deployed on carriers. Admiral William S. Sims, who had commanded US naval forces in Europe, made a strong case for the carrier. He declared that 'a small, high-speed carrier alone can destroy or disable a battleship. . . . [A] fleet whose carriers give it command of the air over the enemy fleet can defeat the latter.'[4] Fast carriers, Sims argued, would be the battleships of the next war.

The 'traditionalists,' headed by Chief of Naval Operations William S. Benson, the Navy's most senior uniformed leader, viewed Sims and other air enthusiasts with deep skepticism. He remarked, 'The Navy doesn't need airplanes. Aviation is just a lot of noise.'[5] Benson did concede that sea-borne aviation could prove useful for the scouting and spotting of naval gunfire. Fighter aircraft would also be needed to screen hostile scout planes away from the fleet, and to neutralize enemy air spotters. Nevertheless, while aviation might assume greater importance, the battleship would remain the fleet's main striking force.

Sims's vision, Benson believed, outstripped technology. Naval aircraft were small, fragile, capable only of short-range flight, and unable to communicate effectively with ships at extended distances. Planes could deliver only meager bomb loads with little accuracy. Benson opposed Sims's recommendation that battleships be equipped with aircraft, and in 1919 initiated a reorganization plan to abolish the naval aviation office, burying its functions under the Naval Operations' Planning and Material Divisions. In addition, a special post-war committee convened by Benson recommended that a decision on constructing the Navy's first carrier be postponed.[6]

Despite Benson's recalcitrance, two factors worked to undermine his position. The first was the 'competition' – the Royal Navy led in carrier technology. For the US Navy, which sought parity with, if not superiority over, Britain, there was a strong incentive to be competitive in all emerging areas of naval warfare. The second factor was the Navy's own embryonic aviation testing. In March 1919, the battleship *Texas* conducted a main-battery gun exercise employing air spotting. Plane spotters greatly enhanced gunnery accuracy and the ability to control the air over both friendly and enemy battle fleets.[7] Impressed with the results, the captain of the *Texas*, N.C. Twining, stated flatly that any naval force 'that neglects aviation development will be at an enormous disadvantage in an engagement with a modern enemy fleet.'[8] In June 1919, the Navy's General Board declared that, 'to enable the United States to meet on at least equal terms any possible enemy . . . fleet aviation must be developed to the fullest extent. . . . A Naval air service must be established, capable of accompanying and operating with the fleet in all waters of the globe.'[9] Additionally, further testing of air power's impact on the surface fleet seemed warranted.

In November 1920, the Navy conducted a classified bombing test against the obsolete battleship *Indiana* with far-reaching, albeit unintended, consequences. Photographs of the stricken *Indiana* appeared in *The Illustrated London News*. Army Air Corps General William 'Billy' Mitchell, an extremely vocal air power advocate, promptly declared to Congress: 'We can tell you definitively now that we can either destroy or sink any ship in existence today.'[10] Mitchell's exploitation of the *Indiana* test results exposed the threat to naval aviation in unmistakable terms. Not only was Mitchell laying claim to the Navy's traditional function as the nation's first line of defense, he also proposed that an independent air service be put in charge of aircraft carriers.[11]

The Navy began closing ranks against a common peril – the US Army. As Rear Admiral Bradley A. Fiske commented in 1920,

> For the sake of the USN and the US America – let's get a Bureau of Aeronautics – pdq [pretty damned quick]. . . . If we don't get that Bureau next session, General Mitchell and a whole horde of politicians will get an 'Air Ministry' established, and the U.S. Navy will find itself lying in the street and the procession marching over it.[12]

As the battle lines between the Navy and Mitchell were drawn, Congress' role proved critical. Representative Fred C. Hicks, of the House Naval Affairs Committee, supported an independent naval aviation arm, as did Senator William Borah, helping fight Mitchell's bid to subsume naval aviation under the Army. In February 1921, Benson agreed to establish the Bureau of Aeronautics, with Rear Admiral William A. Moffett as its chief. Finally, the Navy had an organization to implement a vision that could compete with Mitchell's Army Air Corps.

The bureau's establishment proved timely. In July 1921, Mitchell directed a highly publicized Army bomber demonstration, sinking the former German battleship *Ostfriesland*. Though the ship was at anchor and offered no defense, hardly a test of tactical air power, Mitchell reaped another public relations victory with both the American public and Congress. In response, Moffett and the Navy began to make the case for naval air power.

In addition to vision and organization, the Navy also needed a sense of the operational challenges it would face in future wars to inform them as to how an air arm should be developed. The Americans focused attention principally on the Imperial Japanese Navy, their most likely opponent. In war, the Japanese would likely threaten US possessions in the Western Pacific, in particular the Philippine Islands. Defeating Japan would require the US fleet to steam across the Pacific Ocean from US west coast bases to seek a decisive engagement with the Japanese fleet in its home waters. There, US naval forces would have to overwhelm the enemy's combined fleet and shore-based air forces. Owing to the vast Pacific Ocean and the absence of US forward bases in the region, it was believed that the American fleet would have to bring its own air power. Given the Japanese Navy's size and growing aviation potential, the US Navy would likely require large numbers of aircraft and carriers.[13]

Enablers and Obstacles

Advocates of a revolution in naval warfare had to determine whether the rapid advances in aviation would enable them to realize their vision. They also needed a means for developing the industrial and human resources necessary to sustain future operational concepts. The answer to this challenge was found in the interrelationship between the Naval War College, the newly created Bureau of Aeronautics and fleet exercises – the 'Naval Trinity.'

War-gaming undertaken at the Naval War College represented the first critical element in the trinity. In 1919, Sims, now the college's president, established procedures designed to facilitate an examination of how air power might influence war at sea. The games and simulations exerted strong influence on Navy decisions. Most important, they inspired efforts to enhance naval air power by maximizing the number of aircraft on carriers and compressing the cycle for launching and recovering planes.[14]

At the Bureau of Aeronautics, the trinity's second pillar, Moffett proved a superb bureaucrat and consummate public relations chief. Within the bureau, Moffett developed a cadre of officers who effectively presented the case for naval aviation to Congress. Moffett established himself so well that when the Chief of Naval Operations tried to block Moffett's third consecutive term, President Herbert Hoover personally overrode the chief, ensuring that the bureau would continue to have a determined, vocal advocate.[15]

The third element of the trinity consisted of naval force experiments and exercises as a series of Fleet Problems. These sea maneuvers offered the most visible, and perhaps most persuasive, indication of naval aviation's potential.[16] In combination with Sims's war-games and Moffett's lobbying efforts, the Fleet Problems created an increasing momentum for transformation.

Though the Navy had three worthy enablers to propel change forward there were still good reasons to doubt whether aviation would reach its full potential, especially given the technological uncertainties. Extensive experimentation was one way to reduce incertitude. However, the Washington Naval Treaty of 1922 and tight budgets limited the number of carriers and aircraft available for testing (see Table 10.1). Designers in the Navy's Bureau

Table 10.1: Authorized US carrier construction, 1918–38

Name	Carrier type	Contract Signed	Commissioned
Langley	CV	...	1922
Saratoga	CV	30/10/22	16/11/27
Lexington	CV	30/10/22	14/12/27
Ranger	CV	1/11/30	4/6/34
Yorktown	CV	...	30/9/37
Enterprise	CV	3/8/33	12/5/38

of Construction and Repair did benefit from access to the Royal Navy's carrier plans, enabling the Americans to begin with a state-of-the-art design for its first big carriers, *Saratoga* and *Lexington*. Nevertheless, limited assets and long construction lead times made it problematic to synchronize developments with experimentation results, creating considerable lag between technological and operational advances. The Navy conducted Fleet Problems for seven years before commissioning the *Saratoga* and *Lexington*. The *Ranger* was designed before the carriers achieved a true breakthrough in the Service's Fleet Problems, and both the *Yorktown* and *Enterprise* were designed before the *Ranger* was commissioned.

The Great Depression further slowed carrier construction. At the height of the depression, Moffett, who pressed for more carriers to support experimentation, was only able to get the *Ranger* approved. Even then, the nation's deepening financial crisis delayed the ship's construction. The first carrier whose design was actually based on extensive fleet exercise experience, the *Essex* class, did not emerge until a year after the Japanese attack on Pearl Harbor.

The Navy faced similar challenges in developing planes for its carriers, where, with few resources, the Service had to promote the growth of an entirely new industrial arm. During the 1920s and 1930s, aviation technology itself was marked by rapid change and not a few surprises. The Navy had virtually no experience in designing aircraft. In effecting its transformation to a carrier-based fleet, the visionaries needed an industrial base that would provide the ability to experiment with aircraft in sufficient quantity and variety so as to identify paths that would confirm or refute their vision, while avoiding transformational 'dead ends.' It also required the industrial capacity to scale up production to meet future needs.

In 1916, Navy Secretary Josephus Daniels suggested that the service construct its own aircraft factory to develop prototypes for experimentation. The plant was built a year later at the Philadelphia Naval Yard.[17] Simultaneously, the Navy tentatively drew on advances in civilian technology. Although naval aircraft developments benefited little in their early years from the emergence of civil aviation, the National Advisory

Committee for Aeronautics (NACA) did, over time, promote what today is referred to as 'dual-use technology,' innovations appropriate to both military and civilian purposes. Breakthroughs such as aerodynamic streamlining, supercharged piston engines for high altitude flying, and internally pressured cabins were developed under NACA auspices with the financial and engineering support of the services.[18]

Despite continuing innovation, post-war budget reductions left few dollars for purchasing new aircraft technology. This shortfall was ameliorated to some extent by the Navy's recognition that the rapidly changing nature of aviation made aircraft a rapidly depreciating asset. The Service's approach was to not over-invest scarce resources in aircraft that might rapidly become obsolete. Indeed, with the post-war draw down, the Navy's requirement for new aircraft dropped to just 156 planes in 1921. One downside to these reductions was that they endangered a fledgling American aircraft industry that was heavily dependent on the government for its sustenance. By not buying more planes the Navy threatened the very companies they needed to forge the naval air arm of the future.

Further complicating matters, commercial firms faced competition from the newly established Naval Aircraft Factory (NAF), which soon emerged as one of the country's largest airplane builders. The Navy's dominant manufacturing role troubled Moffett. A healthy civilian aviation sector could contribute to developing new technology, and would be needed to provide the nucleus of an industrial base for wartime expansion. In January 1922, Moffett resolved the problem by limiting the scope of the NAF's efforts. The Navy would concentrate on researching, developing, testing, and evaluating experimental aircraft. In addition, the factory would continue to produce a limited number of aircraft to provide a cost baseline for comparison with commercial manufacturers.

While technology developed, the Navy's inventory of combat aircraft fell by over 50 per cent in the seven years following the First World War (Table 10.2). Yet, despite resource limitations, the Service was relatively generous toward its infant aviation branch during the post-war and arms

Table 10.2: Naval combat aircraft inventory

Year	Combat Aircraft Inventory
1920	1205
1921	1134
1922	780
1923	...
1924	530
1925	491

control-induced cutbacks of the 1920s. Between 1922 and 1925, naval avia-tion's budget remained fixed at US$14.5 million, while the overall Navy budget dropped by 25 per cent. From 1923 to 1929, the naval air arm expanded by over 6,500 personnel (not counting the crews of the manpower-intensive *Saratoga* and *Lexington*), while overall Navy end strength declined by over 1,000.[19]

Meanwhile, Moffett continued to lobby hard for his aircraft program. In 1926, Congress authorized a 1,000-aircraft naval aviation program that the Navy completed in only four years.[20]

The Navy's rapid naval aviation expansion program proved short-lived. Procurement of aircraft also suffered during the Great Depression. For example, the aviation budget for fiscal year 1934, submitted in April 1932, called for US$29.8 million, a reduction of US$3 million from the previous year. By the time the Bureau of the Budget signed off, however, this budget was reduced further to less than US$22 million.

Finding sufficient numbers of high-quality leaders and men to sustain the transformation proved to be an equally daunting challenge. During naval aviation's infancy in the 1920s, the 'Gun Club dominated the Navy,' ardent supporters of traditional battleship tactics. In turn, graduates of the US Naval Academy at Annapolis, the Navy's premier source of commissioning new officers, filled the rank and file of the Gun Club. During this period, more than 80 per cent of academy graduates first went to sea in battleships, and many returned to them during the course of their career, since battle-ship command was virtually a prerequisite for making admiral. Making air power palatable to the Gun Club was essential for gaining a foothold within the officer corps. The naval aviation visionaries were able to institutionalize the new 'branch' of the Service in large part by convincing the Gun Club that aircraft would be necessary for the battleship's continued tactical and operational effectiveness.[21]

Still, institutionalizing naval aviation from a personnel perspective remained a struggle, right up until the eve of the Second World War. In 1921, Moffett declared that the 'lack of trained naval aviators is now a serious consideration and one which requires immediate action if the effi-ciency of Naval Aviation is not to be impaired.'[22] Over the next three years, the shortfall persisted. In 1924, Moffett established a board, headed by Captain Alfred W. Johnson, to address the manning problem. The Johnson Board issued its findings in April 1925, declaring that the shortage of naval aviators required immediate attention.

Navy Secretary Curtis D. Wilbur approved the Johnson Board recom-mendations, but his decision appeared as a direct challenge to senior Navy leaders, who were concerned that officers pursuing an aviation career might become too detached from their professional development as surface naval officers. In response, Rear Admiral William R. Shoemaker, the chief of the Bureau of Navigation, in his own plan argued that naval aviators were no more specialized than other officers, and should therefore perform their share of sea duty before taking on aviation assignments.

The personnel question transcended nearly all other issues and went to the heart of the ongoing dispute within the Navy. The matter came to a head when Shoemaker advocated congressional legislation that would effectively end areas of specialization supporting the aviation program. Moffett appealed to Wilbur who again took up the cause of naval air power and opposed the bill.

While Moffett and other naval airmen continued to argue for independence within the Navy, they firmly rejected the separate air service championed by Mitchell (and adopted by the British, who placed their naval air arm under the Royal Air Force).[23] The solidarity demonstrated by the aviators proved important for building trust and confidence among naval leaders, and for ensuring the close integration of fleet and air efforts. The Service's generally unified, if sometimes strained, approach to operations proved a key element in the fleet's successful transformation. In the end, the Navy reached a compromise solution on personnel assignments that satisfied Moffett. Unfortunately, it took a decade of bitter debate to adequately address the issue. In addition, although the Bureau of Aeronautics succeeded in developing a new career path for naval aviators and associated specialists, the shortage of pilots would continue until the eve of the Second World War.[24]

Resource limitations and the lag time in developing and fielding new systems were sources of friction in the transformation. As a consequence, the Navy tended to focus on examining operational concepts, such as how many carriers should comprise a carrier task force. This contrasted with the option of fully exploiting the advances in technology suggested by the Fleet Problems and Naval War College gaming activities, and advocated so forcefully by Moffett and his Bureau of Aeronautics.

Mapping the Transformation Profile

Barriers, however, did not prevent the Naval Trinity from advancing the cause of transformation. The series of Fleet Problems conducted between 1923 and 1938 demonstrate how the results of the trinity worked to define the place of carrier aviation in modern naval warfare. These exercises reflected the kinds of ambiguities, opportunities and obstacles that present themselves as militaries struggle to account for the role of new technologies.

Building Momentum for Transformation

Fleet Problem I, in 1923, employed two battleships in the role of carriers. In 1925, Fleet Problem V witnessed the Navy's first carrier, *Langley*, a converted collier, launching ten aircraft.[25] The deployment of the *Langley*, despite modest capabilities, came at an opportune time. As the Navy examined the problems associated with a potential war against Japan, planners were not happy at the prospect of risking their battleships against what they anticipated to be strong defense batteries arrayed along the coast of Japan's new island possessions. Moffett, sensing an opportunity, volunteered naval aviation for the task of clearing the battleships' path. He suggested that, 'bombing aircraft, protected by fighting aircraft, both necessarily operating from carriers, could do the job of reducing the [enemy's] defenses.'[26] Thus, aviation experimentation found a wedge into the traditional battleship-focused fleet exercises.

Meanwhile, the Navy continued to fend off attacks by Mitchell. In September 1925, following the crash of Navy dirigible *Shenandoah* and the loss of a demonstration seaplane, Mitchell declared that the two disasters revealed the Services' negligence and incompetence in aviation matters. In response, President Calvin Coolidge appointed prominent lawyer Dwight W. Morrow to head the President's Aircraft Board. Mitchell's complaints inadvertently strengthened the cause of naval aviation. The congressional legislation that followed the board's report established the office of Assistant Secretary of the Navy (Aeronautics), thereby giving naval aviators a voice in senior civilian circles. The legislation also required all aircraft carriers, seaplane tenders and naval air station commanders to be qualified aviators, opening the path to leadership positions for senior air power advocates.

In 1926, a critical boost to naval aviation fortunes occurred when Reeves left the Naval War College to become Commander, Aircraft Squadrons, Battleforce. Reeves began to put into practice the insights he learned from the college's war games. He outfitted the *Langley* with new equipment and adopted revolutionary operational techniques, all designed to maximize the number of planes the carrier could put in the air. These 'test bed' carrier experiments convinced the Navy to adopt a number of innovations.[27]

While offering encouragement to naval aviation enthusiasts, the early exercises also revealed the substantial limitations of carrier-based aircraft. At the time, the only practical way for airplanes to attack surface combatants was with short-range torpedoes that were relatively slow and had to be launched close to their target. They also had a tendency to fail after being released. Worst of all, carrier aircraft simply could not lift torpedoes powerful enough to sink large warships.[28]

Experiments, however, continued to reveal new possibilities. In 1926 Lieutenant Frank D. Wagner led his squadron in the Navy's first demonstration of dive-bombing. The combination of a steep dive attack, employing machine-gun fire and relatively light bombs, proved far more effective than torpedo plane attacks. Follow-on fleet exercises confirmed that carrier torpedo bombers would encounter heavy losses from battleship anti-aircraft batteries, while dive-bombers could attack at far less risk.[29] Meanwhile, aviation engine technology was also progressing, allowing for a rapid increase in bomb payloads.

In light of the Fleet Problems' encouraging results, in 1927 the Navy convened a special board under retired Rear Admiral Montgomery M. Taylor to examine carrier aviation policy.[30] The board established priorities for aircraft requirements with strike aircraft heading the list and torpedo planes last. Though the board viewed aviation's primary purpose as providing air superiority over the battle fleet, its recommendations nevertheless ensured that the carriers would have a substantial offensive capability and that dive-bombing would emerge as the carrier's primary offensive weapon.[31]

Avoiding Lock-in

Within its limited resources, the Navy also hedged against strategic and technological uncertainty by not prematurely settling on a single carrier size and design. Congress appropriated no funds for carriers between 1924 and 1928. This developmental gap forced a strategic pause. Analysis of the lessons learned in the games and early Fleet Problems suggested it was crucial to have carriers deploy as many fighting planes as possible. Moffett argued for small carriers, noting that 'there is a far greater flight deck area available on a large number of small ships than a small number of large ships.'[32] Small-carrier advocates also noted that many ships could patrol a larger area. Moreover, they maintained that to rely on a few large carriers ran the risk of 'putting too many eggs in one basket.' The results of Fleet Problems, studies by the Bureau of Aeronautics and the Naval War College gaming all bolstered these conclusions.

Other factors, however, proved more influential in driving the Navy's design choices. The Washington Naval Treaty of 1922 forbade the construction of new fortifications or military bases in the Pacific island chains. The treaty created a major problem for the Navy, which counted on establishing major bases on Guam, the Marianas and the Philippines. In the absence of forward bases, the Navy would have to bring its own air power across the Pacific, and develop the capability to seize advanced bases to support extended operations. These requirements gave carrier capacity added importance, but the treaty limited each major navy's total tonnage in aircraft carriers at 135,000 tons. The treaty also permitted the conversion of two battle cruisers into aircraft carriers. These factors drove the Navy to elect for the conversion of two cruisers into large carriers, *Saratoga* and *Lexington*. In effect, the treaty limitations helped to prevent the Navy from making the decision exclusively to build small carriers.

Saratoga joined the fleet in November 1927, followed by *Lexington* a month later. Each displaced 36,000 tons, and had speeds in excess of thirty-three knots. They were almost exactly the type of carrier that the Navy studies and experiments told Moffett he should not want. Ironically, they would prove to be almost exactly the kind of carrier the Navy would need fifteen years later. While the treaty-induced *Saratoga* and *Lexington* seemed too large for the aircraft of the time, they would prove well suited for accommodating the rapid advances in aviation technology, which produced bigger, more powerful planes, requiring larger carriers with longer flight decks. The larger carriers, with higher sustained speeds, achieved better survivability and proved more efficient at maximizing aircraft capacity. Since the Navy had not tested their operational concepts with a large number of carriers at sea, they were unaware that their predilection for small carriers was misplaced. Fortunately, external factors discouraged the Navy from prematurely locking into the wrong carrier type.

Transformation Breakpoint

In the 1930s, naval aircraft remained severely limited in bomb-load capacity and range. In battle, carriers would have to get quite close to the enemy ships and loiter until the aircraft were recovered. These vulnerabilities proved readily apparent during the Fleet Problems. Nevertheless, the sea maneuvers moved the notion of carrier attack operations from idea to practice.

Fleet Problem IX proved a major breakpoint in the Navy's transformation. During the exercise, Vice Admiral William V. Pratt (who had recently served as president of the Naval War College) authorized Reeves, commanding the *Saratoga*, to execute a high-speed run toward the Panama Canal. Reeves 'attacked' the canal with a seventy-plane strike force launched 140 miles from the target.[33] On her return, the carrier was located and ruled sunk, but Pratt took a positive view of the *Saratoga* strike. To Pratt, the attack represented a preview of the carrier's potential to conduct attack operations. In 1930, after Pratt became Chief of Naval Operations, he stressed using carriers on the offensive in war games and fleet exercises.

Meanwhile, the Navy's leadership continued to debate the size of future carriers and the value of naval aviation relative to battleships. In 1931, during Fleet Problem XII, Blue Force, comprising the big carriers *Saratoga* and *Lexington*, along with some destroyers and cruisers, was given the mission of stopping an invading Black Force, comprising battleships, cruisers, destroyers, and the smaller carrier *Langley*. Blue split its force into two carrier groups and, instead of going after Black's battle line, attempted to locate and sink the transport ships carrying the landing force. Naval aviators were disappointed when Blue failed and Black effected a landing, although Reeves cautioned that the operation's results should not be incorrectly interpreted, nor the strength of air power underestimated. Clearly, however, some damage was done to the Navy's confidence in air power's potential. Pratt's support for the carrier appeared to wane. He declared the Fleet Problem reaffirmed that the 'battleship is the backbone of the Fleet.'[34]

While the carrier task force would be exercised again, it would not be as an alternative to the traditional battle line.

Fleet Problem XII proved to be only a temporary setback. A year later, 152 aircraft from the *Saratoga* and *Lexington*, under Yarrell's command, executed a surprise attack on Army air bases and facilities in Hawaii. The Army contested the effectiveness of the carrier raid and also claimed their planes had critically damaged the carriers, even though Yarrell's aircraft had conducted two bombing runs on the Army's planes as they sat on the runways. The attack served as important display of the carrier's offensive capabilities.[35]

Fleet Problem XIII followed Yarrell's successful mock air attack on Pearl Harbor. Blue Fleet deployed from Hawaii to support an expeditionary force moving against three unfortified atolls along the US Pacific Coast. Black Fleet operated in defense of the atolls. Yarrell commanded Blue Fleet's air component, to include the *Saratoga* and land-based aircraft in Hawaii. Black Fleet included the *Lexington* and *Langley*. Both Yarrell and his Black Fleet counterpart, Captain Ernest King, focused their efforts on neutralizing the other's air power. King received permission from his senior, Admiral William H. Standley, to operate the *Lexington* independent of the battle force. Keeping the *Lexington* out of the *Saratoga*'s engagement range until

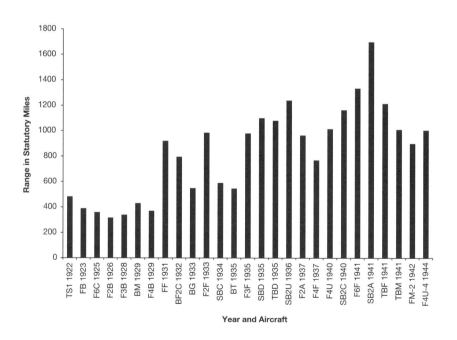

Figure 10.1: Range for USN attack aircraft

191

just the right moment, he launched a devastating forty-nine-plane raid, successfully demonstrating naval aviation's potential as an attack weapon.

Fleet Problem XIV, in 1933, simulated a war with Japan. Black Fleet comprised the two big carriers and an escorting force. The fleet bypassed Hawaii to strike the US West Coast. Black Fleet commander, Admiral Frank H. Clark, a non-aviator, split his force into three groups, with the northern group organized around the *Lexington*, and the southern group around the *Saratoga*. When aircraft from *Lexington* sighted a Blue submarine, Clark directed his cruisers to form a battle column in anticipation of a surface engagement. In so doing, he stripped the *Lexington* of her screen. As she was preparing for a dawn aircraft launch, two Blue battleships emerged from the darkness, one on each side of the carrier. The *Lexington* was quickly ruled out of action. The *Saratoga* proceeded with its strikes, but was attacked and put out of commission by attacks from the *Langley* and other Blue Fleet aircraft. The results were a setback for the carriers, though aviation advocates argued the failure was more a product of poor tactics.

Despite the disappointing results of Fleet Problem XIV, it was becoming difficult to ignore the potential of naval air power. Improvements in aircraft capability were impressive. As Figure 10.1 shows, around 1930, the range of naval attack aircraft leaped from around 400–500 miles to 600–1,000 miles. By the late 1930s, the Navy's combat aircraft boasted ranges of between 800 and 1,200 miles, representing roughly a 100 per cent increase in a decade.

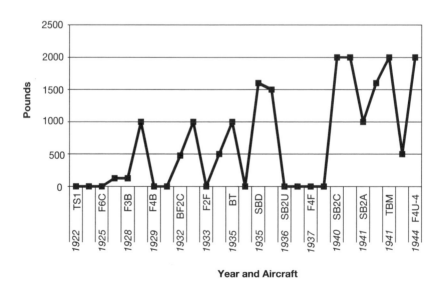

Figure 10.2: Payload for USN attack aircraft

Table 10.3: USN aircraft engine horsepower, 1914–43

Year	Horsepower
1914	100
1918	200–300
1930	700
1939	1,000
1943	2,000

Bomb load-carrying capacity also increased dramatically (Figure 10.2), a result of industry's ability by mid-decade to produce high-performance, all-metal aircraft that incorporated fuel-injected radial engines and variable pitch propellers. Similar to today's advances in computing power, during this brief period the high-performance, single-seat aircraft engine horsepower had an impressive trajectory (Table 10.3). As a result, the Navy's air strike arm more than doubled its range, and simultaneously realized an order-of-magnitude increase in lift capacity. The ability to fly great distances and attack targets with thousand pound bombs made dive-bombers true ship killers. Moreover, dive-bombers were compact enough to be carried in substantial numbers on carriers.[36]

As aircraft range and payloads rapidly increased, concerns emerged over the fleet's ability to provide adequate air defense. The fleet's 'picket line' of destroyers proved inadequate at providing sufficient early warning for effective counter-air operations against long-range, high-flying attack aircraft. Abrogation of the Washington Naval Treaty in the mid-1930s by the Great Powers exacerbated the problem. Nations were no longer constrained in the size of the carrier force. As a result, naval aviation advocates argued that the best defense was to find and strike the enemy's carrier, before its planes were launched against the fleet – and, since the fleet as a whole could not move as fast as the carrier or provide much protection, they saw little virtue in continuing the existing practice of using sea-based aircraft primarily to set the conditions for a fleet battleship engagement.

On the other hand, battleship advocates remained skeptical of the case for independent carrier operations, pointing out that the Japanese could defend against torpedo attacks by armoring or adding impact-absorbing blisters to their ship hulls. The traditionalists also argued that anti-aircraft fire would keep dive-bombers at bay. Finally, they asserted, battleships had remained the centerpiece of the Imperial Japanese Navy, and hence they must remain the US Navy's principal weapon. Battleships were required to defeat battleships.

Given these considerations, it is not surprising that the mainstream Navy had yet to shift to the measures of effectiveness that would show the carrier's advantages in a fleet engagement. Weight of firepower was still the paramount consideration, not firepower as a function of range. As late as 1940, the Naval War College was pointing out to its students that 'it takes 108 planes to carry as many large torpedoes as one squadron of destroyers and 1,200 to carry as many large bombs or large projectiles as one battleship.'[37]

Nevertheless, by the late 1930s, Navy Fleet Problems generally began with opposing carriers placing top priority on seeking each other out, looking for an opportunity to execute a decisive first strike. This tactic generated intense debate. Might carriers operate independently and then, if confronted by an enemy force, might the battleships be employed to protect the carriers, rather than the other way around?

During Fleet Problem XVIII in 1937, White Fleet, with the newest carrier, the 13,800-ton *Ranger*, defended the Hawaiian Islands against Black Fleet, which included the *Saratoga*, *Lexington* and *Langley*. The Fleet Problem revealed a serious disagreement over the operational use of carriers. Admiral Claude C. Bloch, the battle force commander, felt that the carriers were best employed in formation with the battle line, receiving protection from the surface combatants' anti-aircraft guns. The aviators however contended that command of the air should be achieved before the opposing fleets engaged. To accomplish this, the carriers would have to operate independent of the main body, seeking out and destroying the enemy carrier. In the exercise, however, Admiral Bloch restricted the carriers to flying patrols over the battleships and covering the fleet's landing force. Consequently, the *Langley* was sunk, while the *Saratoga* and *Lexington* were heavily damaged by enemy air. After the exercise, when Vice Admiral Frederick J. Horne, commander of all carriers, circulated a paper calling for independent carrier operations, Admiral Bloch had him recall all copies.

The Navy intended Fleet Problem XIX, conducted in 1938, to help resolve the growing dispute over the carriers' role. The scenario divided the fleet into two opposing forces, with Black attempting to establish a coastal base following the destruction of White Fleet. The *Ranger*, along with some land-based aircraft, was assigned to White Fleet. The *Saratoga* and *Lexington* supported the Black Fleet. King saw the exercise as an opportunity to correct what he felt was a serious misuse of the carrier force in Fleet Problem XVIII, but was disappointed when, despite his objections, Black split its forces into two battleship groups, each accompanied by a carrier. Aircraft from the *Ranger* attacked the *Lexington*, and then a follow-on attack by White land-based patrol bombers put the big carrier out of action. The *Saratoga*, as King had feared, was too distant to offer support for *Lexington*. The ambiguous results did little to resolve the dispute over carrier doctrine.

The second phase of Fleet Problem XIX went better for King's carrier force. Blue Fleet was to execute an amphibious landing against a Red Force on Hawaii. Red defenses comprised Army Air Corps planes and Navy patrol bombers. King, allowed to devise his own tactics, had both the *Saratoga* and *Ranger* at his disposal. He directed the *Saratoga* to maneuver northwest of Hawaii to launch a predawn attack on Hawaii. Just before dawn on 29 March, the *Saratoga* launched a successful surprise attack on the Army's Hickam and Wheeler airfields and the Pearl Harbor Naval Air Station.

The third and final phase of Fleet Problem XIX again involved two fleets. In this phase Purple Fleet prepared to launch attacks on Green Fleet's base at San Francisco. King, with the Purple Fleet, again formed an independent carrier strike force with the *Saratoga* and *Lexington*. Breaking off from the battle force, King maneuvered the carriers to launch air strikes on Green's base. Following the strikes, the carriers rejoined Purple Fleet's main body, where their scouting efforts located Green Fleet. Carrier aircraft thereupon attacked the Green Fleet force of cruisers, destroyers and submarines. Although the debate remained inconclusively resolved during the Fleet problems, in 1939 the Navy reorganized its carrier force into Carrier Division 1 with the *Saratoga* and *Lexington* and Carrier Division 2 with the *Yorktown* and *Enterprise*. Naval aviation was emerging as a force in its own right.

On the Cusp

A major influence on the carrier's role was the newly introduced radar technology, which became the Navy's foremost scouting device and a critical enabler for early warning of air attack. The Navy had undertaken radar research during the 1930s, and by 1936 the US Naval Research Laboratory had conducted successful shipboard demonstrations. In 1938, search radar was installed on a battleship and subjected to exhaustive testing during fleet maneuvers in the Caribbean. The tests were a success, with approaching aircraft being detected at ranges of fifty miles.[38]

Over the next two years, the Navy installed radar on all carriers and many surface combatants. By the end of 1939, the United States was testing shipboard radar prototypes for long-range aircraft detection, anti-aircraft fire control and surface tracking. Breakthroughs followed, and radar quickly became vital for defense against fighters, and an indispensable navigational tool.[39] In addition, the growing ability to communicate by radio at extended ranges facilitated greater command and control of air operations.

As technology matured, the carrier began to achieve capabilities that matched the naval aviation vision. Towers, now director of the Bureau of Aeronautics, declared that the carriers must be allowed to operate independent of the battle line. 'I am convinced that carriers must be considered, not as individual vessels, but as part of a striking force,' which would comprise two carriers, four heavy cruisers and four destroyers.[40] Towers also scaled back advocacy for the small carriers, arguing future carriers should be at least as big as the *Yorktown* and *Enterprise* (roughly 20,000 tons each), and with comparable speed (33 knots) and aircraft capacity (72-plane minimum). In addition, he advocated increasing the carrier's fuel capacity to extend its range.[41] The Navy leadership agreed. By January 1940, the basic plans for the *Essex* class of carriers had been formed, displacing 27,000 tons, and emphasizing speed (33 knots) over armament, and higher aircraft numbers (up to 90) in lieu of heavy gunfire support provided by its escort ships. As a result, the Navy prepared to enter the Second World War committed to deploying a force of large carriers, and with it, the nucleus of capabilities needed to fight a new kind of war at sea.

Assessing the Transformation Process

Barriers slowed the transformation process; however, they also helped the Navy to avoid 'locking in' to the wrong class of carriers. Measured developments, extensive experimentation and a modicum of support from Congress also ensured that when war threatened, the United States could quickly 'ramp up' the production of carriers (Table 10.4). 'Buying in' to the revolution at this late date also permitted the Navy to gain the maximum benefit from both technological advances and the insights from its series of war games and Fleet Problems. The Navy proved very effective at 'time-based competition.'[42] The Service had, through a combination of design – and luck – positioned itself to transform quickly into a radically different kind of force. By the late 1930s, the Navy had established enough of a defense industrial base capacity to sustain a rapid buildup in its carrier fleet and the aircraft that would operate off its decks.

Table 10.4: Authorized US carrier construction, 1939–41

Name	Carrier type	Date contract signed	Date commissioned
Hornet	CV	…	24/10/42
Essex	CV	3/7/40	31/12/42
Yorktown	CV	3/7/40	15/4/43
Intrepid	CV	3/7/40	16/8/43
Lexington	CV	9/9/40	17/2/43
Bunker Hill	CV	9/9/40	25/5/43
Wasp	CV	9/9/40	24/11/43
Franklin	CV	9/9/40	31/1/44
Ticonderoga	CV	9/9/40	8/5/44
Randolph	CV	9/9/40	9/10/44
Hornet	CV	…	29/11/43
Bennington	CV	15/12/41	6/8/44
Boxer	CV	15/12/41	16/4/45

Interestingly, the Navy did not have to build a large number of carriers to effect its transformation. Through the end of 1942, the Navy had constructed only eight carriers. Of these, only four – *Saratoga*, *Lexington*, *Yorktown*, and *Enterprise* – approximated the workhorse *Essex*-class carriers that joined the fleet beginning in 1943. Put differently, a small perturbation in the Navy's capital ship program yielded 'revolutionary' results.

Once the Navy had crossed the transformation threshold, it moved aggressively. The battleship was the principal casualty of the Navy's turn to carriers. Only four of six *Iowa*-class ships were built, while the *Montana* class was cancelled altogether. Following the termination of battleship construction, sixteen fleet or fast carriers were commissioned during the war, along with seventy-nine light and escort carriers. Between 1941 and the war's end, the fleet carrier force quadrupled, while the escort carrier force increased from one combatant to seventy-one.

While the transformation from the battleship to carrier was stark, the post-transformation Navy also had a need for 'legacy' systems, combatant ships that were part of the traditional naval battle line. Between 1941 and 1945, the number of submarines and destroyers in the fleet more than doubled (Table 10.5), a feat almost matched by the cruiser force. The Navy's ability to increase rapidly the production of a class of ships that might today be viewed more as experimental prototypes, while also closing off production of a 'sunset' system (i.e., the battleship) and sustaining the production of useful 'legacy' systems, allowed it to effect the revolution in maritime warfare that led to the defeat of the Japanese Navy.

The dynamic of depression-era budgets had much the same effect on aviation programs. If the Navy's aircraft procurement budget was limited, so too was its ability to accumulate a large inventory of aircraft whose value would depreciate rapidly in an environment marked by rapid progress in technology. The Navy seemed to appreciate this. While aviation technology was progressing rapidly and the threat to the United States was relatively low, it consciously avoided 'locking in' to large numbers of aircraft.

Table 10.5: USN active fleet, 1941–45

	1941	1942	1943	1944	1945
Battleships	17	19	21	23	23
Fleet Carriers	7	4	19	25	28
Escort Carriers	1	12	35	65	71
Cruisers	37	39	48	61	72
Destroyers	171	224	332	367	377
Submarines	112	133	172	230	232
Others	445	1,351	3,072	5,313	5,965
Total Active	790	1,782	3,699	6,084	6,768

From 1932 to 1938, inventory of combat aircraft remained essentially stagnant in terms of numbers, though aircraft types increased. During this period alone, the Navy introduced eleven new combat models. Rather than maintain a large inventory of rapidly obsolescing planes, it concentrated on keeping up with technology.

In 1940, as the war in Europe took a turn for the worse and USA–Japan relations became increasingly strained, the Navy was able to move quickly to increase its combat aircraft inventory. From 1940 to 1944, the numbers of airplanes, on average, doubled in size every year, increasing overall by nearly 2,000 per cent.[43]

In summary, given the uncertainties it faced, the Navy achieved a kind of 'hedging' strategy. It created a balanced fleet in which the option remained open to expand the battle line by ramping up construction of substantially better battleships of the *Iowa* and *Montana* class, or to move relatively quickly to increase the number of fast carriers with the *Essex* class.

Baptism by Fire: The Transformation Revealed – and Sustained

The Second World War offered the ultimate 'exercise' of carrier aviation's potential. The war came along just as technology (e.g. advances in aviation, radar and radio communications) had matured to the point where the operations envisioned by the Navy's aviators were not only possible, but necessary.

Still, at the time of the Imperial Japanese Navy's surprise attack on Pearl Harbor in December 1941, the definitive case for the carriers had yet to be made.[44] Admiral Husband E. Kimmel, the commander-in-chief at Pearl Harbor, tended to view carriers as auxiliaries. In fact, the senior air expert on Kimmel's forty-man staff held the modest rank of commander. In the months following the attack, however, the aircraft carrier established itself as the Navy's dominant weapon, not so much because the Gun Club experienced any kind of epiphany, but rather, as Ron Spector has argued, 'because most of the surviving American battleships were too slow and consumed too much fuel for the kind of fast moving hit-and-run warfare the U.S. was now obliged to wage in the Pacific.'[45]

The Battles of the Coral Sea and Midway in May and June of 1942, respectively, confirmed that a transformation in naval warfare had occurred, and that the Navy was well positioned to exploit it. The Coral Sea engagement was the first in history where the fleets did not achieve visual sight of each other. The Battle of Midway, one month later, was also dominated by carrier aircraft, with opposing sides' attacking aircraft seeking out the other's carriers as their principal target. Japan's loss of four of its carriers in the engagement confirmed the U.S. Navy's decisive victory.

At the time of Coral Sea and Midway, neither Japan nor the United States had established a clear lead in aircraft range. As a result, the crucial determinants of success in the carrier war proved to be scouting effectiveness and striking power. Although the US fleets enjoyed the advantage of radar, it was used inefficiently and did not help avert serious damage to American carriers. Thus the advantage was with the offense, and the engagements proceeded much in the way envisioned by aviation enthusiasts during the inter-war years.

Offensive air combat, however, brought with it high attrition and threatened the ability of naval forces to sustain the carrier revolution.[46] A premium was placed on stealth, deception, dispersed forces, and maximum attacking power. The dominance of offense over defense was reflected in carrier air wing composition. In 1942, roughly 75 per cent of a US carrier's air wing comprised attack aircraft.

For the United States, the imperative of offensive operations lessened as the Americans continued to revolutionize the composition of the fleet. As Wayne Hughes insightfully noted, having attack planes comprise three-quarters of carrier wing 'was a good gamble at the beginning of 1942. As early as late 1942 it was a very bad gamble.'[47] The reason for the shift in the odds was the rapidly improving measures for defending the carrier task force. This dramatically enhanced capability rested on the integration of several key technologies, including extended-range communications, radar and anti-aircraft guns. The ability to obtain early warning of an attack, and to mass and coordinate the carrier battle group's defenses (now comprising three or four carriers), combined with the shifting of the carrier air wing mix to approximately 65 per cent fighter aircraft, meant it was no longer critical to attack first. Moreover, with the Japanese carrier threat greatly diminished and the American island-hopping campaign proceeding apace, the US carriers found themselves increasingly in confrontation with Japan's land-based air forces. Thus, where the measure of effectiveness in 1942 had been the number of carriers sunk, it now became the number of naval aircraft destroyed. While Coral Sea and Midway were fought under an 'offensive dominant' regime, the defense, thanks to additional wartime developments, recovered substantially.

Following Coral Sea and Midway, both the United States and Japan also faced the problem of replacing pilot losses, both from combat and severe fatigue. While the Japanese had a reserve of highly qualified aviators, the Americans were not only able to maintain a supply of qualified pilots, but also sent their most experienced pilots back to the United States to train new pilots. In later encounters between the carrier forces of the two fleets, both participants and historians attribute continued American success principally to the far greater skill and experience of US pilots. The United States maintained a dominant position in the new form of warfare, in large measure due to its ability to develop human resources to match advances in technology, offensive and defensive operational concepts, and force structure – in effect combining all the elements that turn transformation into revolution.

Investing in the Revolution

If the phrase 'show me your defense budget and I'll show you your defense priorities' carries any weight, the Navy dramatically changed its priorities promptly following the transformational battles in the spring of 1942. Even after Pearl Harbor, the General Board had resisted moving toward a carrier-centered fleet. The board wanted to increase the number of carriers, but it opposed converting light cruiser hulls into small carriers, and proposed a building program that would lay down only nine additional carriers through 1944.[48]

In May, however, King, now Chief of Naval Operations, unilaterally modified the General Board's recommendations, indefinitely deferring five battleships and replacing them with five carriers and ten cruisers.[49] King was supported in Congress by a powerful ally, Representative Carl Vinson, who in June submitted a bill authorizing the construction of 1.9 million tons of carriers, cruisers and destroyers – but no additional battleships. While to some degree the bill reflected the shortage of battleship armor plate, to an even greater degree it acknowledged that the battleship had been displaced by the carrier as the centerpiece of the fleet.[50] The Navy's wartime construction program proved a watershed in the ascendancy of the carrier force.

Reflections on a Revolution

In its role as the fleet's new main fighting ship, the carrier also showed its weaknesses. Carrier aircraft became the chief naval weapon during daylight hours, but when the sun set, air power lost its grip on control of the sea, and surface combatant engagements proved the norm. In a number of maritime engagements during the Second World War, the battleship dominated.[51] Moreover, battleships were hardly sitting ducks against carrier-based aircraft, particularly when operating as part of a carrier task force. Battleships in the Second World War were equipped with air defenses, perhaps some 100 times greater than those available during the attack on Pearl Harbor.[52]

Still, there could be no doubt as to the carrier's new status in the fleet. This change was reflected not only in budgets and naval operations, but also in the organization of the fleet. The Navy's carrier task forces could launch 'round-the-clock' offensive air operations and sustain themselves for long periods from a mobile fleet train. Battleships filled a new role, supporting carrier task force operations. The age of the carrier battle group had arrived.

Notes

1 The term 'military revolution' has a long and somewhat contentious history. In academic circles, the debate has spanned four decades. See, for example, Geoffrey

Parker, *The Military Revolution* (Cambridge, UK: Cambridge University Press, 1988); Clifford J. Rogers, ed., *The Military Revolution Debate* (Boulder, CO: Westview Press, 1995); Jeremy Black, *European Warfare, 1660–1815* (New Haven, CT: Yale University Press, 1994). In defense policymaking circles, during the latter stages of the Cold War, emphasis was placed on Soviet writings that examined the phenomenon of abrupt advances in military capabilities, typically referred to as 'military–technical revolutions,' or 'revolutions in military affairs.' See, for example, Mary C. Fitzgerald, 'Advanced Conventional Munitions and Moscow's Defensive Force Posture,' *Defense Analysis*, vol. 6, no. 2, 1990, pp. 167–92. Beginning in the late 1980s, the Defense Department began studying the issue. See Fred C. Ikle and Albert Wohlstetter *et al.*, *Discriminate Deterrence* (Washington, DC: Department of Defense, January 1988); Andrew F. Krepinevich, *The Military–Technical Revolution: A Preliminary Assessment* (Unpublished paper, Office of Net Assessment, Office of the Secretary of Defense, July 1992).

2 The building block requirements identified here are drawn from established work in the field of military innovation. See, Stephen Peter Rosen, *Winning the Next War* (Ithaca, NY: Cornell University Press, 1991); Williamson Murray and Barry Watts, 'Military Innovation in Peacetime,' in Williamson Murray and Allan R. Millett, eds, *Military Innovation in the Interwar Period* (Cambridge, UK: Cambridge University Press, 1996); and Andrew F. Krepinevich, Jr., *The Army and Vietnam* (Baltimore, MD: The Johns Hopkins University Press, 1986).

3 Norman Friedman, 'The Aircraft Carrier,' in Robert Gardiner, ed., *The Eclipse of the Big Gun: The Warship, 1906–45* (Annapolis, MD: Naval Institute Press, 1992), p. 38.

4 Clark G. Reynolds, *The Fast Carriers* (Annapolis, MD: Naval Institute Press, 1968), p. 1. Sims presciently defined the fast carrier as 'an airplane carrier of thirty-five knots and carrying one hundred planes.' See also Charles M. Melhorn, *Two-Block Fox* (Annapolis, MD: Naval Institute Press, 1974), pp. 30–33.

5 William, F. Trimble, *Admiral William F. Moffett: Architect of Naval Aviation* (Washington, DC: Smithsonian Institution Press, 1994), p. 71.

6 Benson to OpNav, dispatch ser 82 dtd 7 December 1918. US Department of the Navy (USDN), Record Group 45, Naval Records Collection of the Office of Naval Records and Library: Subject File 1911–27, Box 105.

7 On the effective range-finding system to modern battleship effectiveness, see Jon Tetsuro Sumida, *In Defence of Naval Supremacy* (Boston: Unwin Hyman, 1989).

8 CO, USS Texas, ltr to CincLant Flt dtd 10 March 1919, read into the record of General Board Hearings (GBH), 1919, p. 926.

9 General Board Correspondence (GBC) 449, secret ltr ser 887 to SecNav dtd 23 June 1919, USDN, Record Group 72, Bureau of Aeronautics General Correspondence: Office of CNO 1917–25, Box 345. The General Board also recommended that 'airplane carriers for the fleet be provided in the proportion of one carrier to each squadron of capital ships.' Norman Friedman, Thomas C. Hone, and Mark D. Mandeles, *The Introduction of Carrier Aviation into the U.S. Navy and Royal Navy: Military–Technical Revolutions, Organizations, and the Problems of Decision* (Unpublished paper, 12 May 1994), p. 57. The General Board was the senior uniformed organization that reviewed strategy, policy, ship designs and procurement for the Secretary of the Navy.

10 Melhorn, *Two-Block Fox*, p. 60.

11 Ronald H. Spector, *Eagle Against the Sun* (New York: Free Press, 1985), p. 22.

12 William M. McBride, 'Challenging a Strategic Paradigm: Aviation and the U.S. Navy Special Policy Board of 1924,' *Journal of Strategic Studies*, September 1991, p. 75.
13 Melhorn, *Two-Block Fox*, p. 88.
14 Friedman *et al.*, *The Introduction of Carrier Aviation into the U.S. Navy and Royal Navy*, p. 22; Gardiner, ed., *The Eclipse of the Big Gun*, p. 39; Thomas C. Hone, Norman Friedman, and Mark D. Mandeles, *American and British Aircraft Carrier Development, 1919–1941* (Annapolis, MD: Naval Institute Press, 1999), pp. 33–37.
15 Geoffrey Till, 'Adopting the Aircraft Carrier,' in Williamson Murray and Allan R. Millett, eds, *Military Innovation in the Interwar Period* (New York: Cambridge University Press, 1996), p. 211.
16 The importance of early successes in periods of transformation is discussed in John P. Kotter, 'Leading Change: Why Transformation Efforts Fail,' *Harvard Business Review*, March–April 1995, p. 52.
17 William F. Trimble, *Wings for the Navy: A History of the Naval Aircraft Factory, 1917–1956* (Annapolis, MD: Naval Institute Press, 1990), pp. 7–8.
18 One area where promising developments were not exploited was the turbojet. Another area of the industrial base that suffered from financial shortfalls and lack of attention was torpedo production. I.B. Holley, Jr., 'Jet Lag in the Army Air Corps,' in H. R. Borowski, ed., *Military Planning in the Twentieth Century* (Washington, DC: Office of Air Force History, 1986), pp. 123–53.
19 Wayne P. Hughes, Jr., *Fleet Tactics and Coastal Combat*, 2nd edn (Annapolis, MD: Naval Institute Press, 1999), p. 86.
20 Clark G. Reynolds, *Admiral John H. Towers: The Struggle for Naval Air Supremacy* (Annapolis, MD: Naval Institute Press, 1991), p. 226.
21 Rosen, *Winning the Next War*, pp. 76–80. Another example of transformation-minded officers institutionalizing their agenda by appealing to the dominant culture of their service is the US Army in Vietnam over air mobility. See Krepinevich, *The Army and Vietnam* (Baltimore, MD: Johns Hopkins University Press, 1986), pp. 113–14.
22 Trimble, *Admiral William F. Moffett*, p. 135.
23 On the importance of institutionalization during periods of transformation, and the problems incurred by the Royal Navy with naval aviation, see Rosen, *Winning the Next War*, pp. 96–100; Geoffrey Till, 'Adopting the Aircraft Carrier,' pp. 205–19.
24 Finally, in June 1939, Congress passed legislation authorizing a civilian pilot training program under the new Civil Aeronautics Authority. David C. Evans and Mark R. Peattie, *Kaigun* (Annapolis, MD: Naval Institute Press, 1997), p. 326.
25 Reynolds, *The Fast Carriers*, p. 17.
26 Ronald H. Spector, 'Winning With Second Best Technology: Naval Aviation in the Pacific, 1941–44' (Unpublished paper), p. 7.
27 Friedman *et al.*, *The Introduction of Carrier Aviation into the U.S. Navy and Royal Navy*, p. 77; Evans and Peattie, *Kaigun*, p. 323; Friedman, 'Aircraft Carrier,' p. 39; Reynolds, *Towers*, p. 205.
28 Friedman, 'Aircraft Carrier,' p. 187.
29 Reynolds, *Fast Carriers*, p. 17; and Friedman *et al.*, *The Introduction of Carrier Aviation into the U.S. Navy and Royal Navy*, pp. 90, 188. While Lt. Wagner's demonstration helped pave the way for carrier strike operations, Marine aviators pioneered dive-bombing in Haiti in 1919. Trimble, *Admiral William F. Moffett*, pp. 209–10.
30 The board was comprised of many naval aviation proponents, including Moffett, Reeves, Mitscher, and Yarnell.

31 Hone *et al.*, *American and British Aircraft Carrier Development*, pp. 46–47.

32 Trimble, *Admiral William F. Moffett*, p. 212n.

33 *Saratoga* carried 110 planes and 100 pilots, an enormous leap in capability from the *Langley's* few dozen aircraft (Fleet Problem IX, National Archives Publication M964, 'Report of the CINC, U.S. Fleet,' pp. 23, 26, 71). *Saratoga's* revolutionary exploit was the product of chance. She was detached from the battleship force because the battleships' destroyer screen did not have sufficient fuel to keep up with her.

34 'Admiral Reeves' Comments,' Fleet Problem XII, Office of the Secretary, Confidential Correspondence, Modern Military Records, US National Archives; and 'Remarks of Admiral W.V. Pratt . . . at the Critique of Fleet Problem XII,' Bristol Papers.

35 For a summary of the Army's protest see Reynolds, *Admiral John H. Towers*, pp. 237–38.

36 Roy A. Grosnick, *Dictionary of American Naval Aviation Squadrons*, vol. 1 (Washington, DC: Naval Historical Center, Department of the Navy, 1955), pp. 453–508; Gordon Swanborough and Peter M. Bowens, *United States Navy Aircraft Since 1911* (Annapolis, MD: Naval Institute Press, 1990).

37 George W. Baer, *One Hundred Years of Sea Power* (Stanford, CA: Stanford University Press, 1993), p. 136.

38 Evans and Peattie, *Kaigun*, pp. 394, 411.

39 Hughes, *Fleet Tactics*, pp. 116–11.

40 Reynolds, *Admiral John H. Towers*, p. 292n.

41 *Ibid.*

42 For a discussion of the concept of 'time-based competition,' see George Stalk, 'Time – the Next Source of Competitive Advantage,' *Harvard Business Review*, July–August 1988, p. 41.

43 Deputy Chief of Naval Operations and The Commander, Naval Air Systems Command, *United States Naval Aviation 1910–80* (Washington, DC: Government Printing Office, 1981), pp. 381–82.

44 In a number of important respects the US Navy trailed its Japanese counterpart. At the time of its attack on Pearl Harbor, the Japanese had ten carriers in the Pacific; the US Navy had only three. In April 1941, the Japanese created the First Air Fleet, comprising three carriers, two seaplane divisions, and ten destroyers. American carriers, on the other hand, were still being brought together in an *ad hoc* manner for exercises. The First Air Fleet represented the single most powerful concentration of naval air power in the world and constituted a revolutionary change in naval organization. The Pearl Harbor operation might not have been conceived, let alone executed, without the First Air Fleet's existence (Evans and Peattie, *Kaigun*, pp. 349, 351–52).

45 Spector, 'Winning With Second Best Technology,' p. 15.

46 In December 1941 the United States possessed seven fleet carriers, *Saratoga*, *Lexington*, *Ranger*, *Yorktown*, *Enterprise*, *Wasp* and *Hornet*. A year later, only one, *Ranger*, had not been sunk or seriously damaged.

47 Hughes, *Fleet Tactics and Coastal Combat*, p. 110.

48 Joel R. Davidson, *The Unsinkable Fleet* (Annapolis, MD: Naval Institute Press, 1996), p. 34.

49 Chief of Naval Operations to the Secretary of the Navy, 8 May 1942, Subject: 1943–44 Combatant Shipbuilding Program, 00 Files 1942–47, Box 1, Folder 1, Naval Historical Center, Washington, DC.

50 Robert L. O'Connell, *Sacred Vessels* (Boulder: CO: Westview Press), p. 316.

51 Apart from the raid on Pearl Harbor, the annihilation of the Japanese convoy and escort force by US Army Air Force bombers at the Bismarck Sea, and the

cruiser and battleships actions off Guadalcanal on 12–15 November 1942, there were seventeen named battles between Japanese and American naval forces during the first two years of the war. Four were carrier battles, and thirteen were ship-to-ship engagements.

52 Bernard Brodie, *Sea Power in the Machine Age* (New York: Greenwood Press, 1969), pp. 418–19.

11

US OBJECTIVES AND PLANS FOR WAR WITH THE SOVIET UNION, 1946–54

David Kaiser

Any war plan raises a sequence of questions that need to be answered before embarking upon a war with any confidence. First, what is the political objective of the war, and more specifically, to what extent must we force our enemy to submit to achieve it? The next two critical questions address the military and political impact of the plan upon the enemy that one hopes to compel. First, what are the chances that the plan, if executed, will have the desired *military* impact upon the enemy? Second, assuming that the plan *does* have the desired military effect upon the enemy, what are the chances that it will therefore have the desired *political* impact upon him as well – that is, what are the chances that the enemy will make peace on our desired terms? To estimate the chances of the overall success of the plan, one must then multiply those two estimated probabilities together. While this is not an exercise that can achieve mathematical exactitude, it is nonetheless useful in broadly weighing possible outcomes.

To illustrate, let us look for a moment at the most famous war plan in modern military history, the Schlieffen Plan, which was designed to encircle the French army, take Paris, and quickly force France to make peace with Germany. Looking first at its execution in purely military terms, we find that it failed, although many have argued that it might have succeeded. For the sake of argument, and without getting into the merits of the complex questions involved, I shall assign a 60 per cent probability of military success to the plan, implying that had the Germans been able to execute it ten times, it would have achieved its military objectives on six occasions. We must then ask, however, whether that would have persuaded the French government to make peace on acceptable terms, as another French government did in 1940, or whether France, supported by both Russia and Great Britain, would have continued to resist in 1914 anyway, as France had in 1870–71. If we rate the chances of a quick peace at only 50 per cent, and then multiply that figure by 60 per cent, we get only a 30 per cent chance that the plan would really meet its political, as well as military, objectives.

When one does such calculations realistically and analyzes the result before war begins, they can encourage some re-evaluation of the importance of what one is trying to achieve in the war, and perhaps even spur a change of political objective. Had Bethmann Hollweg and the rest of the Germans calculated that they had less than a 50–50 chance of knocking France out of the war, they might well have re-evaluated the question of whether the war was worth it – as most of us, I think, would now agree that it was not. Germany then might have accepted the idea that the era in which one great European power could simply conquer one or more others at an acceptable cost was over. The same process might have encouraged the Germans to re-evaluate the extent of the threat they faced from Russia. In short, the preparation and evaluation of war plans can help a nation define or redefine its national security interests through a kind of intellectual feedback loop that forces politicians and strategists to re-evaluate their objectives in light of the viability of their strategies.

To a remarkable extent, these questions were both addressed and answered during the early Cold War – specifically the years 1946–54 – when American military and political authorities seriously considered a possible war with the Soviet Union for the first time.[1] But while planners and members of the National Security Council raised these questions from time to time, they seldom gave them the attention they seemed to require. Even with respect to the purely military effectiveness of their plans against the Soviet Union, planners relied upon extremely optimistic assumptions. The issue of the circumstances under which the Soviet Union might surrender received much less attention. Finally, given that these war plans relied largely upon atomic and thermonuclear weapons of unprecedented destructive power, a third question eventually emerged. Was it possible that, given the death, destruction, and chaos that would result from a successful American atomic offensive against the Soviet Union, a victory would leave the United States face to face with an impossible situation? This question eventually reached the highest levels of government in 1954, but it was not allowed to interfere with the general thrust of American military planning.

Had these questions been more systematically addressed, they might have led to more extended discussions of the bases of national policy as well. *Was* it really necessary or sensible to plan for the total destruction of the Soviet Union in the event of a war? What exactly *would* justify an American decision to fight? In what circumstances *would* the United States actually be able to use atomic or nuclear weapons? And was the Soviet Union – faced with a similar range of choices – really likely to undertake a war? As it turned out, the war plans written and approved in the Eisenhower Administration took the possibility of all-out war very seriously, and also called for the use of atomic and nuclear weapons in a variety of local contingencies. But in practice, one could argue, the considerations that planners generally tended to ignore intruded upon decision-makers – especially in the most severe crises – and forced American leaders into a curious kind of doublethink in an effort to reconcile their plans and force posture with political and military realities. Faced with real choices, they often declined to execute their plans.

When American military planners took a first sustained look at post-war relations with the Soviet Union in 1944, they reached remarkable conclusions. In preparation for the Dumbarton Oaks Conference, on 28 July the Joint Strategic Studies Committee submitted a paper on fundamental military factors and their relationship to arrangements for the post-war world. The paper surveyed the strategic situation that victory over the Axis was likely to create. After the defeat of Japan, they wrote, 'the United States and Russia will be the strongest military powers in the world . . . the relative strength and geographic positions of these two powers are such as to preclude the military defeat of one of these powers by the other, even if that power were allied with the British Empire.' This remarkable paper, which General Marshall forwarded to the Secretary of State on 3 August, certainly implied that the two victorious powers would have to live with one another when the war was over, and that any conflict between them would have to stop far short of any attempt at total victory.[2] Sixty years later the military planners' appreciation of the situation looks rather prescient, but it did not guide the planning that began just two years later for a possible new war.

Instead, by 1946, the emergence of various political conflicts between the Soviet Union and the United States on the one hand and the successful development of the atomic bomb on the other had led American military planners to think in terms of a complete victory over the Soviet Union. In his careful study, *American War Plans 1945–1950*, Steven Ross shows how the Joint Chiefs of Staff began directing the preparation of plans for war against the Soviet Union in 1946 despite the lack of much specific political guidance. The first few plans, including Pincher, first published on 2 March 1946, Charioteer of 3 December 1947, Broiler of 8 November 1947, and Frolic of 17 March 1948, all assumed that the Soviet Union could overrun most of the Middle East, the north coast of the Mediterranean, and Western Europe at the outset of a war. The plans counted upon a sustained strategic air offensive – one relying upon atomic bombs – to achieve victory over the Soviet Union. They initially planned to mount the offensive with B-29s based in the United Kingdom, in the Cairo–Suez area, possibly in North China, and in northwestern India, the area which was about to become West Pakistan. Later, more pessimistic assessments suggested that more distant bases, including Iceland, Morocco, and Okinawa, might have to be used instead. Despite the lack of specific political guidance, at least one plan, Broiler, foresaw an attempt to force a Soviet withdrawal to the 1939 Soviet borders and somehow to make it impossible for any Soviet government to begin war anew.[3]

These initial plans were developed in the absence of the capabilities needed to implement them, especially with respect to the atomic weapons themselves. The United States had only nine available unassembled atomic bombs in mid-1946, thirteen a year later, and fifty two years later.[4] The JCS in October 1947 called for the production of 400 atomic bombs to make these plans feasible,[5] but many critical questions about the effectiveness of the bombs, American inability to locate critical targets, and Soviet air defenses remained unanswered. During 1948, as tensions with the Soviet Union increased, leading military and civilian figures began to raise basic questions about these plans.

In April 1948, CNO Admiral Denfield criticized Frolic, the latest plan, on the grounds that the Western European nations would be gravely demoralized by its abandonment of them to Soviet control, and that it made no provision for the possible failure of an atomic offensive. The other Chiefs, including Army Chief of Staff General Omar Bradley, overruled him.[6] More importantly, President Truman in May of 1948 ordered the preparation of a conventional war plan both because he questioned whether the American people would approve the first use of atomic weapons and because he still hoped such weapons might be outlawed or placed under international control. Secretary of Defense James Forrestal, however, ordered the abandonment of this planning exercise a few months later, after the Soviet blockade of Berlin had begun. In NSC 30 of 16 September 1948, Truman specifically reserved the decision to use atomic weapons for the President, but authorized planning to use them in the event of war.[7]

Forrestal also started the first real debate over American objectives with respect to the Soviet Union. Concerned by the Soviet threat and by Truman's continuing reductions in the American defense budget, on 10 July 1948 Forrestal asked the State Department – still the body thought responsible for the definition of American interests and objectives – to prepare a statement of the peacetime and wartime objectives of American policy toward the Soviet Union and the means required to achieve them. George F. Kennan, who as director of State's Policy Planning Staff was trying to give American policy in the Cold War a broad and flexible character, replied with a Policy Planning paper of 25 August. Rather than spend much time analyzing objectives and strategies should war occur, the paper argued that the Soviet Union was most unlikely to undertake war in the near future for a variety of domestic and international reasons, and seemed to imply that the possibility of war with the United States would probably deter Soviet military aggression for the foreseeable future. In a separate paper, Kennan defined American peacetime objectives *vis-à-vis* the Soviet Union very broadly as the reduction of Soviet power and influence 'to limits where they will no longer constitute a threat to the peace and stability of international society,' and argued that the United States should 'create situations which will compel the Soviet Government to recognize the practical undesirability of acting on the basis of its present concepts and the necessity of behaving, at least outwardly, as though it were the converse of those concepts that were true.' In the event of war, however, Kennan listed American objectives that would require the complete or near-complete defeat of the Soviet Union. These included the destruction of Soviet authority outside Soviet borders, the elimination of the international Communist apparatus, the reduction of any remaining Communist or non-Communist post-war regime or regimes to military insignificance, and the end of any iron curtain. Kennan opposed, however, any attempt to determine the nature of post-war regimes or any post-war de-communization program.[8]

For reasons that are unclear, the final draft of what the National Security Council approved as NSC 20 / 4 on 23 November 1948, 'U.S. Objectives with Respect to the USSR to Counter Soviet Threats to U.S. Security,' took a much more alarmist line regarding Soviet objectives than Kennan's paper. 'Communist ideology and Soviet behavior,' it read, 'clearly demonstrate that the ultimate objective of the leaders of the USSR is the domination of the world,' and although the Soviet Union was probably not planning for war in the near future, war 'in communist thinking is inevitable.' NSC 20 / 4 also included a statement of American objectives in the event of war based closely upon Kennan's earlier effort. Since it remained policy until 1954, it deserves to be quoted in full.

> In the event of war with the USSR we should endeavor by successful military and other operations to create conditions that would permit satisfactory accomplishment of U.S. objectives without a predetermined requirement of unconditional surrender. War aims supplemental to our peacetime aims should include:

A   Eliminating Soviet Russian domination in areas outside the borders of any Russian state allowed to exist after the war.

B   Destroying the structure of relationships by which the leaders of the All-Union Communist Party have been able to exert moral and disciplinary authority over individual citizens, or groups of citizens, in countries not under communist control.

C   Assuring that any regime or regimes which may exist on   t raditional Russian territory in the aftermath of war:
    (1) Do not have sufficient military power to wage aggressive war.
    (2) Impose nothing resembling the present iron curtain over contact with the outside world.

D   In addition, if any Bolshevik regime is left in any part of the Soviet Union, insuring that it does not control enough of the military–industrial potential of the Soviet Union to enable it to wage war on comparable terms with any other regime or regimes which may exist on traditional Russian territory.

War, in short, should reduce any surviving Soviet regime to something comparable to the situation following the Treaty of Brest-Litovsk, and this would obviously require something not far from unconditional surrender. Although this language closely followed the paper Kennan had written earlier in the year, within six months the Director of Policy Planning began taking a very different line.

It was during the year 1949 that the American government came the closest to re-evaluating both its policy and strategy in a possible war with the Soviet Union, but 1950 opened with existing concepts more firmly established than ever. Inside the Pentagon, Secretary Forrestal, who of all Truman's senior advisers obviously took the possibility of war most seriously, asked the Air Force for a more detailed evaluation of the effectiveness of an atomic offensive against the Soviet Union, and the JCS commissioned the Harmon Report from a committee chaired by Air Force Lt. General Hubert Harmon. Despite the extremely optimistic assumption that the Strategic Air Command would successfully strike seventy Soviet cities, the Harmon Report of 12 May 1949 concluded that the offensive would neither cripple Soviet offensive capabilities nor induce the regime or the population to capitulate. The report became the focus of a serious interservice split within the Pentagon, as Navy leaders seized upon it as proof that the strategy of relying upon atomic weapons – and the Air Force-dominated defense budgets which resulted from this strategy – would not effectively defend the United States. Truman himself was simultaneously raising questions about the nation's dependence upon atomic weapons, and in April 1949 he asked Secretary of Defense Louis Johnson, who had taken office after Forrestal's nervous breakdown, for studies of the effectiveness of the atomic offensive. Johnson himself received the Harmon Report on 28 July, but the Secretary, for reasons that are not clear, managed to keep it from reaching the President and gave him a somewhat misleading account of its conclusions.[9] Meanwhile, on 23 September 1949, Truman announced that the Soviet Union had exploded an atomic bomb, significantly increasing concern about a possible war.

Had the Harmon Report reached the State Department, it would have come as a surprise and an encouragement to George Kennan, who was trying to raise other sorts of questions about American policy and strategy as talk of war became more widespread. In a discussion at State on 11 October, he specifically backed away from the war objectives he had laid down a year earlier, while raising doubts parallel to those of the Harmon Report.

> On the one hand, there seemed to be an acceptance throughout the Government of the infallibility of the Joint Chiefs of Staff, and on the other hand, it was obvious that the Joint Chiefs drew their conclusions from the maximum capabilities of the enemy which they based on the improbable to a greater degree than on the probable course of events. He stated his belief that there is no clear-cut

Government concept of what our objective would be if we got into a war with Russia. His own view is that neither total annihilation nor complete surrender of the enemy is possible and, therefore, that limited rather than total warfare should be our objective. . . .

[Regarding the atomic bomb], Mr. Kennan pointed out that the only decision to date on this subject is that the President will determine whether or not to use it; but, in the meantime, it was his opinion that the military have been basing all their plans on the use of the bomb, thus making it difficult if not impossible to do anything else when the time comes to make a decision. He also added that he and the others in the Department who were supposed to be Russian experts were against atomic bombing of Russian cities. They feel that the most probable result would be to stiffen the courage and will to resist of the Russian people. From this he went on to say that if we decided it would be unfeasible to use the atomic bomb in the first instance there might be some advantage in then agreeing with the Russians that neither of us would use it at all.[10]

The same issues arose in a talk among Kennan, Secretary of State Acheson, and Soviet expert Llewellyn Thompson in December, in which Kennan suggested that the American guarantee of NATO had been given mainly for political reasons, and that the United States should simply try to halt a Soviet advance and not even 'contemplate trying to occupy all of Russia and Siberia' should war occur. Acheson raised the same questions in a memorandum he dictated for his own use on 20 December.[11] The State Department seemed to be edging toward the position that the United States should adopt limited objectives in a possible conflict with the Soviets.

These views might also have encouraged new diplomatic approaches to the Soviets, but trust between the United States and Stalin's Soviet Union had reached an all-time low, and despite these doubts about the probability of war, the appropriateness of unlimited objectives, and the workability of American strategy, the United States was not even exploring any diplomatic initiatives that might have led to some kind of *détente*. Partly, perhaps, for this reason, the only specific issue that now had to be resolved in light of these new developments was a military one: whether to develop a thermonuclear or hydrogen bomb in response to the Soviet atomic test and new revelations of Soviet atomic spying. Kennan, who had already stepped down as head of the Policy Planning Staff and was planning to leave the government, tried to make the hydrogen bomb decision the occasion not only to re-evaluate a military strategy based upon the indiscriminate, immediate use of nuclear weapons, but also to question whether nuclear weapons had any political utility at all. In a memorandum of 20 January 1950, he argued that these weapons fell into a new category precisely because, in his opinion, they could *not* be used to secure worthwhile political objectives.

By and large, the conventional weapons of warfare have admitted and recognized the possibility of surrender and submission. For that reason, they have traditionally been designed to spare the unarmed and helpless non-combatant . . . as well as the combatant prepared to lay down his arms. This general quality of the conventional weapons of warfare implied a still more profound and vital recognition: namely that warfare should be a means to an end other than warfare, an end connected with the beliefs and the feelings and the attitudes of people, an end marked by submission to a new political will and perhaps to a new regime of life, but an end which at least did not negate the principle of life itself.

The weapons of mass destruction do not have this quality. They cannot really be reconciled with a political purpose directed to shaping, rather than destroying, the lives of the adversary. They fail to take account of the ultimate responsibility of men for one another, and even for each other's errors and mistakes.[12]

Doubts among both scientists and State Department officials had already led President Truman to reappoint a special NSC committee on atomic energy including Acheson, Louis Johnson, and David Lilienthal to study the issue of the H-Bomb, but by the time Kennan wrote these words, the JCS had submitted a memo arguing firmly in favor of developing the weapon to Truman, arguing that a situation in which the Soviets acquired it but the United States did not would be intolerable. The Chiefs, in an indirect reply to Kennan, also suggested that to forgo the weapon might signal a disastrous American renunciation of any nuclear weapons, and added that a successful H-Bomb would have significant military advantages. The President found their arguments convincing and approved the development on 31 January 1950. Truman went ahead despite having received a relatively pessimistic briefing on the effects of an atomic offensive on 23 January.[13]

The JCS approved a new war plan, Offtackle, in the same month. Offtackle, while committing the USA to the defense of Western Europe, assumed that the Soviets would probably drive American forces from the continent, but planned to return via the Rhône Valley after a prolonged atomic air offensive against the Soviets mounted from Britain, Okinawa, the continental United States, and the Middle East. Establishing another pattern, Offtackle also estimated rather arbitrarily that the Soviet Union would have about thirty atomic bombs by late 1950. On 7 April 1950, NSC–68 revised that estimate downward slightly, but predicted that the Soviets would have 25–45 atomic bombs by mid-1951, 45–90 by mid-1952, and 70–135 by mid-1953. As a matter of fact, the Soviets did not even test a deliverable bomb until 24 September 1951, and the best estimates suggest that they had fewer than fifty atomic bombs even by 1953.[14] Although as we shall see the American Army apparently regarded such plans as temporary expedients, they had nothing else to propose at present.

Thus, despite the doubts of a number of leading Americans, including President Truman, George F. Kennan, the Harmon Committee, and various senior naval officers, the Truman Administration had committed itself to a policy of seeking the virtually complete defeat of the Soviet Union during a general war and a strategy based upon an atomic air offensive to secure this objective. The American Army, however, was still trying to expand its role in the defense of Western Europe. Since the United States could never deploy sufficient forces for a conventional defense itself, such a strategy had to rely upon the rearmament of European nations, including West Germany – a step which the Joint Chiefs formally proposed in May 1950, before the Soviet attack on Korea. That attack led immediately to wide-ranging discussions of command arrangements and deployments for the conventional defense of Europe, although complex and difficult arguments over the proper form of German rearmament held up any definite decisions for well over a year. After a long Senate debate in the first half of 1951, the Administration dispatched four divisions to Europe.[15]

During the years 1950–52, the preparation of NSC–68 by Kennan's successor Paul Nitze, the outbreak of the Korean War, the Chinese Communist intervention in that war, and continuing plans for NATO conventional defense led to a series of intense debates over national security policy within the Truman Administration and a major defense build-up, but neither American policy objectives nor strategy were ever seriously reviewed again during that time. New debates focused on Soviet intentions rather than American objectives, and eventually reached somewhat more frightening conclusions than those prevailing in the late 1940s. In the summer of 1951, Charles Bohlen, the new Counselor to the Department, challenged Nitze's estimate in NSC–68 that the Soviets were determined to achieve world domination, or that the Korean War represented a new willingness on Moscow's part to take risks. Bohlen eventually secured some significant changes of emphasis in a new policy statement, NSC 114/2 of 12 October 1951, which restored language more in the spirit of Kennan's 1948 appreciations and recognized that the Soviets would not risk their existing position to extend their power.[16] Similar arguments led to compromise language in an annex to NSC 135/1 of 22 August 1952, which extensively discussed the restraints inherent in Soviet policies and strategies, but which added that the Soviets 'would probably deliberately initiate general war' should they conclude that they could eliminate American power without 'serious risk to the maintenance of their regime.'[17] Meanwhile, the Joint Chiefs in August of 1950 had tried to start a re-examination of US objectives in the event of global war with the Soviets. This project, entitled NSC–79, was never completed, but a December 1952 draft by Louis Halle of the Policy Planning Staff continued to plan for the destruction of the Soviet regime in the event of war.[18]

During 1951, State Department and JCS representatives reached some interesting conclusions regarding the circumstances in which the United States would go to war. They specifically limited such cases to an attack on the United States, Canada, Alaska, NATO, West Germany, Austria, Trieste, Japan, or American overseas bases, or direct Soviet intervention in the Korean War. But the United States would take no action if the Soviets attacked Finland or Afghanistan, and would probably confine itself to lesser military actions in the event of Soviet attacks on Yugoslavia, Greece or Turkey, or Iran. Even the American response to Soviet attacks on West Germany or Austria was left open, as was American action in response to other aggression in the Far East.[19] In short, while adhering to a strategy of maximum ends and means should war with the Soviets occur, the Truman Administration was thinking carefully about exactly what stakes would justify undertaking such a war by the time that it left office.

The issue of European defense had also received extensive further consideration, culminating at the Lisbon Conference of 20–25 February 1952, at which NATO set goals of forty-one divisions in place and ninety available within a month of the outbreak of war by 1954, while also agreeing in principle upon a European army, the European Defense Community, including German contingents rising to twelve divisions.[20] In the same year, however, the enormous financial strain of meeting such goals led British planners to propose to the Americans a strategy based more on the American atomic deterrent and new tactical atomic weapons. The Chairman of the Joint Chiefs of Staff, Army General Omar Bradley, replied skeptically about the effects of an atomic air offensive against the Soviet Union, added that tactical nuclear weapons would not be available for several years, and continued to push for the agreed expansion – an important indication, once again, that the Army did not accept the idea that war against the Soviets could and should be waged mainly from the air.[21] By late 1952 the United States had recognized that the Europeans would probably fail to meet the long-term Lisbon goals, and NATO Commander General Matthew Ridgway was undertaking an assessment of the effect of tactical atomic weapons on defense requirements.[22] The Truman Administration bequeathed this problem to its successor.

Immediately upon entering office in January 1953, the Eisenhower Administration began a thorough review of national security policies and strategies. The new Administration – particularly its Secretary of the Treasury, George Humphrey, and President Eisenhower himself – especially feared the long-term budgetary and economic effects of current policies. Eisenhower defined the issue that most dominated their review on 25 March 1953, when he suggested that the NSC might ask for a report 'as to whether national bankruptcy or national destruction would get us first.'[23] Even before taking office, Eisenhower had apparently adopted the opinion of Admiral Arthur Radford, who as CINCPAC had discussed these issues with the President-elect on his return from Korea in December 1952, and who became Chairman of a new cast of Joint Chiefs a few months later, that the United States had too many forces in too many parts of the world.[24] In the wake of Stalin's death, the obviously new tone which his successors immediately adopted in their public statements, and the Korean armistice, the new Administration played with some basic changes in policy objectives, but in the end, Eisenhower reaffirmed the strategy of all-out nuclear war should it prove necessary.

In May 1953 Eisenhower commissioned Project Solarium, a new study in which separate teams developed three different policy alternatives: a continuation of existing policy; a public declaration that any Communist military advances beyond a specified line would lead immediately to general war; or an immediate attempt to roll back some Communist gains, specifically in Southeast Asia and China. The second and third options obviously presented enormous difficulties, and when the NSC first discussed the reports on 16 July, Eisenhower somewhat confusedly asked for a reconciliation of their differences, and later became angry when the teams – not surprisingly – could not bring this about. But the President also raised some of the most basic problems associated with American planning for nuclear war, expressing his belief 'that the only thing worse than losing a global war was winning one; that there would be no individual freedom after the next global war,' and adding, 'What would we do with Russia, if we should win in a global war?'[25]

No one as yet systematically addressed these issues, but the Chiefs, under enormous pressure to cut future defense budgets, proposed at least some peacetime strategic changes in late August. In an effort to cut costs and improve enlistment and retention rates in American military forces, they proposed redeploying a large number of American troops from overseas to the continental United States, while maintaining the overseas air bases necessary for a nuclear offensive against the Soviet Union. About ten days later, Secretary of State Dulles raised the possibility of a general settlement with the Soviets, including both mutual withdrawals of Soviet and American forces from Eastern and Western Europe and an arms control agreement.

Eisenhower, who was vacationing in Colorado, showed interest in this proposal, while adding that if the Soviets would *not* accept arms control, the United States might have to consider unleashing a preventive war to avoid an indefinite arms race and the dictatorial American state that would probably result from it.[26] Dulles, apparently following up, insisted on 30 September that a new statement of Basic National Security Policy, NSC 162, drop language stating that any new agreements with the Soviet Union would have to *improve* the western position, and specifically suggested that the United States might want to recognize certain aspects of the status quo. This, however, was apparently the end of this discussion.[27]

Faced with its continuing budgetary dilemma, the Administration decided to make savings not by scaling down objectives or trying to defuse the Cold War, but by explicitly relying more heavily on atomic weapons. Chairman of the Joint Chiefs Admiral Arthur Radford suggested on 13 October that he could not adopt a new and less expensive strategic concept unless the Administration either approved the Chiefs' ideas on redeployment or specifically authorized increased reliance upon atomic weapons. This new emphasis took two specific forms. First, the final version of NSC 162, adopted on 30 October, defined the first requirement of defense against the Soviet threat as 'A strong military power, with emphasis on the capability of inflicting massive retaliatory damage by offensive striking power.' The Joint Chiefs – led by CNO Admiral Carney – tried to alter this wording to make this merely one aspect of needed military power, but President Eisenhower himself on 29 October insisted that the nation had to set specific military priorities.[28] In addition, NSC 162 stated, 'In the event of hostilities, the United States will consider nuclear weapons to be as available for use as other munitions.' Later policy statements went considerably further down this road, and changes in force structure eventually left the military unable to undertake almost any major military operation without atomic weapons.[29] The paper concluded by reaffirming the wartime objectives laid down in NSC 20 five years earlier, but the NSC also decided to restudy those objectives now.[30]

Admiral Carney and General Matthew Ridgway, the new Chief of Staff of the Army, apparently decided to use the redefinition of objectives to question the recently agreed-upon priorities in military strategy – priorities which confined their services to a secondary role, and which obviously doomed the long-planned build-up of NATO conventional forces. Their attempts led to a clear Presidential statement regarding the nature and objectives of a future war with the Soviet Union. On 4 March 1954, Radford presented a draft of NSC 5410, 'U.S. Objectives in the Event of General War with the Soviet Bloc,' to the full NSC. The draft listed twelve separate war objectives, including:

1. To achieve a victory which will insure the survival of the United States as a free nation and the continuation of its free institutions;
2. To preserve and retain as many of its allies as possible and
3. To reduce by military and other measures the capabilities of the USSR to the point where it has lost its will or ability to wage war against the United States and its allies.

Combined with a further objective of ensuring 'that postwar regimes in the former enemy territories will not follow totalitarian and aggressive policies and practices that would threaten the security and freedom of other peoples,' these objectives amounted to unconditional Soviet surrender.[31]

Radford reported that the JCS had been unable to agree upon these objectives. Eisenhower's own comments on the draft paper showed that he understood how difficult the problem would be, but that he was now less willing to ask whether the United States should therefore reconsider its basic policies and strategies.

> The President pointed out that we could anticipate in the aftermath of a third world war a tremendous swing toward isolationism in the United States. Moreover, the colossal job of occupying the territories of the defeated enemy would be far beyond the resources of the United States at the end of such a war. While the President therefore said he agreed that it was right to keep this problem of war objectives in mind, he believed that the chaos resulting from a third world war would be so great as to render it impossible for the National Security Council to determine in advance our precise objectives and courses of action in the event of such a war.
>
> As regards the kind of government we would attempt to set up in a defeated Russia, the President said it was hard to debate. A totalitarian system was the only imaginable instrument by which Russia could be ruled for a considerable interval after the war. By and large, concluded the President, the main purpose served by the paper was to emphasize how vital it was to avoid a third world war.[32]

Eisenhower, while well aware that even victory would produce a most unsatisfactory situation, did not raise the option of lesser American objectives.

The Army and Navy, however, insisted on debating fundamental objectives and the strategies they required. At another NSC meeting on 25 March 1954, Admiral Radford explained that Admiral Carney and General Ridgway wanted to introduce new considerations into the definition of American war objectives that would question the entire policy of seeking the total defeat of the Soviet Union and the strategy of using nuclear weapons to do so. To some extent, as Radford seemed to suggest, Carney and Ridgway may simply have been trying to secure a larger share of the reduced defense budget by questioning the Administration's reliance upon nuclear weapons, but their views also reflected a broader consideration of the consequences of a possible war. Specifically, Ridgway and Carney wanted to revise objective 3, above, as follows:

> To reduce by military and other measures the military capabilities of the USSR, and of the Soviet satellites and Communist China as may be necessary, to the point where they have lost their will or ability to continue to wage war, either individually or collectively, against the United States and its allies – bearing in mind that the

application of military measures must be with discrimination and at the minimum practicable cost in postwar political, social and economic dislocation.

Ridgway and Carney also wanted to reduce US objectives with respect to the post-war regime in Soviet territory, ensuring only that any such regime would not 'threaten the security of the United States or of its principal allies.' Taken together, these changes clearly indicated that these two Chiefs wanted to prepare for a limited rather than an unlimited war with the Soviets, one that might end on terms far short of unconditional surrender, and that they wanted to limit the application of American military power in light of the situation which maximum force might create. Summarizing their views, Admiral Radford – who disagreed – brought up a historical parallel.

Quoting from the portions of the memorandum which set forth the views of Admiral Carney and General Ridgway, Admiral Radford indicated their fear that full exploitation of our nuclear capability might inflict such chaos and destruction and suffering in the Soviet Union as had not been known in Europe since the end of the Thirty Years' War. Indeed, in the circumstances it was impossible to visualize how the United States could cope with the victory it might achieve over the Soviets, or how it might hope to establish a workable occupation regime. In sum, any proposed assault upon the capabilities of the USSR to wage war ought to be evaluated in terms both of the possible contribution to victory and in light of the limiting factors discussed above.

Carney and Ridgway, having helped design a war plan to achieve the objectives specified by the highest political authorities, had also taken note of the situation which even the successful execution of the plan would create, and were now asking whether that situation would in fact serve the interests of the United States. That question, obviously, lay within the competence of the political authorities, but one cannot fault their temerity in raising it, since they might reasonably have wondered whether their civilian superiors had indeed given these questions the attention they deserved. They were in a sense following the injunction of Clausewitz, who wrote that a nation's political objective is not 'a tyrant,' but 'must adapt itself to its chosen means, a process which can radically change it.'[33] When Radford was finished, President Eisenhower replied at length, confirming that he had thought about the issues raised by the paper, and indicating that he now knew exactly where he stood.

At the conclusion of Admiral Radford's statement, the President, with considerable vehemence and conviction, expressed the opinion that the subjects that Admiral Radford had discussed came pretty close to the area of prerogatives of the Commander-in-Chief. He said he was speaking very frankly to the Council in expressing his absolute conviction that in view of the development of the new weapons of mass destruction, with the terrible significance which these involved, everything in any future war with the Soviet bloc would have to be subordinated to winning that war. This was the one thing that must constantly be borne in mind, and there was little else with respect to war objectives that needed to worry anyone very much. . . . In illustration of his point, the President turned to paragraph 1 of the draft report, which read: 'To insure a victory which will insure the survival of the United States as a free nation and the continuation of its free institutions in the post-war period.' This, said the President, he would change by putting a period after 'victory' and deleting the rest of the paragraph, if not the rest of the paper. We can't tell what we will do after we achieve a victory in what will be total and not in any sense limited warfare. Accordingly, he disagreed, said the President, with the limitations and qualifications suggested.

 . . . Obviously we were desperately anxious to maintain our free institutions, and we were anxious to help our friends and allies abroad, but we were in no position to count on it or plan on it, in view of the catastrophic nature of the third world war if it should come. . . . He could assure the Council that with respect to any decision he might be obliged to make regarding a war plan, his decision would be based on his judgment of just how much such a war plan would hurt the enemy. For the time being, at least, no other considerations would be of significance. This, of course, did not mean that he would exclude from his judgment the question of how much harm or hurt the United States itself would suffer as a result of the methods chosen to prosecute the war. . . . The President concluded by admitting that his point of view might seem brutal, but in view of the fact that we would never enter the war except in retaliation against a heavy Soviet atomic attack, he simply could not conceive of any other course of action than the course of action which would hit the Russians where and how it would hurt most.

Paragraph 1 was accordingly revised, although the period was placed after 'United States' instead of 'victory,' and the paragraphs on the postwar situation in enemy territory were dropped altogether. The President offered to discuss these issues privately with Admiral Carney and General Ridgway, but it is not clear that such a discussion ever took place. NSC 5410 / 2, as amended, was adopted.

Eisenhower's exposition raises some difficult questions that his Administration subsequently resolved in an even more frightening manner. His statement that the American war plan would only be executed 'in retaliation against a heavy Soviet atomic attack' probably owes something to the language of NSC 162, which he had approved a few months earlier, and which referred, as we have seen, to the need for a 'retaliatory' capability. However, subsequent war planning in the Eisenhower Administration – for which we as yet lack data comparable to that for the Truman Administration – called for a major atomic offensive in the event of any war against the Soviet Union, including one that broke out in Europe.[34] And only a few months after this conversation, on 17 December 1954, NATO adopted MC 48, which, closely following Eisenhower's own ideas, called for the immediate – and in practice, quite possibly preemptive – use of nuclear weapons tactically and strategically to stop and defeat a Soviet attack on Europe. NATO commander General Lauris Norstad received advance authorization to use nuclear weapons, thus giving him, in principle, the right to choose the moment for their use – possibly even before a Soviet attack had started.[35] And although in the remaining six years of his Administration Eisenhower sometimes questioned the need for the United States' increasingly extensive nuclear arsenal and the remarkably comprehensive targeting plans that went with it, it does not seem that the issue of American objectives in the event of war was ever discussed by his Administration again.

Those who intermittently questioned the wisdom of these American objectives and strategies in a possible war with the Soviet Union were raising very serious questions, and might have raised a good many more. In particular, one might ask how such plans could have been reconciled with the American aim of preserving a free Western Europe, which undoubtedly would have suffered very severely from Soviet nuclear forces in a possible war by the mid-1950s. The issue of the possible use of the foreign bases essential to carry out the planned strategic air offensive against the Soviets created a good deal of controversy in relations between Washington on the one hand and Ottawa and London on the other, and would probably have become considerably more tense had war come closer. Meanwhile, although so far as we know the Air Force did not re-authorize studies similar to those of the Harmon committee, the question of whether such an offensive even would have brought about the defeat of the Soviet Union remained an open one until the 1960s, when the U.S. fielded Minuteman and Polaris missiles. It is far from clear, in short, that American war plans from 1946 through 1954 or even 1960 could have accomplished their military objectives, quite uncertain whether they would have forced the Soviets to surrender, and even less clear that their execution could in any meaningful sense have served the interests of the United States.

Why, then, did successive Administrations stick with these objectives and strategies? In my opinion, the policy behind the plans was simply a logical extension of American foreign policy during the Second World War, as it had come to be understood in the post-war period. In the Second World War the United States, using air, naval and ground forces and fighting with allies, achieved the unconditional surrender of two expansionist, totalitarian enemies, Germany and Japan. Many senior American officials – although *not* Russian experts like Kennan and Bohlen – had immediately begun viewing the Soviet Union in the same way when the Cold War began, and military planners in 1946–47 assumed in the absence of political guidance that war with the Soviet Union would be fought to the same kind of finish. When NSC 20 was issued in 1948, it confirmed this view, and neither Kennan nor Ridgway and Carney managed to secure any serious reconsideration of it. Because the Soviet Union seemed to represent the same kind of regime as Nazi Germany and Imperial Japan, its destruction became the goal of American strategy.

As I have recently argued elsewhere, this view may have oversimplified the choices faced by the United States and by President Franklin Roosevelt in particular in 1940–41.[36] Although Roosevelt recognized Nazi Germany as a threat to the United States after the fall of France, he initially committed himself only to a more effective defense of the Western Hemisphere, and then, by early 1941, to assisting in the defense of Great Britain. Not until after the German attack on the Soviet Union, however, did he definitely try to secure American entry into the war, and this may well have been because it was only then that it seemed possible, as well as desirable, for the United States to help secure the total defeat of Nazi Germany – and if need be, Japan as well – at an acceptable cost. Lacking any land ally of sufficient power to assist in a possible post-1945 war with the Soviet Union, the United States might have drawn the conclusion that the possibility of total victory was too remote to pursue. In its planning, however, the United States stuck to objectives amounting to unconditional surrender.

The United States and its government, one might suggest, had enormous difficulty accepting the results of their victory in the Second World War, which had inevitably left the Soviet Union as the world's second strongest power and condemned the United States to an indefinite period of unfriendly coexistence and a political struggle on many fronts. In practice, as some Europeans argued throughout the Cold War, the United States and the Soviet Union worked out a mutual accommodation;[37] in theory, the United States only rarely accepted the possibility of proceeding on such a basis as long as the Soviet Union remained a Communist state, and planned to destroy the Soviet Union in the event of war.

Some will argue that the western victory in the Cold War vindicated American strategy. Yet American success in the Cold War may owe more to the realities that constrained the actions of both sides than to the quality of the analyses of our civilian and military planners. During relatively quiet times planners spoke in terms of all-out war and total victory, but to paraphrase Dr. Johnson, in crises the prospect of being incinerated within a fortnight tended to concentrate Soviet and American minds wonderfully, leading them to re-evaluate the significance of issues like access to Berlin and missiles in Cuba and Turkey and to avoid war over them. On the other hand, *had* war ever broken out, it would obviously have been in the interests of all humanity for it to remain a war of limited objectives, and only once, to my knowledge, did an American President ever suggest how, in the case of Berlin, this might have been done. This was President Kennedy, who on 22 January 1963 told the NSC that Cuba had become a Soviet hostage in the same way that Berlin was an American hostage, and suggested that the United States must retain the option of attacking Cuba in response to a Soviet seizure of Berlin.[38] Kennedy's concept, one might argue, reflected roughly the same conclusion that American military planners had reached back in 1944: that neither the United States nor the Soviet Union could plan realistically for the defeat of the other in a general war. Nuclear weapons had not altered that fact, especially after both powers achieved the capability of striking the other.

The issue of appropriate political objectives remains critical in the post-Cold War world. In Iraq and in Kosovo, the United States showed an impressive new willingness to content itself with limited objectives in conflicts against evil regimes, but the second Bush Administration's National Security Strategy now calls for the elimination of any dangerous and hostile regimes, and has now led us into Iraq. The end of the Cold War has increased American ambitions, and the United States may now once again have a difficult time in reconciling its ends and means, and in understanding the relationships between the two. Any political objective, no matter how noble, may become a tyrant, leading a nation to pursue strategies that, even if successful, will leave all parties far worse off than before.

Notes

1 My main sources on war planning itself are Steven T. Ross, *American War Plans 1945–50* (London, 1996), and two well-known articles by David Alan Rosenberg, 'American Atomic Strategy and the Hydrogen Bomb Decision,' *Journal of American History*, vol. 66, no. 1, June 1979, pp. 62 87, and 'The Origins of Overkill: Nuclear Weapons and American Strategy, 1945–60,' *International Security*, vol. 7, no. 1, Spring 1983, pp. 3–71. My information on higher-level political discussions comes from the *Foreign Relations of the United States* (hereafter *FRUS*) series, and specifically from the volumes on Basic National Security Policy.

2 *FRUS*, 1944, vol. I, pp. 699–703. See also Mark A. Stoler, *Allies and Adversaries* (Chapel Hill, NC, 2000), pp. 171–5.

3 Ross, *American War Plans*, pp. 25–75.

4 Rosenberg, 'The Origins of Overkill,' p. 14.

5 Rosenberg, 'The Hydrogen Bomb Decision,' pp. 67–68.

6 Ross, *American War Plans*, pp. 72–75.

7 Rosenberg, 'The Origins of Overkill,' pp. 12–13.

8 *FRUS*, 1948, vol. I, part II, pp. 588–92, 599–601, 609–11, 615–24.

9 Ross, *American War Plans*, p. 107; Rosenberg, 'The Hydrogen Bomb Decision,' pp. 72–77.

10 *FRUS*, 1949, vol. I, pp. 399–403.

11 *Ibid.*, pp. 413–16, 612–17.

12 *FRUS*, 1950, vol. I, p. 39.
13 Rosenberg, 'The Hydrogen Bomb Decision,' pp. 82–84.
14 Ross, *American War Plans*, pp. 112–19; for NSC 68 (7 April 1950) see *FRUS*, 1950, vol. I, p. 251; David Holloway, *Stalin and the Bomb* (New Haven, CT, 1994), pp. 219, 322.
15 Walter S. Poole, *The Joint Chiefs of Staff and National Policy, vol. IV, 1950–1952* (*History of the Joint Chiefs of Staff*, vol. 4) (Washington, DC, 1998), pp. 95–136.
16 *Ibid.*, 12 October 1951, pp. 182–92.
17 *FRUS*, 1952–54, vol. II, part 1, pp. 89–94. For the slightly amended final version, NSC 135 / 3, approved 25 September, see pp. 142–56.
18 *Ibid.*, pp. 197–201.
19 *FRUS*, 1951, vol. I, pp. 865–74. This paper does not seem to have gone to the NSC.
20 Poole, *The Joint Chiefs of Staff and National Policy*, pp. 149–52.
21 *Ibid.*, pp. 159–60.
22 Robert A. Wampler, 'Conventional Goals and Nuclear Promises: The Truman Administration and the Roots of the NATO New Look,' in Francis H. Heller and John R. Gillingham, eds, *NATO: The Founding of the Atlantic Alliance and the Integration of Europe* (New York, 1992), pp. 363–69.
23 *FRUS*, 1952–54, vol. II, pp. 258–64.
24 Robert J. Watson, *The Joint Chiefs of Staff and National Policy 1953–54* (*History of the Joint Chiefs of Staff*, vol. 5) (Washington, DC, 1986), p. 15.
25 *Ibid.*, pp. 323–28, 383–98.
26 *Ibid.*, pp. 443–54, 457–63.
27 *Ibid.*, pp. 491–503.
28 Watson, *The Joint Chiefs of Staff and National Policy*, pp. 22–23.
29 David Kaiser, *American Tragedy: Kennedy, Johnson, and the Origins of the Vietnam War* (Cambridge, MA, 2000), pp. 15–19.
30 *FRUS*, 1952–54, vol. II, pp. 577–96.
31 NSC 5410, 19 February 1954, Eisenhower Library.
32 *FRUS*, 1952–54, vol. II, pp. 635–36.
33 Carl von Clausewitz, *On War* (trans. Michael Howard and Peter Paret) (Princeton, NJ, 1976), p. 87.
34 Watson, *The Joint Chiefs of Staff and National Policy*, pp. 93–103. Continuing disagreements among the services left the precise role of conventional forces in such a war rather undefined. It is not clear whether these plans, unlike the Truman Administration's plans, expected to halt a conventional Soviet advance in Western Europe.
35 Marc Trachtenberg, *A Constructed Peace* (Princeton, NJ, 1999), pp. 156–82. Some evidence suggests that SAC Commander General Curtis LeMay also anticipated launching a strike on the Soviet Union on his own authority, should the need arise: see Fred Kaplan, *The Wizards of Armageddon* (New York, 1983), pp. 132–34, referring to a conversation between LeMay and Richard Sprague in 1957.
36 Kaiser, *American Tragedy*, pp. 485–87.
37 This is also the theme of Trachtenberg, *A Constructed Peace*.
38 Kaiser, *American Tragedy*, p. 199.

12

FROM THE FALL OF FRANCE TO THE *FORCE DE FRAPPE*

The Remaking of French Military Power, 1940–62

Charles G. Cogan

France emerged from the Second World War with its Army discredited, its economy shattered, and its population humiliated after four years of German occupation. A civil war had raged in 1943–44 between the internal Resistance, heavily influenced by the Communists, and the *milice* of the Vichy regime. General Charles de Gaulle, the most senior political figure to emerge from the Second World War with honor, was able to unite the country only briefly, before it descended into its pre-war constitutional pattern of parliamentary bickering and weak governments.[1]

Before leaving Government, however, de Gaulle in October 1945 created the Commissariat for Atomic Energy (CEA), with the clear intention of making France an atomic military power. During a visit to Ottawa in July 1944, de Gaulle had received an 'off-line' briefing on the Allied wartime atomic bomb project from three French scientists who broke their secrecy agreement to inform him.[2]

Although the armed forces were cut back drastically at the end of the war, conscription, long considered an essential aspect of citizenship in Republican France, continued, and indeed draftees were used in helping suppress Communist-led insurrectionary strikes that peaked at the end of 1947. And the Army, discredited after the war, soon had to be brought into play again as France, more than any other country, had to endure the twin shocks of the Cold War and decolonization.[3]

A disproportionate number of troops had to be employed in the French Union (mainly in Indochina) and in North Africa. Maintaining France's overseas possessions was seen in the post-war era as the surest route to France's return to grandeur. In Indochina, where Ho Chi Minh had declared independence in September 1945, the French were unwilling to come to a real agreement with him, and after a year of intermittent negotiations, the first Indochina War began at the end of 1946.

In Europe, France's entry first into the Brussels Pact and then into the North Atlantic Treaty affirmed the country's role as a key European ally in the Cold War. It also renewed the Second World War tradition of a continuing and intensifying dependence on American equipment and military command. By the time of the French defeat at Dien Bien Phu in 1954, the USA was providing 80 per cent of the cost of the Indochina War,[4] in addition to helping provide equipment for French divisions serving in NATO's defense of Western Europe.

The failure of the European Army plan in 1954, due to French fears of a rearmed Germany, only strengthened the authority of the NATO integrated command over the Allied armed forces, including those of France. Nevertheless, it is a fact perhaps too often overlooked, that the massive American military assistance to France in the 1940s and 1950s played a significant role in the remaking of the country's military power.

A second colonial war broke out in Algeria immediately after the Indochina defeat, and this time draftees were used in a conflict that lasted from 1954 until 1962. Increasingly unpopular, it led in 1958 to the return of de Gaulle as a putative mediator between the Army in Algeria and the Government in Paris, the latter being unable to put down the challenge to its authority launched by a group of Army officers exasperated at what they saw as a half-hearted policy toward the nationalists' revolt.

But de Gaulle, in an about-face, eventually proceeded to negotiate independence for Algeria and the liquidation of virtually the rest of the French Union. This in turn led in 1961 to a revolt of a number of senior officers in the 500,000-man French Army in Algeria, who expressed a long-smoldering frustration at the lack of support from the civilian authorities in Paris.[5] De Gaulle crushed the revolt and proceeded to assert mastery over the armed forces.

Though suffering heavy losses in Indochina and Algeria, the French Army found its expiation in these two wars; this, together with France's nuclear weapons capability, brought to fruition by de Gaulle in the 1960s, restored France's parity with Britain as the two ranking Western military powers after the United States.

In the meantime, de Gaulle gradually broke his ties with the NATO military command while remaining within the North Atlantic Alliance. In so doing, he was able, as he saw it, to restore France to full independence, which has been a *leitmotif* in French strategic thinking since the country's fall from grace in 1940. Independence became a national obsession. As André Martel observed, referring to the immediate post-war period, 'An independent France must recreate its military independence.'[6] The core of this independence was the *force de frappe*, which finally became operational in 1969, and which in theory could be employed anywhere on the globe and against any adversary (the so-called 'all azimuth' (*tous azimuth*) doctrine).

Introduction: the Bitter Legacy of the Second World War

In one sense, France's inter-war period began in May–June 1940, when France was defeated by Germany. In another sense, the inter-war period began in 1945 when France, thanks to the magisterial arrogance of Charles de Gaulle, wound up on the side of the victors of the Second World War. Although de Gaulle's feat was prodigious, it was a hollow victory for France, having suffered the humiliation of four years of German occupation and the *de facto* dethronement of France from its status as a major power.

In yet another sense, there was no inter-war period for France, which plunged itself immediately after the Second World War into a succession of insurrectionary wars in two of the territories it had conquered in the nineteenth century: Indochina and Algeria. Thus it can be said that France, or elements of France, were continually at war from 1939 until 1962, when peace finally descended with Algerian independence.

The Reconstitution of the French Fighting Forces, 1940–45

At the end of July 1940, only a few weeks after his break with the Pétain Government[7] and his arrival in Britain, Charles de Gaulle had some 7,000 troops at his disposal,[8] many of whom were members of the French expeditionary force withdrawn from Norway who were located in Britain at the time of the Armistice.

Thereafter, de Gaulle's goal was to attract as many French soldiers and volunteers as possible to return to the war against Germany. After some notable failures, this effort began to pick up steam, particularly after de Gaulle arrived in Algiers following the Allied landings in North Africa. Over the course of 1943, de Gaulle won out in a power struggle against his American-sponsored rival, General Henri Giraud, and was able, at least nominally, to establish authority over the Resistance in France. This meant that he had won control over the three components of French fighting forces: his own Free French forces; the Resistance forces, known as the French Forces of the Interior (FFI); and the French Army elements in North Africa that had been under the Vichy Government. Among the three, de Gaulle himself recognized the preponderance of the French North African Army component.

The core of the French Army which went into combat with the Allies in Italy and France in 1943–44 consisted of eight divisions of French regulars mandated by the Casablanca Conference of January 1943. An agreement was reached between French and American authorities to equip mainly French military elements in North Africa which were being returned to the war after the Allied landings there in November 1942. The so-called Anfa Plan, approved by President Roosevelt on 24 January 1943, and modified at the beginning of 1944, called for the equipping of five infantry and three armored divisions.[9] Two of these were Free French divisions already in existence: the First Free French Division (1er D.F.L.), already in existence but being converted from British to American equipment.;[10] and the Second Armored Division (2e D.B.) under General Philippe Leclerc. Two others were Moroccan divisions, a third Algerian, and a fourth Black African; all were commanded by French officers.

In addition to recruits from North Africa, volunteers from the French overseas territories and escapees from France continued to swell the ranks of this reconstituted French Army. By 1 September 1944, France had been able to recruit 560,000 men from outside the Metropole,[11] of whom 300,000 were from the indigenous populations of North Africa, Black Africa and Oceania.[12] Beginning in 1944, the eight French divisions were augmented by divisions created out of the internal Resistance in France, three of them in 1944 and four of them in 1945.[13] By May 1945, when the war in Europe ended, the French Army had grown to 1,300,000 men (See Table 12.1).[14]

The French forces were equipped and armed by the United States, and moreover had been under American overall command, a situation that irked de Gaulle. As Maurice Vaïsse observed, 'The Allied army could have won the war without the French; but without the allied army, the French Army could not even have fought.'[15]

Table 12.1: The size of the French army, 1940–45

Date	Free French (FFL)	Army of NA	FFI	Total
July 1940	7,000[a]	400,045[b]	–	–
1942	50,000[c]	110,000[d]	70,000[e]	–
May 1943	50,000[f]	80,000[g]	–	–
Sept 1944[h]	–	–	400,000[i]	560,000[j]
May 1945	–	110,000[k]	–	1,300,000[l]

Notes

a. Doise and Vaïsse, *Diplomatie et outil militaire,* p. 456.
b. Christine Levisse-Touze, 'La poursuite de la lutte en Afrique française du Nord,' in Institut d'histoire des conflits contemporains (IHCC), *Les armées françaises pendant la Second Guerre mondiale*, Paris, 7–10 May 1985, p. 95. Services Historiques de l'Armée de Terra (SHAT), 7N2471, dossier 5: 'Situation des effectifs à la date de l'armistice.'
c. J.N. Vincent, 'Typologie et motivation des Forces Françaises Libres,' in IHCC, *op. cit.*, p. 138. Commandant Etchegoyen, Historique des FFL, archives du SHAT (4O1 to 4P 10).
d. Levisse-Touze, 'L'armée d'Afrique: armée de transition pour une grande revanche? 1940–42,' in *Revue historique des armées*, no. 3, 1992, p. 12.
e. André Corvisier, ed., *Histoire militaire de la France*, vol. 4 (Paris: Presses universitaires de France, 1994), p. 163.
f. *Ibid.*, p. 83.
g. Doise and Vaïsse, *Diplomatie et outil militaire*, p. 459.
h. The FFL were dissolved in 1943.
i. SHAT, 7P 59, telegram from the General Headquarters of National Defense (EMGDN), 23 October 1944.
j. Doise and Vaïsse, *Diplomatie et outil militaire*, p. 477.
k. J. Vernet (chef de battalion), *Le réarmement et la réorganisation de l'armée de terre française, 1943–1946* (Vincennes: SHAT, 1980), p. 99.
l. Doise and Vaïsse, *Diplomatie et outil militaire*, p. 477; *Histoire militaire de la France*, vol. 4, pp. 258–59.

The *Force de Frappe*

There seems little doubt that de Gaulle had in mind the development of a French atomic weapon when he created the Commissariat of Atomic Energy (CEA) in October 1945. Equipping France with such a weapon could constitute a key element in compensating for the country's reduced position at the end of the war. In particular, it would give France permanent leverage over Germany, and it would help restore France to its previous position of military parity with Britain.

The language of the ordinance which created the CEA leaves little doubt as to the intention behind it. Article 1 states in part: 'The Commissariat for Atomic Energy [will] pursue scientific and technical research with a view towards the utilization of atomic energy in various areas of science, industry and national defense.' A military officer with the rank of general was included in the CEA as a representative of the defense establishment. And finally, as noted by Aline Coutrot, a note dated 27 October 1945 by the Commissioner General for Atomic Energy, Raoul Dautry, made mention of the 'atomic bomb,' but the word 'bomb' was scratched out and replaced by the word 'energy.'[16]

However, only a few months after the creation of the CEA, de Gaulle resigned from office. He did not return to power for 12 years. Work on the militarization of France's atomic energy capability did not begin until 1954.

The Departure of de Gaulle and the Downgrading of the French Military

As the war approached its end, a dispute broke out between two of de Gaulle's ministers in the Provisional Government, Pierre Mendès France, Minister of the Economy, and René Pleven, Minister of Finance. The latter was the more important ministry of the two, and Pleven had been at de Gaulle's side since the early days of the Resistance in London. In the days when the Provisional Government was installed in Algiers, Mendès France held both portfolios. In his view, a policy of rigor was in order: wage and price controls and a tight monetary policy were imperative in order to prevent an onset of inflation. Pleven's approach was focused on the short term and was aimed at alleviating the suffering of the French people after four years of occupation. His recipe was a raise in public sector salaries (of 40 per cent) and the floating of a national 'Liberation Loan.'[17] The result was a sharp increase in inflation. On 18 January 1945, Mendès France resigned and spelled out his concerns in a letter to de Gaulle: 'General, I appeal to you, to your inflexibility, to everything which causes the French to have confidence in you, to institute measures of national salvation.' Though de Gaulle kept Mendès France briefly in the Government, he decided in favor of Pleven. Mendès France left in April 1945.

While de Gaulle recognized that a strong military was a mark of a country's power and prestige, the policy of 'grandeur' was unsustainable in the immediate post-war.[18] At the same time de Gaulle recognized the need to devote resources for rebuilding France's shattered economy.[19] For a country that was prostrate economically, maintaining a large army was untenable.

In November 1945, the Socialists proposed a reduction of 20 per cent in defense expenditures. De Gaulle fought this off, but the Constituent Assembly debate reflected a deeper constitutional struggle between the Assembly and the Executive over the relative powers of the two branches, at a time when a new Constitution was being drafted.

The parliamentary debate of 31 December 1945–1 January 1946 led to the resignation three weeks later, of de Gaulle who found it impossible to govern with a majority of the Assembly opposed to his program. According to Robert Frank, 'The departure of de Gaulle was probably not just linked to the internal institutional crisis; it marked also the failure of the French policy of "grandeur" in the world as it was in 1946.'[20]

Though he enjoyed enormous personal prestige, no consensus was available to de Gaulle to carry through with even a modest military program aimed at restoring French grandeur.

Following de Gaulle's departure, a compromise was reached in early 1946 whereby defense expenditures were reduced by five per cent, but with the General's departure from the scene, even more drastic reductions were called for, including the 'dissolution of the Army.'[21] The armed forces' share of the national budget declined precipitously, from a high of September 1945 when this share totaled 41 per cent.[22] Army personnel were cut back sharply as well, by nearly two-thirds.

Table 12.2: French military budget as percentage of national budget, 1945–55

Year	Percentage of national budget
1945	40.7
1949	20.6
1950	18.3
1951	27.6
1952–54	33.3
1955	27.8

Notes
a.Doise and Vaïsse, *Diplomatie et outil militaire*, p. 518.
(N.B. In a New Year's message on 1 January 1949,
General Georges Revers observed that the armed forces'
share of the budget had been progressively reduced from
40 per cent in 1945 to 30 per cent in1948, to 17.5 per cent
in 1949 *Informations Militaires* (*IM*), 1949, No. 127, p.2).

Change and Turbulence in the Officer Corps

In September 1939, the French Armed Forces included around 35,000 officers. Of those, 1,200 were killed, 800 were gravely wounded or missing, and
10,000 were taken prisoner in the 1940 campaign. After the Armistice, and
before November 1942, some 1,000 fled and joined de Gaulle's Free French
forces. Of the 10,000 in the Unoccupied Zone, 4,200 were in the Army of the
Armistice. Overseas there were 5,000 in North Africa, 4,000 in West Africa
and 2,000 in Indochina. After the German occupation of all of France in
November 1942, 4,500 officers in the Unoccupied Zone took no part in the
rest of the war, while 1,100 made it to North Africa and 4,000 joined the
internal Resistance.[23]

As the Germans were being driven out of France, the country was still
in the after-shock of a civil war that had raged in 1943–44 between the
Resistance and the Vichy regime. The purges of collaborators that
followed the collapse of the Vichy Government continued into 1946 and
affected particularly the Government administration as well as the Armed
Forces.

In 1944–45, the French Army underwent the double shock of purges on
the one hand and integration of officers from the internal Resistance on the
other. In the purge hearings, 6,630 officers whose cases were heard were rein-
stated, 650 were retired, and 2,570 were dismissed.[24] In the integration
process, some 5,000 officers from the internal Resistance were integrated
into the regular armed forces.[25]

In addition, the officer ranks swelled in 1945 by those returning from the
prisoner-of-war camps in Germany. And yet a plan of 8 March, 1946
projected a reduction of the Army by June 1946 to 460,000 from a high of

Table 12.3: French force levels, 1945–52

Year	Army	Navy	Air Force	Total
1945	1,300,000[a]	85,000[b]	152,000[c]	1,537,000[d]
1946[e]	400,000	45,000	50,000	495,000
1948[f]	465,000	58,000	77,000	600,000
1950	–	–	–	659,000[g]
1952	–	–	–	885,000[h]

Notes

A Doise and Vaïsse, *Diplomatie et outil militaire*, p. 477.

b. *De Gaulle et la Nation*, p. 178.

c. *Ibid.*

d. N.B. Robert Frank in *De Gaulle et la Nation* (p. 178) puts the total of the French Army at
   1.25 million as of March 1945. The total used in this table is that of Maurice Vaïsse and
   André Corvisier (1.3 million as of May 1945).

e. *Informations Militaires* (*IM*), 1946, No. 46, p. 6.

f. *IM*, 1948, No. 115, p. 4.

g. *IM*, 1950, No. 154, p. 7.

h. Doise and Vaïsse, *Diplomatie et outil militaire*, p. 518.

1,300,000 in June 1945. The actual figures for the Armed Forces for 1946 are shown above in Table 12.3.

The result was that the drastically downsized French military was top-heavy with officers. As announced on 21 February 1946 by the Minister of the Armies, Edmond Michelet, whose Ministry had been created three months earlier, there would have to be a reduction in the officer corps. This would involve the demobilization of some 10,000 to 15,000 active duty officers.[26] By the end of 1946, the Armed Forces counted 22,000 officers, in contrast to 1939 when the total was 35,000.

Because of trouble in the French Empire, the proportion of troops needed overseas was unusually high. The troop level in Metropolitan France had to be reduced accordingly to 110,000, causing General Jean de Lattre de Tassigny to observe that financial imperatives had brought the French Army in the Metropole down to the same level as the Army of the Armistice [of 1940].[27]

Military Planning Structures

France's defense planning structures that emerged in the post-war were basically on two levels: the level of *defense*, which constituted a blend of civilian and military authorities; and a level of *armed forces*, which was strictly military. The structures reflected the uneasy symbiosis in French civil–military relations that has been a hallmark of French history since the Revolution. They represented an effort by essentially weak governments, who were at the mercy of shifting parliamentary majorities, to establish civilian control over the military.

In the immediate aftermath of the Liberation in 1944, de Gaulle, as head of the Provisional Government, instituted a centralized defense planning system. He wanted a strengthened Presidency, with the Chief of State in charge of defense, an element that had been missing in 1940.

At the apex of the system was the National Defense Committee (CDN), headed by de Gaulle. It was composed of civilians and military personnel, including the Minister of Armies, the Minister of Armaments, and the Service Chiefs.[28] Directly underneath was the supreme military body, the General Headquarters of National Defense (EMGDN), headed by General Alphonse Juin, the former commander of the French Expeditionary Corps

Table 12.4: Size of French officer corps, 1939 and 1946

Year	Number of officers
1939	35,000
1946	22,000[a]

Note
a. Doise and Vaïsse, *Diplomatie et outil militaire*, p. 487.

in Italy. The 1946 Constitution, promulgated after de Gaulle's departure, placed national defense under the authority of both the President (largely a figurehead under the new Constitution) and the Prime Minister. Gradually the authority over national defense was parceled out, and the role of the military within it, exercised at the highest level in the EMGDN, became weakened with the departure of its chief, General Juin, in 1947. The Prime Minister delegated defense to the Defense Minister in 1948, and authority then largely devolved to the civilian ministers in charge of the Army, the Navy and the Air Force. These ministries were headed mainly by representatives of the different parties within the tripartite governing coalition (Socialists, Communists, and Christian Democrats), which ruled until the spring of 1947. Thereafter, by a decree of 24 April 1948, secretaries of state became the civilian chiefs over the three services. These secretaries of state each disposed of their own budget, further weakening the centralizing authority of the Defense Minister.[29]

The EMGDN was transformed into an organization that was part civilian and became the General Secretariat of National Defense in 1950. Authority for military planning was split between central organizations on one hand (the Committee of Chiefs of Staff and the Headquarters of the Armed Forces), and the three armed services on the other hand.[30]

This atomization of authority continued into the 1950s. The void in strategic direction at the head of the French Government, during which time the military was forced into a succession of colonial wars, was to be filled by the military.[31] The Headquarters of the Armed Forces, which was the working element under the Committee of Chiefs of Staff, grew in importance, and a further step toward centralization took place in 1953 with the creation of the post of Chief of the General Staff of the Armies (i.e. the three services). General Paul Ely was the first to serve in this position until he was called away in mid-1954 to supervise the French retreat from Indochina. He returned to the post with increased powers in February 1956 and served through the Suez crisis and the Army revolt in Algiers, leaving in May 1958.

France's Strategic Objectives

At a meeting of the National Defense Committee on 2 October 1944, French strategic objectives were laid out by General Alphonse Juin. The presentation showed de Gaulle's stamp and his reflections on defense going back to the 1930s.

The first objective was the creation of a standing intervention force, deemed necessary to repair the error of the 1930s, when the French General Staff took the position that France could not go into action militarily except by first calling a general mobilization.[32] This requirement left France immobile during the crisis occasioned by Hitler's remilitarization of the Rhineland in 1936.

During the meeting of the National Defense Committee of 2 October 1944, it was made clear that the intervention force was destined for the European Theater, in particular against a German offensive.[33] The force would be in a position to intervene not only in Western Europe, but also to be deployed to protect French interests and colonies in French North Africa and French West Africa.[34]

The second objective was to assure the permanent security of the French Empire.[35] The issue of the Empire emerged with the end of the war: a bloody revolt erupted in Sétif, in eastern Algeria, starting on V-E Day on 8 May 1945, and spread to nearby Guelma and to other parts of the country, resulting in the deaths of scores of European *colons*. Quelled with great ferocity by the French, the revolt of the Algerian Muslims would begin again definitively in 1954. At the end of 1946, hostilities began in earnest in Indochina between the French Army and the forces of the self-proclaimed Democratic Republic of Vietnam led by Ho Chi Minh. Only three months later, on 30 March 1947, an insurrection broke out on the island of Madagascar, requiring considerable French forces to put it down.

To assure the 'permanent security' of the French Empire, the armed forces would have to avail themselves of strategic bases for effective deployment as the need arose. These would have to be far enough away to remain operational in the event of an attack on the Metropole and were, namely, Dakar, Beirut, Diego-Suarez, and Camranh Bay.[36]

The third strategic objective was a more traditionally French one: the training of a force of reservists who could be mobilized to defend the country in the event of a total war,[37] a possibility that seemed to haunt de Gaulle more than other Western leaders. This objective related to the French desire to maintain a conscript Army as a hallmark of France's commitment to 'Republican' virtues and to counteract any tendencies on the part of the overwhelmingly conservative officer corps to stage a coup and install strong-man rule (encompassed by the term 'Bonapartism').

Distribution of Forces

In the Spring of 1947, the new War Minister, Paul Coste-Floret, stated that France needed fifteen years of peace, during which time it would have to be content with 'an army of transition.'[38] Accordingly, he laid out two priorities: the security of the French Union and military training for the French nation.

Forces levels were relatively static. On 31 May 1948, the new Minister of Defense, Pierre-Henri Teitgen, projected minimum force levels in a period of peace at 600,000, with the breakdown as shown in Table 12.5. This peacetime projection, however, had already been exceeded overseas by 50,000 due to France's participation in the Indochina war.[39] Whereas Table 12.5 represents the overall distribution, Tables 12.6 and 12.7 reflect the changes that

Table 12.5: Location and size of French forces, 1946–52

Year	Total	Metropole	Germany	North Africa	Indochina	Other Territories
1946[a]	400,000	110,000	–	102,000	116,000[b]	–
1948[c]	600,000 [d]	195,000	60,000	110,000	150,000[e]	–
1950[f]	659,000	–	–	–	150,000	–
1952[g]	885,000	–	–	–	200,000	47,000

Notes
a. Doise and Vaïsse, *Diplomatie et outil militaire*, p. 491.
b. This figure includes all of the Far East, not just Indochina.
c. *Informations Militaires* (*IM*), 1948, No. 115, p. 4.
d. Of this total, the Army included 465,000, the Air Force 77,000 and the Navy 58,000 (*ibid.*).
e. This figure includes Indochina and other overseas territories (except North Africa) (*ibid.*).
f. *IM*, 1950, No. 160, p. 5.
g. Doise and Vaïsse, *Diplomatie et outil militaire*, p. 518.

took place first in Indochina and then in Algeria. The wars beyond the Metropole were thus consuming more and more troops and resources.

The Emergence of the Soviet Threat and the End of French 'Neutrality'

With France consumed by colonial wars and fears of a resurgent Germany, it is not surprising that French threat assessments after the Second World War did not mention the Soviet Union as a potential enemy. In fact, during a visit to Moscow in December 1944, de Gaulle had signed a Friendship Treaty with the Soviet Union, in effect a collective defense agreement against Germany.[40]

However, it gradually became apparent that the overwhelming focus on Germany was out of keeping with post-war realities. Germany had been so thoroughly crushed, that it would take at least a generation to reconstitute itself as a credible military threat.

In the late spring of 1947 – a pivotal year in France in terms of its positioning between East and West – President Vincent Auriol and his chief military confidant, General Jean de Lattre de Tassigny, agreed that a conflict between the United States and the Soviet Union was (a) possible, and (b) infinitely more probable than a conflict arising from a resurgent Germany.[41]

On 20 April 1947, shortly after President Truman announced that the USA would come to the aid of Greece and Turkey against the threat of Communism, Foreign Minister Georges Bidault came to an understanding with his American counterpart, George Marshall. France considered itself an integral part of the Western camp in the developing struggle with the Soviet Bloc, and that the French Communists would not remain for long in the Government in Paris. (They were ejected from the Cabinet of Prime

Table 12.6: Size of French forces in Indochina, 1946-54[a]

Year	Size of force
1946	89,000
1948	118,000
1949	120,000
1950	154,000
1952	200,000
1954	204,000[b]

Notes

a. Doise and Vaïsse, *Diplomatie et outil militaire*,
   p. 554. N.B. French troops were out of Indochina by 1956.
b. In the period roughly 1950–54, the number of
   French in the total remained stable at around
   60,000. The increase came in the number of
   North African and Indochinese troops (*ibid.*, p. 554).

Minister Paul Ramadier in the following month.) However, as Georges-Henri Soutou has pointed out, 'It took another two years . . . for this fundamental agreement to be translated into reality, reflecting just how large were the divisions and hesitations in France.'[42]

The prevailing slogan at the time was that of anti-fascism which, as François Furet has demonstrated, was a vehicle for promoting anti-capitalism.[43] The prestige of the Red Army and the Soviet Union, as the power that had had the main role in the defeat of Nazi Germany, was at an all-time high in the immediate post-war, and the Communist Party was a potent force on the French political scene. As Georgette Elgey, a leading historian of the French Fourth Republic, noted, 'With nearly a million members, five ministers in the Government, [and] 160 deputies in the Constituent Assembly, the Communist Party dominate[d] French political life.'[44]

In September 1947, the French military, through a memorandum by the General Headquarters of National Defense (EMGDN) to the President, took the position that neutrality was impossible for France and that it should join the Anglo-American camp for fundamental political reasons (one of them being that if Paris were to choose the side of Moscow in the event of a war with the Soviet Union, the 'Anglo-Saxons' would seize the territories of the French Empire).[45]

The EMGDN memorandum, authored by its chief, General Humbert, argued that Western Europe stood a reasonable chance of defending itself against an invasion by the Soviet Union, supported by substantial US military aid.[46]

In a restricted Cabinet meeting of 23 September 1947, Prime Minister Ramadier refused to accept the recommendations of General Humbert, arguing that there were still two options that remained open for France, neutrality or siding with the Anglo-Americans. One of the reasons behind this hesitation was the realization that if France were to throw in its lot with the Anglo-American camp, this would mean acquiescing to a likely

Table 12.7: Size of French forces in Algeria, 1954-58a

Date	Size of force
Nov 1954	80,000
Aug 1956	400,000
1957	450,000[b]
1958	500,000[c]

Notes

a. Doise and Vaïsse, *Diplomatie et outil militaire*, p. 570
b. Of this number 335,000 were French, and of the latter, 80 per cent were draftees. These figures do not include the Air Force (30,000) and the Navy (3,000), nearly all of whom were French (*ibid.*).
c. Of this number, 55,000 were officers (*ibid.*, p. 580).

push by the USA for Germany's rearming.[47] Opinion, led on the military side by General de Lattre but opposed by General Juin and many other officers, warned against an American 'vassalization' of France that had begun with the Marshall Plan and would be intensified by a military alliance.[48]

The situation changed drastically in France when the Communists, still excluded from the Government, launched a series of insurrectional strikes in November–December 1947. The Government responded by activating draftees in order to quell the riots and acts of sabotage. On 19 December 1947, Bidault obtained from the Cabinet the admission that neutrality was not a solution for France and that instead there should be mutual military and security arrangements drawn up by the US, the UK, and France.

The coup of Prague in February 1948 finally ended the hesitations of France about allying with Anglo-Americans. The Brussels Pact, a collective security accord between Britain and France plus the Benelux countries, went into effect in March 1948. It marked a turning point away from Germany and towards the Soviet Union as the main threat to Europe (although Germany remained the only explicit potential enemy in the Treaty text). It also represented for France an invitation for American military assistance, based on the perception that Europe needed US help in its defense.

As East–West tensions mounted over Germany in the spring of 1948, with the Anglo-American adoption of a common currency in their occupation zones, followed by the Soviet blockade of Berlin in June, an American military re-engagement was becoming inevitable. The sense of alarm in Western Europe was underlined by the realization that it was not in a position to defend itself against the huge Soviet Army, given the rapid Allied demobilization that had followed the war. At the time of the German surrender, American, British and Canadian forces totaled 5 million; a year later there were only 880,000.[49]

The heightened sense of threat in Western Europe meant that the 'forward defense' thesis was to win out. The Brussels Pact Defense Ministers declared in September 1948 that the defense of Europe should be undertaken as far to the east of the Rhine as possible. At the same time, the Ministers set up a military headquarters for the Pact at Fontainebleau.

The American military re-engagement in Europe brought with it the military subordination of Europe to the USA. The North Atlantic Treaty of 4 April 1949 superimposed itself over the Brussels Pact. With the return of General Eisenhower at the beginning of 1951 to head up a North Atlantic Treaty Organization Headquarters at Rocquencourt, the Brussels Pact Military Headquarters at Fontainebleau was eclipsed.

American Military Aid to France

The North Atlantic Treaty was accompanied by a series of bilateral military assistance agreements between the United States on one hand and the rest of the treaty members on the other. France was expected to provide the bulk of the ground troops for the defense of Western Europe. The overall military assistance program, known as the Mutual Defense Assistance Program (MDAP), which was a follow-up to the North Atlantic Treaty, was voted for by Congress on 30 September 1949 and signed by President Truman on 6 October. The MDAP program provided that for the Fiscal Year beginning 1 July 1949, the USA would provide military credits to a number of foreign countries in the amount of US$1,314,100,000.[50] Of the portion for the North Atlantic Treaty countries (US$1,148,000,000), approximately one-half would go to France. The latter would be expected to furnish 55 per cent of the troops drawn from the Brussels Pact powers for the defense of Western Europe.[51]

Although the rearmament of France was a tangible sign of an increase in the country's power, it was accompanied by a diminution of France's independence, since France was to become part of the integrated NATO command under General Eisenhower as the Supreme Allied Commander Europe (SACEUR).[52]

At this time in the late 1940s, however, the onerous nature of the military arrangements of the North Atlantic Treaty was overshadowed by the sense of French weakness in the face of the Soviet Union and the realization that the United States could redress this balance. Furthermore, in the West–West context, the rearmament process could be a way of bringing France back to parity with Great Britain.

On 15 March 1950, both houses of the French Parliament approved the bilateral military accord for mutual defense between France and the United States, which had been signed on 27 January 1950. According to the stipulations of the accord, the assistance furnished by the USA was to be in the framework of an integrated defense of the North Atlantic region. There was to be no unauthorized use of the weaponry and no transfers to third countries without prior agreement.

On 25 June 1950, North Korea attacked the South and, as Maurice Vaïsse put it, 'The Korean conflict abolished in a single instant all the obstacles to rearmament.'[53] A French Government memorandum of 7 August 1950 to the USA and other members of the North Atlantic Pact acknowledged Paris' dependence: 'This [the French rearmament] effort cannot be realized except by means of external assistance.'[54]

In February 1952, the NATO Council meeting at Lisbon decided on 'force goals' for the defense of Western Europe, within the framework of the projected European Army (officially known as the European Defense Community – EDC). These were as follows: fourteen French divisions; twelve German divisions; twelve Italian divisions; five divisions from Belgium and the Netherlands combined; and four British divisions with their own air support – Britain being in association with the EDC, but not a member *per se*.

The Lisbon 'force goals' proved unrealistic, and in any event, the EDC project was killed in the French Parliament two years later. In spite of France being projected to supply the most forces, its continuing need to divert troops for the defense of its Empire meant that it was unable to provide its share of troops. Instead, with German rearmament in the mid-1950s, Germany carried the largest burden of a ground defense against a possible Soviet attack. Notwithstanding, American military assistance to France was considerable: it totaled US$4,154,600,000 from Fiscal Year 1950, when it began, through Fiscal Year 1965.[55] (The aid ended when France withdrew from the NATO in March 1966.)

France's Emergence as a Nuclear Power

Although American assistance in the buildup of France's conventional forces in the early Cold War was significant and even critical, the USA did little to help and actually impeded France's efforts in the nuclear area. This was essentially done in two ways. The first was through amendments in the 1950s to the postwar McMahon Act, which had prohibited exchanges with foreign countries on atomic energy matters. In the 1950s amendments, which opened the door to cooperation with the British, hedges were introduced to bar France, most notably, that to qualify for exchanges of information, a nation had already to '[have] made substantial progress in the development of nuclear weapons.'[56]

The second attempt to obstruct the development of the French atomic bomb was through the US proposal at the beginning of the 1960s to create a Multilateral Force (MLF): a nuclear force would be created out of the European members of NATO, but the USA would retain a veto over its employment. The British also demanded a veto, which the USA never ruled out. France declined the proposal, viewing it as part of an attempt to divert France from developing its own nuclear program.

The development of France's atomic bomb did not begin with de Gaulle, but preceded his return to power in 1958. In 1954, the Prime Minister, Mendès France, created a committee on nuclear explosions. A new impetus was given to weaponization when the Soviets, during the Suez crisis, made veiled threats to drop atomic bombs on London and Paris, to which the Americans responded mainly by privately belittling the threats. In the aftermath of Suez, and for a brief period, France entered into a cooperative venture in nuclear development with West Germany and Italy, but this was quashed in early 1958 by the Defense Minister, Jacques Chaban-Delmas, at the instance of de Gaulle, who was still out of power at the time. On 11 April 1958, Prime Minister Félix Gaillard set a date of early 1960 for the first French atomic explosion. This took place in February 1960, with de Gaulle back in power.

Although the leaders of the Fourth Republic saw a nuclear weapons program as enhancing France's position in negotiating with the other great powers, de Gaulle saw it as a way to retain France's sovereignty. In the 1960s a strategy was developed that would henceforth govern French thinking on how the country would exploit its possession of atomic weapons. As Maurice Vaïsse has pointed out, it consisted both of *persuasion* (what in the USA is often referred to as compellence) and *deterrence* ('dissuasion'), and he referred to the words of de Gaulle himself:

> Possession by a country of atomic weapons means being in a position to reduce to submission a country that does not have them. But it is also a means of dissuading any nation possessing such weapons from proceeding to atomic aggression; because the latter would consist in unleashing death and immediately receiving the same.[57]

The *deterrence* side of the coin is expressed in the French formula of the 'deterrence by the weak of the strong' ('*la dissuasion du faible au fort*'); that is to say, that the French threat to destroy as many of the enemy as the total of the French population – 60 million – would be sufficient to dissuade an adversary possessing a wide margin of superiority over France in nuclear weapons.

The *persuasion* side of the coin is rarely enunciated, because in effect it reflects a continuing French aim for nuclear hegemony in Western Europe. As the US Ambassador to France, Charles Bohlen, observed in 1965, this was tied to France's objections to the MLF:

> From the nature of the objections which the French have brought forward to the MLF, it would appear to me that the real French objection is the recognition that any form of NATO (or outside NATO) nuclear force in which some continental Europeans would participate would inevitably do away with the French monopoly of

European nuclear weapons. . . . This central aim of French policy has rarely been enunciated.[58]

The emphasis on 'continental Europe' reflects a focus on Germany that has been present from the beginning. In a meeting of top officials in December 1954, Prime Minister Mendès France noted the particular advantage that France, once it had obtained the atomic bomb, would then have over Germany, which was prohibited from developing nuclear weapons.[59]

The French nuclear force became operational in 1969[60] and came to be based on a triad of land-based missiles (*Albion Plateau*); air-launched missiles, by Mirage aircraft; and missiles launched by submarine (*sous-marin nucléaire lanceur d'engins – SNLE*).

France's Insurrectionary Wars 1: Indochina

As noted in the summary above, Ho Chi Minh seized power in Hanoi in September 1945, declaring a 'Democratic Republic' for the whole of Vietnam. He attempted to fill the vacuum created by the Japanese ouster of the Vichy French administration in March 1945. But already, after the Second World War, de Gaulle had sent an expeditionary corps under General Philippe Leclerc to restore French authority in Indochina. De Gaulle also named Admiral Thierry d'Argenlieu as the leading civilian authority with the title of High Commissioner. The two worked to some degree at cross-purposes, with d'Argenlieu attempting to restore the French colonial presence and Leclerc seeking accommodation with Ho Chi Minh.

On 6 March 1946, Leclerc came to an agreement with the Viet Minh. Ho's Democratic Republic of Vietnam (DRV) was recognized as the legitimate government of the country, occupying the position of a free state of the Indochina Federation, which was in turn part of the French Union. In return, Ho allowed the French to put 25,000 troops into the northern part of Vietnam, 10,000 of whom were to be Vietnamese; and to withdraw these troops in tranches of one-fifth annually until the occupation ended five years later.[61]

The 6 March agreement also provided for a referendum in Cochinchina, in southernmost Vietnam, which had been converted by the French into a separate colony. The referendum was to determine if Cochinchina would become part of Vietnam, which the Vietnamese had always considered it to be anyway.[62] It was the French failure to carry through with this referendum that became the principal bone of contention which prevented the implementation of the 6 March agreement and which in turn led to the violent clash between Ho and the French at the end of 1946.

With open warfare having broken out between the Viet Minh and the French, the latter then turned to Bao Dai, the former Emperor, and there followed a long period of mutual jockeying, with the focus being on the terms unity and independence. Unity basically meant reattaching Cochinchina to the rest of Vietnam. This was essentially accomplished through a vote in the French National Assembly on 23 April 1949.[63]

Independence was a more complicated concept. The question was how much independence would Vietnam enjoy as an 'Associated State' within the French Union.

Nevertheless, the difference in interpretation over the concept of independence was papered over in an accord signed between Bao Dai and French President Vincent Auriol on 8 March 1949, the so-called Elysée Agreement.[64]

Until this point, the USA, while explicitly hoping for both an association of Vietnam with France and a fulfillment of Vietnamese aspirations for self-government,[65] remained aloof from the French negotiations with Bao Dai.

Later in 1949, the triumph of the Communists in China reinforced the feeling in Washington that the United States was in danger of losing the Cold War. As the French National Assembly finally ratified the Elysée Accords of ten months earlier, a rapid polarization of international attitudes toward Indochina occurred. India regarded Bao Dai as a French puppet with no popular support and refused to recognize his regime; other Asian countries generally followed India's lead.[66] On 19 January 1950, the new Communist regime in China recognized Ho Chi Minh as the leader of the legitimate government of Vietnam. Twelve days later the Soviet Union followed suit, and subsequently several European satellite countries followed. The United States' recognition of the Bao Dai regime, on 2 February 1950, was followed by the recognition of Great Britain and twenty-five other Western powers.[67] On 14 February 1950, China and the Soviet Union signed a treaty of friendship. The Cold War had arrived in Southeast Asia.

US military assistance soon followed. From a modest beginning, the aid to the French for the Indochina War rose sharply, reaching a total of US$2,753,000,000 at the time the war concluded in July 1954 with the Geneva Conference.[68] This figure represented more than half of the overall total of US$4,154,600,000 in US military assistance to France in the period from Fiscal Year 1950 through Fiscal Year 1965.[69]

According to Pentagon estimates, France spent US$7 billion in the pursuit of the Indochina War from 1946 to 1954. Thus, together with the American contribution of US$2.7 billion and that of the Associated States (Vietnam, Cambodia and Laos), which came to US$250 million, the financial cost of the war amounted, on the Allied side, to almost 10 billion dollars.[70]

American military support was significant. By July 1954, when aid ceased, the USA had provided the following: 1,800 combat vehicles; 30,887 motor transport vehicles; 361,522 small arms and machine guns; 2,847 artillery pieces; 438 naval craft; two Second World War aircraft carriers; and about 500 aircraft.[71]

The battle of Dien Bien Phu, which ushered in the end of the Indochina War,[72] had resulted from a grave military misjudgment: the French commander, General Henri Navarre, had calculated that the Viet Minh could be lured into a conventional battle and decimated. That a native army without a single plane or tank could defeat a well-equipped Western force seemed inconceivable. The Viet Minh did, however, have artillery, supplied by the Chinese, and along with anti-aircraft weapons this helped to spell the difference. An estimated 60,000 artillery shells supplied by the Chinese fell on the remote basin-outpost of Dien Bien Phu in northwest Vietnam during the battle there (13 March–7 May 1954).[73]

The French Army lost 7,115 – killed, wounded or missing at Dien Bien Phu. The conqueror for the Viet Minh, General VO Nguyen Gap, took 10,000 prisoners.[74] Overall, in the years 1945 to 1954, the French Expeditionary Corps suffered 92,000 killed.[75] Of this total nearly 20,000 were Europeans, the remainder being Vietnamese or French colonial troops from the Maher or, to a lesser extent, Black Africa. Of the Frenchmen, nearly all were officers or non-commissioned officers. A total of 2,000 of the former died;[76] among whom were 800 St. Cyr graduates.[77] Table 12.8 details the origins of French Army personnel in Indochina, as of 1949.

France's Insurrectionary Wars 2: Algeria

Out of the 1954 cease-fire agreement that accompanied the Geneva Conference, many of the French Army prisoners were repatriated. The battle-hardened French Army units in Vietnam were then transported to Algeria to handle the revolt that had broken out there on 1 November 1954, three months after the conclusion of the Geneva Conference. The French Army officers arriving in Algeria, in particular those of the elite parachute regiments, were determined not to allow what happened in Indochina to take place in Algeria.[78] This sentiment reflected both a bitterness at the indifference of the people and the Government of the Metropole toward this ill-starred army of professionals in remote Indochina, as well as a desire to take a more dominant role in the formulation of a strategy of counter-insurgency.

In the view of these Army officers, Algeria was (and was to be) very different from Indochina. Algeria, which was considered to be an integral part of France, was on the doorstep of the Metropole instead of being halfway around the world. Additionally, the proportion of Europeans was

Table 12.8: Size of the French Expeditionary Corps in Indochina, 1949[a]

French	Legionnaires	North Africans	Black Africans	Vietnamese	Total
44,000	15,000	15,000	7,000	39,000	120,000

Note

a. Doise and Vaïsse, *Diplomatie et outil militaire*, p. 549.

different – 40,000 in Indochina in 1945 in a population numbering 30 million, as compared to 1 million in Algeria in the 1950s out of a population totaling 10 million. Europeans were omnipresent in Algeria, although outnumbered nine to one by the native Muslim population.

'La Guerre Révolutionnaire'

A period of strategic introspection took place in the French Army in the 1950s, coincident with the battle of Dien Bien Phu. A new theory arose to help explain this defeat and prevent further ones. It was called 'Revolutionary War' ('la Guerre révolutionnaire'), promulgated by a small group of officers led by Colonel Lacheroy. An entire issue of *Revue Militaire d'Information*, the successor to *Informations Militaires* as the primary journal of the military, was devoted to the new doctrine, in February 1957.[79]

The idea behind 'la Guerre révolutionnaire' was somewhat similar to the 'hearts and minds' campaign of Colonel Edwin Lansdale that worked well in the Philippines and was transplanted to South Vietnam, with some initial success, in the late 1950s. The key to victory in 'la Guerre révolutionnaire' was winning over the national population through persuasion and civic works: building of schools and hospitals and other public works, and administering health care and educational services. A new French Army bureau, the Fifth Bureau, was created to carry out this activity.

What gave 'la Guerre révolutionnaire' its special and flawed emphasis was the syncretistic link between native independence movements and international Communism. It was strongly asserted that 'la Guerre révolutionnaire' did not reach its full development until the advent of the Soviet Union:

> It is a question of getting a clear idea of this method of combat, which became perfected worldwide following the creation of the Union of Soviet Socialist Republics and particularly in our [French] overseas territories since the end of the Second World War.[80]

Thus the Algerian nationalist fighter ('fellagha') was painted as an agent of Marxism–Leninism, a doctrinal linkage that served to obscure the indigenous roots of the Algerian independence movement. In the Messianic parlance of 'la Guerre révolutionnaire,' the French Army was seen as doing the West's (and Christianity's) work in Algeria, although not as an offensive against Islam but against international Communism. From the opposite point of view, that of the indigenous population, the inner core of the independence movement was in essence the rejection of the West by an Arab, Muslim civilization. The theory of 'la Guerre révolutionaire,' widely accepted in the French Army, failed to take into account the real basis for independence among the indigenous population.

From Insurrectionary Wars to Insurrection

The war in Algeria was the catalyst for de Gaulle's return to power. The revolt of the Army in Algiers and the proclamation of a 'Government of Public Safety' there threatened civil war and impelled the French Chief of State René Coty to call de Gaulle out of retirement and ask him to form a Government. On 1 June 1958, de Gaulle was voted in legally as Prime Minister by the National Assembly.

Three days after his investiture, de Gaulle traveled to Algiers and told a massed throng of mostly Europeans in the Forum that he understood them ('Je vous ai compris!'). He was not more specific than that, though each of the parties at stake, the Europeans and the Muslims, took his words as a sign of encouragement. Bit by bit, however, the military officers and *colons* came to realize that the man they had championed as an antidote to the vacillating policies of the Fourth Republic was about to compromise with the anti-colonialist forces. This evolutionary process took place against a backdrop of increased terrorist acts by the Algerian *Front de la Libération Nationale* (FLN) following its defeat in the battle of Algiers and its abortive attempts to breach the French-built Morice Line aimed at keeping out infiltrators from neighboring Tunisia. Concessions by de Gaulle reinforced the feeling among the military die-hards that their 'victory' was being snatched away from them.

When de Gaulle announced the principle of self-determination for Algeria in a speech on 16 September 1959, the seeds of further Army revolts were sown. They recognized that although they could defeat the FLN militarily, they had already lost politically.

Sensing the unrest in the Army, de Gaulle made a visit to Algeria in December 1960. In addressing a group of officers, de Gaulle admonished them that they must obey the laws of the state: 'The Army is not at the service of any clan, any faction, or any interest. It simply serves France.'[81]

The decisive moment came on 11 December 1960, during de Gaulle's visit, when the Muslims' pent-up desire for independence expressed itself in a massive demonstration. The French Army stood aside. In an Army that was 80 per cent made up of draftees, the influence of de Gaulle was telling. At this point all but a group of extremists in the officer corps realized that the die was cast: Algeria would achieve its independence. The *putsch* of the Generals, which followed in April 1961, was doomed. The bulk of the Army would not follow along; de Gaulle denounced the revolt in a public speech; and the movement ended four days later. As Maurice Vaïsse has written of the aftermath of Algeria, 'The military, conquerors on the ground, had to abandon the battlefield to become the managers of the *force de frappe*, the instrument of national independence.'[82] In the eight-year Algerian war, 32,000 Frenchmen died, 25,000 in combat, and 7,000 in accidents.[83]

Conclusion

The year of Algerian independence, 1962, also brought about the essential end of the French Empire: it was the first time since 1830 that the French Army as a whole found itself inside the Metropole.[84] But in a deeper sense, 1962, with its bereaved families and embittered officers who resigned or were dismissed from the service, marked the final stage of reconciliation between the French military and the French Republic – two institutions that had been locked in a dubious and ambiguous relationship since the *Ancien Régime* had been overthrown by the Revolution. One of de Gaulle's aims, as de la Gorce has also pointed out, was to 'assure with more certainty the integration of the officer corps into a French society from which it had been separated for too long.'[85]

The Army prior to the Second World War served as a state within the state. As there was no significant 'Right' in the French Parliament, the Army served as a surrogate 'Right.' This was the case through the nineteenth century, as *coups d'Etat*, or attempted *coups d'Etat*, alternated with Republican-inspired uprisings. At the end of the century, the Dreyfus affair had pitted a wrong-headed Army against the defenders of human rights and 'Republican' virtues. As we have seen in this study, it was elements of the Army that pushed aside the civilian rulers to conclude a dishonorable peace in 1940; and it was the Army that virtually took over the governance of Algeria in the 1950s and challenged the Government in Paris on several occasions to keep Algeria part of the French Empire.

The French Army, though torn by dissension, did not emerge from that war with a sense of defeat.[86] Algeria was different from Indochina: there was no 'long march' of prisoners from the final battle, as at Dien Bien Phu.

Though the malaise of defeat was not present in Algeria, there was a different kind of unease, as this mainly draftee Army returned to France and a suspicious French public. The French Army had been drawn into an implacable counter-guerrilla war in Algeria, both in the countryside and in the cities, a war that was far from conventional and which, in the widespread use of torture, offended its honor.

Taken together, the 'useless' wars of Indochina and Algeria, constituted the rebirth of the French military, which had been since 1940, to borrow a phrase from François Furet, *en mal d'expiation* ('yearning for expiation'). This *aggiornamento* was accompanied by a transition in the mid-1950s away from a dependence on American equipment and toward the creation of a purely French armaments industry focused on armor and aircraft and, ultimately, nuclear weapons and delivery systems.

It is perhaps ironic that France's experience in dealing with insurrectionary warfare from 1945 until 1962, disastrous though it was from a political point of view, has had a carryover effect. France, along with Britain, is one of the two powers in Europe today with a capacity and a willingness to intervene outside the original defensive zone of NATO in Western

Europe. It is perhaps unnecessary to remind ourselves also that the reflex of intervention goes deep in these two countries that possessed the greatest empires in the age of colonialism.

Note

1 For an analysis of this period of the war and its aftermath, see *De Gaulle et la Nation face aux problèmes de Défense (1945–1946)*, the proceedings of a conference organized by the Institut d'Histoire du Temps Présent and the Institut Charles-de-Gaulle, 21–22 October 1982 (Paris: Collection Espoir / Plon, 1983); also see Jean Doise and Maurice Vaïsse, *Diplomatie et outil militaire, 1871–1991* (Paris: Seuil, 1992); and Charles G. Cogan, *Oldest Allies, Guarded Friends: the United States and France since 1940* (Westport, CT: Praeger, 1994).
2 Bertrand Goldschmidt, *Le Complexe atomique* (Paris: Fayard, 1980), p. 32. Cited in *De Gaulle et la Nation*, p. 129.
3 Doise and Vaïsse, *Diplomatie et outil militaire*, p. 501.
4 *The Pentagon Papers. The Defense Department History of United States Decisionmaking on Vietnam*, The Senator Gravel Edition (Boston: Beacon Press, 1971), vol. I, p. 54. The exact figure cited was 78 per cent.
5 For an analysis of French civil–military relations since the Second World War see Samy Cohen, *La défaite des généraux: Le pouvoir politique et l'armée sous la Ve République* (Paris: Fayard, 1994); also see Jean Planchais, *Une Histoire politique de l'Armée. 2. 1940–1967: de De Gaulle à De Gaulle* (Paris: Seuil, 1967); Paul Marie de la Gorce, *La République et son Armée* (Paris: Fayard, 1963).
6 *De Gaulle et la Nation*, p. 30.
7 Marshal Philippe Pétain agreed to head the Vichy government which was located in the unoccupied zone France.
8 Doise and Vaïsse, *Diplomatie et outil militaire*, p. 456.
9 Jacques Vernet, 'L'Armée de Terre au 8 mai 1945,' in *De Gaulle et la Nation*, p. 33.
10 The 1er D.F.L. was the first French unit to engage the Germans after the French defeat in 1940.
11 Doise and Vaïsse, *Diplomatie et outil militaire*, p. 477.
12 *Ibid.*, p. 467. (N.B. The figures cited by Jacques Vernet as being of the same date (1 September 1944) are not markedly different: 295,000 indigenous out of 550,000 total (*De Gaulle et la Nation*, p. 34).)
13 *Ibid.*, p. 477.
14 *Ibid.*
15 *Ibid.*, p. 468.
16 *De Gaulle et la Nation*, p. 132.
17 Jean Lacouture, *De Gaulle. 2. Le politique* (Paris: Seuil, 1985), p. 122.
18 Robert Frank, 'Les crédits militaires: contraintes budgetaires et choix politiques (mai 1945–avril 1946),' in *De Gaulle et la Nation*, p. 174.
19 *Ibid.*, p. 177.
20 *Ibid.*, p. 174.
21 Doise and Vaïsse, *Diplomatie et outil militaire*, p. 480.
22 Planchais, *Une histoire politique de l'armée*, p. 117.
23 Doise and Vaïsse, *Diplomatie et outil militaire*, p. 486.
24 *Ibid.*
25 *Ibid.*, p. 487.
26 *Informations Militaires* (*IM*), no. 46, 1946, p. 6.
27 Doise and Vaïsse, *Diplomatie et outil militaire*, p. 491.

28 *Ibid.*, p. 482.
29 *Ibid.*, pp. 504–05.
30 *Ibid.*, p. 505.
31 *Ibid.*
32 Jean Delmas, 'Naissance d'une politique de défense (1944–8 mai 1945),' in *De Gaulle et la Nation*, p. 86.
33 *Ibid.*
34 *Ibid.*
35 *Ibid.*, p. 87.
36 *Ibid.*
37 *Ibid.*, p. 88.
38 Doise and Vaïsse, *Diplomatie et outil militaire*, pp. 480–81.
39 *IM*, no. 115, 1948, p. 4.
40 Jean Laloy, *Yalta: Yesterday, Today, Tomorrow*, trans. William R. Tyler (New York: Harper & Row, 1988), p. 58.
41 Georges-Henri Soutou, 'La sécurité de la France dans l'après-guerre,' in *La France et l'OTAN* (Paris: Editions Complexe, 1996), p. 31.
42 *Ibid.*, p. 30.
43 François Furet, *Le passé d'une illusion: essai sur l'idée communiste au Xxe siècle* (Paris: Robert Laffont / Calmann-Lévy, 1995), p. 424.
44 Georgette Elgey, *La République des illusions, 1945–1951* (Paris: Fayard, 1965), p. 15.
45 Soutou, 'La sécurité de la France dans l'après-guerre,' pp. 31–32.
46 *Ibid.*, p. 32.
47 *Ibid.*, p. 33.
48 *Ibid.*, p. 38.
49 Doise and Vaïsse, *Diplomatie et outil militaire*, p. 479.
50 Lawrence S. Kaplan, *A Community of Interests: NATO and the Military Assistance Program, 1948–1951* (Washington, DC: Office of the Secretary of Defense Historical Office, 1980), p. 116, Table 6.
51 *IM*, no. 151, 1950, p. 8. (N.B. Although it is not stated outright that the amount allocated to the North Atlantic Treaty countries was $1,148,000,000, it appears from the context that this was the case.)
52 Doise and Vaïsse, *Diplomatie et outil militaire*, p. 509.
53 *Ibid.*, p. 514.
54 *IM*, no. 160, 1950, p. 4.
55 *Annual Report of the Secretary of Defense for Fiscal Year 1965*, Appendix, p. 426, Table 42.
56 For further elaboration on this issue, see Cogan, *Oldest Allies, Guarded Friends*, pp. 132–33.
57 Doise and Vaïsse, *Diplomatie et outil militaire*, p. 613. Reference is to de Gaulle's press conference of 23 July 1964.
58 Lyndon Baines Johnson Library, National Security Files, Europe and USSR, Box 170, France: Vol. 5, 12 / 64–2 / 65, Paris telegram 3798, 5 January 1965, Section 2, pp. 1–2. Cited in Cogan, *Oldest Allies, Guarded Friends*, p. 130.
59 Doise and Vaïsse, *Diplomatie et outil militaire*, p. 598.
60 *Ibid.*, p. 620.
61 *The History of the Joint Chiefs of Staff (HJCS). The Joint Chiefs of Staff and the War in Vietnam. History of the Indochina Incident, 1940–1954* (Wilmington, DE: Michael Glazier, 1982), p. 103.
62 *Ibid.*, p. 104.
63 *Ibid.*, p. 131.
64 *Ibid.*, p. 130.

65 *Ibid.*, p. 132.
66 *Ibid.*, p. 146.
67 *Ibid.*, p. 148.
68 *Ibid.*, p. 487.
69 *Ibid.*, p. 28.
70 *Ibid.*, p. 485.
71 *The Pentagon Papers*, vol. I, p. 200. (N.B. Missing from this list are artillery pieces, artillery shells, and small arms ammunition rounds which according to JCS estimates established at the end of June 1953, a year before the end of the war, totaled 2,847, 5 million and 220 million respectively (*HJCS*, p. 261).)
72 The French customarily call the war of 1946–54 the Indochina War, and the American-led war of 1961–75 the Vietnam War.
73 Chen Jian, 'China and the First Indochina War,' *China Quarterly*, March 1993, p. 102.
74 Jean Planchais, 'La chute de Dien Bien Phu,' *Le Monde*, 9 May 1989, p. 2.
75 De la Gorce, *La République et son Armée*, p. 677.
76 Doise and Vaïsse, *Diplomatie et outil militaire*, p. 558.
77 *Ibid.*, p. 549.
78 Jean-Raymond Tournoux, *Secrets d'Etat* (Paris: Plon, 1960), p. 197.
79 *Revue Militaire d'Information (RMI)*, February 1957.
80 *Ibid.*, p. 10.
81 Quoted in de la Gorce, *La République et son Armée*, p. 650.
82 Doise and Vaïsse, *Diplomatie et outil militaire*, p. 594.
83 *Ibid.*, p. 571.
84 De la Gorce, *La République et son Armée*, p. 671.
85 *Ibid.*, p. 670.
86 *Ibid.*, p. 669.

13

CONCLUSION

Seven Lessons about the Fog of Peace

Talbot Imlay and Monica Duffy Toft

This edited volume, the product of two conferences organized by Harvard University's John M. Olin Institute for Strategic Studies, addresses the subject of peacetime military and strategic planning under conditions of uncertainty. Two goals motivated the editors throughout the project: to impress upon scholars the importance of the subject and to provide some useful guidance to practitioners confronted with the difficult task of piercing the 'fog of peace.' The approach adopted is a qualitative one that focuses on several historical case studies, partly because the editors believe in the intrinsic value of this approach and partly because anything resembling a comprehensive study lay well beyond the resources available. With these goals in mind, the editors gathered together historians and political scientists to examine cases from four different time periods: 1815–54, 1871–1914, 1919–39 and post-1945.

The authors of the individual chapters discuss concrete cases of military and strategic planning. Military planning concentrates on preparing armed forces for war and involves a variety of elements, including force structure, weapons systems, doctrine and tactics, and command arrangements. Strategic planning looks beyond the military aspects to encompass political, economic and other factors. Although the two types of planning differ in their focus, both share a common difficulty – that of uncertainty. As the future is never completely determined in advance, planners necessarily operate in an environment of uncertainty, which renders their task immensely complex and error-prone. The difficulties of uncertainty are heightened in periods of peace, those periods in which war appears to be neither impossible nor imminent. Uncertainty comes in many forms, but it can be usefully divided into three elements: (1) the difficulty of identifying friend and foe; (2) the difficulty of understanding the nature of future war; and (3) the difficulty of determining its timing. Each chapter highlights one or more elements of uncertainty, and the goal of this concluding chapter is to consider seven common points or lessons that emerge from the eleven historical case studies.

Lesson 1: Effective War Planning Requires as Many Inputs as Possible

Although most of the seven lessons directly address the issue of uncertainty, the first lesson concerns two questions: who is responsible for military planning and how is it undertaken? The first lesson is that military and strategic planning requires as many inputs as possible. A balance of civilian and military input is indispensable for effective planning under conditions of uncertainty. One mistake is to leave planning to military planners alone: military planners are especially effective when it comes to the military aspects of planning, but less skilled when it comes to working out the broader grand-strategic and political implications of war planning.

In his contextual chapter on the pre-1914 period, for example, David Stevenson shows that while the professionalization of the general staff improved military planning, it also fostered an excessive focus on military factors at the expense of non-military factors. Interestingly, Stevenson's chapter suggests that what is needed is not only a proper mix of military and civilian inputs, but also a balance between short-, medium-, and longer-term planning. Here, widening the circle of planners beyond general staff officers is important since the latter tend to concentrate on military preparations for war in the immediate future, regularly updating preparations in light of developments. While this practice works against a rigid attachment to the status quo, as witnessed by the evolution of the military plans of the Great Powers before 1914, excessive attention to immediate needs can hamper the proper consideration of longer-term factors. Thus, planners before 1914 neglected such factors as nationalism and technological developments, both of which helped to produce stalemate between 1914 and 1917.

Louise Richardson, whose chapter examines the earlier, post-Napoleonic period, reinforces Stevenson's argument by showing that diplomats of the period proved more flexible and imaginative than military officers. While diplomats adapted to the new international system characterized by the Concert of Europe, military planners adopted a 'business as usual' approach; they appeared incapable of recognizing the new order that helped to produce and sustain the Concert for several decades. Discussing the Prussian and British cases, Richardson notes that while Prussia created the general staff as part of its military reforms following the Napoleonic Wars, these efforts proved short-lived: the reformers were soon cashiered, replaced by Kaiser Wilhelm's impulsive and uncoordinated planning. Similarly, the British Army remained entrenched in its ideas, a complacency that Richardson attributes to Wellington's victory against Napoleonic France. Although Wellington's success at Waterloo provided him with extraordinary legitimacy, his authority was insufficient to overcome the effects of Britain's decentralized system of military planning. Exacerbating matters was the fact that Wellington himself resisted centralizing efforts for fear of undermining his authority as Commander in Chief. Overall, Britain's military and strategic planning lacked coordination, seriously impeding its planning efforts. From the British case, Richardson suggests that defeat might be a better teacher than victory, though Prussia's stalled military reforms indicate that victory alone does not ensure reform. In any case, Richardson's chapter offers a warning to contemporary planners: in periods of uncertainty, military planners are apt to prefer the familiar and the comfortable to change since the latter tends to increase rather than decrease existing uncertainty.

In line with Stevenson and Richardson's interest in those responsible for planning, Frederick Kagan, in his chapter on Russian war planning in the first half of the nineteenth century, shows that committees comprising of military and civilian participants could plan effectively. This was especially true in the case of *ad hoc* committees charged with responding to immediate crises. Such committees, however, proved less effective when it came to longer-term strategic planning, which reinforces the point that it is not simply the civilian–military balance in planning, but also the time frames of planners that matters. It seems that longer-term planning is not something that comes naturally to planners, whether military or civilian, but something that they must be specifically tasked to do. Poor long-term planning contributed to Russia's defeat in the Crimean War, which was the result not only of confused policies but also of a lack of resources and of backwardness. While Britain, France, and Prussia were modernizing their industries and militaries, Russia maintained serfdom, a system that hampered industrial development. The lack of industrial development impeded Russia's war effort, especially when it came to railroads and the transporting of troops and supplies across its vast territorial expanse. Faced with several potential military fronts, Russia, more than other great powers of the time, needed to harness the capabilities afforded by the rail system for rapid deployment. The question is whether Russian planners understood the trade-offs involved. Russia fielded one of the largest armies in the world, but one that cost the country dearly to sustain. Had railroads been properly integrated into the Russian planning system, the size of the army could have been reduced as troops could be more effectively transported from one front to another. Such trade-offs, however, needed to be identified and resolved in advance – tasks for which a system based on *ad hoc* committees, charged with dealing with immediate crises, proved inappropriate. Kagan's chapter thus drives home the point that effective military and strategic planning demands a combination of military and civilian inputs as well as the consideration of several time frames. While the present and immediate future necessarily demands attention, this should not come at the expense of a longer-term vision.

David Kaiser's chapter on US military planning after 1945 provides an example in this regard, showing how the possession of nuclear weapons confounded planners' thinking about how to achieve victory in a war against the Soviet Union. According to Kaiser, effective war planning involves combining in coherent fashion military means with political goals. In a war against the Soviet Union, the political goals would vary depending on circumstances, including a withdrawal from Eastern Europe, the elimination of the communist regime, or a simple return to the *status quo ante*. However, given that atomic weapons possessed the potential for total destruction of the enemy, could the military means employed not be reconciled with any of these goals? As Kaiser argues, US planners do not appear to have come to terms with the problem of reconciling the two. Once the Soviets possessed their own nuclear capacity, the problem became still more insoluble. Victory in a war with the Soviet Union was defined as the 'survival of the United States,' yet it was far from apparent how even this more limited objective could be achieved in the wake of a nuclear exchange. Here greater civilian input and leadership might have been helpful, but rather than confront the problem, the Eisenhower Administration left it to later administrations to work through the thorny issues of a balance between burgeoning nuclear capacities and the political objectives that might reasonably be secured by them.

Lesson 2: Balance Short-term and Long-term Perspectives in Planning

The remaining lessons deal more directly with the role of uncertainty. The first of these concerns uncertainty about the timing of war. There are two related questions regarding timing and war planning: (1) the question of long- versus short-term planning; and (2) the question of when exactly the next war will begin. Regarding the first question, as the previous comments on time frames suggest, the balance between short- and long-term planning is difficult to draw, especially during periods of rapid political, economic, technological, and other change. Given that war is always possible, if not always probable, planners must closely follow short-term events and developments, tailoring their plans to unexpected changes. At the same time, given that many of the factors that Affect planning work over decades, a long-term planning vision is necessary to avoid falling victim to what Pierre Renouvin termed the 'profound forces' of history.

The obvious lesson then is that it is dangerous to focus exclusively either on the short term or on the long term when planning for future war. Kagan's chapter underlines clearly the dangers of devoting excessive attention to short-term problems. Similarly, Holger Herwig, in his chapter on German planning before 1914, highlights the unfortunate effects of what he terms a 'command decision-making' system headed by the Kaiser. Not only did this system impede a coordinated approach to planning between military and civilian planners, with disastrous results for Germany in 1914; it also placed Wilhelm II – a man lacking either the discipline or temperament to balance short - and long-term considerations – in the position of supreme commander. Impulsive to a fault, the Kaiser reacted in unpredictable and contradictory fashion to immediate events, forcing German war planning to lurch along without consistency or continuity. The case of inter-war French planning, by contrast, underscores the danger of emphasizing the long term at the expense of the short term. French planners, expecting a future war to resemble that of 1914–18, prepared their military forces with a long war in mind. The problem was that preparations for a long war left the French without the type of rapid reaction forces that might have deterred Nazi Germany's *blitzkrieg* gamble in the spring of 1940.

Lesson 3: Hedge Your Bets

In terms of the development of weapon systems, another lesson is the importance of hedging research and development bets. Andrew Krepinevich, in his chapter on American carrier aviation between the wars, discusses the hedging strategy pursued by the US Navy in a period of rapid technological change regarding aviation and naval warfare. US Navy planners decided to construct a balanced fleet rather than focusing on one or two elements to the exclusion of others. As Krepinevich argues, this hedging strategy had the distinct advantage of leaving open the option of further developing one or more elements in response to an unpredictable future. The alternative, to concentrate on one element of naval warfare, risked 'locking-in' the American navy to a type of warfare that might prove sub-optimal in the future. This danger of 'lock-in,' moreover, is especially strong at the beginning of the development cycle, when a weapons system and its technological basis are in the early stages of development.

In the case of Britain's RAF, John Ferris provides an excellent overview of the challenges and perils facing a service that develops one mission over others. During the inter-war period, the RAF devoted a great deal of thought and resources to developing strategic bombing as a means of seriously hampering an adversary's war-making capacity. Although the RAF succeeded in creating one of the best strategic bombing commands in the world, its effectiveness during the Second World War is open to question, and the investment in strategic bombing arguably cost more than it gained. The focus on strategic air drained resources from air support for the army and naval aviation, causing damage not only to the army and the Royal Navy, but, also to Britain as a whole. At the same time, however, a side-effect of the fixation with strategic bombing was an interest in air defense against bombing attacks, a capacity the RAF also developed between the wars – a capacity that would prove its worth during the Battle of Britain.

Given that the course of future developments is especially difficult to foresee, planners need to avoid closing down options that might prove to be valuable later, since in wartime it is much harder to create something from scratch than to build upon pre-existing capabilities. During peacetime, military forces should strive, within financial and other limits, to develop an array of weapons systems, doctrines, and force structures, accepting that some of them may turn out to be less useful than expected in a future war.

Lesson 4: The Need for Flexibility in Identifying Friends and Foes

Another element of uncertainty is the difficulty in identifying friend from foe. During immediate pre-war and wartime periods, enemies and friends are generally known. Planners thus possess a good sense of who their likely enemies and allies will be, the resources to which they will have access, and the potential and actual military fronts. In cases of peacetime planning, where war remains a possibility but not in a fairly fixed future, such knowledge is often sparse or absent. Potential friends might conceivably become enemies and vice versa. To take one example, Russia was the ally of Germany until the 1890s, when it became the ally of France. Even then, however, some German leaders remained hopeful and some French leaders remained fearful that Russia might revert to its former partner. One possible answer to this source of uncertainty is to consider everyone as a potential enemy. As Jon Sumida notes in his chapter on British naval planning, mastery of the seas before 1914 was premised on a global strategic perspective in which 'yesterday's enemy might be tomorrow's ally, and vice versa.' Yet this approach not only demands financial and other resources that are beyond the scope of any one country, but also, as Sumida shows, can produce confusion and even paralysis as innumerable plans, responding to different contingencies, compete with and cancel out one another. Britain's strategy thus represents an extreme, and in the event debilitating, form of the realist argument that states are in the end responsible for their own security and as such, cannot afford to make 'friends' or 'enemies' in any lasting sense.

But if this extreme position is counterproductive, a more moderate position is potentially more useful. Planners must remain flexible when it comes to identifying possible enemies and they must avoid focusing on present foes to the exclusion of other, less immediate ones. In his chapter on the Russian case after 1815, Kagan notes that planning was marred by a focus on Turkey, Sweden, and Poland rather than on Britain and France, who turned out to be Russia's adversaries in the Crimean War. Similarly, Lawrence Sondhaus, in his chapter on the German Confederation's war planning, describes the months spent 'in acrimonious planning for a French invasion of the German states, which the new French regime of Louis Philippe had not threatened and had no intention of undertaking.' The importance of flexibility in identifying enemies is reinforced by the point that one's enemy influences greatly the type of war one might have to fight. In the case of the inter-war United States, while the navy focused on Japan, which fostered interest in aircraft carriers and expeditionary forces (the Marines), the army looked more to land warfare requiring large divisions. Similarly, Charles

Cogan, in his chapter on French military planning after 1945, explains that the French military was divided between two enemies and two types of warfare. The first enemy was colonial independence movements, which required a heavy commitment of resources in manpower and conventional weapons. The second enemy was the Soviet Union, which to de Gaulle's mind required nuclear weapons (*force de frappe*). That nuclear weapons would also enhance France's prestige in the world and confirm its place among the great powers were no doubt additional reasons for the French leader's enthusiasm. France, however, lacked the resources to pursue both options, and it was only when de Gaulle succeeded in ending the Algerian War that the military could devote itself to acquiring a nuclear capability. As Cogan's chapter illustrates, de Gaulle had a longer-term view of France's potential foes than most military officers, which allowed him to see beyond the immediate needs of colonial wars.

Lesson 5: Formal Allied Planning Requires Effective Preparation

If the task of identifying one's enemies can be hazardous, so can that of planning with one's allies. Most major wars are between groups of states – a point recently underscored by the international make-up of the coalition during the 1991 Gulf War and, to a lesser extent, its sequel in 2003. To maximize effectiveness, a wartime coalition requires formal planning in peacetime between its potential members. Without joint planning, the danger arises of wrongly assuming that one's presumed partner will act in wartime as one desires him to do. For example, Stevenson shows that war planning before 1914 between the Germans and Austrians was practically non-existent, with the result that the two allies went to war with contradictory rather than complementary war plans. Equally to the point, Sondhaus in his chapter underscores the difficulties of coordinating resources and planning in multi-member coalitions. Not only did the rivalry between Austria and Prussia exclude effective planning between the Confederation's two principal members, but the smaller states also remained hesitant for fear of being dragged into the Austro-Prussian rivalry. Yet, it is not smaller states alone that fear, or should fear, being dragged into war. Prior to the First World War Germany and Russia faced this possibility as a result of their alliances with Austria-Hungary and Serbia, respectively.

There is the additional danger that allies will become substitutes for effective planning. Richardson, in her chapter on Concert planning after 1815, explains that the existence of allies rendered war planning more difficult than it would otherwise have been, since it bred over-optimism: the British, believing that the Concert system itself furnished them with security, neglected both war planning and their army after 1815. Without the Concert, British planners might have been forced to think harder about a future war. Similarly, although the Austrian Chief of the General Staff

Franz Conrad recognized that his army strength was inadequate to deal with the multiple fronts Austria was likely to face, he overestimated the amount of help its ally Germany would provide in 1914. According to Stevenson, 'Over-optimism about the German rather than the Austrian army caused his downfall.' Had Conrad had a better assessment of Germany's role in a general European war, he might not have mobilized his forces so readily, causing Russia to mobilize, which proved to be a decisive step in the immediate origins of the First World War. Thus, although alliances may provide additional security in terms of extra resources, expertise, and manpower, planning with allies requires a good deal of foresight and preparation. In a coalition, planning must be conceived as a combined and integrated effort among partners.

Lesson 6: Balance of Power Within an Alliance May Undermine Planning

If planning in a coalition context is often inevitable, it is also important to beware of the potential pitfalls of the task. Planners therefore need to work hard not only on their own planning efforts but also on those of their possible allies. To this lesson, Lawrence Sondhaus suggests another one: that effective war planning within a coalition requires a dominant partner. In his chapter on the German Confederation, Sondhaus explains that the Austro-Prussian rivalry proved especially debilitating because the two states were roughly equal in power and influence. Neither one could impose its views on the other, with the result that planning suffered. In effect, a coalition appears to be more effective when there is one dominant power, which can prevent states from using the coalition to advance their own interests and to undermine the united purpose of its members.[1] The United States arguably played this role during the Cold War with the Western Alliance, as did the Soviet Union with the Warsaw Pact.

If true, the overwhelming military dominance of the United States might be a cause for current optimism. The wars in Iraq and Kosovo demonstrate the power of a dominant state to forge an alliance in short order. That said, however, a gross imbalance of power between allies not only raises the overconfidence problem, but also a free-rider problem, as weaker states are content to leave the financial, military and other burdens to the dominant member. At the same time, as Charles Cogan argues, planners and statesmen are jealous of their state's independence; independence, that may be threatened by joining an alliance. This factor is especially relevant in the case of an alliance in which one state clearly predominates, for the weaker state has reason to fear being overshadowed, if not excluded completely from decision making. For de Gaulle, resistance to the possibility of American dictation contributed to the desire for an independent nuclear force that would allow France to remain a major player both within and without the Western Alliance.

Lesson 7: Be Flexible for Effective Military and Strategic Planning

If there is one overall lesson to draw from the evidence presented in the case studies, it is that flexibility in the planning process is vital if a state is to achieve its military and strategic objectives.[2] The ability of a system to adapt to uncertainty is the result of sound planning and foresight. Flexibility, in other words, does not happen by accident. Evidence of the value of flexibility or the harm of inflexibility is provided in nearly every case presented in this volume, and perhaps the most famous example of the perils of inflexibility remains the mobilization plans of the great powers leading into the First World War. These rigid, fixed plans have been singled out as a leading, if not *the*, cause of the First World War, despite Stevenson's claim that '[T]he very universality of these failures of foresight suggest it may be unreasonable to expect strategic planners to have anticipated the evolution of the conflict.'

Richardson's insight about the proper balance between military and civilian planning was premised on the idea that diplomats of the era possessed a more flexible and visionary outlook than did their military counterparts. The lack of flexibility in terms of outlook was personified and actuated in the German decision-making system under Kaiser Wilhelm, as discussed in Herwig's chapter. Additionally, although Russia did not have a formal system of war planning to deal with the numerous crises it faced during the early part of the nineteenth century, Kagan's discussion revealed that the system of forming *ad hoc* committees as crises emerged allowed for relatively effective management of these crises. Similarly, the hedging strategy adopted by the US Navy in the development of weapons systems is premised on flexibility, while France's ability to meet the security challenges facing it following the Second World War was hampered by inflexible thinking and doctrine. In the French case, it was the inability to adapt to a new era marked by the end of formal empires. Only major warfare in Algeria and Indochina and the loss of enormous blood and treasure convinced de Gaulle, and eventually the French military, that France's empire was no longer an asset but rather a threat to France's security. Only then could France free up the needed resources for a nuclear program, thereby enhancing its independence, status, and security.

Conclusion

Since the attacks on the World Trade Center and Pentagon on 11 September 2001, a 'war on terror' has dominated American military and strategic policy. With this in mind, we review lessons outlined above in terms of the war on terror.

The first lesson, that effective planning requires as many inputs as possible, is clearly relevant to the war on terror. The terrorist threat is a multi-faceted one in which the military aspect is not necessarily the most important. Indeed, given the United States' overwhelming military superiority, any intelligent terrorist would likely choose not to engage the United States on the battlefield, opting instead to attack vulnerable military and non-military targets off the battlefield.[3] This simple point highlights the need to involve a wide range of viewpoints and not just those of the military, when considering the nature of the terrorist threat. In addition to traditional inputs from the military, diplomats, and scholars, a host of other voices need to be considered if the United States and other countries are to respond effectively to what is a complex and evolving threat. Among these new and diverse set of voices that might provide needed insights and intelligence are financial and banking experts, computer programmers, and shipping companies.

No less relevant to the war on terror is the second lesson concerning the need to balance short-term and long-term perspectives in planning. Terrorism is a short-term and long-term threat and planners need to consider both aspects. Understandably, the short-term perspective looms especially large: planners need to anticipate new attacks and devise concrete policies to eliminate or at least reduce the effectiveness of terrorists. Yet the long-term perspective should not be lost sight of, since terrorism partially finds its origins in political, economic, demographic and other processes that unfold over decades. Planners must track these processes and strive to understand their implications for the terrorist threat in the immediate and longer-term future. At the same time, while it is important for planners to possess a short-term and long-term perspective, it is equally vital to prevent one perspective from sabotaging the other. In the case of the war in Iraq, one motive was to encourage the spread of democracy in the Middle East, a long-term goal that, if successful, promised to reduce terrorism at its roots. Arguably, however, this long-term goal has been undermined by events in Iraq. Not only has the invasion and occupation drained resources that might otherwise have been employed more directly against Al Qaeda and its allies, but prolonged American occupation has encouraged the recruitment of new members into the terrorist ranks. Although the future is uncertain, the situation in Iraq suggests that planners need to consider carefully the relationship between long-term aims and short-term effects.

Lesson three, on the value of hedging strategies, is also important in the war on terror. In intelligence, doctrine, and force structure, the United States had invested almost all its resources in building and maintaining a military capable of countering threats from other states or coalitions of states. The rising terrorist threat therefore caught the United States largely unprepared to meet the particular needs of a counterinsurgency fight. The trick now will be to build a military capable of engaging shadowy foes in distant lands without simultaneously dissipating US capital invested in conventional warfighting and planning capabilities.

Lesson four, which urges flexibility in identifying friend and foe, is equally important in any war against terror. Pakistan and Saudi Arabia are both US allies in the war on terror yet at the same time a major source of sanctuary and support for the terrorists themselves. The United States is currently fighting an insurgency in Iraq with the aim of establishing a democracy there, yet neither Pakistan nor Saudi Arabia (nor Kuwait for that matter) have been pressured by the United States to become more democratic. China may prove a thorn in the side of US policy regarding the peaceful re-integration of Taiwan with mainland China, but an ally in the war on terror and in efforts to keep North Korea from becoming a future source of fissile material to terrorists. In short, the war on terror will demand a return to diplomatic excellence and alliance flexibility not seen in the West since the nineteenth century.

Lessons five and six, which are both concerned with the advantages and disadvantages of planning in an alliance context, are particularly relevant to the war on terror. American planners have thus far concentrated largely on military capabilities, an approach that has fostered a tendency to downplay the importance of allies. Clearly, in any war, military capabilities are important. But in unconventional wars excessive attention to military capabilities neglects others aspects that can be as – if not more – important. Equally to the point, many of the non-military aspects of the war require the cooperation of other countries – of potential allies. For example, to choke the financial resources of terrorists calls for a concerted effort among international and national financial institutions. In the case of Iraq, Washington's neglect of its real and potential allies has undermined American efforts to create a peaceful and stable regime. In the eyes of many Iraqis and non-Iraqis, the largely unilateral American actions in Iraq and elsewhere lack legitimacy, a viewpoint that encourages resistance. Had American planners been more attuned to non-military factors, such as the importance of diplomacy and not being seen going to war alone, they might have realized that however paltry their military contribution, allies could contribute legitimacy.

Finally, lesson seven, which calls attention to the relationship between political goals and military means, is also relevant to the war on terror. Regarding the definition of political goals, the aim of an outright victory against terrorism seems patently unrealistic. Given the low barriers to entry for terrorists, it is likely impossible for the United States to eliminate completely the terrorist threat. How would one even know when the goal of eliminating the terrorist threat had been achieved? Unfortunately, some level of threat will continue for a long time, if not indefinitely. Perhaps a more realistic goal is to reduce the threat of terrorism to acceptable proportions, even if this leaves open the question of who defines acceptable and on what bases. The notion of acceptability is important because it raises the question of ends and means. If absolute victory means undermining basic freedoms at home or waging perpetual war abroad, the price may be too high. In the end, the war on terror suggests that neither political goals nor military means should be viewed in absolute terms. Planners must strive instead for a balance, remaining sensitive to the trade-offs between the two.

If this volume has shown anything, it is that the fog of peace can never be entirely pierced. Flexibility and constant cultivation of the ability to question received wisdom and to reconsider assumptions are the best security against catastrophic failure in a future war, regardless of whether that war resembles a more traditional interstate war or the current war on terror. This in turn highlights the problem of guaranteeing that multiple viewpoints are represented throughout all stages of planning, and this in planning environments that tend to systematically discriminate against opposing points of view.

Notes

1 For a related argument see Robert O. Keohane's *After Hegemony* (Princeton: Princeton University Press, 1984), in which he argues that dominant powers are necessary for providing collective goods that often persist and help maintain peace even after the hegemon's power declines.
2 For an essay arguing that flexibility should become a formal principle of war, see Robert S. Frost, 'The Growing Imperative to Adopt "Flexibility" as an American Principle of War,' Strategic Studies Institute monograph, 15 October 1999.
3 On this point more broadly, see especially Ivan Arreguín-Toft's *How the Weak Win Wars: A Theory of Asymmetric Conflict* (New York: Cambridge University Press, 2005).

BIBLIOGRAPHY

Andrew, C.M. *Secret Service: The Making of the British Intelligence Community* (London: Heinemann, 1985).

Arreguín-Toft, I. *How the Weak Win Wars: A Theory of Asymmetric Conflict* (New York: Cambridge University Press, 2005).

Ash, A. *Sir Frederick Sykes and the Air Revolution* (London: Frank Cass, 1998).

Baack, L.J. *Christian Bernstorff and Prussia: Diplomacy and Reform Conservatism, 1818–1832* (New Brunswick, NJ: Rutgers University Press, 1980).

Baer, G.W. *One Hundred Years of Sea Power* (Stanford, CA: Stanford University Press, 1993).

Berend, I.T. *Decades of Crisis: Central and Eastern Europe Before World War II* (Berkeley, CA: University of California Press, 1998).

Best, A. *Britain, Japan and Pearl Harbor: Avoiding War in East Asia, 1936–41* (London: Routledge, 1995).

Best, G. *Humanity in Warfare: The Modern History of the International Law of Armed Conflicts* (London: Weidenfeld & Nicolson, 1983).

Biddle, T.D. *Rhetoric and Reality in Air Warfare: The Evolution of British and American Ideas about Strategic Bombing, 1917–1945* (Princeton, NJ: Princeton University Press, 2002).

Billinger, R.D. Jr. *Metternich and the German Question: States' Rights and Federal Duties, 1820–1834* (Newark, DE: University of Delaware Press, 1991).

Birn, D.S. *The League of Nations Union, 1918–1945* (Oxford: Oxford University Press, 1981).

Black, J. *European Warfare, 1660–1815* (New Haven, CT: Yale University Press, 1994).

Bloomfield, A.I. *Monetary Policy under the International Gold Standard, 1880–1914* (New York: Federal Reserve Bank of New York, 1959).

Bond, B. *British Military Policy Between the Two World Wars* (Oxford: Oxford University Press, 1980).

Boyle, A. *Trenchard, Man of Vision* (London: Collins, 1962).

Bridge, F.R., and Bullen, R. *The Great Powers and the European States System, 1815–1914* (London: Longman, 1980).

Brinkley, A. *The End of Reform: New Deal Liberalism in Recession and War* (New York: Alfred A. Knopf, 1995).

Brodie, B. *Sea Power in the Machine Age* (New York: Greenwood Press, 1969).

Bruce Lincoln, W. *Nicholas I: Emperor and Autocrat of All the Russias* (DeKalb, IL: Northern Illinois University Press, 1989).

Bucholz, A. *Moltke, Schlieffen, and Prussian War Planning* (Providence, RI: Berg, 1991).

Chapman, H. *State Capitalism and Working-Class Radicalism in the French Aircraft Industry* (Berkeley, CA: University of California Press, 1991).

Charmley, J. *Churchill, The End of Glory: A Political Biography* (London: Hodder & Stoughton, 1993).

Clarke, I.F. *Voices Prophesying War, 1763–1984* (London: Oxford University Press, 1966).

Cogan, C.G. *Oldest Allies, Guarded Friends: The United States and France since 1940* (Westport, CT: Praeger, 1994).

Copeland, D.C. *The Origins of Major War* (Ithaca, NY: Cornell University Press, 2000).

Corum, J.S. *The Roots of Blitzkrieg: Hans von Seeckt and the German Military Reform* (Lawrence, KS: University Press of Kansas, 1992).

Craig, G.A. *The Politics of the Prussian Army, 1640–1945* (London: Oxford University Press, 1964).

Dallek, R. *Franklin D. Roosevelt and American Foreign Policy, 1932–1945* (Oxford: Oxford University Press, 1979).

Davidson, J.R. *The Unsinkable Fleet* (Annapolis, MD: Naval Institute Press, 1996).

De Cecco, M. *Money and Empire: The International Gold Standard, 1890–1914* (Oxford: Blackwell, 1974).

Deist, W. *et al. Germany and the Second World War*, vol. 1 (Oxford: Oxford University Press, 1990).

Desch, M.C. *Civilian Control of the Military: The Changing Security Environment* (Baltimore, MD: The Johns Hopkins University Press, 1999).

Doughty, R.A. *The Seeds of Disaster: The Development of French Army Doctrine, 1919–1939* (Hamden, CT: Archon Books, 1985).

Driver, H. *The Birth of Military Aviation: Britain, 1903–1914* (London: Royal Historical Society / Boydell Press, 1997).

Eichengreen, B. *Globalizing Capitalism: A History of the International Monetary System* (Princeton, NJ: Princeton University Press, 1996).

Feis, H. *Europe: The World's Banker, 1870–1914* (New York: Council on Foreign Relations, 1964).

Feldman, G.D. *Army, Industry and Labor in Germany 1914–1918* (Princeton, NJ: Princeton University Press, 1966).

Ferguson, N. *The Pity of War* (New York: Basic Books, 1998).

Ferris, J.R. *Men, Money, and Diplomacy: The Evolution of British Strategic Policy, 1919–26* (Ithaca, NY: Cornell University Press, 1989).

Fischer, F. *War of Illusions: German Policies from 1911 to 1914* (London: Chatto & Windus, 1975; translation of German original, 1969).

Förster, S. and Nagler, J. (eds). *On the Road to Total War: The American Civil War and the German Wars of Unification, 1861–1871* (Cambridge: Cambridge University Press, 1997).

Friedberg, A.L. *The Weary Titan: Britain and the Experience of Relative Decline, 1895–1905* (Princeton, NJ: Princeton University Press, 1988).

Fuller, W.C. Jr. *Strategy and Power in Russia, 1600–1914* (New York: Free Press, 1992).

Gaddis, J.L. *et al.* (eds). *Cold War Statesmen Confront the Bomb: Nuclear Diplomacy Since 1945* (Oxford: Oxford University Press, 1999).

Gaddis, J.L. *The Long Peace: Inquiries into the History of the Cold War* (Oxford: Oxford University Press, 1987).

Gardiner, R. (ed.). *The Eclipse of the Big Gun: The Warship, 1906–45* (Annapolis, MD: Naval Institute Press).

Gillingham, J. *Coal, Steel, and the Rebirth of Europe, 1945–1955: The Germans and the French from Ruhr Conflict to Economic Community* (Cambridge: Cambridge University Press, 1991).

Glantz, D.M. and House, J.M. *When Titans Clashed: How the Red Army Stopped Hitler* (Lawrence, KS: University Press of Kansas, 1995).

Gooch, J. *The Plans of War: The General Staff and British Military Strategy, c. 1900–1916* (London: Routledge & Kegan Paul, 1974).

Gordon, A. *The Rules of the Game: Jutland and British Naval Command* (Annapolis, MD: Naval Institute Press, 1996).

Goulter, C.J.M. *A Forgotten Offensive: Royal Air Force Coastal Command's Anti-Shipping Campaign, 1940–1945* (London: Frank Cass, 1995).

Habeck, M.R. *Storm of Steel: The Development of Armor Doctrine in Germany and the Soviet Union, 1919–1939* (Ithaca, NY: Cornell University Press, 2003).

Haggie, P. *Britannia at Bay: The Defence of the British Empire Against Japan 1931–1941* (Oxford: Oxford University Press, 1981).

Halpern, P.G. *The Mediterranean Naval Situation, 1908–1914* (Cambridge, MA: Harvard University Press, 1971).

Harris, J.P. *Men, Ideas and Tanks: British Military Thought and Armoured Forces, 1903–1939* (Manchester: Manchester University Press, 1995).

Harrison, M. (ed.). *The Economics of World War II: Six Great Powers in International Comparison* (Cambridge: Cambridge University Press, 1998).

Haslam, J. *The Soviet Union and the Struggle for Collective Security in Europe, 1933–1939* (London: Macmillan, 1984).

Herrmann, D.G. *The Arming of Europe and the Making of the First World War* (Princeton, NJ: Princeton University Press, 1996).

Herwig, H.H. *The First World War: Germany and Austria-Hungary 1914–1918* (London: Arnold, 1997).

——'*Luxury' Fleet: The Imperial German Navy 1888–1918* (London and Atlantic Highlands, NJ: Allen & Unwin, 1987).

——*The German Naval Officer Corps: A Social and Political History 1890–1918* (Oxford: Oxford University Press, 1973).

Hobson, R. *Imperialism at Sea: Naval Strategic Thought, the Ideology of Sea Power, and the Tirpitz Plan, 1875–1914* (Boston: Brill, 2002).

Hogan, M.J. (ed.). *Paths to Power: The Historiography of American Foreign Relations to 1941* (Cambridge: Cambridge University Press, 2000).

Holloway, D. *Stalin and the Bomb* (New Haven, CT: Yale University Press, 1994).

Hone, T.C., Friedman, N. and Mandeles, M.D. *American and British Aircraft Carrier Development, 1919–1941* (Annapolis, MD: Naval Institute Press, 1999).

Howard, M.E. *The Continental Commitment: The Dilemma of British Defence Policy in the Era of the Two World Wars* (London: Maurice Temple Smith, 1972).

——*The Franco-Prussian War: The German Invasion of France, 1870–71* (London: Hart-Davis, 1961).

Hughes, W.P. Jr. *Fleet Tactics and Coastal Combat*, 2nd edn (Annapolis, MD: Naval Institute Press, 1999).

Huntington, S.P. *Political Order in Changing Societies* (New Haven, CT: Yale University Press, 1968).

——*The Soldier and the State: The Theory and Politics of Civil–Military Relations* (Cambridge, MA: Harvard University Press, 1957).

Hyde, H.M. *British Air Policy Between the Wars, 1919–1939* (London: Heinemann, 1976).

Ikenberry, G.J. *After Victory: Institutions, Strategic Restraint, and the Rebuilding of Order After Major Wars* (Princeton, NJ: Princeton University Press, 2001).

Ikle, F.C. and Wohlstetter, A. *et al. Discriminate Deterrence* (Washington, DC: Department of Defense, January 1988).

Iriye, A. *The Origins of the Second World War in Asia and the Pacific* (London: Longman, 1987).

——*After Imperialism: The Search for a New Order in the Far East, 1921–1931* (Cambridge, MA: Harvard University Press, 1965).

Janowitz, M. *The Professional Soldier: A Social and Political Portrait* (Glencoe, IL: Free Press, 1960).

Jervis, R. *System Effects: Complexity in Political and Social Life* (Princeton, NJ: Princeton University Press, 1997).

Kagan, F.W. *The Military Reforms of Nicholas I: The Origins of the Modern Russian Army* (New York: St. Martin's Press, 1999).

Kaiser, D.E. *American Tragedy: Kennedy, Johnson, and the Origins of the Vietnam War* (Cambridge, MA: Harvard University Press, 2000).

——*Economic Diplomacy and the Origins of the Second World War: Germany, Britain, France, and Eastern Europe* (Princeton, NJ: Princeton University Press, 1980).

Kaplan, F.M. *The Wizards of Armageddon* (New York: Simon & Schuster, 1983).

Kaplan, L.S. *A Community of Interests: NATO and the Military Assistance Program, 1948–1951* (Washington, DC: Office of the Secretary of Defense Historical Office, 1980).

Kayser, C. *et al. War with Iraq: Costs, Consequences, and Alternatives* (Cambridge, MA: American Academy of Arts and Sciences, 2002).

Keep, J.C.H. *Soldiers of the Tsar: Army and Society in Russia, 1462–1874* (Oxford: Oxford University Press, 1985).

Kennedy, D.M. *Freedom from Fear: The American People in Depression and War, 1929–1945* (Oxford: Oxford University Press, 1999).

Kennedy, P.M. *The Rise and Fall of British Naval Mastery* (London: Ashfield Press, 1994).

—— *The Rise and Fall of the Great Powers* (New York: Random House, 1987).

—— (ed.). *War Plans of the Great Powers, 1880–1914* (London: Allen & Unwin, 1979).

Keohane, R.O. *After Hegemony* (Princeton, NJ: Princeton University Press, 1984).

Khong, Y.F. *Analogies at War: Korea, Munich, Dien Bien Phu, and the Vietnam Decisions of 1965* (Princeton, NJ: Princeton University Press, 1992).

Kier, E. *Imagining War: French and British Military Doctrine Between the Wars* (Princeton, NJ: Princeton University Press, 1997).

Kiesling, E.C. *Arming Against Hitler: France and the Limits of Military Planning* (Lawrence, KS: University Press of Kansas, 1996).

264

Knox, M. *Hitler's Italian Allies: Royal Armed Forces, Fascist Regime, and the War of 1940–43* (Cambridge: Cambridge University Press, 2000).

——*Common Destiny: Dictatorship, Foreign Policy, and War in Fascist Italy and Nazi Germany* (Cambridge: Cambridge University Press, 2000).

Kraehe, E.E. *Metternich's German Policy, volume 2: The Congress of Vienna, 1814–1815* (Princeton, NJ: Princeton University Press, 1983).

Krepinevich, A.F. Jr. *The Army and Vietnam* (Baltimore, MD: The Johns Hopkins University Press, 1986).

Laloy, J. *Yalta: Yesterday, Today, Tomorrow*, trans. W.R. Tyler (New York: Harper & Row, 1988).

Lambert, N.A. *Sir John Fisher's Naval Revolution* (Columbia, SC: University of South Carolina Press, 1999).

Lambi, I.N. *The Navy and German Power Politics, 1862–1914* (Boston: Allen & Unwin, 1984).

Langhorne, R.T.B. *The Collapse of the Concert of Europe: International Politics 1890–1914* (London: Macmillan, 1981).

Lebow, R.N. *Between War and Peace: The Nature of International Crisis* (Baltimore: Johns Hopkins University Press, 1981).

Leffler, M.P. *A Preponderance of Power: National Security, the Truman Administration, and the Cold War* (Stanford, CA: Stanford University Press, 1992).

Leslie, R.F. *Polish Politics and the Revolution of November 1830* (London: 1956).

Luvaas, J. *The Military Legacy of the Civil War: The European Inheritance* (Lawrence, Kansas: University of Kansas Press, 1988).

Lyons, F.S.L. *Internationalism in Europe, 1815–1914* (Leyden: A.W. Sythoff, 1963).

Mackay, R.F. *Fisher of Kilverstone* (Oxford: Clarendon Press, 1973).

Marder, A.J. *The Anatomy of British Sea Power: A History of British Naval Policy in the Pre-Dreadnought Era, 1880–1905* (London: Cass, 1964 [reprinted edition]).

——*From the Dreadnought to Scapa Flow: The Royal Navy in the Fisher Era, 1904–1914* (London: Oxford University Press, 1961).

Mazower, M. *Dark Continent: Europe's Twentieth Century* (New York: Alfred A. Knopf, 1999).

McElwee, W. *The Art of War: Waterloo to Mons* (London: Weidenfeld and Nicolson, 1974).

McKercher, B.J.C. *Transition of Power: Britain's Loss of Global Pre-Eminence to the United States, 1930–1945* (Cambridge: Cambridge University Press, 1999).

McNeill, W.H. *The Pursuit of Power: Technology, Armed Force, and Society since AD 1000* (Oxford: Blackwell, 1983).

Mearsheimer, J. *The Tragedy of Great Power Politics* (New York: W.W. Norton, 2001).

Melhorn, C.M. *Two-Block Fox* (Annapolis, MD: Naval Institute Press, 1974).

Menning, R.R. *The Art of the Possible: Documents on Great Power Diplomacy, 1814–1914* (New York: McGraw-Hill, 1996).

Miller, S.E. (ed.). *Military Strategy and the Origins of the First World War* (Princeton, NJ: Princeton University Press, 1985).

Milward, A. *War, Economy and Society, 1939–1945* (Berkeley, CA: University of California Press, 1977).

Mombauer, A. *Helmuth von Moltke and the Origins of the First World War* (Cambridge: Cambridge University Press, 2001).

Monger, G. *The End of Isolation: British Foreign Policy 1900–1907* (London: Thomas Nelson, 1963).

Mueller, J. *Retreat from Doomsday: The Obsolescence of Major War* (New York: Basic Books, 1989).

Murray, W. and Millett, A.R. (eds). *Military Innovation in the Interwar Period* (Cambridge: Cambridge University Press, 1996).

——*Calculations: Net Assessment and the Coming of World War II* (New York: Free Press, 1992).

Murray, W. *Strategy for Defeat: The Luftwaffe, 1933–1945* (Maxwell Air Force Base: Air University Press, 1983).

Neidpath, J. *The Singapore Naval Base and the Defence of Britain's Eastern Empire, 1919–1941* (Oxford: Clarendon Press, 1981).

Neilson, K. *Britain and the Last Tsar: British Policy and Russia, 1894–1917* (Oxford: Clarendon Press, 1995).

Nye, J.S. *Bound to Lead: The Changing Nature of American Power* (New York: Basic Books, 1990).

O'Connell, R.L. *Sacred Vessels* (Boulder, CO: Westview Press, 1993).

Offer, A. *The First World War: An Agrarian Interpretation* (Oxford: Oxford University Press, 1989).

Overy, R. *Why the Allies Won* (New York: Norton, 1995).

——*War and Economy in the Third Reich* (Oxford: Oxford University Press, 1994).

——*The Air War, 1939–1945* (London: Europa, 1980).

Pape, R.A. *Bombing to Win: Air Power and Coercion in War* (Ithaca, NY: Cornell University Press, 1996).

Paris, M. *Winged Warfare: The Literature and Theory of Aerial Warfare in Britain, 1859–1917* (Manchester: Manchester University Press, 1992).

Parker, G. *The Military Revolution* (Cambridge: Cambridge University Press, 1988).

Parkinson, R. *Clausewitz: A Biography* (New York: Stein & Day, 1971).

Pick, D. *War Machine: The Rationalization of Slaughter in the Modern Age* (New Haven, CT: Yale University Press, 1993).

Poole, W.S. *The Joint Chiefs of Staff and National Policy, vol. IV, 1950–1952* (Washington, DC: Office of Joint History, Office of the Chairman of the Joint Chiefs of Staff, 1998).

Porch, D. *The March to the Marne: The French Army 1871–1914* (Cambridge: Cambridge University Press, 1981).

Posen, B. *The Sources of Military Doctrine: France, Britain, and Germany Between the World Wars* (Ithaca, NY: Cornell University Press, 1984).

Powers, B. *Strategy Without Slide Rule* (London: Croom Helm, 1976).

Ralston, D.B. *The Army of the Republic: The Place of the Military in the Political Evolution of France, 1871–1914* (Cambridge, MA and London: MIT Press, 1967).

Ránki, G. *The Economics of the Second World War* (Vienna: Bohlau Verlag, 1993).

Reiter, D. and Stam, A.C. *Democracies at War* (Princeton, NJ: Princeton University Press, 2002).

Reynolds, C.G. *Admiral John H. Towers: The Struggle for Naval Air Supremacy* (Annapolis, MD: Naval Institute Press, 1991).

——*The Fast Carriers* (Annapolis, MD: Naval Institute Press, 1968).

Reynolds, D. *Britannia Overruled: British Policy and World Power in the Twentieth Century* (London: Longman, 2000).

Reynolds, D. *et al.* (eds). *Allies at War: The Soviet, American, and British Experience, 1939–1945* (New York: St. Martin's Press, 1994).

Riasanovsky, N. *Nicholas I and Official Nationality in Russia, 1825–1855* (Berkeley, CA: University of California Press, 1967).

Richards, D. *Portal of Hungerford* (London: Heinemann, 1977).

Ritchie, S. *Industry and Air Power: The Expansion of British Military Aircraft Production, 1935–1941* (London: Frank Cass, 1997).

Ritter, G. *The Schlieffen Plan: Critique of a Myth* (London: Wolff, 1958).

Robertson, S. *The Development of RAF Strategic Bombing Doctrine, 1919–1939* (Westport, CT: Praeger, 1995).

Rogers, C.J. (ed.). *The Military Revolution Debate* (Boulder, CO: Westview Press, 1995).

Rosen, S.P. *Winning the Next War: Innovation and the Modern Military* (Ithaca, NY: Cornell University Press, 1991).

Ross, S.T. *American War Plans 1945–50* (London: Frank Cass, 1996).

Rothenberg, G.E. *The Army of Francis Joseph* (West Lafayette, IN: Purdue University Press, 1976).

Russett, B.M. *Grasping the Democratic Peace: Principles for a Post-Cold War World* (Princeton, NJ: Princeton University Press, 1993).

Salerno, R.M. *March to the Oceans: The Mediterranean Origins of an Imperial War* (Ithaca, NY: Cornell University Press, 2002).

Sater, W.F. and Herwig, H.H. *The Grand Illusion: The Prussianization of the Chilean Army* (Lincoln: University of Nebraska Press, 1999).

Schroeder, P.W. *The Transformation of European Politics, 1763–1848* (Oxford: Clarendon Press, 1994).

——*Austria, Great Britain, and the Crimean War: The Destruction of the European Concert* (Ithaca, NY: Cornell University Press, 1972).

——*Metternich's Diplomacy at its Zenith, 1820–1823* (Austin, TX: University of Texas Press, 1962).

Schuker, S.A. *The End of French Predominance in Europe: The Financial Crisis of 1924 and the Adoption of the Dawes Plan* (Chapel Hill, NC: University of North Carolina Press, 1976).

Schweller, R. *Deadly Imbalances: Tripolarity and Hitler's Strategy of World Conquest* (New York: Columbia University Press, 1997).

Shay, R.P. *British Rearmament in the Thirties: Politics and Profits* (Princeton, NJ: Princeton University Press, 1977).

Sherry, M.S. *The Rise of American Air Power: The Creation of Armageddon* (New Haven, CT: Yale University Press, 1987).

Showalter, D. *Railroads and Rifles: Soldiers, Technology, and the Unification of Germany* (Hamden, CT: Archon Books, 1976).

Smith, M. *British Air Strategy Between the Wars* (Oxford: Oxford University Press, 1984).

Snyder, J.L. *Democratization and Nationalist Conflict* (New York: Norton, 2000).

——*The Ideology of the Offensive: Military Decision-Making and the Disasters of 1914* (Ithaca, NY: Cornell University Press, 1984).

Sondhaus, L. *In the Service of the Emperor: Italians in the Austrian Armed Forces, 1814–1918* (Boulder, CO: East European Monographs, 1990).

Spector, R.H. *Eagle Against the Sun* (New York: Free Press, 1985).

Spiers, E.M. *Haldane: An Army Reformer* (Edinburgh: Edinburgh University Press, 1980).

Stam, A.C. *Win, Lose, or Draw: Domestic Politics and the Crucible of War* (Ann Arbor, MI: University of Michigan Press, 1992).

Steinberg, J. *Yesterday's Deterrent: Tirpitz and the Birth of the German Battle Fleet* (London: MacDonald, 1965).

Stevenson, D. *Armaments and the Coming of War: Europe, 1904–1914* (Oxford: Oxford University Press, 1996).

Stoler, M.A. *Allies and Adversaries* (Chapel Hill, NC: University of North Carolina Press, 2000).

Strachan, H.F.A. *The First World War. Vol. I: To Arms* (Oxford: Oxford University Press, 2001).

Sumida, J.T. *In Defense of Naval Supremacy: Finance, Technology, and British Naval Policy, 1889–1914* (Boston: Unwin Hyman, 1989).

Swanborough, G. and Bowens, P.M. *United States Navy Aircraft since 1911* (Annapolis, MD: Naval Institute Press, 1990).

Till, G. *Air Power and the Royal Navy, 1914–1945: An Historical Survey* (London: Macdonald and Jane's, 1979).

Trachtenberg, M. *A Constructed Peace: The Making of the European Settlement, 1945–1963* (Princeton, NJ: Princeton University Press, 1999).

——*Reparation in World Politics: France and European Diplomacy, 1916–1923* (New York: Columbia University Press, 1980).

Trimble, W.F. *Admiral William F. Moffett: Architect of Naval Aviation* (Washington, DC: Smithsonian Institution Press, 1994).

——*Wings for the Navy: A History of the Naval Aircraft Factory, 1917–1956* (Annapolis, MD: Naval Institute Press, 1990).

Vagts, A. *The Military Attache* (Princeton, NJ: Princeton University Press, 1967).

van Creveld, M. *Supplying War: Logistics from Wallenstein to Patton* (Cambridge: Cambridge University Press, 1977).

Van Evera, S. *Causes of War: Power and the Roots of Conflict* (Ithaca, NY: Cornell University Press, 1999).

Wallach, Y.L. *The Dogma of the Battle of Annihilation: The Theories of Clausewitz and Schlieffen and Their Impact on the German Conduct of Two World Wars* (Westport, CT: Greenwood, 1986).

Walt, S. *The Origins of Alliances* (Ithaca, NY: Cornell University Press, 1987).

Waltz, K. *Theory of International Politics* (Reading, MA: Addison-Wesley, 1979).

Wandycz, P.S. *The Twilight of French Eastern Alliances, 1926–1936: French–Czechoslovak–Polish Relations from Locarno to the Remilitarization of the Rhineland* (Princeton, NJ: Princeton University Press, 1988).

Watson, R.J. *The Joint Chiefs of Staff and National Policy 1953–54* (Washington, DC: Joint History Office, 1986).

Watt, D.C. *How War Came: The Immediate Origins of the Second World War, 1938–1939* (London: Heinemann, 1989).

Webster, C and Frankland, N. *The Strategic Air Offensive Against Germany, 1939–1945, Vol. 1* (London: HMSO, 1961).

Weinberg, G.L. *World in the Balance: Behind the Scenes of World War II* (Hanover, NH: University Press of New England, 1981).

Westwood, J.N. *Russia against Japan, 1904–05: A New Look at the Russo-Japanese War* (Basingstoke: Macmillan, 1986).

Williams, W.A. *The Tragedy of American Diplomacy* (New York: Dell, 1962).

Williamson, S.R. *Austria-Hungary and the Origins of the First World War* (Basingstoke: Macmillan, 1991).

——*The Politics of Grand Strategy: Britain and France Prepare for War, 1904–1914* (Cambridge, MA: Harvard University Press, 1969).

Wright, R. *Dowding and the Battle of Britain* (London: Macdonald & Co., 1969).

Zimmerman, D. *Britain's Shield: Radar and the Defeat of the Luftwaffe* (Stroud: Sutton, 2001).

Zisk, K.M. *Engaging the Enemy: Organization Theory and Soviet Military Innovation, 1955–1991* (Princeton, NJ: Princeton University Press, 1993).

INDEX

Dutch invasion of (1831) 57; rebellion against Netherlands 55–56;
revolution in (1830) 29
Benson, William S. 181
Berchtold, Count Leopold 120
Berend, Iván T. 155n15
Berenhorst, Georg Heinrich von 100,
121, 122
Berghahn, Volker R. 123n37
Berlin 55–57, 61–63, 67–68, 74n55, 85,
92, 121; access to, Cold War negotiations on 221–22; Berlin-to-Baghdad
railway project 77; Conference in
(1831–32) 54, 58–60; Congress of
(1878) 78; 'focal point of international relations' 111; General Staff in
105–6; Soviet blockade of 208,
221–22, 236; Tirpitz headquarters in
113–14; visions of military policy in,
two distinct 117–18, 120; War
Ministry in 116
Bernstorff, Count Christian von 56–58,
60
Bethmann Hollweg, Theobald von 108,
116, 120, 206
Beyerchen, Alan 177n55
Bidault, Georges 234, 236
Biddle, Tami Davis 157n37
Billinger Jr., Robert D. 72n14
Birn, Donald S. 156n24
Bismarck, Otto von 6, 47, 55, 67, 68, 78,
79, 81, 86, 93, 101, 106, 107, 109,
111–12, 120
Black Sea 27, 35–36, 45
Bloch, Admiral Claude C. 194
Bloch, Ivan S. 76, 86, 95n1
Bloomfield, A.I. 95n11
Bogdanovich, M.I. 49n34
Bohlen, Charles 213, 221, 239–40
Bologna 57
Bolsheviks 144
Bomber Command, RAF 163, 169, 170,
174
Borah, Senator William 182
Bosnia 71; annexation crisis (1908–9) 78
Bradley, General Omar N. 208, 214
Britain 12, 13, 29, 91–92; Admiralty
contingency planning 136–37;
Anglo-German naval race 80; battle
cruisers, power projection by 131,
132–33, 135; battle fleet concentra-
tion, danger in 133; battleship
construction, for and against

126–27, 128; colonies and communications, protection of 135–36;
Committee of Imperial Defence 152;
Copenhagen attacked by (1807) 135;
costs of naval supremacy 127–28;
Crimean War 20, 23–24, 45–47;
defence policy, long-term nature of
fundamental shifts 136–37; economy
of, preeminence of 19; European
allies of 43; Field Service
Regulations (1912) 86, 88; financial
problems for naval build-up 131–32,
136; Fisher's naval build-up, major
issues for 132; Fisher's naval
reforms, opposition to 132; Fisher's
revolutionary concept of naval
warfare 126, 130–31; flotilla defence
133, 134, 135; geography and
economics, defence requirements
and 127; interwar years (1919–39),
power of 140–41; Joint Intelligence
Committee 152; Liberal government
in (1906) 131–32; London
Agreement (1840) 60; 'Long Peace'
and absence of military planning in
16–19; manpower shortages in
volunteer navy 128–29; military
conditions in (1815–56) 17; Naval
Defence Act (1889) 80; naval power
of (1815–56) 18–19; naval technology, developments in 130–31;
naval technology, developments in
(1815–56) 23; preparation for global
naval war (1904–14) 126–37; savings
and administrative reforms, naval
costs and 129–30; tensions with
Japan (1919–39) 142; torpedoes,
development of 128; 'Triple *Entente*'
with France and Russia 80, 87, 89,
90–91; US bases in 207; wariness of
continental entanglements 143–44;
Whig ascendancy in 40; World War
I, naval strategies 134–35
British Expeditionary Force 88
Brodie, Bernard 204n52
Brunswick 56, 66
Brussels Pact 224, 236, 237
Bucholz, Arden 72n13, 123n19
Bulgaria 68
Buol-Schauenstein, Count Karl von
67–68
Burroughs, Peter 25n10
Bush, President George W. 70, 74n57

Europe: arms limitation and arbitration calls 78; Cold War defence of 214; commercial expansion of 76–77; economic trends in 77–78; European Defence Community (EDC) 238; geo-strategic factors in interwar (1919–39) 144–45; Great Powers of 75–78, 79–80, 81–91; liberalism in 40; preoccupation with war between France and Germany 75, 76; rearmament post World War II of 213, 237–38; tensions of 1870s and 1880s in 79; withdrawal of US investment capital from 141; *see also* Austria; Austria-Hungary; Britain; France; Germany; Italy; Prussia; Russia; Soviet Union
European Army Plan (1954) 225
European Coal and Steel Community (ECSC) 148

Falkenhayn, General Erich von 108, 115
Falkland Islands 94–95
Fashoda Crisis (1898) 80
Feis, H. 95n13
Feldman, Gerald D. 156n19
Ferguson, Niall 155n14
Ferrara 57
Ferris, John 5, 7, 154, 159–78, 253, x
Fighter Command, RAF 169, 170
Finland 214
Fischel, Admiral Max von 113, 114
Fischer, Professor Fritz 92, 120
Fisher, Admiral Sir John 7, 8, 126, 129–34, 136
Fiske, Rear Admiral Bradley A. 182
Die Flotte 113
Forrestal, James 208, 210
Förster, Stig 97n34, 98n67, 123n36
France 12, 13, 18, 29, 31, 40–41, 43, 51, 66, 70, 91–92, 100, 129, 254, 255; Algeria, war in 242–43; American military aid to 237–38; *ancien regime* in 16; Army Law (1814) 16; aspirations for European hegemony in check (1815–56) 22; Belgian intervention (1831) 57–58; bitter legacy of World War II for 225–26; Commissariat for Atomic Energy (CEA) 224, 228; Communist Party in 235; Crimean War 45–47; demographic and economic weakness of 143; distribution of forces post World

War II 233–34; downgrading military post de Gaulle 228–29; dreadnought construction, late start to 132; *force de frappe* 228, 244; Free French 226–27, 230; French Forces of the Interior (FFI) 226; Friendship Treaty with Soviet Union 234; General Headquarters of National Defence (EMGDN) 235; Indochina, war in 240–42; July Revolution (1830) 54, 55; military planning structures, post World War II 231–32; military power of, remaking (1940–62) 224–46; Minie bullet and rifle invented 23; naval technology, developments in (1815–56) 23; 'neutrality,' post World War II end of 234–37; nuclear power 238–40; officer corps, change and turbulence post World War II 230–31; Plans XVI and XVII 81, 88–89, 91; preoccupation with war with Germany 75, 76; *rapprochement* with Germany 80; reconstitution of fighting forces (1940–45) 226–27; 'Revolutionary War' of 1950s in 243; Soviet threat, emergence of 234–37; strategic objectives, post World War II 232–33; tensions with Japan (1919–39) 142; 'Triple *Entente*' with Britain and Russia 80, 87, 89, 90–91; Vichy regime in 230
Francis I, Emperor 57
Frank, Robert 229, 246n18
Franz Joseph, Emperor 67, 82
Friedberg, Aaron 95
Friedman, Norman 201n3
Friedrich II (Frederick the Great) 107, 109, 121
Friedrich Wilhelm I 107
Friedrich Wilhelm III 58, 60
Friedrich Wilhelm IV 60, 61–62, 68, 103
Frieser, Karl-Heinz 8–9n5
Frimont, General Count Johann 57
Front de la Libération Nationale (FLN) 244
Frost, Robert S. 260n2
Fuller, J.F.C. 168
Fuller, W.C. 98n61
Furet, François 235, 245

Gaddis, John Lewis 9n6
Gaillard, Félix 239
Gap, General VO Nguyen 242

hedging bets in 253–54, 258; identification of friends and foes, flexibility in 254–55, 259; impact of Concert of Europe on strategic and 15–23, 24–25; importance and difficulties of 2–3; industrial developments (1871–1914) 83–85; international environment (1871–1914) 75–80; international politics, changing nature in interwar (1919–39) years 148; interventionism of interwar (1919–39) governments 145–47; interwar (1919–39) planners and nature of future warfare 150–53; interwar period (1919–39) 139–54; land power, difficulties of coastal defence for 44–45; legacy of World war I for 139–50, 153–54; 'Long Peace' and absence of 16–22, 24–25; military history, influence on 85–91; nature of RAF planning 164, 166–68; organizational basis for Russian war planning (1815–56) 30–34; political objective of 205; political uncertainties for strategic planners (1871–1914) 81–85; revolutions in military affairs (RMAs) 5, 153–54, 159–75; Russian strategic vision, post-1815 26–29; scholarship on 3; scientific threshold, acceleration of 152–53; shifts in wealth and power (1871–1914) 92–93; strategic air warfare, RAF planning for 167–69; strategic planners, role of (1871–1914) 81–91; structures in France 231–32; technological change and interwar (1919–39) planning 152–53; technological developments during 'Long Peace' 22–23; technological uncertainties for strategic planners (1871–1914) 83–85; terrorism, countering threat of 1, 257–60; total war, theory of 150; Turkey, Russian planning for war against (1816–29) 34–40; uncertainties in 1–3, 4; uncertainties of 249; uncertainties of interwar (1919–39) years 147–53; US military planning for Cold War 205–22; war planning in Russia (1815–56) 26–49
Miliutin, D.A. 33
Miller, Steven E. 8n4
Millett, Allan R. 8n3

Minuteman missile 220
Mitchell, General William 'Billy' 182, 187, 188
Modena 57
Moffett, Rear Admiral William A. 182, 183–88, 190
Mohammad Ali of Egypt 40, 43
Moldovia 37
Moltke, General Helmuth von 23, 90, 105, 115, 116–18, 120–21
Moltke the Elder, Count Helmuth 47, 55, 85, 105–6, 107, 110, 111–12
Mombauer, A. 98n68
Monger, George 137n6
Montenegro 89
Moravia 66
Moroccan Crisis (1905–6) 78, 80
Morocco 207
Morrow, Dwight W. 188
Mueller, John 8n1
Müller, Admiral Georg Alexander von 108, 109, 120
Munchengratz agreement 13
Murray, Williamson 8n3
Mussolini, Benito 149

Napoleon, Louis 13
Napoleon Buonaparte 8, 12, 14–15, 16, 20, 27–28, 50
Napoleon III 85
Napoleonic Wars 11, 14, 15–16, 24, 27
NATO (North Atlantic Treaty Organization) 25, 69–71, 211, 214, 216, 220, 225, 237–38; NATO-Russia Council 70–71
Navarre, General Henri 242
Nazi Germany 6, 143–44, 146–47, 149–50, 221, 253
Near East 78
Near Eastern Crisis (1840) 23, 54, 59–60, 63
Nessel'rode, Count 39
Netherlands 29, 51, 59, 116, 238; Belgian rebellion against 55–56; invasion of Belgium (1831) 57; tensions with Japan (1919–39) 142
Nicholas I, Tsar 13, 20–21, 26, 29, 31–40, 40–44, 45–46
Nicholas II, Tsar 80, 83
Nitze, Paul 213
Normandy 76
Norstad, General Lauris 220
North Atlantic Treaty 224, 237